WPAS IN TRANSITION

WPAS IN TRANSITION

Navigating Educational Leadership Positions

Edited by

COURTNEY ADAMS WOOTEN
JACOB BABB
BRIAN RAY

UTAH STATE UNIVERSITY PRESS
Logan

© 2018 the University Press of Colorado

Published by Utah State University Press
An imprint of University Press of Colorado
5589 Arapahoe Avenue, Suite 206C
Boulder, Colorado 80303

All rights reserved
Manufactured in the United States of America

 The University Press of Colorado is a proud member of
The Association of American University Presses.

The University Press of Colorado is a cooperative publishing enterprise supported, in part, Adams State University, Colorado State University, Fort Lewis College, Metropolitan State University of Denver, Regis University, University of Colorado, University of Northern Colorado, Utah State University, and Western State Colorado University.

∞ This paper meets the requirements of the ANSI/NISO Z39.48-1992 (Permanence of Paper)

ISBN: 978-1-60732-632-8 (paperback)
ISBN: 978-1-60732-633-5 (ebook)
https://doi.org/10.7330/9781607326335

Library of Congress Cataloging-in-Publication Data

Names: Wooten, Courtney Adams, editor. | Babb, Jacob, editor. | Ray, Brian, 1982– editor.
Title: WPAs in transition : navigating educational leadership positions/ edited by Courtney Adams Wooten, Jacob Babb, Brian Ray.
Other titles: Writing program administrators in transition
Description: Logan : Utah State University Press, [2017] | Includes bibliographical references and index.
Identifiers: LCCN 2016049467| ISBN 9781607326328 (pbk.) | ISBN 9781607326335 (ebook)
Subjects: LCSH: Writing centers—Administration. | College administrators—Vocational guidance. | College teacher mobility.
Classification: LCC PE1404 .W67 2017 | DDC 808/.0420711—dc23
LC record available at https://lccn.loc.gov/2016049467

Cover illustration © Jodi Baglien Sparkes / Shutterstock.com.

CONTENTS

Acknowledgments   ix

Introduction: Travels, Transitions, and Leadership
  Courtney Adams Wooten and Jacob Babb   3

SECTION 1: POWER AND AGENCY

1. A State of Permanent Transition: Strategies for WPA Survival in the Ever-Present Marginal Space of HBCUs
  Karen Keaton Jackson   25

2. Suddenly WPA: Lessons from an Early and Unexpected Transition
  Chris Blankenship   37

3. Servers, Cooks, and the Inadequacy of Metaphor
  Jennifer Riley Campbell and Richard Colby   51

4. "An Exercise in Cognitive Dissonance": Liminal WPA Transitions
  Talinn Phillips, Paul Shovlin, and Megan L. Titus   70

SECTION 2: IDENTITIES AND SUBJECTIVITIES

5. Defining Disciplinarity at Moments of Transition: The Dappled Expertise of the Multidisciplinary WPA
  Andrea Scott   87

6. The Joys of WPAhood: Embracing Interruption in the Personal and the Professional
  Kate Pantelides   100

7. Metaphors We Work By: New Writing Center Directors' Labor and Identities
  Rebecca Jackson, Jackie Grutsch McKinney, and Nicole I. Caswell   111

8. Get Offa My Lawn! Generational Challenges of WPAs in Transition
  Beth Huber   126

9. Performance Attribution and Administrative (Un)Becoming: Learning to Fail While Trying to Fly

   Steven J. Corbett 139

10. Reseeing the WPA Skill Set: GenAdmins Transitioning from WPA to University Pedagogical Leadership

    Amy Rupiper Taggart 153

SECTION 3: COLLABORATIONS AND DIALOGUES

11. "You Say Goodbye, I Say Hello": Transitions as Two Programs Consolidate

    Letizia Guglielmo and Beth Daniell 171

12. Command and Collaboration: Leading as a New WPA

    Laura J. Davies 188

13. The Collaborative WPA: Bringing a Writing Center Ethos to WAC

    Tereza Joy Kramer, Jaquelyn Davis, Holland Enke, and Reyna Olegario 204

14. There and Back Again, Sort Of: Returning as WPA (and Preparing to Leave)

    Chris Warnick 219

SECTION 4: DISRUPTION AND ACTIVISM

15. Revolving Doors and Settled Locks: Staying Put in an Undesirable Place

    Sarah Stanley 233

16. Connection, Community, and Identity: Writing Programs and WPAs at the Community College

    Mark Blaauw-Hara and Cheri Lemieux Spiegel 245

17. Fostering Ethical Transitions: Creating Community as Writing Program Administrators

    Bradley Smith and Kerri K. Morris 260

18. Writing Center Professionals, Marginalization, and the Faculty/Administrator Divide

    Molly Tetreault 272

19. Transitioning from Contingent to Tenure-Track Faculty Status as a WPA: Working toward Solidarity and Academic-Labor Justice through Hybridity

Liliana M. Naydan   284

Conclusion: Transitions and Transfer

Brian Ray   297

About the Authors   305
Index   311

ACKNOWLEDGMENTS

We would all like to thank our contributors—their dedication to and excitement for this collection has kept us energized throughout the process, and we are proud of the work that everyone brought together. In particular, we would like to recognize Amy Rupiper Taggart, whose passing last year affected us and many others in the field. We are saddened by this loss but grateful that we can publish one of her pieces. We would also like to thank Michael Spooner, Laura Furney, and everyone else at Utah State University Press who shepherded this project forward.

Courtney would like to thank her family and friends for their support, especially her grandparents and parents for supporting her moves to pursue her career; her siblings—Colby, Ansley, Tyler, Heather, Bethany, and Hayleigh—for always being available to hang out whether virtually or face-to-face; and Ali, my sister from another mother. And, of course, I appreciate the two people who put up with me on both my best and worst days, Mikell and Megan; their support keeps me going and reminds me that there is much in my life to be thankful for. I would also like to thank Jacob and Brian for their amazing work on this project; I'm excited to keep working together in the future and am thankful for their support.

Jacob would like to thank his wife Niki for her support, her love, and her enduring patience. He simply couldn't do the work he does without that support. He would also like to thank his kids Annabelle and Oliver for giving their dad time to work when he needs it. Jacob would also like to thank Indiana University Southeast for institutional support in the form of a summer research grant in 2016 that provided needed time and resources for editing this collection. Finally, Jacob thanks Courtney and Brian for being great collaborators—this isn't the first project and it isn't the last.

WPAS IN TRANSITION

Introduction
TRAVELS, TRANSITIONS, AND LEADERSHIP

Courtney Adams Wooten and Jacob Babb

This is a book about the transitions writing program administrators (WPAs) experience in numerous iterations, whether it's a junior faculty member taking over as director of composition for the first time or a senior scholar passing along the role to someone else and contemplating what's next. Our contributors provide narratives and frameworks useful for others transitioning into or out of roles as WPAs, or even for those whose transitions are more lateral, as they take on new tasks within their existing WPA positions.

In some ways, this collection is also about metaphors and the hard work of making meaning with language. Some of the authors in the collection, such as Jennifer Campbell and Richard Colby in "Servers, Cooks, and the Inadequacy of Metaphor" and Rebecca Jackson, Jackie Grutsch McKinney, and Nicole I. Caswell in "Metaphors We Work By," explicitly contemplate the role of metaphors in articulating or clarifying their transitions. Other contributors seek terms to elucidate concepts of transition otherwise difficult to capture, such as Liliana M. Naydan in "Transitioning from Contingent to Tenure-Track-Faculty Status as a WPA" and Talinn Phillips, Paul Shovlin, and Megan Titus in "An Exercise in Cognitive Dissonance," all working to articulate the difficulties of being WPAs as contingent faculty members, graduate students, or somewhere between those positions and more stable full-time positions. With this emphasis on metaphor and language in mind, we offer our own metaphor for WPA transitions: travel.

Traveling is never easy. Trips often involve sweat, tears, crying children, barking dogs and meowing cats, moving trucks, crowded airplanes, and cheap food. However, trips also open up new lives, lead to laughter and memories, and hold the promise of the unimagined and exciting. As Harold Ramis and John Hughes's 1983 classic travel film

Vacation demonstrates, travel changes people even when the destination—Walley World, in this case—ends up not being what they expected. We offer travel as a metaphor for the kinds of transitions individuals make when they take on or step out of roles as WPAs, such as directors of first-year writing programs, writing centers, writing-across-the-curriculum programs, and undergraduate writing majors. This is the metaphor that shapes our own understanding of WPA transitions, likely because our own experiences as WPAs involve a great deal of travel.

In the summer of 2014, when we began having the conversations that inspired this collection, we were in the middle of several different "trips" emanating from the same graduate program in North Carolina, where we all completed our PhDs in rhetoric and composition. Courtney had just accepted a tenure-track position as a WPA at Stephen F. Austin State University, a regional university in Texas. Jacob had accepted a tenure-track position at Indiana University Southeast, a regional commuter university, the year before, and had just transitioned into the role of WPA at the end of his first year. And Brian had accepted a tenure-track position at the University of Nebraska at Kearney two years before; like Jacob, he became a WPA during his first year at his institution. (Brian has since accepted a position at the University of Arkansas at Little Rock to serve as WPA—another journey, another transition.) Counting all the flights for campus visits and all the driving to transplant ourselves and our families to new places, we accumulated thousands of miles of travel. It's no wonder travel and transition culminated in our particular metaphorical lens.

As we all dispersed across the United States to assume these positions, we were struck by the physical and emotional tolls transitions can take on any person but especially on those who are moving into leadership positions. Making such huge moves while simultaneously having to act like and become leaders—fake it 'til you make it, as the popular mantra goes—of a sometimes unknown group of people is a daunting proposition. Many in the field of rhetoric and composition experience transitions into and out of leadership positions during their careers. We wondered how these transitions impact us as people, partners, parents, friends, scholars, leaders, and, most pertinent to this collection, WPAs. How does this *amount* of movement, both literal in terms of geography and figurative in terms of career tracks, positively and negatively affect our professional and personal lives? How can we develop frameworks to better understand and productively move through these changes?

It seems we were not the only ones contemplating similar questions. When Courtney issued a call on the WPA listserv for participants to assemble a panel about the transitions WPAs in different institutions and at different stages of their careers face, to be presented at the Council of Writing Program Administrators (CWPA) conference in 2014, more WPAs than the panel could accept replied, their responses demonstrating a vast array of responses to the notion of transition. This overwhelming reaction prompted our realization that the field needed to engage in a larger discussion regarding the impact of leadership transitions on scholars' lives, especially since so many in the field of writing studies go through such transitions routinely (not the least when brand-new PhDs move into new positions). Drawing on their own experiences moving into and out of WPA positions, authors in this collection offer some answers to questions about WPA transitions and develop frames through which all leaders—whether WPAs or not—can reenvision their experiences. Some authors discuss the influence of transitions on their persons; some discuss the influence of transitions on their careers; others discuss the influence of transitions on their institutions, programs, and the field. All draw attention to the often tumultuous times when leaders find the road, retread the road, or clear the road so as we pass similar milestones, we can learn how to make the trip more reflexively and clearly, if not more easily.

Before discussing some of the ways this collection contributes to our current understandings of WPA transitions, we must note the way in which we have approached the first two parts, *writing program*, of this administrative title. The debate about definitions of *writing program* on the WPA-L in summer 2015 sparked our own awareness about the ways different people continue to think about what a writing program is and what this definition means both theoretically and practically. From the CFP for the 2014 CWPA panel to the CFP for this collection, we have sought to keep the meaning of *writing program* as broad as possible, seeking individuals who administer sites of writing of all types to apply, and we have maintained this inclusivity in our selections for this collection (seen in the WPAs, assistant WPAs, WCPs, and National Writing Program site directors who have contributed). Further, we have deliberately avoided separating the collection into parts governed by these position types, which would, we think, potentially prohibit some of us from identifying, connecting with, and using frameworks that can be useful to all of us as we experience different transitions. In other words, we believe the collection and our field both are strengthened when we seek out the similarities and overlaps in our experiences as WPAs.

Despite the rich scholarship on writing program administration, which is so often attentive to issues of labor and equity (Bousquet, Scott,

Parascondola 2004; Strickland 2011), cultural/political and institutional forces that shape the teaching of composition (Adler-Kassner 2008; Goldblatt 2007; Rose and Weiser 2010), and assessment (Inoue 2015; O'Neill, Moore, and Huot 2009; White, Elliot, and Peckham 2015), scholars have yet to examine in a systematic way how transitioning into and out of administrative roles impacts people's careers and their scholarly and personal identities. Others have already begun analyzing leadership transitions in ways rhetoric and composition—and English studies in general—has yet to do in scholarship. One clear finding that directly relates to the field is the growing emphasis on asking "less experienced leaders from lower levels in the organization . . . to make tremendous leaps upward in leadership scope and into unfamiliar territory" (Paese and Wellins 2007, 3). The field of writing program administration has itself debated the growth of the pretenured or untenured WPA position that asks those with limited experience and not much institutional power to assume leadership positions in writing programs (see Charlton et al. 2011; Horning and Dew 2007).

Despite such debates, job ads continue to call for applicants to fill such positions, partially in response to the same economic forces Paese and Wellins (2007) point to as the root cause of the influx of younger leaders in business fields and partially in response to the rapid growth of jobs for WPAs that has not yet been accompanied with a corresponding growth in those who are qualified to take on these positions. For example, a brief examination of the Academic Jobs Wiki for jobs in rhetoric and composition during the 2014–2015 year shows 57 of 242 advertisements for full-time positions sought candidates who would engage in some form of writing program administration, including directing first-year writing programs, writing centers, and writing-across-the-curriculum programs. Of those fifty-seven advertisements, twenty-eight were for tenure-track assistant professors, with another six billed as assistant/associate searches and four that were fully open rank. The remaining advertisements for WPAs sought associate/full professors (nine) or non-tenure-track instructors (ten). Therefore, two-thirds of the positions were open to tenure-track assistant professors, while almost half specifically called for assistant professors. These trends illustrate how prevalent WPA positions are in the field (around one-quarter of the 2014–2015 jobs listed on the wiki) and the many transitions that take place as people move into and out of the positions, most notably among early-career scholars filling assistant-professor positions. As so many in our field make personal and professional adjustments during these times of movement both into and out of administrative positions, it is imperative that we better understand what these adjustments are and how they affect our lives.

Lack of scholarship about administrative transitions in our own field does not, however, indicate a complete dearth of frameworks to guide our travels. One of the most obvious sites where leadership transitions have been discussed is in relation to corporations and businesses. This information is written from the ultimate perspective of helping businesses expand—with the aim of growing their bottom lines—by helping leaders form, develop, and succeed. Such texts, typically written as advice manuals by business leaders to other business leaders, often include heuristics for planning and surviving transitions from both company and personal positions. For example, Richard Elsner and Bridget Farrands posit that transitions occur in three phases (arriving, surviving, thriving), that each stage has its own obstacles, and that there are certain techniques new leaders can implement to avoid failure (Elsner and Farrands 2012). David L. Dotlich, James L. Noel, and Norman Walker offer a slightly different tactic, outlining thirteen common "leadership passages," both in work and home life, leaders need to be prepared for (Dotlich, Noel, and Walker 2004). Both provide a look at different stages that can occur during a leadership transition and how individuals can prepare for and survive these. Kevin Eikenberry and Guy Harris take on a different kind of project: defining a specific type of transition and how to handle its particular issues. They focus on those who are transitioning into their first leadership positions and on the resulting issues, including how to lead those who were previously one's colleagues (Eikenberry and Harris 2011). The rhetoric of these books often resembles that of a motivational speaker: Eikenberry and Harris's book begins "Congratulations! You are now the supervisor. The manager. The foreman. The boss. Your role has changed and you are asked to be a leader. There is no better word than to say 'Congratulations!'" (1). Such a voice isn't the measured, methodical, analytical tone we value in academia, and it feeds into the hierarchies that often govern businesses and increasingly influence higher education contexts. Although the business model is one faculty often explicitly resist, some of these concepts are useful to consider in relation to our work as leaders in our field, institutions, and programs. In other words, we should not let our resistance to the commodification of education blind us to the useful insights to be gained about leadership transitions from the business world.

Other fields such as nursing, information technology, and education have also scrutinized leadership transitions from the perspective of helping those in the field acclimate to new leadership positions. In nursing, Schumacher and Meleis (1994) wrote a review of literature focused around the concept of transitions and how they have been approached in the field of nursing, including "situational transitions" when nurses move into and out of particular positions (120). Their review of 124 articles from 1986 to 1992 found three conditions necessary to successful transitions: subjective well-being, role mastery, and well-being of relationships (124). Such extensive research indicates the level of scrutiny other fields have already given to transitions. In the field of information technology, Marilu Goodyear and Cynthia Golden specifically speak about leadership transitions in the context of high turnover in the field (Goodyear and Golden 2008). They identify four "areas of interaction between leaders and followers" they claim are "critical for success during a transition: Partnering in decision making; Focusing on the successful implementation of new directions; Challenging the new leader as appropriate; Understanding and providing the unique support the new leader requires" (53). Their goal is to give IT professionals who often face transitions between positions some guidance, even if brief, about how to manage the interpersonal relationships that often determine the failure or success in leadership. A little closer to home, though far above the typical WPA's tax bracket, books intended to help top-level education administrators transition have become more common. One example is James Martin and James E. Samels's collection *Presidential Transition in Higher Education: Managing Leadership Change*, which addresses the growing number of presidential transitions at colleges and universities (Martin and Samels 2004). The authors in this volume speak to a variety of stakeholders involved in these types of transitions and tactics for handling them. The ultimate aims of these texts are often more in line with our own goals than with the goals of business models (despite the growing attention in higher education to recruitment, retention, and similar corporate-like practices): to help people become better leaders and be successful without necessarily worrying about a company's profitability.

Apart from these somewhat expected areas in which leadership transitions might gain attention, the issues and problems that often arise from any type of leadership transition have led to increased attention to many different sorts of transitions not typically accounted for in previous work. For example, Tom Dale Mullins (2015) discusses religious-leadership transitions in *Passing the Leadership Baton*. Further, organizations have been built to help those in different types of positions acclimate to new or exit previous positions. The Leadership Transition Institute offers academics and business leaders focused attention to leadership transitions.[1]

With the proliferation of writing programs across and outside the United States and the many types of WPA positions being created, filled, and refilled, WPAs cannot afford to ignore the insights needed to help them through their own leadership transitions that can be generated not just from other scholarship but from our own lived experiences. These various scholarly and popular perspectives not only offer us a starting point through which to consider our own work but also highlight the importance of creating our own frameworks through which to theorize and prepare for transitions into and out of administrative positions. In the remainder of the introduction, we discuss specific concepts we have found useful in adapting to leadership transitions, particularly as WPAs, and we conclude by providing an overview of the chapters that comprise this book.

TRACING THE ROAD ALREADY TRAVELED: THEORY AND PRACTICE IN WPA TRANSITIONS

Although English studies in general, rhetoric and composition as a field, and writing program administration as a related field have explored leadership transitions very little, scholarship has indirectly focused on similar issues, particularly when scholars explore the connections between their professional and personal lives. Diana George's collection *Kitchen Cooks, Plate Twirlers and Troubadours* served as an initial inspiration for this collection in its focus on lived experience as an important site of knowledge making (George 1999). While those authors did not particularly look at moments in their lives as transitionary, many of them were talking about transitions of different kinds; for example, in "The WPA as Father, Husband, Ex," Doug Hesse discusses his transitions into and out of familial roles while serving as a WPA (Hesse 1999). Similarly drawing on narrative as knowledge making, Peggy O'Neill, Angela Crow, and Larry W. Burton's collection *A Field of Dreams* provides programmatic narratives of independent writing programs that often involve transitions of entire programs, particularly in the movement of writing programs out of English departments (O'Neill, Crow, and Burton 2002). Two of the most explicit contributions about WPA leadership transitions are David E. Schwalm's "Writing Program Administration as Preparation for an Administrative Career" (Schwalm 2002) and Susan McLeod's "Moving Up the Administrative Ladder" (McLeod 2002), both reflecting the familiar road some WPAs take from WPA to other administrative positions. However, these pieces have not been recently taken up to consider the work WPAs engage in. We encouraged authors in our collection to similarly relate and reflect on their own experiences as they sparked conversations about how WPAs transition into and out of positions and how we can better understand these transitions. Lived experience serves as the central hallmark of these chapters around which authors have thoughtfully constructed frameworks to help us all better understand their own and similar situations.

Despite the lack of scholarship about leadership transitions in writing studies, the many responses to our call for proposals for this collection illustrate the need to consider times of leadership transitions and how they affect our lives, those around us, and the institutions and programs we are part of. Paese and Wellins (2007) found that many leaders, especially those at the midlevel or midcareer, place "making a transition at work" as the second most challenging event in their lives, second only to separation or divorce (6). Anecdotally, transition points are similarly disruptive and stressful for WPAs, whether we are moving to new locations to take charge of new programs or moving into new positions at the same institutions. Rather than having to develop concepts from scratch through which to theorize and reconsider our practices during transitions, there are already some available frameworks that, when adapted to our specific locations, can be useful.

Two texts, both of which deserve more attention from rhetoric and composition scholars and WPAs, discuss transitions particular to faculty in higher education. Ronald J. Henry's *Transitions between Faculty and Administrative Careers* provides a variety of perspectives from faculty who became administrators (Henry 2006). One of the chief differences between these experiences and those of newer-generation WPAs is that WPA training has recently become a formal part of many rhetoric and composition programs, with questions and information about graduate courses in writing program administration often appearing during conferences and on the WPA listserv. Therefore, graduate students with such training often see WPA work and, consequently, university leadership as important aspects of their professional identities from the time they become faculty members, unlike many of those in this collection whose paths to leadership, as Henry puts it, were "somewhat serendipitous" and "not deliberate" (1). Nevertheless, this collection provides useful perspectives for all faculty to consider as they move into administrative roles. Focusing on the end-of-career timeline, Claire A. Van Ummersen, Jean M. McLaughlin, and Lauren J. Duranleau's collection *Faculty Retirement: Best Practices for Navigating the Transition* explores issues related to faculty retirement, including psychological effects of retirement and institutional support for retirees (Van Ummersen,

McLaughlin, and Duranleau 2014). Although they address faculty at large and not academic leaders or WPAs in particular, Van Ummersen, McLaughlin, and Duranleau's collection reflects recent discussions at the Conference on College Composition and Communication (including the establishment of a special-interest group for senior, late-career, and retired professionals) and at the Conference for Writing Program Administrators, as well as discussion on the WPA listserv about the role of retirees in the profession. WPAs are particularly invested in the issue of retirement, as they must simultaneously transition out of academic life and out of leadership positions through which they have helped build and sustain programs. (As a retiring faculty member and former WPA at Jacob's institution noted, only half joking, "I'm probably going to hate any changes you make to my program.") This book, like Henry's, provides some general information about transitions WPAs and other rhetoric and composition faculty who have moved into leadership positions may find useful.

Pushing against our tendency to resist concepts useful in corporate America fruitfully provides more specific road signs to help us mark, plan for, and successfully navigate routes through administrative transitions. The Corporate Executive Board Company (CEB), a corporation focused on business management, is influential as a sponsor of information about leadership transitions. In "High-Impact Leadership Transitions," the CEB calls on organizations and leaders to think in terms of what *type* of transition is occurring and how they can best prepare for that kind of transition rather than in hierarchical (someone moving up or down) or entry-point (someone moving into or out of the company) terms (Corporate Executive Board Company 2012). Claiming that "these approaches both fail to account for differences in the circumstances that each transitioning leader must face" (4), it hypothesizes that there are five transition types that account for 97 percent of all leadership transitions: smooth sailing, replacing an icon, following a train wreck, jump starting, and breaking ground (4). Their descriptions of each transition type, with definitions of important priorities in each situation, can help those entering new leadership positions, such as new WPAs or WPAs moving into different administrative positions, to better understand what type of situation they are entering and how they can best approach it. For example, of the breaking-ground transition, where someone steps into a newly created position, they claim, "To succeed in this transition it is critical to clearly define the responsibilities and objectives of the role and gain a better understanding of the stakeholder universe" (13). Translated to WPAs, this recommendation asks us to make sure it is clear what work expectations are, particularly when work must be justified for course releases, additional pay, or other compensation, and to pay attention to the many stakeholders involved in the work of writing programs, including students, other faculty, upper administration, parents, and the culture at large, not to mention tenure and promotion committees who must weigh our work as WPAs. Focusing on each type of transition is useful in directing our attention to different priorities depending on the kind of transition we are a part of. Further, the CEB's information about how often the different types of transition occur in organizations (smooth sailing: 3 percent; replacing an icon: 18 percent; following a train wreck: 27 percent; jump starting: 19 percent; breaking ground: 31 percent) encourages WPAs to consider what transition types typically occur for us and how we can differently approach various kinds of transitions.

Focusing more specifically on how new leaders can prove themselves and garner respect and support, Mark E. Van Buren and Todd Safferstone outline the concept of the "collective quick win" they argue is common among strong new leaders (Van Buren and Safferstone 2009). A collective quick win is "a new and visible contribution to the success of the business made early in [a new leader's] tenure" (56), something that requires the effort of a group of people, doesn't require additional resources, and gets noticed by others (Van Buren and Safferstone specify "by people two levels above the new leader" [57]). The effect of collective quick wins, they claim, is "a crucial form of reassurance to the leaders' bosses, who hope they have made the right promotion decision; to team members deciding whether to place confidence in their new manager; and to peers trying to determine whether an equal has joined their ranks" (57). Although Van Buren and Safferstone strangely don't indicate how quickly this action should take place (perhaps an acknowledgment that the time frame is contingent on the workplace), they do provide a set of questions, or a diagnostic, to help leaders determine which opportunity might work as a collective quick win. In the case of WPAs, such action could involve setting up workshops led by faculty in the writing program in order to create digital assignments or collaboratively writing or revising student learning outcomes (see Babb and Wooten 2016). The idea of the collective quick win points out the strengths of working with others once in a new position to build something the group takes pride in and that others can recognize as having a positive impact on the program.

Speaking about movement into leadership positions generally, Paese and Wellins found that dealing with internal politics was a significant challenge for the six hundred managers from around the world that they surveyed: "At first and mid levels, politics is the top challenge, with almost half of first-level leaders and one third at level two [of three] saying that they have been unable to address this challenge effectively. Senior leaders rate politics as the fourth most difficult challenge" (Paese and Wellins 2007, 10). WPAs are not naïve about the many political entanglements they may face, particularly if they are nontenured. Paese and Wellins don't offer particular advice about this problem, but they note, "It's worth reflecting on the amount of organisational time and effort managing these conflicting interests must inevitably consume" (10). As any WPA who has spent hours agonizing over one e-mail knows, internal politics can consume much of our time.

Perhaps a more helpful note in Paesc and Mitchell's related article is their finding that survey respondents said it was difficult to establish "a new network appropriate to their level," and they recommend that organizations help "facilitate peer-to-peer support networks for newly promoted managers" (Paese and Mitchell 2007, 11) that might minimize politics. The need to help new leaders network is one echoed by Van Buren and Safferstone, who encourage companies to "engage the support network" of the new leader's "manager, peers, and direct reports" (Van Buren and Safferstone 2009, 61). The importance of networking across campus and what campuses could do to facilitate this process must be emphasized. As new WPAs, we have often expressed our frustrations to one another that there is no clear way to meet others across campus besides approaching them whenever we need to communicate with them about a particular project or issue, which are times when preexisting relationships would facilitate our communication. Developing more ways to network or encouraging institutions to help new faculty members in general to network not just with other faculty—and not with just new faculty, as often happens in orientation sessions—would establish useful inroads for WPAs navigating some of the politics involved in their positions.

This brief trip through some of the scholarship available is certainly not exhaustive. Instead, it is intended to earmark some of the information already available about leadership transitions WPAs might find useful to tap into and consider in relation to our administrative positions. Even if scholars resist or outright reject the business- and profit-oriented terminology and rhetorical strategies employed in some of these texts, the authors still offer us valuable ways through which to examine our own lived experiences and on which to begin building our own theories about transitioning into and out of WPA and other administrative positions.

Thus, these texts serve as trails we can trace and outline even as we forge our own. We hope more WPAs will travel these roads and produce scholarship to enrich and build more frameworks to facilitate our transitions.

THE TRAVELER'S ROAD MAP

Because of the diversity of perspectives offered by the contributors to this collection, we could have used any number of different organizational strategies. However, our focus on not just the narratives but also on the frameworks authors construct to understand the transitions they faced as WPAs—and our desire for others to interact with, question, push against, and employ these frameworks—led us to organize the chapters based on the overall focus authors presented as they talked about the transitions they had gone through. Thus, we have created four sections that address overarching issues in WPA scholarship, rhetoric and composition as a field, and the wider higher education community. It is our hope that readers will find all these perspectives useful for examining their own experiences and developing their own frameworks for understanding professional transitions.

Power and Agency

In one of the most often-cited articles on WPAs and power, Edward M. White (1991) asserts that "administrators, including WPAs, cannot afford the luxury of powerlessness. The only way to do the job of a WPA is to be aware of the power relationships we necessarily conduct, and to use the considerable power we have for the good of our program" (White 1991, 12). The opening section of this collection contains four chapters that contemplate the amount of power WPAs actually have, the role that power plays in their efforts to support and develop their programs, and the agency they have as WPAs.

First, Karen Keaton Jackson, in "A State of Permanent Transition: Strategies for Surviving in an Ever-Present Marginal Space," deconstructs the ideas of leader and manager often inherent in WPA positions to argue that the interplay between these roles can help those WPAs, such as herself, who find themselves in nearly constant states of transition. Next, in his chapter about job-position negotiations, "Suddenly WPA: Lessons from an Early and Unexpected Transition," Chris Blankenship explores the limits of the time and energy we should be willing to give up to become WPAs even as he notes the power of privilege he may have had as a white male to negotiate for time and space to assume this position. Jennifer Riley Campbell and Richard Colby's "Servers, Cooks, and the Inadequacy of Metaphor" asks us to question the limits of the metaphors we use to describe our work and argues that assistant directors in writing programs must carefully consider their institutional power and agency as they assume and carry out their work, especially as they balance their workloads and take on leadership positions with those who were formerly their colleagues.

The concluding chapter for this section, "'An Exercise in Cognitive Dissonance': Liminal WPA Transitions" by Talinn Phillips, Paul Shovlin, and Megan L. Titus, draws attention to an unrecognized or temporary WPA position, the liminal WPA who often performs the tasks of a WPA but does not have institutional status as a WPA. Through their interviews with four liminal WPAs who were transitioning into and out of their roles, they explore the positive and negative aspects of these positions and how departments and programs can help those in these positions, arguing that these positions may not be preferable but that they are not disappearing.

Identities and Subjectivities

One of the large questions driving this collection is one about how our work as WPAs impacts our professional and personal identities and how our subjectivity shapes and is shaped by our role as administrators. The six essays that comprise this section take on some of these issues, particularly drawing our attention to the subjectivities we inhabit and what these mean as we transition into WPA positions. They serve as road signs directing us to possible paths and offering us choices about the journeys we wish to make and how we think of these journeys. Andrea Scott's "Defining Disciplinary at Moments of Transition: The Dappled Expertise of the Multidisciplinary WPA" begins this section with a broad call for WPA scholarship to better account for the productive connections between literary studies and composition as she discusses her transition from one job to another very different job. Her tracing of the overlaps and differences in these fields, which productively helped her transition as a WPA, asks readers to consider what it means if we extend our disciplinary roots to include all those who engage in WPA work.

The next chapter draws attention to what it means to inhabit particular bodies in particular places and times. "The Joys of WPAhood: Embracing Interruption in the Personal and the Professional" by Kate Pantelides explores the personal interweaving of parental identities with WPA work. She argues that conceptualizing WPA work through the lenses of adaptation and interruption can help us see how disruptions to the status quo can be beneficial and how our personal and professional identities can productively speak to each other. Focusing on new WPAs, "Metaphors We Work By: New Writing Center Directors' Labor and Identities" by Rebecca Jackson, Jackie Grutsch McKinney, and Nicole I. Caswell, draws on interviews with nine writing center directors during their first year on the job, focusing on the metaphors these WCDs use to describe their work as "perilous and tenuous" while also building a sense of "excitement and pride." Jackson, McKinney, and Caswell emphasize the on-the-job nature of much of the training these WCPs went through and call for institutions to set up more realistic expectations for WCP workloads.

In "Get Offa My Lawn!: Generational Challenges of WPAs in Transition," Beth Huber offers the stories of four generational shifts in one writing program. Huber addresses the challenges of leaving WPA positions and watching new WPAs shift the priorities of writing programs, claiming such changes occur naturally over time and must happen incrementally. Exploring a topic many WPAs avoid—failure—Steven J. Corbett's "Processes of Administrative (Un)Becoming: Learning to Fail While Trying to Fly" extends the field's inquiry into failure in writing classes to WPAs, asking us what it means to learn to fail in our work as we transition into new positions and places and, ultimately, as we leave them.

Finally, Amy Rupiper Taggart's "Re-seeing the WPA Skill Set: GenAdmins Transitioning from WPA to University Pedagogical Leadership" calls on WPAs to consider what happens when we move through GenAdmin identities as WPAs into other administrative positions on campus. She argues that we need to identify other options for work besides WPA positions and that we need to be more aware of the skills we possess and how these may translate to other kinds of work.

Collaborations and Dialogues

Just as in road trips for which we often plan the routes and read maps together, WPA work frequently involves collaborations between programs, WPAs, other administrators, teachers, students, staff, and so forth. The chapters in this section explicitly present situations in which collaborations occurred during WPA transitions and what we can glean about our own work from these experiences and the conversations that took place around them. Letizia Guglielmo and Beth Daniell's chapter, "'You Say Goodbye, I Say Hello': Transitions as Two Programs

Consolidate," recounts their experiences of transitioning into and out of a WPA position on the same campus while this campus simultaneously merged with another institution at the behest of the board of regents at the University of Georgia. Their chapter exposes the subject positions they found themselves in during this time and how they continue to negotiate these based on a shared commitment to the writing program.

Examining the leadership strategies needed during transitions into WPA positions, Laura J. Davies's "Command and Collaboration: Leading as a New WPA" turns attention to power structures that exist in WPA work, arguing that command and collaboration are complementary leadership theories that must be further considered as she recounts her time as a jWPA at the United States Air Force Academy. In the next chapter, Tereza Joy Kramer, Jaquelyn Davis, Holland Enke, and Reyna Olegario speak to the importance of working with those around us, including students, who are vital parts of our writing programs. In "Integrating Approach and Ethos: Creating a Writing Center/WAC Program through Collaborative Leadership," they argue that dialogue and collaboration are essential to leadership growth, recounting how these relationships have fostered unique opportunities for faculty and student collaboration in their Center for Writing Across the Curriculum.

In the concluding chapter for this section, "There and Back Again, Sort of: The WPA as Literacy Broker," Chris Warnick builds on Deborah Brandt's theory of literacy brokers to analyze his return to a WPA position after an eight-year hiatus; he offers this theory as useful for WPAs because it helped him embrace the "creativity and imagination" and reflection needed in order to collaborate with others in his program for the second time. Taken together, the chapters in this section highlight some of the ways in which collaboration during WPA transitions can enrich the work we do and strengthen our programs and their reach across campuses.

Disruption and Activism

The final section of the book includes chapters that describe how WPA transitions may tap into the potentially creative energy of disruption. For some of the authors, such disruptions lead to new perspectives on their career paths or directions for their programs. For others, disruption takes the form of activism, particularly regarding questions of labor. The section's opening chapter, Sarah Stanley's "Revolving Doors and Settled Locks: Staying Put in an Undesirable Place," questions the dominant narrative of GenAdmin, exploring her own identity outside this group and arguing that "staying put" in a particular place rather than moving often between positions affords more opportunities to contribute to both writing programs and the communities we live in. Speaking in the context of community colleges in "Connection, Community, and Identity: Writing Programs and WPAs at the Community College," Mark Blaauw-Hara and Cheri Lemieux Spiegel argue that connections to the larger WPA community are essential to addressing feelings of loneliness and isolation, particularly in institutions where writing programs and WPA positions are relatively unfamiliar territory, and to creating a holistic approach to writing-program decisions.

Perhaps one of the most difficult transitions involves passing the torch on to someone else. Employing the metaphors of space/rooms and travelers, Bradley Smith and Kerri K. Morris, in "Fostering Ethical Transitions: Creating Community as Writing Program Administrators," recount the creation of a writing program from the ground up. They discuss how these metaphors help them see the community of writing teachers they are in the process of creating and argue that such frameworks can serve as useful ways for a current WPA and a next-in-line WPA who is still a faculty member to negotiate their relationship with each other while they are both working with the same writing program. Complicating the ways in which different positions are seen in our field, Molly Tetreault's "Reconsidering Marginalization: One Writing Center Director's Perspective" questions the privileging of faculty writing center director positions over staff positions and asks us to consider what it would mean to stop focusing on job status as a measure of marginalization and to recognize instead the solidarity among all of us. In discussing moving from a contingent WPA position (which might be seen as liminal) to a tenure-track WPA position, Liliana M. Naydan argues, in "Transitioning from Contingent to Tenure-Track Faculty Status As a WPA: Working toward Solidarity and Academic Labor Justice through Hybridity," that in order to enact labor activism, those such as herself who have transitioned from contingent to tenure-track status must listen to other contingent faculty members' stories, exchange stories with them, and seek to unearth solidarity among all faculty as the basis on which labor reform can occur. Taken together, these chapters offer three new landmarks to guide our discussion about labor and marginalization as they affect WPA identities and the future of our field.

Conclusion

Successful transition requires awareness and reflection about the interstitial realms of our work, something we hope our collection inspires in readers. Our own experiences have taught us that the few months at the beginning, end, or between jobs are hardly dead time. These are periods of intense transformation, in both positive and negative ways. They are filled with new expectations, learning curves, and anxiety. Their importance necessitates the kind of in-depth exploration given here. All the narratives may not apply to our immediate contexts, but they offer strategies and tools for our use when we do encounter similar circumstances. In turn, they should also prompt us to think about our own positions and programs from different perspectives. They may bring to light challenges and resources we have yet to consider.

As all three of us continue to face transitions both large and small, professional and personal, we keep looking around as we make our journey, consulting maps, planning trips, reading road signs, finding landmarks, making rest stops, and exiting and entering the highway. Since human beings are in a constant state of flux, we don't anticipate these transitions ending; we only hope we learn as we go and become better at handling them. These chapters offer all WPAs as well as others in and out of our field who find themselves in leadership positions some starting points for considering what it means to be a "leader" and how we move into, through, and out of these positions.

Note

1. See the Leadership Transition Institute's website at http://www.executiveboard.com/exbd/leadership-transition/index.page.

References

Adler-Kassner, Linda. 2008. *The Activist WPA: Changing Stories about Writing and Writers*. Logan: Utah State University Press.

Babb, Jacob, and Courtney Adams Wooten. 2016. "Traveling on the Assessment Loop: The Role of Contingent Labor in Curriculum Development." In *Contingency, Exploration, and Solidarity: Labor and Action in English Studies*, edited by Seth Kahn, William Lalicker, and Amy Lynch-Biniek, 169–82. Fort Collins, CO: WAC Clearinghouse.

Bousquet, Marc, Tony Scott, and Leo Parascondola, eds. 2004. *Tenured Bosses and Disposable Teachers: Writing Instruction in the Managed University*. Carbondale: Southern Illinois University Press.

Charlton, Colin, Jonikka Charlton, Tarez Samra Graban, Kathleen J. Ryan, and Amy Ferdinandt Stolley. 2011. *GenAdmin: Theorizing WPA Identities in the Twenty-First Century*. Anderson, SC: Parlor.

Corporate Executive Board Company. 2012. "High-Impact Leadership Transitions: A Transformative Approach." https://www.cebglobal.com/top-insights/leadership-transition/resources.html?referrerTitle=High-Impact%20Leadership%20Transitions.

Dotlich, David L., James L. Noel, and Norman Walker. 2004. *Leadership Passages: The Personal and Professional Transitions that Make or Break a Leader.* San Francisco, CA: Jossey-Bass.

Eikenberry, Kevin, and Guy Harris. 2011. *From Bud to Boss: Secrets to a Successful Transition to Remarkable Leadership.* San Francisco, CA: Jossey-Bass.

Elsner, Richard, and Bridget Farrands. 2012. *Leadership Transitions: How Business Leaders Take Charge in New Roles.* Philadelphia, PA: Kogan Page.

George, Diana, ed. 1999. *Kitchen Cooks, Plate Twirlers and Troubadours: Writing Program Administrators Tell Their Stories.* Portsmouth, NH: Boynton/Cook-Heinemann.

Goldblatt, Eli. 2007. *Because We Live Here: Sponsoring Literacy Beyond the College Curriculum.* New York: Hampton.

Goodyear, Marilu, and Cynthia Golden. 2008. "Leadership Transitions: Key for Success." *EDUCAUSE Quarterly* 31 (1): 52–54.

Henry, Ronald J., ed. 2006. *Transitions between Faculty and Administrative Careers.* Danvers, MA: Wiley Periodicals.

Hesse, Doug. 1999. "The WPA as Husband, Father, Ex." In *Kitchen Cooks, Plate Twirlers and Troubadours: Writing Program Administrators Tell Their Stories*, edited by Diana George, 44–55. Portsmouth, NH: Boynton/Cook-Heinemann.

Horning, Alice, and Debra Frank Dew. 2007. *Untenured Faculty as Writing Program Administrators: Institutional Practices and Politics.* Anderson, SC: Parlor.

Inoue, Asao. 2015. *Antiracist Writing Assessment Ecologies: Teaching and Assessing for a Socially Just Future.* Fort Collins, CO: WAC Clearinghouse and Parlor.

Martin, James, and James E. Samels. 2004. *Presidential Transition in Higher Education: Managing Leadership Change.* Baltimore, MD: Johns Hopkins University Press.

McLeod, Susan H. 2002. "Moving up the Administrative Ladder." In *The Writing Program Administrator's Resource: A Guide to Reflective Institutional Practice*, edited by Stuart C. Brown and Theresa Enos, 113–24. Mahwah, NJ: Erlbaum.

Mullins, Tom Dale. 2015. *Passing the Leadership Baton: A Winning Transition Plan for Your Ministry.* Nashville, TN: Thomas Nelson.

O'Neill, Peggy, Angela Crow, and Larry W. Burton, eds. 2002. *A Field of Dreams: Independent Writing Programs and the Future of Composition Studies.* Logan: Utah State University Press.

O'Neill, Peggy, Cindy Moore, and Brian Huot. 2009. *A Guide to College Writing Assessment.* Logan: Utah State University Press.

Paese, Matt, and Simon Mitchell. 2007. *Leaders in Transition: Stepping Up, Not Off.* Pittsburgh: Development Dimensions International.

Paese, Matt, and Richard S. Wellins. 2007. "Leaders in Transition: Stepping Up, Not Off." http://www.ddiworld.com/ddi/media/trend-research/leaders-in-transition-stepping-up-not-off_mis_ddi.pdf.

Rose, Shirley K., and Irwin Weiser. 2010. *Going Public: The WPA as Advocate for Engagement.* Logan: Utah State University Press.

Schumacher, Karen L., and Afaf Ibrahim Meleis. 1994. "Transitions: A Central Concept in Nursing." *Image: The Journal of Nursing Scholarship* 26 (2): 119–127. https://doi.org/10.1111/j.1547-5069.1994.tb00929.x.

Schwalm, David E. 2002. "Writing Program Administration as Preparation for an Administrative Career." In *The Writing Program Administrator's Resource: A Guide to Reflective Institutional Practice*, edited by Stuart C. Brown and Teresa Enos, 125–35. Mahwah, NJ: Erlbaum.

Strickland, Donna. 2011. *The Managerial Unconscious in the History of Composition Studies.* Carbondale: Southern Illinois University Press.

Van Buren, Mark E., and Todd Safferstone. 2009. "The Quick Wins Paradox." *Harvard Business Review* 87 (1): 54–61. https://hbr.org/2009/01/the-quick-wins-paradox.

Van Ummersen, Claire A., Jean M. McLaughlin, and Lauren J. Duranleau. 2014. *Faculty Retirement: Best Practices for Navigating the Transition.* Sterling, VA: Stylus.

White, Edward M. 1991. "Use It or Lose It: Power and the WPA." *WPA: Writing Program Administration* 15 (1–2): 3–12.

White, Edward M., Norbert Elliot, and Irvin Peckham. 2015. *Very Like a Whale: The Assessment of Writing Programs.* Logan: Utah State University Press.

SECTION 1

Power and Agency

1
A STATE OF PERMANENT TRANSITION
Strategies for WPA Survival in the Ever-Present Marginal Space of HBCUs

Karen Keaton Jackson

Full-time faculty member. Part-time administrator. Fundraiser. Fund seeker. Conference-proposal organizer. Advisor. Mentor. Hustler. Semi-stalker (I'll explain). Othermother. Big Sister. Auntie. Godmother. Data gatherer. Survey creator. Advocate. Report writer. Assessment coordinator. Tutor trainer. Faculty resource. Cheerleader. Manager. Leader.

I can recall early in my career being pointed to the Portland Resolution, that wonderful document from 1992 that spells out the acceptable work conditions and roles we all should expect as WPAs at our institutions. When I was hired at my institution as a tenure-track assistant professor over ten years ago, I had no idea that just a few short months later, I would be asked to revitalize the then-writing center and oversee the first-year writing program. But, I did not fear, for I armed myself with "The Portland Resolution" (1992), feeling confident my department chair would see these guidelines and ensure my responsibilities were delegated accordingly.

I was so naïve.

Ten years later, I chuckle at the wonderful descriptions of what should have been in place when I accepted the dual, really triple, role of directing the writing center, which included designing and implementing a campus-wide writing-intensive program and directing first-year composition, all in the second year of my tenure-track journey. (It wasn't until after I received tenure that I was relieved of first-year writing.) In truth, none of those guidelines from the Portland Resolution were fulfilled for me: "clear job descriptions or role statements . . . clearly defined administrative structure . . . informed guidelines for assessing the work of a WPA fairly . . . access to those individuals and units that influence their programs . . . the power to request, *receive, and allocate* funds sufficient for the funding of the program" ("The Portland Resolution" 1992, 88–91; my emphasis). As a junior faculty member and lone compositionist, I struggled with saying no, for I didn't want to be seen as uncollegial or unwilling to do the work given to me. Many junior faculty members often confront this very issue, as even Liliana M. Naydan discusses in chapter 20 of this edited collection. In her chapter, she points out that "many WPAs engage in administration prior to or sometimes at the expense of attaining tenure and the greater job security that accompanies it" (284–85). So, I knew I had to work smarter, not harder, and find ways to make this new arrangement work. And in terms of the writing program itself, I had to figure out how to be a visionary in creating this new presence on campus while simultaneously managing the day-to-day operations of the program and the new Writing Studio (formerly writing center).

The editors of this collection asked for submissions from colleagues moving into or out of various roles within the academy, implying that one role is left behind when a new one is added. The purpose is for WPAs to engage in dialogue about the experience of moving from one role to the next, thus ensuring an increased chance of success. But, what about those colleagues, such as myself, who essentially live in a state of transition, constantly moving between the aforementioned roles consistently, simultaneously, and permanently? Colleagues at large research institutions often have the luxury of focusing on one, at most two, formal job roles at a time with ample resources to support each one. However, for those of us at smaller institutions, especially historically black universities (HBCUs) such as mine that are teaching centered and have fewer funding options, wearing multiple hats becomes the norm. This phenomenon causes us to have questions such as what current leadership research exists that can be applicable to WPAs in this position? What is both gained and lost by existing in a marginal leadership space on a consistent basis? What are some best practices and effective strategies used by WPAs in this position to ensure success?

To help frame this discussion, I cite John Kotter's 2001 article "What Leaders Really Do" to help define our ideas of leadership. What his article essentially shows is that occupying these multiple roles forces individuals to be both managers and leaders, which at its core is problematic as the two roles often are in opposition. In this article, I also draw from the works of Donna Strickland (2011) and Tony Scott (2009) to critically deconstruct notions of managers and leaders to work toward a new philosophy that helps WPAs more successfully navigate between the two roles. Ultimately, I argue that despite what the majority of leadership research suggests, it is possible to place the two roles of manager and leader in conversation with each other so each distinctive need is fulfilled and the WPA has a better chance of success (and sanity).

In the business world, there is a plethora of literature about how leaders and managers differ, though sometimes the two roles are conflated. In his *Harvard Business Review* article, "What Leaders Really Do," John Kotter (2001) explains how we can appreciate the strengths of each role. Managers "brin[g] order and predictability to a situation." They plan and budget, control and solve problems, and handle organizing and staffing. In short, managers "manage" the day-to-day operations in a specific work environment. In contrast, leaders set the direction, help align people (finding the right fit between the people and the vision), and motivate and inspire others. In short, they are the visionaries who set the tone and direction of where the organization is headed. Both roles are necessary and complement each other well. Yet, when one is called to be both manager and leader simultaneously, it can be difficult at times to separate the two. It's hard to step back and be a visionary when caught up in the daily grind of problem solving and putting out fires.

In composition scholarship, those of us who embody this double consciousness (to borrow from W.E.B. DuBois) are called "managerial intellectuals" by Marc Bousquet (2003). According to Bousquet, though many composition faculty do desire to become true intellectuals, or visionaries and leaders who impact the field, the reality is that many of us become managers or bosses in charge of writing centers, first-year writing programs, institutional writing programs, and so forth. (Bousquet 2003, 8–9). Donna Strickland (2011) goes even further to state the field of composition is operating in a "managerial unconscious," for we have omitted opportunities to think critically about the work of management and how the field ultimately is impacted (15). To dream big and inspire others when feeling down because we see the daily stumbling blocks that prevent us from being so great is difficult, to say it mildly. So, then, how does one negotiate the two roles and make the best of the situation?

At this point, it is necessary that I step back and give a brief history of the founding of HBCUs and a description of our contexts, particularly the ways in which faculty and students engage with one another. Historically black colleges and universities, or HBCUs, were founded because blacks were not allowed to attend predominately white institutions, or PWIs. The first HBCU was founded in 1837 (Cheyney University in Pennsylvania), and the majority of the others were founded by abolitionists and religious groups after the end of the Civil War. Currently, there are approximately one hundred HBCUs in existence, and they received their official designation as HBCUs from Congress in 1965. Specifically, an HBCU is defined as an institution whose "principal mission was and is the education of black Americans [and] was accredited and . . . established before 1964" (United Negro College Fund n.d.). At HBCUs, we pride ourselves on having smaller class sizes, which allows for a more intimate and personalized learning process. Our primary focus is on teaching, with service and research following behind. As a result, we have higher teaching loads than those at research institutions (usually a 4/4 load or higher); however, because most HBCUs are primarily undergraduate institutions, we most often teach our courses and grade all assignments without the help of graduate assistants, thus giving students direct access to us at all times.

Though in current times HBCUs are becoming more diverse racially, the primary student clientele, particularly at the undergraduate level, is composed of African American students, and many of the traditions in terms of curriculum, classroom structure, and student-faculty interactions still exist today. Another interesting aspect of the HBCU student population is just how academically diverse it is. On the one hand, we stay true to our historical missions: we recruit "diamonds in the rough," or those students who on paper are not ideal or have not been the most academically prepared; we then polish them up and send them to be change agents in the world. It is essential also to note here that most are not in the best academic shape, not because of intelligence or innate ability but because of a lack of access, opportunity, and exposure (which usually is connected to socioeconomic status). Our classrooms are full of some of the most intelligent and competitive students, who choose to attend HBCUs over large research or Ivy League universities because of family legacy and tradition, personal obligations, or perhaps because their K–12 experiences were ones in which they were part of a handful of blacks in their high schools or in their honors classes and they want to experience four years in a safe space where they can embrace the fullness of and diversity within the black culture.

I've often been told by my students, "You're like the big sister I never had," though that was in my younger teaching days, or "You remind me of my auntie," or "You're like my academic mom," which I promptly replace with "academic godmother," as in my mind, I am nowhere near old enough to have an nineteen- year-old child. However, what these statements demonstrate is how many African American instructors at HBCUs serve as "othermothers" or even "otherfathers" to hundreds of students on a daily basis. Our campus-wide approach is labeled an *intrusive* one, for we essentially are tasked with engaging with our students by any means necessary. We female faculty and staff often stand in the gap and represent mother figures who gently nudge or give life advice to young people transitioning into adulthood. African American male faculty and staff offer young men and women visual images of positive black males, for we know the media rarely takes the opportunity to highlight black males in a positive light. I often have students with fathers who are in prison and have been there for most of the students' childhoods, if the fathers are present at all. Yet, these are young people determined to make different choices and select an alternate life path for themselves; still, they often need encouragement and sound advice on how to navigate this new space, for they may come from families or communities where they are the first to blaze this new trail. Thus, it is imperative to keep the unique HBCU context in mind while reading this chapter, as it very much shapes the WPA experience.

I admit that when I was a new WPA, the leadership piece came much more easily than the managerial piece. I had attended conferences and spent my summers reading writing center and writing-across-the-curriculum theory and pedagogy, all in an effort to determine what I wanted our new Writing Studio to look like and feel like; I wanted to see how I could inspire faculty members to implement our new writing intensive (WI) program in their academic departments. So, I focused on being a leader first. I changed the name of our writing center to the Writing Studio (I was inspired by Duke University's and Georgia State University's Studios), and I referred to our tutors as consultants, all to help bring about a positive new presence on campus and eliminate the negative stigma often attached to receiving tutorial services. After spending some time focusing on those "big-picture" items, I then realized I had to turn my focus to the day-to-day managerial tasks.

Those tasks included developing training materials, facilitating the consultant training, creating needed policies and procedures so the Writing Studio would run smoothly, and developing an assessment plan for the WI faculty so we could evaluate exactly what was happening in the courses. The deeper I got into the managerial piece, the harder it was to stay upbeat and continue being that visionary. But, rather than stay discouraged (though I still have my moments), I began to look at the benefits of being in two places at once, of being in a marginal leadership space and still able to effect change.

The first time I was introduced to the concept of marginal space, or liminal space, was in my undergraduate thesis course at Hampton

University. To prepare us for scholarly work, our instructors required us to read Henry Louis Gates's 1988 *The Signifyin' Monkey: A Theory of African-American Literary Criticism*. In that text he gives an historical account, connecting African mythological and cultural beliefs with present-day African American dialect, illustrating how being in a marginal space is like being in two worlds. For the people of Yoruba, it meant that Esu-Elebara, a trickster figure of Yoruba mythology, literally had one foot in heaven and one foot on earth. He could go between both worlds, acting as a liaison for both humans and the heavenly world because of his ability to communicate in both spaces effectively. In African American culture, it means having the ability to speak in multiple dialects, including African American Vernacular English and Standard English (though we know the two are not mutually exclusive). Often, being in a marginal space is seen as negative, for it can be perceived as not being fully seen or valued in any real way. Yet, Gates posits that being in a marginal space can be positive, for it allows one to move easily from one role to the next, sometimes without even being noticed, seamlessly and rather effortlessly. In some ways it keeps others on their toes when it comes to you, for they don't always know what role you will occupy and when those transitions will take place.

This theme of WPAs occupying multiple roles is one that permeates this very text. Talinn Phillips, Paul Shovin, and Megan Titus in chapter 5 of this edited collection discuss WPAs who exist in a liminal space. They define liminal WPAs as adjuncts or graduate students or perhaps even tenure-track faculty. The assumption is that once one earns tenure or a permanent position, the liminality disappears. Yet, I posit that at smaller institutions, that liminal situation never goes away.

At my institution, I'm essentially the only one who is a part of or meets with all writing constituents on campus on a consistent basis. The advantage is that I am "insider" and in the know for essentially every writing sect. Thus, I think people in all areas are less guarded around me and are 100 percent real rather than censoring themselves to give the "appropriate" response. Also, I genuinely show interest for each group's concerns as related to student writing; I think there's an established trust I have with each of these groups so that even if I push back, disagree, or share another perspective, they understand I am bringing those ideas with everyone's best interests at heart.

Here's a very basic example: no matter how many classroom presentations we give or times I tell faculty members to give us advanced notification when they want to send several students to us at the same time, we inevitably have professors who require their entire class to come have their assignments "proofread" by someone in the Writing Studio before handing them in. In many instances, this requirement comes from the professors who refuse to allow us to give classroom presentations about our services. Consequently, most often these are the students who come in with less-than-enthusiastic attitudes about their appointments. They don't care to be actively engaged and would prefer to have someone else edit their paper while they sit back and relax. My consultants loathe these appointments. Hence, they have asked me if we can forbid any student whose teacher has not invited a presentation from receiving services because their students are never prepared to be participant learners. In the same vein, they have asked that we not allow faculty members to require students to come. I think the request is partially tongue in cheek, but I know there is some real truth behind the request. Similarly, they have asked if we can refuse to see students who come in for assistance the same day their papers are due. In both cases, I give an emphatic no and go on to explain why we cannot refuse students in our spaces.

In the first instance, the students would be suffering essentially because the faculty member was not proactive enough to get us involved before sending students to us. While we can educate students about our true purpose once they arrive in our space, it is not necessarily their fault they don't know that purpose in advance. Several faculty members with good intentions send their students with instructions to have someone proofread, not realizing their actions go counter to everything we hold sacred as writing center professionals. I remind my staff that many of these faculty members actually are trying to support us by sending students, so we have an obligation to serve those students. Simultaneously, I use that assignment as an opportunity to reach out to the faculty and explain our true purpose and pedagogy. Moreover, often it's those students who come unwillingly their first time who end up appreciating the space and who come back repeatedly on their own. I explain to the consultants that often I require my first-year writing students to visit the Studio, with the hope that they will see the benefit and return again. Sometimes, it's just a necessary "evil" or first step.

In the second instance of students wanting to be served at the last minute, again I make clear that my staff is obligated to help all students as best they can. While it's too late to do much to improve the students' current assignments, it's a chance to explain how more help could have been given if the students had come earlier. It's an opportunity to let the students know of our true purpose and encourage them to come again better prepared. In both instances, even if the consultants do not like my answer, I believe they respect it more because they know I value their concerns and that, ultimately, I always have their backs.

These examples illustrate the benefit of occupying a marginal space. Because I am a faculty member, I understand their perspective and can more effectively share that with the writing consultants. But because they know I advocate for them whenever I can, they listen and actually respect my opinion (rather than being suspicious of me, as they are of many other faculty members), even when I push back.

Another great benefit of occupying multiple positions is that I am able to bring together the many campus stakeholders who value writing. After sitting in several meetings in which the upper-level writing-intensive (WI) faculty wondered what happens in those first-year writing classes and vice versa, I realized it only made sense to have everyone convene for a single conversation. Recently, I gathered representatives from our WI faculty, first-year writing faculty, our campus-wide Communicating to Succeed program, and even the student writing consultants (it's never too early to get them involved in these kinds of professional conversations). Because of my multiple roles, each constituent trusts me to represent their concerns, so gathering everyone was fairly easy. The meeting was quite productive, as each group got to hear what the other group valued related to student writing. Similarly, the writing consultants gained a better understanding of the reasons some professors design assignments in specific ways and have certain expectations (sometimes unrealistic ones) about what we're able to do in the Writing Studio. In addition, this meeting gave the writing consultants the opportunity to explain our true purpose and how we operate inside tutorial sessions. The conversation in which we engaged was fruitful and eye opening for everyone. My marginal space made me equipped to communicate to everyone fairly easily, accurately, and effectively. Now, that doesn't mean any issues are resolved necessarily, but it does mean true meaningful dialogue begins and I can ensure it is sustained.

WPAs who are both cheerleaders and players can be more invested in seeing a vision come to fruition. Managers most often are executing someone else's vision, someone else's passion, so the personal commitment to see a plan succeed is not always there. Yes, managers may be invested as much as they believe their paychecks say they should be, but that personal drive and enthusiasm for a project more often is lacking. Thus, the leaders who also are managers are more willing to keep going when the task becomes difficult and obstacles are in the way. According to Abraham Zaleznik (2004), often considered the first to theorize about the difference between managers and leaders, managers "maintain minimal emotional involvement [and] lack empathy" when relating to others; they also create goals out of necessities, "take an impersonal, passive outlook," and avoid risk (3). Leaders "relate to others directly, intuitively, empathetically," focus on how their decisions impact the participants, "change how people think about what's desirable and possible . . . shape rather than respond to ideas . . . and seek risk when opportunities appear promising" (3). Yet, it is impossible for managers who also serve as leaders to not feel emotionally connected to their work. Leaders are invested in seeing their visions come to life, and managers who are involved in creating that vision will work harder to see it happen.

For example, I have been the director of the Writing Studio for just over ten years now. When I first took the position, the then-writing center was a small space barely known outside the English department. Few students outside English classes or beyond their first year sought out our assistance. I had no budget. The Writing Studio was not a line item on any department's budget, so I had to rely on soft money, including Title III federal grant money and "leftover" funding from other departments, to purchase supplies and pay the student tutors. While it was frustrating and time consuming to go to different colleagues asking for resources, I saw it as "paying my dues" and a necessary evil for earning the respect of administrators on campus.

Ten years later, I still have no budget, and I'm no closer to getting one. (Another feature of HBCUs is our limited funding for numerous reasons, including fewer grant dollars coming into our institutions because with a 4/4 or 4/5 teaching load, finding the time to complete and submit applications is nearly impossible.) Granted, it is easier for me to obtain funds from other departments because I have an established rapport with colleagues, so people trust that I will use their funds wisely. Yet the energy exerted and time spent continuing to search for assistance is beyond frustrating. I have collected data to show our growth and impact on campus. The year before I became director of the Studio, the previous director estimated they held two hundred tutorial sessions with students. This past year, we held over thirteen hundred sessions and served an additional one thousand students via classroom presentations and campus-wide workshops. We went from having only about 30 percent of our clients making appointments in advance to approximately 84 percent of our students making their appointments in advance; moreover, 74 percent of our students were repeat clients. We believe this growth is evidence of a changing culture, of students actually planning in advance rather than waiting until the last minute to complete their writing assignments and of students seeing the value of our services. This example also shows how the manager and leader positions work together, for the manager's role is to collect and maintain sufficient data and the leader's role is to use that evidence to advocate for betting resources and working conditions.

I am convinced I only stuck with this position and work as hard as I do to make the Writing Studio a success because it is my own vision I have been working to implement. I would not have been as passionate about ensuring the Writing Studio thrived if it were someone else's dream I was fulfilling. Thus, in this instance, being both leader and manager has worked in the best interest of the Studio because it has a manager who is willing to jump through a few more hoops than the average person would. I can see what the Studio is doing for both our clients and our student staff members, so I constantly am recharged each year.

It has become the norm for my graduate-student staff members to present at local and regional conferences. Yes, as is the case with all other funding, securing travel funds is a challenge, as well. But because so many of my graduate students have aspirations of entering doctoral programs or becoming community college professors, I know these professional experiences will be invaluable in helping them become more marketable and competitive. Again, that "big sister" and "othermother" vision of seeing my students achieve is what pushes me to knock on many doors and complete endless amounts of paperwork to make the conference travel a reality. Ultimately, some staff members have gone on to doctoral programs in English, others have become high-school and community college instructors who have been involved in course design and administrative roles, and one even became an assistant writing center director at a local university.

Ultimately, occupying both roles has kept me informed and somewhat energized to fulfill each one to the best of my ability. The downfalls of both roles for me, and I imagine for many others too, is that maintaining adequate enthusiasm, energy, and time (literally) to fulfill each one successfully becomes extremely difficult. It is physically and emotionally taxing to fight seemingly endless battles in the name of saving the Writing Studio. I think short term the positives can outweigh the negatives when establishing a writing center; but long term, these conditions can easily lead to burnout and complacency.

According to Zaleznik (2004), managers feel a part of the organization, while leaders often feel separated from it (18). I find this observation to be quite interesting; because leaders are so passionate about their unit's success, I never considered that they would see themselves as not being a part of it. However, he explains that because managers are so involved in the day-to-day hustle, they can more easily connect to everyone on an individual basis, forging meaningful and effective relationships. But because leaders are creating visions yet unseen by others, taking risks when colleagues may see that as ridiculous, they must be willing to stand apart, sometimes alone, as they work to help others see that vision become a reality. This position is both an advantage and a constraint. On the one hand, because I do hold so many managerial roles, I still have quite a close relationship with my graduate and undergraduate writing consultants. Many have become like younger siblings or nieces and nephews, sharing with me their concerns about next steps in life, graduate and professional programs, and life relationships, even after they have graduated. More seasoned alumni come to me for advice on everything from marriage to parenting without even giving it a second thought. I treasure those relationships and hate the thought of losing them. But in all honesty, as my leadership role increases and I get a bit more help (staffing) at the manager level, I do think some of the student workers feel I am less accessible. When we were a smaller unit, I did all managerial things, so it was inevitable that the relationships would form. Now, I must make a concerted effort to chat with my staff members more off the record, initiating conversations about their classes and life beyond college. It's not as effortless as it used to be. And yet because I believe so much in how the consultants benefit from their roles as workers in the Studio, and because I take my role as mentor so seriously, I want to ensure they have good heads on their shoulders when they leave my space. As Jane Hindman (2009) notes, this outsider-within stance (Patricia Hill Collins; see Collins 1990) is not static, but rather is always changing. As certain aspects of my roles expand and change, I am forced to constantly recalibrate my positions and the tasks within them.

So, is it desirable to try to stay in two worlds—manager and leader? Administrator and faculty member? My heart says yes because the benefits are so great. But my body often says no, for it is taxing and draining trying to occupy two spaces physically and mentally at one time. In William McCauley and Nicholas Mauriello's 2007 edited collection *Marginal Words, Marginal Works? Tutoring the Academy in the Work of Writing Centers*, several writing center administrators talk about the benefits and drawbacks of occupying marginal spaces on their campuses. Essentially, recurring questions in each chapter are how marginal (or not) do I want to be at my own institution? and might the strategy in this chapter work on my campus? No author gives any prescriptive answers, but they challenge us to weigh the costs and benefits of positioning ourselves in specific ways through the strategies and practices in which we are willing to engage.

As Tony Scott (2009) points out in his article "How We Do What We Do?," rarely are the contradictions in our roles discussed in a scholarly or academic forum, nor are we usually prepared for the matrix that is WPA life: "Discussions of pedagogy and literacy theory rarely deal with the material conditions of teaching and writing in the university. . . . Our contradictions therefore are carried forward year to year without acknowledgements or efforts at reconciliation" (44). In other words, most of us ponder how much we're willing to give and to whom. Ultimately, we must question what makes sense given our own institutional contexts, missions, and goals. Being in the margins means the rules are still being formulated, and often we can determine how much of a part we want to play in that process.

References

Bousquet, Marc. 2003. "Composition as Management Science." In *Tenured Bosses and Disposable Teachers: Writing Instruction in the Managed University*, edited by Marc Bousquet, Tony Scott, and Leo Parascondola, 11–35. Carbondale: Southern Illinois University Press.

Bousquet, Marc, Tony Scott, and Leo Parascondola. 2003. *Tenured Bosses and Disposable Teachers: Writing Instruction in the Managed University*. Carbondale: Southern Illinois University Press.

Collins, Patricia Hill. 1990. Black *Feminist Thought: Knowledge, Consciousness, and the Politics of Empowerment*. New York: Routledge.

Gates, Henry Louis. 1988. *The Signifyin' Monkey: A Theory of African-American Literary Criticism*. New York: Oxford University Press.

Hindman, John. 2009. "Inviting Trouble: The Subversive Potential of the Outsider Within Standpoint." In *The Writing Program Interrupted: Making Space for Critical Discourse*, edited by Donna Strickland and Jeanne Gunner, 99–113. Portsmouth, NH: Boynton/Cook.

Kotter, John P. (1990) 2001. "What Leaders Really Do." Special leadership issue, *Harvard Business Review*. https://hbr.org/2001/12/what-leaders-really-do.

McCauley, William J., and Nicholas Mauriello, eds. 2007. *Marginal Words, Marginal Work? Tutoring the Academy in the Work of Writing Centers*. New York: Hampton.

"The Portland Resolution: Guidelines for Writing Program Administrator Positions." 1992. *WPA: Writing Program Administration* 16 (1–2): 88–94.

Scott, Tony. 2009. "How We Do What We Do: Facing the Contradictory Political Economics of Writing Programs." In *The Writing Program Interrupted: Making Space for Critical Discourse*, edited by Donna Strickland and Jeanne Gunner, 41–55. Portsmouth, NH: Boynton/Cook.

Strickland, Donna. 2011. *The Managerial Unconscious in the History of Composition Studies*. Carbondale: Southern Illinois University Press.

United Negro College Fund (UNCF). n.d. Accessed June 17, 2016. http://www.uncf.org.

Zaleznik, Abraham. 2004. "Managers and Leaders: Are They Different?" *Harvard Business Review* (January). https://hbr.org/2004/01/managers-and-leaders-are-they-different.

2
SUDDENLY WPA
Lessons from an Early and Unexpected Transition

Chris Blankenship

When I was interviewed for a tenure-track position at Emporia State University in 2012, I was told in no uncertain terms that, should I be offered the job, I would be expected to step into the role of director of composition once I received tenure. Knowing the difficulties faced by jWPAs (Dew and Horning 2007), I felt the stipulation was fair, even generous, and I readily accepted the position after it was offered a few days later. When I started the job that fall, I immediately began helping with the composition program as a member of the standing Composition Committee, but the administrative responsibilities of the program remained entirely with the tenured director.

Just after midterm during my third semester at ESU, the director of composition informed me that she would be stepping down from her position for health reasons, effective at the end of the semester. Despite the verbal assurances during my interview, no restrictions against taking this position pretenure existed in my official contract. It quickly became clear that the rest of the department, as well as the dean and provost, expected I would immediately and gladly take the position—one that received limited reassignment time in exchange for responsibilities in placement, scheduling, training and supervising graduate teaching assistants, hiring and supervising contingent instructors, transfer-credit decisions, test-out evaluations, program assessment, and a slew of other minor duties. Having read scholarship about jWPAs, particularly Alice Horning's (2007) argument about the questionable ethics of such positions (40), I was reluctant to accept the job so far from tenure; however, my options were limited, and after several meetings, the chair, dean, and I came to terms I found acceptable. In the spring of 2014, I officially became the WPA.

DOI: 10.7330/9781607326335.c002

This chapter details my journey through the perilous waters of dealing with departmental pressures to take the job and negotiating contract modifications with administrators within a very short time frame. I reflect on the victories I achieved, the concessions I made, and the lessons I learned in going through this process while also considering what role my privilege as a white male played in these outcomes. It is my hope that my experiences may provide a touchstone for how to (or not to) use negotiations to resist the "do-more-with-less" mentality that seems to pervade higher education, particularly with the ballooning responsibilities assigned to writing program administration.

INSTITUTIONAL CONTEXT

Emporia State University is a regional, postbaccalaureate comprehensive institution of approximately six thousand students (four thousand undergraduates) in a small town in east central Kansas. The student population is fairly homogenous; the vast majority (83 percent) are in-state students and 69 percent are white. The institution is teaching focused: all faculty teach the equivalent of twelve credit hours a semester with a sixteen-to-one student-faculty ratio (College Portraits 2014). Opportunities for reduced teaching loads for research and administration are very limited, particularly in the College of Liberal Arts and Sciences, where most general education courses are taught.

The composition program is housed in English, Modern Languages, and Journalism, a department of fifteen tenure-line faculty, five to eight non-tenure-track faculty (both part and full time), and ten to twelve graduate teaching assistants in the master of arts in English program. The composition program itself comprises those who teach three courses: Basic Writing, Composition I, and Composition II. Among the tenure-line faculty, only the two rhetoric and composition specialists regularly teach sections of these three courses. The majority of composition courses are taught by GTAs (e.g., fifty out of seventy-two available sections during the 2014–2015 academic year).

While the department chair and graduate director have some input into certain aspects of the program, such as the hiring of GTAs, the director of composition is otherwise an autonomous authority. At the point at which I took over, the program had been in place for eighteen years, founded and run by the former WPA throughout this entire time save for a single semester sabbatical during which a non-tenure-track instructor, a former graduate student from the program, served as temporary director. As the only rhetoric and composition specialist on faculty, the former WPA was solely responsible for all program development. Even the standing department Composition Committee generally went without members and meetings until another new hire, and I agreed to serve on it as part of our service responsibilities in 2012, an unfortunate reflection of the traditional reliance on, yet inattention to, composition we see in traditional, literary-studies-focused English departments (Crowley 1998).

PERSONAL CONTEXT

The position I was hired into was a new one, the culmination of a long-argued point by the WPA that a department with the responsibility to provide expert composition instruction and up-to-date training for graduate-student teachers required more than a single specialist in rhetoric and composition. When I started work at Emporia State in fall 2012, I was assigned two composition courses and two split-level undergraduate/graduate courses in rhetoric and composition theory. On the service side, I immediately threw myself into working with the composition program by serving on the newly reinvigorated Composition Committee and taking the lead on designing an assessment protocol for the program, something I quickly learned our accreditor, the Higher Learning Commission, expected us to have in place by their next visit in 2015.

Near the end of my second semester, the WPA and I decided we should formalize the work I had been doing by creating a nominal assistant-director position.[1] The responsibilities would be limited to running our new portfolio-assessment program, working with the second-year GTAs (who received less supervision than the first-year GTAs), and advising the director on other program-development matters. This role would still count only as service for retention, tenure, and promotion purposes; however, it would allow me to start working with the GTAs more directly and provide more recognition of my expertise and professional status during the implementation and administration of our new portfolio-assessment program. I officially took on these responsibilities at the end of the spring 2013 semester as we conducted a small pilot of the assessment. As it would turn out, I would only spend one semester in this role.

Beyond my role at the university, it's important to acknowledge aspects of myself that certainly played a role in my negotiation process: namely, I am a white, heterosexual, cisgender male. My "invisible knapsack" of unearned privilege (McIntosh 2012, 74) is quite a large one. These privileges become more conspicuous in small-town Kansas, even in a university setting. As I noted above, the demographics of the students are fairly homogenous, and the same can be said of the faculty and administration here, with a "faculty of color" percentage of 12 percent and "women faculty" of 47 percent (College Portraits 2014). As a feminist, I believe awareness of these intersections of social power is vital to understanding any process of negotiation, especially when negotiating for and with positions of authority.

SUDDENLY WPA

Around mid-October in 2013, just after midterm during my third semester at ESU, the WPA informed me she would be stepping down from the position. She wanted to let me know ahead of the department meeting where she would be announcing it because the clear "heir apparent" to the position would be me, especially given that I had voluntarily taken on the newly created role of assistant director.

After taking a few days to collect my thoughts, I met with the WPA again to talk to her about the responsibilities of being director of composition. Because she had built the program from scratch when she was hired nearly two decades earlier, there was no official list of responsibilities for the position; the duties of the WPA had simply developed organically over time. She noted that, in recent years, the responsibilities had expanded, primarily due to a greater emphasis at the university level on assessment and reporting requirements. Using the notes from this meeting, I compiled a document listing all the job responsibilities, organized into four categories: program administration, supervision of instructors, coordination and placement, and university duties (see app. A for full list). I realized that trying to accomplish all the work on this list while also teaching three courses a semester would jeopardize my chances at earning tenure.

The next week, the WPA announced her decision to step down at our monthly department meeting. After applause acknowledging her years of hard work, all heads turned toward me expectantly. After a moment of silence, one senior member of the faculty declared she was nominating me for the position, a motion quickly seconded by a second senior faculty member. Luckily, the department chair pointed out that this was a matter for discussion, not voting. He asked me what I thought about the situation. Because of the (much-appreciated) prior notice the WPA had given me, I had prepared for this question. I thanked the faculty for their vote of confidence but explained my hesitance to accept the position simply as it stood. I pointed out that in the years since the position was created, the responsibilities had expanded and (with emphatic nodding from the WPA) that the work required to do the position well simply required more time per week than a single reassigned course represented. I expressed my willingness to speak with the dean about the position with the hopes that an arrangement could be made that would make it possible for me to do the job well while still allowing me to feel somewhat comfortable with my ability to earn tenure.

What I hadn't prepared for was the mixed response from my colleagues. Some, particularly those who were also untenured, empathized with my concerns and encouraged me to negotiate with the dean about the position. Others seemed put out by my hesitance, saying everyone in the department was overworked and undercompensated for that work and that I should step up and do my part. One other faculty member, a Spanish-language-and-literature professor, also asked with interest about the compensation available for the WPA work. Before the discussion could go any further, the chair thanked me for my willingness to talk about taking the position, said he would arrange a meeting with the dean, and moved the meeting on.

Given the response I received from my colleagues, I realized negotiations would be more difficult than I had thought. It wouldn't simply be enough to point out work that went into the position; I would need to demonstrate the impacts of the work, particularly when it isn't done well. Using the list of responsibilities, I decided upon a starting point for my negotiation: reassigned time for two courses a semester rather than one. By way of a tradeoff, I would propose that the fall GTA support course, the Teaching Practicum, should be revised to a full three-credit-hour course rather than one credit hour . This change would keep the WPA position mathematically at 50 percent reassigned time from the typical twelve-credit-hour load while also making a valuable change to the GTA training program, providing more support for these new teachers in their first semesters. Fortunately, I had the support of the graduate director (also the department chair) and the WPA in this revision to the curriculum; in fact, the WPA herself had proposed the change several years earlier, though it had been rejected by the previous dean.

A second place of likely negotiation would be the contract length. As with most schools on a semester system, regular faculty contracts are nine months, from mid-August to mid-May. The director's contract spanned ten months, the beginning of August through the end of May. The WPA informed me that despite this contract length, she was expected to work those two off-contract months scheduling courses, fielding questions about placement, evaluating test-out materials, administrating summer test-out sections of composition, communicating with GTAs, and attending meetings dealing with general education. I decided that, in order to be compensated for this work, I would also ask for an eleven-month contract.

A few days later, during the first week of November, the chair and I met with the dean in her office. After some brief pleasantries, the dean asked what I thought of becoming the director of composition. I had brought copies of the list of responsibilities of the position, so, using that as a reference, I explained my concerns and proposed the above changes to the position.

Although the dean was a senior professor in music, she had also served as the interim department chair in English a few years back and was already somewhat familiar with the WPA position. While she was generally silent during my opening argument, she surprised me by noting that other program directors across campus with similar kinds of responsibilities often received reassigned time similar to what I was asking for, though the contract lengths and types varied, a comparative study I wished I had thought to conduct myself. Following this, she asked me a series of questions about different contract scenarios: if the contract were to be eleven months, which month would I be off contract? If it were ten months, would I want the same time frame as the current WPA? Would I be willing to teach a summer course as part of my contract as department chairs are required to do? As much as possible, I stuck to the position revisions I started with. The dean was sympathetic to my arguments but never made any promises or assurances other than that she would take all the information forward to the provost, who would be the final arbiter of the decision.

Less than a week after this meeting, the chair called me into his office and relayed the provost's response; he would allow the position to include 50 percent reassigned time in the fall, 25 percent in the spring, and an eleven-month contract with a required summer course as a part of that contract. The next day, I sent my response to the chair (names truncated for the sake of privacy):

> Chair,
>
> Yesterday, you informed me that Provost C. has offered to change the Director of Composition position to a 2/3 load with an 11 month contract and a mandatory course taught during the summer as part of that extended contract. After putting in a great deal of thought, I have decided that I cannot accept the position with these adjustments. The current position requires six courses over ten months and the proposed

position requires six courses over 11 months. While that would be a moderate increase in pay, it would not be a reduction in overall workload, which was my primary concern in accepting the position, especially as an untenured faculty member.

When I met with you and Dean M. about the position, the 2/2 load and 11 month contract I spoke of was a good faith statement of the bare minimum requirements for me to be able to do the job effectively. Not only would I be taking over all of the duties that the director has done in the past, I would be adding in implementation, oversight, and data analysis of the new program assessment as well as the additional data collection and analysis that we have begun in the last year involving grade distribution, transfer credit, and retention. The amount of work that these responsibilities entail is simply more than the work of teaching a single course. Additionally, as Dean M. pointed out during our meeting, a 2/2 load is commensurate with the administrative reassign time of other program directors across campus with similar responsibilities. Given the great value that we place on the composition sequence by requiring it of every student, it seems to me that the time given to the director should at least match that of other academic programs.

Please pass on my decision to Dean M. and Provost C. If you believe that the provost would be amenable to continuing this conversation, please feel free to schedule a meeting. I would be happy to further explain my rationale behind these requirements and answer any questions he may have.

Chris

Less than twenty-four hours later, the chair and I had another meeting scheduled with the dean. In the meeting, the dean explained the provost's main concern: 50 percent reassigned time and an eleven-month contract was too similar to what department chairs receive. Only in his first year at our university, the provost wasn't willing to risk the ire of other department chairs if he approved what could be perceived as compensation for a second "chair" position for our department.[2] The dean asked whether there were any concessions I would be willing to make, given that the provost wouldn't accept my original requirements. Deciding that time was more important than money, I said that I would be willing to accept 50 percent reassigned time in both semesters on the existing ten-month contract but that I would not accept any offer that included a required summer course as part of the contract. The dean thanked me for my flexibility and said she would take the new offer to the provost.

Within a few days, the provost had accepted my terms, and the dean formally offered the revised position of director of composition to me. I accepted and signed my new contract near the end of November, confirming that I would start my WPA work in January.

LESSONS LEARNED

Don't be afraid to say no. The most important lesson from my negotiation process is the power of *no*. My not immediately accepting the position and willingness to reject the initial offer created the opportunity to revise an under-supported WPA position into something manageable for an untenured professor. As long as you can provide good reasons and evidence for why the current level of support is inadequate to the job, you have the option to stand your ground and advocate for fair compensation, in both reassigned time and money, for the valuable and necessary work that goes into being an effective WPA.

I should note here that the straightforward, argumentative discourse style I used in my negotiations is a traditionally masculine one that was likely more expected and tolerated due to my privilege as a white male. In many ways, I dug into my invisible knapsack for the tools to make my argument that others may not readily have access to. As the former WPA told me, she once tried to step down from the position, and the dean at the time, a man, threatened to find her in breach of contract (she was originally hired with a job ad specifically asking for a WPA), revoke her tenure, and fire her. Of course, the process wouldn't have been as simple as that, but she chose not to fight him on it. In my case, I was a male negotiating with a female dean who, in turn, negotiated on my behalf with a male provost. With this "buffer" in place, I honestly can't say how much of my argumentation even made it to the provost or to what extent the dean adapted my arguments to her own discourse style. Other mitigating factors include the fact that this dean, although she had not announced it at the time of my negotiations, would be retiring at the end of that academic year, perhaps giving her a reason to be more aggressive with her advocacy on my behalf; the fact that this dean had close ties to my department (as opposed to the previous dean, who had a notoriously adversarial one); and the fact that it was the provost's first semester at the university.

In the end, I can't say how much my social privilege impacted my negotiations for this position. It's possible these administrators would not have tolerated an answer of no from someone without my privilege; it's also possible I was simply lucky in having a new provost and an amenable, experienced dean. I will say, though, that as overworked and as underappreciated as so many WPAs are, if my privilege allowed me to better argue for positive, lasting changes to this WPA position, I'm willing to accept the discomfort I feel as a feminist for using these advantages.

Understand you're eventually going to have to say yes. Although being willing to say no to taking on administrative responsibilities that aren't in your contract and/or may damage your ability to earn tenure can help you during negotiations, your final answer will still probably have to be yes. Many smaller programs simply won't have enough qualified faculty who could take on the role of a WPA. If you completely reject the role of a WPA, these responsibilities are likely to (1) be required of the department chair, who is likely just as overworked as the WPA, or (2) be taken over by an unqualified faculty member who likes the idea of the reassigned time, extra contract time, or authority, or simply doesn't feel empowered to say no when the first choice for the position refuses. The first situation can cause resentment from someone who likely has significant control over your future at that institution. The second can cause you stress and frustration as you deal with the influence and authority of someone whose experience with composition pedagogy and theory may be quite limited, such as the Spanish-language-and-literature professor mentioned above.

For a junior faculty member, WPA work can be stressful and time consuming, but it also provides you with valuable experience that can open up a lot of opportunities. Resist the push as much as you can to get the best compensation for your work that you can, but know you may, in fact, be the best person at your institution for the job. In my case, had the administration rejected my counteroffer and refused to budge any more than they already had, I probably would have relented and taken the position anyway. I remember how terrifying it was being a master's student teaching for the first time. The support and expertise of my WPA was what got me through. If I'm honest with myself, I knew from the beginning I would end up taking the position, regardless of how the negotiations went.

Beyond this reason, though, I also had more pragmatic concerns. Resisting too strongly can damage relationships essential not only to effective WPA work but also to future tenure and promotion decisions, especially in smaller departments. If I had ultimately refused to take up the role, it would have left the WPA and the chair, two of my biggest allies in the department, scrambling to figure out how to cover the work. And, as Fox and Malenczyk (2013) note in their chapter on institutional politics in *A Rhetoric for Writing Program Administrators*, unhappy upper administration can have a detrimental effect on both WPA work *and* job security, especially for those without the protection of tenure or a union.

Get the responsibilities in writing. The fact that the duties of the director of composition had been ill defined was a primary reason I felt my negotiations were necessary; it's vital for anyone considering WPA work of any kind to get the responsibilities of the position in writing, often called a *statement of mutual expectation* (also see Taggart's chapter in this volume). Having clear expectations from all involved parties makes it much easier to draw limits when needed or to renegotiate a position if it becomes necessary to your work to take on additional responsibilities.

My chair and dean agreed to use the list of responsibilities I had compiled as the basis for the revised director of composition position; however, in retrospect, I would have made the language in this document more closely mirror that in "Evaluating the Intellectual Work of Writing Administration," which was developed by the Council of Writing Program Administrators (1998). For instance, had I used *faculty development* rather than *supervision of instructors* (app. A), I could have emphasized the pedagogical nature of the administrative work rather than reinforcing the unfortunately common perception of WPA as "manager" (Charlton et al. 2011, 118). Similarly, articulating what I term *clerical duties* in my document instead as *program-related textual production* would describe the same responsibilities but with a more professional framework. Having the backing of a professional organization to help you make the case for your administrative work toward retention, tenure, and promotion is incredibly important, especially with administrators who come from other fields of study.

There will be unhappy/angry people. Although I received a great deal of support in my negotiations, there were others who resented my efforts. As I noted above, some of my colleagues felt I was shirking a responsibility to the department to get this necessary work done. They felt my position as a rhetoric and composition specialist not only qualified me but *obligated* me to do this work with a minimum amount of fuss, despite their experiences with the former WPA's struggles.

Even after I had accepted the position, I had to deal with anger from yet other colleagues who resented the fact that I *had* been successful in my efforts. Many members of the department had traditionally done extracontractual work across campus with little to no recognition or compensation. For example, ESU has a very successful creative-writing minor, built and maintained largely due to the efforts of one professor. She advises fifty-plus undergraduate students, directs the graduation projects of most graduate students working in creative writing, organizes events, and teaches workshops, all without any reassignment time or additional pay. While she wasn't angry with me per se, I had become a symbol for an unfair system. I simply had to listen with a sympathetic ear and acknowledge that, yes, my success is simply another indication that the system is sexist/racist/ageist. I can't say it's a pleasant experience, but, as I've acknowledged, she certainly wasn't wrong. I hope those who have the ability to stand their ground, especially with the protection of tenure, will feel empowered to refuse to add even more uncompensated labor to faculty positions that already require so much for so little.

Assess thyself. White's Law: "Assess thyself or assessment shall be done unto thee" (Elliot and Perelman 2012, 1) Anytime you successfully make an argument about job responsibilities, workload, or compensation, you'll want to be able to demonstrate that the changes made to the position are warranted and appropriate. When I started as WPA, I kept a log of the time I spent on the responsibilities of the position. I wanted to ensure I could justify the new reassignment time for the position should budget cuts or new administrators question the resources going into the position. Doing this work myself also allowed me to control, to some extent, how this work would be evaluated. By categorizing according to the established responsibilities, I would also be able to show just how much time I was spending training and supervising GTAs (a lot, as it turns out) versus dealing with university-level bureaucracy (not as much as I expected). While I never had to use this data to argue for the position itself, I was able to use it in my retention materials to help demonstrate the work I was doing for those on our Faculty Recognition Committee.

THREE SEMESTERS LATER

When I first wrote this chapter, I had just finished my third semester as WPA. I feel that my negotiated reassignment time was put to good use. Over those three semesters, I was able to implement our new portfolio assessment, for which the composition program received praise from our Office of Institutional Research and Assessment as well as from the accreditors from the Higher Learning Commission. I was able to devote more time to training and supervision of the GTAs, helping improve retention in the program. And I was able to set a precedent for providing full-time positions for our contingent faculty by only hiring instructors in part-time roles when there were not enough courses to provide full-time work.

Most noteworthy, though, is the change to the director of composition position itself. In 2015, I moved to Utah for a new job (I loved my WPA work, but my spouse and I captured the unicorn of two tenure-track positions at the same school). The new WPA at ESU has the same reassigned time I had. Even though I have moved on, my negotiations have had a lasting impact at ESU. Even though I'm still not comfortable with the exercise of privilege that likely led to my success, leaving behind a better, more sustainable WPA position is definitely something I can be proud of.

APPENDIX

Responsibilities of the Director of Composition

1. Program Administration:
   - Teaching and Pedagogy
     - Modify and maintain program learning objectives and teaching techniques that keep up with best practices in the profession
     - Oversee the updating of the *Composition Manual* to reflect best practices
     - Coordinate with the library on the development of information literacy instruction for composition students
     - Evaluate textbooks for program†††matic use
   - Data Collection and Assessment
     - Organize and run portfolio assessment each semester
     - Analyze the data gathered from portfolio assessment
     - Collect and analyze course data (ie: failure rates, discrepancies in transfer student grades)
   - Clerical Duties
     - Establish and maintain personnel files on all GTA's and adjunct instructors
     - Schedule and staff 30+ courses a semester in consultation with the EMLJ chair
     - Complete data entry for scheduled courses
     - Submit regular reports to the EMLJ chair
2. Supervision of Instructors:
   - Graduate Teaching Assistants (10–14 individuals teaching two sections a semester)
     - Provide pre-semester training (approximately one week) for new GTA's in both fall and spring

- Teach GTA training courses (EG 895 in fall and EG 790 in spring)
- Track GTA progress through course observations, lesson plan workshops, graded paper sets, and course evaluations (both mid-term and end-of-semester) discussions
- Advise GTAs on student issues (plagiarism, disruptive behavior, etc)
- Adjunct Instructors (5–8 individuals teaching 1–4 sections a semester)
  - Hire new adjuncts when necessary
  - Provide any necessary training in program-specific learning outcomes
  - Oversee instructor teaching through course evaluations
  - Advise adjuncts on student issues (plagiarism, disruptive behavior, etc)
- Tenured and Tenure-Track Professors (3–5 individuals teaching 0–2 sections a semester)
    Coordinate instruction to align with program learning objectives

3. Coordination and Placement:
- Composition Students
  - Advise students seeking to enter composition
  - Administer and evaluate placement tests for Basic Writing and Composition II
  - Arbitrate student complaints dealing with composition courses
- Advising Office
  - Assist with decisions over composition transfer credit
  - Work with course assignments, section distribution, and course caps

4. University Duties:
- General Education
  - Coordinate with the General Education Council
  - Report to the Director of General Education and Dean of LAS
- Representation
  - Attend and vote in annual KBOR Core Outcomes meeting
  - Submit program information to regional and national composition program initiatives
- Advocacy
  - Represent the Composition Program with administration and faculty governance bodies
  - Consult with EMLJ chair and Writing Center Director regarding Writing Center pedagogy, training, oversight, and advocacy
  - Conduct workshops on writing pedagogy across campus

Notes

1. The parameters of the position were ad hoc, determined entirely by the individual strengths and preferences of myself and the WPA. We planned to formalize the role to a greater degree during the next year in order to distribute the responsibility more systematically (see Phelps 2002), but, due to the short time I was in this role, that process never moved forward.
2. I have since learned that this "second-chair" argument has been made by upper administration at other universities. It is worthwhile to note that negotiations for WPA positions may need to include arguments for why the job responsibilities of a WPA are distinct from those of a department chair. In my case, the distinctions involved the nature of the labor of those teaching in the program (non-tenure-track faculty and graduate assistants) as well as the larger role the WPA played in the training and supervision of teachers within that program.

References

Charlton, Colin, Jonikka Charlton, Tarez Samra Graban, Kathleen J. Ryan, and Amy Ferdinandt Stolley. 2011. *GenAdmin: Theorizing WPA Identities in the Twenty-First Century*. Anderson, SC: Parlor.

College Portraits. 2014. "Emporia State University College Portrait." http://www.collegeportraits.org/KS/ESU.

Council of Writing Program Administrators. 1998. "Evaluating the Intellectual Work of Writing Program Administration." *WPA: Writing Program Administration* 22 (1–2): 85–104.

Crowley, Sharon. 1998. *Composition in the University: Historical and Polemical Essays*. Pittsburgh, PA: University of Pittsburgh Press.

Dew, Debra Frank, and Alice Horning, eds. 2007. *Untenured Faculty as Writing Program Administrators: Institutional Practices and Politics*. West Lafayette, IN: Parlor.

Elliot, Norbert, and Les Perelman, eds. 2012. *Writing Assessment in the 21st Century: Essays in Honor of Edward M White*. New York: Hampton.

Fox, Tom, and Rita Malenczyk. 2013. "What Are Institutional Politics?" In *A Rhetoric for Writing Program Administrators*, edited by Rita Malenczyk, 313–23. Anderson, SC: Parlor.

Horning, Alice. 2007. "Ethics and the jWPA." In *Untenured Faculty as Writing Program Administrators: Institutional Practices and Politics*, edited by Debra Frank Dew and Alice Horning, 40–57. West Lafayette, IN: Parlor.

McIntosh, Peggy. 2012. "White Privilege: Unpacking the Invisible Knapsack." In *Race, Class, and Gender: An Anthology*. 9th ed., edited by Margaret L. Anderson and Patricia Hill Collins, 74–78. Belmont, CA: Cengage.

Phelps, Louise Wetherbee. 2002. "Turtles All the Way Down: Educating Academic Leaders." In *The Writing Program Administrator's Resource: A Guide to Reflective Institutional Practice*, edited by Stuart C. Brown and Theresa Enos, 3–40. New York: Psychology.

3
SERVERS, COOKS, AND THE INADEQUACY OF METAPHOR

Jennifer Riley Campbell and Richard Colby

In their article on composing a WPA-themed game, "Praxis and Allies," Tom Sura et al. (2009) determine that one important quality of WPA scholarship is that of narratives. They write, "Narratives are ubiquitous throughout WPA scholarship because they help WPAs situate their reader within an otherwise possibly foreign context. It is through narrative that WPAs are best able to share with a larger audience what they do and why and how their work is intellectual" (80). This anthology is inspired by *Kitchen Cooks, Plate Twirlers & Troubadours*, itself a "collection of stories" (George 1999, xi). Yet, as that collection represents, so often our narratives turn to metaphor and comparison with what is familiar, both in our understanding of those tales and in the way we convey those tales to others. While the WPA wears "many, many hats" (Brown and Enos 2002, xvii), there is no WPA milliner, so our comparisons attempt to define our work, sometimes in roles familiar to the academy, such as teacher (Gebhardt 2002, 35) or scholar (Council of Writing Program Administrators 1998). However, we also construct metaphors to convey frantic multitasking, whether plate twirling (Pinard 1999, 58) or juggling (Brueggemann 2003, 88), and metaphors of wielding our power against foes (White 2003, 113). There are metaphors of parenting and of being a flight attendant (Micciche 2002, 442), nurturing and serving others, and metaphors of creative producers, such as the film auteur (Janangelo 2002, 143). The profession is not lacking in metaphorical comparisons, mostly because WPA positions are in constant flux but also because we are learning to survive in roles outsiders cannot readily observe in practice.

More telling, however, is that metaphors can serve a powerful purpose of helping us better understand ourselves and our identity (Baker et al. 2005, 40). In a collection of WPA narratives that appeared in 2005, one of the authors loosely classifies the many metaphors by which we

DOI: 10.7330/9781607326335.c003

define WPA work using comparisons to other professions, entertainers, family, or Velcro (Baker et al. 2005, 36–39), settling on the idea that "the validity of each metaphor creates a need for larger metaphors" (39). Metaphors can help us differentiate the work we do both at the local level and beyond; so much of administrative work varies from place to place and person to person, so we seek to convey both our differences and our similarities through such comparisons. For example, Lynn Bloom's 2002 Labor Day e-mail query to WPAs about what makes such work "fun" shows a diversity as great as that of the nine writing center directors Rebecca Jackson, Jackie Grutsch McKinney, and Nicole Caswell report on in this collection. We understand, as George Lakoff and Mark Johnson famously wrote, that "no metaphor can ever be comprehended or even adequately represented independently of its experiential basis" (Lakoff and Johnson 2003, 19), so we use narrative to convey our experiences and share our sense of how we inhabit these positions and what we choose to make of them.

In this article, we present two narratives, buttressed by two metaphors, that make a case that the position often doesn't define the administrative role as much as the WPA's personality and previous experiences do. We are friends and colleagues who share many of the same attitudes about teaching, service, and scholarship. While we are writing from two ends of one trajectory—the outgoing assistant director and the incoming assistant director—we both envision the position in different ways. When discussing how we conceptualize and experience our administrative positions, we found we had both spent years in the food-service industry, and our rather different experiences and attitudes toward duties there shaped how we envisioned and enacted the AD role. However, as we described ourselves as servers and cooks, we realized these metaphors for WPA work are limiting. Even in our short experiences, we both see the limits of a single metaphor for the work we do. Seeing novel work only through the lens of the familiar can turn such work into a familiar source rather than a new target, limiting the possibilities of enriching WPA work. We both are ambivalent about the metaphors we have identified with, even though they are the identities that so often helped us find our way. As new WPAs, but also of a generation of composition and rhetoric scholars who participated in graduate courses and workshops on WPA work, we also wonder whether the conflation of WPA work with our pasts says more about who we are than it does about any inherent realities of the position. The metaphors we construct of WPA work affirm that they are "similarities as experienced by people" (Lakoff and Johnson 2003, 154) and not objective comparisons of the roles and jobs we describe. More important, we contend that the metaphors we construct here and that have been written about previously seem to suggest a longing for well-trodden paths toward well-defined goals rather than the more thorny transitions and transformations WPA work often affords.

CONTEXT

The stand-alone writing program at the University of Denver (DUWP) was created in 2006, consisting of nineteen full-time, non-tenure-track lecturers, a non-tenure-track writing center director, and a tenured director. As the program grew, two imperatives led to the addition of an assistant-director-of-first-year-writing position (AD). One was that a single director was not enough to fully support faculty and students in a writing program that had expanded in enrollments and faculty lines. Creating an assistant-director position to handle most duties related to first-year writing allowed the program's executive director, Doug Hesse, to focus on other aspects of program administration and national service.[1] The other imperative was our program's commitment to professional development and shared governance. In 2011, interested lecturers were invited to apply for the newly created AD position. After interviews and input from program faculty, the first AD was hired to a three-year term, and the program is currently in transition to a new AD. In the midst of this transition, our university approved a significant restructuring of faculty roles, converting full-time lecturer positions to teaching professorships with opportunities for promotion and extended contracts.[2]

As a preface, then, we recognize our situation often approximates Richard Miller's utopian vision of a program "comprised of fully-intending, free-willed subjects happily engaged in the composing process; collaborative projects that lead faculty members across the university to share the responsibility for providing sustained writing instruction; [and] resolutions for creating working conditions where writing teachers are accorded the respect and salaries they deserve" (Miller 1999, 8). In a program comprised of non-tenure-track teaching assistant and associate professors, we have not faced many of the challenges of jWPAs on the tenure track. When we work with faculty in the DUWP and across campus, we aren't made to feel "contingent," and our expertise is (usually) valued. This doesn't mean, however, that the AD role isn't fraught with unclear expectations or uneasy power dynamics.

SERVICE WITH A SMILE: JENNIFER'S EXPERIENCE

While the lore is full of tales from reluctant WPAs, I really wanted this job. I had served on various iterations of the committee responsible for first-year curriculum and assessment from the beginning of the program and had developed relationships across campus through the faculty senate. I had studied writing program administration under Ed White and Theresa Enos and served as assistant director of composition in the large English department at Auburn University. The summer after I began as AD at DUWP, the program funded my participation in the WPA workshop led by Shirley Rose and Dominic Delli Carpini, so I was well prepared and even eager to tackle the various duties this position entailed (see app. for the full position description). While this preparation certainly informed my practice, looking back, I didn't draw enough on my theoretical and practical training while serving as the AD. I remember repeatedly referencing a grid shared in the workshop about prioritizing my duties based on effort and impact, but time and again I was distracted by smaller, immediate claims on my attention, and I spent most of my time on "administrivia" and putting out fires. But while much of the WPA scholarship laments or denigrates the time-consuming managerial or clerical aspects of our positions, I see scheduling, advising, and creating documentation for stakeholders across campus as critical to the success of a program, and I actually enjoyed this part of my work as AD.

Perhaps I was well suited to the hectic pace of WPA work because, from the time I was fifteen until I started grad school, I was a server, a bartender, and a bar manager. I was used to running around, trying to make everyone happy. I also had part-time jobs in retail, framing, groundskeeping, and editing. Everything I did was about serving others—making everything run efficiently and look nice. I generally enjoyed this work, and I was good at it. I learned early in my serving career the importance of "saving steps"—organizing items and grabbing a lot at once to make delivery more efficient. Naturally, I was eager to make the writing program more efficient and handle tasks that had been neglected. For example, one of my first missions was to replace a messy, paper-based system for soliciting faculty course and scheduling preferences with an online form, and I mastered the puzzle of developing schedules that made the lecturers happy while meeting program needs. I developed a similar system for managing our online portfolio assessment and worked with faculty on scoring and applying assessment data.

While I had to learn a fair bit on the fly during this transition into middle management, the expectations and timeframes for scheduling and assessment were pretty well defined. Other responsibilities had more blurred edges, and most of these involved what Mara Holt, Leon Anderson, and Albert Rouzie describe as the emotion work of WPAs: "Most WPAs feel ambivalent about emotion work. On one hand, they find it fulfilling, internally rewarding, and sometimes enlightening. On the other hand, they find that it can grow like kudzu to push out institutionally rewarded activities such as scholarship" (Holt, Anderson, and Rouzie 2003, 156). Ironically, some of the duties that required significant time and emotion management were combined into one bullet point on the job description, as being "program ombudsperson" entailed addressing student and DUWP faculty concerns related to the first-year writing sequence, resolving all transfer requests, and assisting with student questions and concerns during each registration period and the opening weeks of each term.

Take the last item. I developed informative and attractive materials to make advising more effective and employed my front-of-house skills to host and participate in multiple orientations and advising events. I really felt in my element when helping students register for classes or pointing faculty, students, and (increasingly) parents to the resources they needed. I liked serving all these groups, doing so efficiently but with a personal touch. But having demonstrated competence in this sort of work, I ended up doing more. A student's question about writing courses could turn into a half-hour advising and registration session, and a few even came to me for help after they had completed our required courses. Students are often fairly stressed or even downright emotional by the time they have landed in the AD's office, so these meetings demand a combination of institutional and emotional intelligence, and some issues just won't have easy or quick resolutions. How long should you spend with the crying student who came in to ask which class to take but actually isn't even sure if she should be at DU or in school at all right now? How many diplomatic and well-crafted e-mails should you exchange with an upset student before ignoring them?

It also wasn't uncommon for people within our program and across campus to contact me with questions technically beyond my purview, illustrating that the boundaries of my role were still somewhat fuzzy. When our long-time office manager moved on and we hired one replacement, and too shortly thereafter another, I took on even more managerial and logistical tasks. Regardless of our defined academic duties, WPAs are often pulled into nurturing or managerial roles, but my gender, service background, and "assistant" position within the program likely made this work more central to the position than it might be for others. Some of the "housekeeping" tasks felt like the side work that had irritated me as a server—as Richard takes on the AD role, we are working to shift these tasks back to the office manager—while the interaction with students and colleagues, the emotion work central to the role, was "*crucially important, often fulfilling, but not officially recognized*" (Holt, Anderson, and Rouzie 2003, 152; emphasis in original).

I found that much of what I saw as important front-of-house work wasn't particularly visible except to those I was serving directly. Part of this invisibility was the nature of the position, but another matter was how much I should communicate with our director, Doug Hesse. Communicating directly with the chair or director was a top-three essential activity cited by administrators surveyed in 1989 and 2012 (Rose et al. 2013, 52), but I had made the mistake of contacting him only when I saw a potential issue developing or came upon a situation I couldn't handle myself. In an effort to save Doug from mundane concerns and too many e-mails, I generally handled day-to-day matters myself, making much of my work invisible to him and others in the program. This certainly wasn't the best way to showcase my efforts and successes. Doug said he assumed all was well because he received no complaints, but he wished I had copied him on more things and that we could have met more frequently to discuss issues in the program. In the latter half of my tenure, I made more efforts on this front, and I suggest that any AD should keep specific records of all their work and communicate with other administrators early and often, as others have argued (Jackson, Grutsch McKinney, and Caswell, this volume). Despite this advice, this is still a transition in process, as "bothering" the director is a concern Richard has as well.

In an annual-review letter during my second year as AD, the director praised my work in managerial and logistical areas but said he wished I were more present in big-picture discussions of the program. In a follow-up discussion, we agreed it would be nice if I could do more of the "intellectual work" of the WPA, but I also wanted to point out that such big-picture work wasn't necessarily in the job description, and there wasn't enough time in the day. I would now also argue, however, that many of the AD duties, such as discussions with colleagues and especially assessment work, are intellectual labors that drew on my expertise and shaped the program (though perhaps subtly) rather than service tasks that could be handled just as well by an office manager. It is in this overlap of duties that the server metaphor breaks down because the WPA works out front and behind the scenes, alternating between routine tasks and innovative problem solving, sometimes as a humble servant but sometimes as benevolent dictator.

Another difference between WPA work and restaurant work is that, with the latter, you clock out, go home, and don't worry about the restaurant until your next shift. As AD, however, I embraced the "being accessible" expectation for WPAs (Rose et al. 2013, 52–53) to a fault. Although I had release time, I was still teaching classes, so I spent evenings and weekends attending to the lesson planning and grading displaced by managerial tasks throughout the day, and those AD duties extended beyond business hours as well. I answered calls during my commute, checked messages while making dinner, and went back to work after putting my daughter to bed. One critique of our over-worked director had been about his tendency to respond to e-mails in a less-than-timely fashion, so I always responded within twenty-four hours (and often much more quickly). Once, a lecturer e-mailed me on Friday evening; when I hadn't responded by Sunday afternoon, she sent another (somewhat impatient) e-mail asking whether I was okay because she assumed I was sick when it took me so long to reply.

The truth is that I faced a number of physical and personal challenges, and these outside factors significantly influenced my experience and abilities during my time as AD. For example, in my second year, I shattered my right humerus two days before winter quarter started. I was lucky the director volunteered to take over my class for the term, but I was determined to keep up my administrative duties, so I compressed my teaching-observation schedule and took notes left-handed on my phone while I sat through classes in pain. Then my father passed away. Then I was diagnosed with fibromyalgia. I was "in the weeds" more than I care to admit, often working until I literally couldn't anymore and feeling worse when I dropped the ball on even small things. The best piece of advice I can give anyone entering WPA work is that you *must* take care of yourself[3] and ask for help when you need it. As Richard began assuming AD duties, I strongly encouraged him to set better boundaries than I had, both in terms of task creep and time (ah, the mythical work-life balance) and in how personally he might take the job and interactions with the director and other faculty.

While the regular bureaucratic work of the position could be taxing, navigating relationships with other lecturers as I transitioned into administration caused far more anxiety. Experiences throughout my time as AD confirmed Donna Qualley and Elizabeth Chiseri-Strater's contention that "the vulnerability that often leaves us feeling unsure and off-balance as administrators and teachers is also what keeps us positioned as learners continually having to renegotiate our positions" (Qualley and Chiseri-Strater 2007, 172). Because I was the first AD, I had to not only negotiate the parameters of the position but also my changing relationships with colleagues. My first discomfort arose in the hiring process, as a number of colleagues I had been teaching with for five years also applied for the position, and the other two finalists were not only colleagues but also good friends. I knew when I was hired that two people I cared about were disappointed. Thus, I quickly realized I would face no-win situations that might strain my existing relationships.

In both my application letter and interviews, I was candid about my concern over duties that would require me to evaluate my fellow teachers, and these evaluations did in fact become the most stressful aspects of the position. The new position came with a fairly clear list of responsibilities, but there was still uncertainty among the faculty about the nature of the position. This uncertainty was illustrated early on when a colleague and friend introduced me to someone: "She's kind of my boss, but she's kind of one of us." Shifting between professional and social interactions with peers could be challenging, and as I continued in the position, I found myself attending fewer social events with colleagues. When I inevitably made mistakes or had to make tough decisions, I agonized over them and worried about how my peers would respond, another example of the emotional demands of the role.

My propensity to be a people pleaser was problematic when many decisions were going to make at least one party unhappy. I lost sleep wondering how to best serve the program, the faculty, and our students—especially when they had conflicting desires. Handling student complaints about my colleagues was a tricky matter, even if I could draw on a wealth of experience from my previous jobs in addressing complaints diplomatically. I quickly learned the importance of not rushing to judgment and of recognizing the value of approaches to teaching that differed (sometimes considerably) from my own. Later, when there were more serious concerns about a colleague, I realized it would be best for me to gather information for the director, who could have the more uncomfortable discussions with faculty members when their annual evaluations or positions might be affected. I was much more comfortable serving my colleagues than censuring them.

During my first full year as AD, I undertook the rather daunting responsibility of observing all lecturers, providing formative feedback, and writing evaluations of their teaching for annual review. Assessing my peers' teaching was one of the most challenging rhetorical situations I've faced. In an effort to not let my personal relationships bias my work, during my first round of observing and writing letters, I tried to channel what I thought upper-level administrators might be looking for and how they would write. I learned this was not the best strategy when a respected colleague, for whom I thought I had written a glowing letter, e-mailed me with some concerns. I had praised how she handled a long silence during class conversation but hadn't considered that she was expecting the students' confusion and had planned the following activity in advance. A comment about classroom management was seen as "damning by faint praise." She suggested that my tone and advice might be appropriate for newer lecturers but not for teachers with more experience. Another lecturer e-mailed to let me know I'd confused the theorist she discussed that day with her reference to a previous discussion and asked that I foreground the more positive aspects of my observation rather than presenting it in chronological order, for fear that other administrators might not read the whole thing.

Initially, I felt defensive and wondered whether they would send such e-mails to the director, but then I reread their e-mails and embraced them as a learning experience. The first was thoughtful and constructive, representing how my approach might have rubbed others the wrong way as well, and the second demonstrated the importance of attention to detail and the need to consider the multiple audiences for these letters in a more nuanced way. Most important, I realized the observation letters from the assistant director should be more descriptive than evaluative. I then had similar concerns about the fairly lengthy annual-review letters I had written for each faculty member at about [the] same time. While a couple of my colleagues said they appreciated [the] work and care, I feared others might have found the new review [pro]cess off-putting. I took the feedback from my two colleagues serio[usly] and I spoke with others about this aspect of the position in keep[ing] with Qualley and Chiseri-Strater's advice: "Only when individuals in a community have rhetorical agency can they work together to examine and mediate their practices and create changes that make equity a reality for all participants" (Qualley and Chiseri-Strater 2007, 177). I discussed my concerns with the director, and we decided that from then on, the assistant director would review all course evaluations and teaching materials, preparing numbers and notes on strengths and potential weaknesses for the director, who could then review particular features and write the evaluation letters himself. This reduced my load, both in terms of time and angst. I also began "being myself" in observation letters, writing as a colleague rather than a manager. I felt more comfortable with the process (though it still took forever), and the lecturer who originally expressed the most concern e-mailed to thank me for my insights.

Negotiating my role and authority with my peers was certainly one of the most challenging aspects of transitioning into the developing AD role, but by the end of my time in the position, I felt I had earned the trust of my colleagues. Perhaps this was because when I made mistakes, I quickly owned them, apologized, and did what I could to correct them (another habit from my time as a server and manager). In other situations in which there were disagreements, I always tried to be open-minded and sympathetic while explaining my rationale. Over time, quite a few colleagues contacted me with policy questions or stopped by the office to discuss concerns or ideas. I finally felt I had settled into my role and that the systems I had put in place would allow time to explore more intellectual and future-oriented aspects of administration. Naturally, that's when my appointment was up.

Transitioning out of the AD role led to another bout of identity negotiation. As Doug Hesse (1999, 2013) has written, being a WPA becomes part of your identity, and in some ways it had superseded my identities as teacher and scholar. To reclaim my teaching identity, I taught a first-year seminar I love but that WPA work hadn't allowed for, and I redesigned my writing courses. I've enjoyed the extra time for lesson planning and the reinvigoration that comes from learning new things with my students. The way I approach teaching is inflected by my service ethos, too, however, and my husband says I've just shifted from spending all time taking care of the program to spending all my time taking care ore students—no longer managing, but still mothering. Aside from ongoing work-life balance issue, that's fine by me.

 was also able to start writing again. During my tenure as AD, I was like ie poster child for how WPA work can derail scholarship: I went from presenting at several conferences a year to attending one if I was lucky, I didn't publish, and I had trouble keeping up with WPA-L, much less publications in the field. Now, I can do more research and writing, but the bulk of my research in the coming year will be dictated by a project I started as AD and is still in direct service to the program. So much of my scholarship has been framed in this way that I've promised myself I'll soon work on an article that has nothing to do with WPA work or pedagogy.

Another nice part of the transition was the liberating feeling of forwarding admin-related e-mails to Richard and realizing those weren't problems I needed to solve. And yet, leaving the AD position left me once again trying to adjust my role in relation to others. To extend the server metaphor a bit, consider how a good server delivers everything diners need to enjoy their meal and then leaves them alone while keeping an eye and an ear out in case anyone needs anything. I've taken the same approach with leaving administration. I've stepped back, speaking less in faculty meetings and participating in fewer program initiatives, in part because I need the rest but more because I fear my colleagues have heard enough from me. Transitions rarely allow you to go back to where you started. They propel you out the other side, bruised and weary, but wiser. In my case, despite the catharsis of forwarding those e-mails to Richard, I feel a tinge of longing for when I was so needed, connected to the program and the campus.

Richard and I were fortunate that we had an overlap quarter when we began sharing the AD duties, so I was able to share what I had learned, answer questions, and discuss plans for the future. However, in the rush of establishing the new position, creating new systems and processes, and navigating various roles and issues, I had found it challenging to keep good records. My plan to create a quarterly guide for the new AD kept getting put off, and the resulting document was little more than a collection of key contacts in various departments, roughly what should be done when, and assorted documents he could use with a little editing. Like Diana George's grandmother, who baked a mean cake but left no recipe (George 1999, xi), I established a position but left no instruction manual.

CREATIVE COOKING: RICHARD'S EXPERIENCE

This is my fifteenth year teaching. While I spent a few of those years as a wet-behind-the-ears graduate student, the time is still significant to me because I have now been in the profession for as long as I worked previously in the only other job I ever had. Around the same time I was born, my dad took over the restaurant his parents started some fifteen years prior in a small mountain community. From then on, I grew up around the restaurant business. As a little kid, I remember weaving through the aisles, bussing tables (probably more obstacle than help), and the occasional experiments in the kitchen, a few smells of which still linger in my memory. It wasn't until I was about fifteen that I began regular, hourly paid labor as an apple peeler. My dad was the type of boss everybody respected not only because of his relaxed attitude but also because he was always the hardest-working person in the place. If something wasn't getting done, rather than reprimand, he would quietly insert himself into the flow and make sure it got done, then just as quietly go on to another job that needed doing. My academic self is modeled a great deal on my dad's work and management ethic, an origin tale faintly echoing my current boss's (Hesse 1999, 44). Of course, my "boss" loathes that title, as it highlights the exploitation of labor in composition programs, at least as James Sledd (2013) and Marc Bousquet (2003), among others, have argued. And yet, we still use the term, sometimes tongue in cheek, sometimes unaware, and sometimes as an imperfect metaphor, as Jennifer conveyed in her story of being introduced by a peer. As a boss in transition, thinking about my dad and my own sense of what it means to do WPA work, I want to shift into why my tale of transition is not a conversion narrative but more a confession.

Growing up in a restaurant meant I tried a lot of different jobs. Cooking food, washing dishes, cleaning toilets, shooing black bears, consoling employees, dealing with customer complaints, and repairing equipment were just everyday occurrences, sometimes many all in the same day. The restaurant business seems the perfect preparation for the role of WPA; my qualifications aside, I want to share a bit about my second-favorite job and my least-favorite job at the restaurant.

Ask anyone who has worked in the industry, and they will tell you the most financially lucrative job in any restaurant is server. The year before I entered college, I took a turn at waiting tables for a season. While there is an art and science to it, it serves as first and last contact for demands and complaints and in the end produces nothing. The server life is not for me; there is no worse job. My second-favorite job in the restaurant is the job I did for almost ten years before leaving for Ohio and my PhD program—and that is cook. I loved cooking for customers. I wanted everything that came out of that kitchen to satisfy the cravings of those who drove sometimes two hours or more to come to our little restaurant in the mountains of Southern California. Cooking is building; it's a creative act, but it also is about audience and purpose, so it is the most rhetorical of acts—and yet, it is behind the scenes. As I graduated from the kitchen into teaching, it is that cook identity I have most translated into my classroom. I want to produce assignments and lessons for students that inspire them to want to produce their own creations; I never want to be just a server of somebody else's work.

As the incoming AD, I am, one might think, approaching the opportunity with a bit of optimism and idealism; after all, I had to apply and be vetted for the job, unlike some at other universities who stumbled into WPA work because nobody else was interested or because they were simply in need of a job. So now it comes time for the confession. I never wanted to be a WPA. Jennifer and I represent second- or maybe third-generation WPAs, with degrees in rhetoric and composition and coursework specifically devoted to being a WPA. I'm informed about the rewards as well as the challenges of WPA work, and to be clear, the

AD position I am transitioning into, while piled with responsibilities and challenges, is well supported and in a program respected and funded by our university. I wanted *this* job.

My confession and ambivalence is really about WPA work in general—what troubles me about the WPA position is the split between administration and teaching (much as I find troubling the split between teaching and research). As we indicated earlier, our position is comprised 30 percent of service, but often the service faculty do extends well beyond traditional notions of serving on a committee. Our faculty do writing center work on and off campus, do various sorts of outreach work, offer workshops across the disciplines, and run efforts to showcase student work, including publications. There is plenty of valuable work, but very little of it is program-level administration. It's easier for faculty to see Doug's role as manager of that domain and the rest of us doing other, highly valuable work. Much as my dad has managed by example, showing how we all can do what needs to be done and not just delivering commands, I expect faculty to do more administrative tasks in addition to the other types of service they are doing. When I offered a version of this line of reasoning while interviewing for the AD position, I remember Doug taking a stern but thoughtful tone in saying, "That all may be true, but at the end of the day, somebody has to make a decision." While he is correct, I still think expecting a "boss" or manager or server to take care of certain tasks can make those tasks invisible and thus neither valued nor understood by the faculty.

Despite my ambivalence, I was excited about becoming the new AD. What I wanted to bring to the role was the very thing Jennifer wished she had spent more time doing—building. While she had created some program materials and some loose documents, we still didn't have a robust adjunct manual. We also needed a more central hub for the myriad tasks that go on in our program. We have an active faculty who participate on many committees and produce a great deal of material, but most of it gets filed away on a hard drive equivalent of Warehouse 13. My building and silent worker-manager ethos wanted to create resources out of that knowledge and work to inform not only our program faculty but faculty across campus, an important task of WPA work, as Karen Bishop (2002) has argued. I still hold on to that idealism, and come fall quarter, I will endeavor to make it a reality.

However, within a few weeks of accepting this role, I ran into some managerial difficulties of the position. My first official task was to begin classroom observations, a process Jennifer has already revealed to be difficult on many levels. For me, however, I could only think, what cook doesn't relish watching other cooks at work? Sure, communicating these observations to the faculty is a tricky rhetorical situation, but I felt confident in using description coupled with pedagogical questions to avoid the hint of evaluative judgment that Jennifer, even in her most diplomatic voice, confronted. What became difficult for me was that, about four letters in, I grew bored with writing the standard four-paragraph professional letter. I didn't think I was building anything of any worth to the reader—they felt arhetorical. So then I began experimenting. One class I observed was about writing effective opening lines, which also led to a discussion about the professor's writing pet peeves—I integrated all his pet peeves into his letter. For another professor, who I knew was a Star Wars fan, I framed the letter in a Star Wars-inspired narrative. After a few of these, I began to second-guess this process because we had just approved a significant revision of the university's appointment, promotion, and tenure document that changed the nature of our positions and the stakes of our annual reviews. After much work across the university, our university transitioned full-time, nontenured appointments into nontenure teaching professor lines. Part of this change was a policy that faculty within the departments and programs would serve on internal committees to make judgments about promotion rather than, as it was before, just our director. Before, an observation letter or teaching reflection would be read by Doug, but these new letters I was writing were going to be seen by more people, potentially people outside our department. An observation letter that might be perceived as too flippant or not professional could reflect more negatively on the faculty than it would on me. The lesson, as I complete the final letters for this year, is that I can't always cook—I must know when to just serve the food.

The second lesson of my transition was that even when I could be a cook, I was never the head chef. A few weeks into the transition, a couple of faculty members ran into an issue of plagiarism. These were experienced faculty, one of whom was also a founding faculty member. Nevertheless, they asked me for advice about the situation. I took this cue to write a one-thousand-word plagiarism advice document with university policy procedures, three approaches to talking with a student about plagiarism, and some strategies for determining whether something is plagiarism or just patchwriting. This is the type of "macrolevel teaching" Richard Gebhardt (2002, 35) celebrates in WPA work and that I looked forward to since our teaching-intensive positions have us only interacting with first-year students. I was also building something I thought might be a useful addition to our program manual, adjunct training, and WAC resources. However, while I was thanked initially for my document, I soon received an e-mail that complained I was not respecting the pedagogical experience this faculty member had with the issue. Much as Jennifer found with her observation letters, colleagues we used to routinely talk with about teaching and research suddenly took our observations or comments in a totally different fashion once we donned the AD apron. My idealism is still intact, but I suspect my wish to stay in the back of the house, cooking up materials to support the program's mission and our faculty's teaching, cannot be a prix faire menu—I need to remain aware of the full constraints of the rhetorical situation.

As I transitioned more into the role, another lesson arose. One of the AD's major responsibilities is in the hiring and support of adjuncts. The DUWP is fortunate in that we haven't had to rely much on adjuncts, and a couple have taught here for years. Jennifer began holding an orientation and workshop day for adjuncts, which hadn't happened in the past. Her system worked well when everyone we hired already had experience teaching composition and several were familiar with DU's approach. In her last half year, however, we offered adjunct positions to several PhD students from DU's English department who had consulted in the writing center but either hadn't taught first-year writing or weren't familiar with our rhetorical approach or with teaching qualitative and quantitative research. We did what we could during our fall orientation, but Jennifer realized she could have offered more supervision and support during the PhD students' first quarters of teaching each class. I wanted to add a more robust support mechanism for adjuncts, so I started quarterly workshops around a theme. The first was on assignment design, the second on commenting on writing, and the third on teaching various research methodologies. In these paid workshops, adjuncts are asked to share artifacts from their teaching while I present teaching research and other approaches to enrich their pedagogical approaches. I have further begun to integrate a lot of this material into an ongoing adjunct manual that focuses more on helping new faculty with pedagogical approaches than on the bulleted lists of promotion and review information in the manual for the full-time faculty.

The lesson I learned isn't embedded in these workshops and support strategies, which others might find useful. The lesson came when, because adjuncts are a clearly defined responsibility of our AD position, I tried to once again step from cook to head chef, much to the chagrin of our boss. As enrollments have increased, and as one of our faculty filled in as interim writing center director and another took leave for a term, I began hiring more adjuncts. Even though we have had few in the past, I saw a need to hire more to cover the approaching spring term. Beyond offering enough seats for our students, I was excited about setting the new adjunct faculty up from the very beginning with the expectation that the program would offer substantial orientation and professional development and support through workshops and informal gatherings so the position would help them become better teachers at DU and beyond. However, as the director pointed out to me, the solution to the spring enrollment crunch was to raise caps for the full-time faculty rather than fill the ranks with yet more underpaid adjuncts (the university sets the amount of money we can pay our adjuncts, currently $3,000 per course). I saw an opportunity to engage in the more intellectual work Jennifer missed out on (and that Doug encourages), but the reality of our positions is that the tactical, and managerial, is often the preferred method. That's not to suggest that the workshops and orientations I will offer are any less useful, only that the constraints of our role, and the need to consider others' positions, define us more often than we would like.

My life in the restaurant prepared me for WPA work, but the disconnects between that life and the responsibilities of the AD position and further academic responsibilities ultimately make it not the best training. The constraints and expectations of WPA work are not the same as those in restaurant work, whether managing, cooking, serving, or performing one of the myriad other jobs that inhabit the space. But our position as teaching professors is also not the same as other professorial roles. For example, we don't have research expectations aside from showing up to a few conferences. And while the program values our experience and aspires to shared governance, we do have an experienced and high-profile director, so we are sometimes redirected by an often-wiser strategic decision from his office. Perhaps I cling to the cook metaphor because I long for the simpler times of staying in the kitchen with little scrutiny from others, even though my job before AD life (and after) has had me in front of colleagues, students, and scholars for some time.

Jennifer has expressed the challenges of her transition from colleague to administrator, and that is a particularly jarring experience; however, we are also in a privileged position as internal hires into the AD position. We, along with our founding colleagues, were instrumental in building the program. We not only know the course goals and assessment processes, but we know why they are there. We have a sense of institutional history that allows us to see where change is possible and where it is not. If we are advocating anything here it is that, as so many have argued before, WPA work requires more than just one hat or identity. Even though we have toyed with the evolution of our own identities, born through working in food service, we recognize an attempt to create a comprehensive metaphor for the work of a WPA is probably futile—maybe because our identities are somewhat fragmented by the position. We cannot identify with the position as if it were simply flight attendant (Micciche 2002) or film director (Janangelo 2002). We also cannot identify as "boss" (Bousquet 2003; Sledd 2013). However, we see in our own narratives how our personalities and the nonacademic jobs we have had inform how we see the work of AD, and that is ultimately what metaphorical comparisons have led us to—seeing where we can excel in the vast landscape of WPA work. Our diversity in life experience and teaching led to similarly diversity in administrating. Even though many of our duties are defined by the job description, each person who enacts this role will approach those responsibilities, and others that inevitably emerge, in their own way. It is helpful to draw on the metaphors shared by others and to recognize how the metaphors we identify with most closely can shape our experience. No single metaphor can capture the fluidity of our administrative roles, but as we question existing metaphors and develop new ones, we can transition between the WPA role as it is and as we want it to be.

APPENDIX

Duties of the Assistant Director for First-Year Writing

The Responsibilities of Assistant Director for First-Year Writing include

- Serve as program ombudsperson. Address student and WRIT faculty concerns related to the WRIT sequence. Resolve all transfer requests. Assist with student questions and concerns during each registration period and the opening weeks of each term.
- Plan WRIT course offerings each year; work closely with the Office Manager to schedule faculty teaching assignments.
- Review teaching in WRIT courses. Provide formative feedback as the opportunity or need arises. Write annual evaluations of teaching for each lecturer and adjunct.
- Hire, train, support, develop, and review adjunct faculty..
- Coordinate the assessment of WRIT courses, including drafting the annual assessment report. Participate in research and faculty development related to assessment.
- Serve ex officio on the WRIT committee. Participate in discussions of curriculum and pedagogy.
- Represent the Writing Program on the FSEM committee. Serve as liaison between the Writing Program and Academic Advising.

- Perform other duties as assigned by or negotiated with the Executive Director of Writing.

Several lecturers joked that our director had cleverly constructed this position to cover his least favorite aspects of WPA work, and the number and seriousness of responsibilities the AD would be undertaking as a lecturer shocked some tenured colleagues across campus. The first bullet entails a range of duties that probably warrant bullets of their own, but this variety of duties allows for a rich professional-development experience. One point of discussion among the faculty has been the potential for dividing these duties among multiple assistant directors to increase faculty involvement and reduce the demands on the single AD, but at this time, there has been no movement on that front.

Notes

1. As explained in the program's faculty handbook, "The Executive Director is ultimately responsible for all aspects of the program, including the first-year curriculum and assessment; all hiring, professional development, and review; coordinating the ASEM program; providing faculty development and support for writing across campus; serving as supervisor to the Writing Center Director and other leadership; developing the program budget and representing program interests both on campus and off."
2. It should be noted that, while some programs' teaching professorships base 90 percent of annual-review and promotion decisions on teaching alone, positions in the DUWP consist of 60 percent teaching, 30 percent service, and 10 percent scholarship and contributions to the profession. We followed the same distribution as lecturers prior to the restructuring.
3. Just as my position was being created, Doug Hesse (2013) addressed this issue in "What Is a Personal Life?" While Doug gives excellent advice about setting boundaries, claiming personal time, and the like, neither of us has followed it very well.

References

Baker, Anthony, Karen Bishop, Suellynn Duffey, Jeanne Gunner, Rich Miller, and Shelley Reid. 2005. "The Progress of Generations." *WPA: Writing Program Administration* 29 (1–2): 31–57.
Bishop, Karen. 2002. "On the Road to (Documentary) Reality: Capturing the Intellectual and Political Process of Writing Program Administration." In *The Writing Program Administrator as Theorist: Making Knowledge Work*, edited by Shirley K. Rose and Irwin Weiser, 42–53. Portsmouth, NH: Heinemann.
Bloom, Lynn Z. 2002. "Are We Having Fun Yet? Necessity, Creativity, and Writing Program Administration." *WPA: Writing Program Administration* 26 (1–2): 57–70.
Bousquet, Marc. 2003. "Tenured Bosses and Disposable Teachers." In *Tenured Bosses and Disposable Teachers: Writing Instruction in the Managed University*, edited by Marc Bousquet, Tony Scott, and Leo Parascondola, 1–8. Carbondale: Southern Illinois University Press.
Brown, Stuart C., and Theresa Enos, eds. 2002. *The Writing Program Administrator's Resource: A Guide to Reflective Institutional Practice*. Mahwah, NJ: Erlbaum.

Brueggemann, Brenda Jo. 2003. "The Juggler." In *Composition Studies in the New Millennium: Rereading the Past, Rewriting the Future*, edited by Lynn Z. Bloom, Donald A. Daiker, and Edward White, 88–94. Carbondale: Southern Illinois University Press.
Council of Writing Program Administrators. 1998. "Evaluating the Intellectual Work of Writing Program Administration." *WPA: Writing Program Administration* 22 (1–2): 85–104. http://wpacouncil.org/positions/intellectualwork.html.
Gebhardt, Richard. 2002. "Administration as Focus for Understanding the Teaching of Writing." In *The Allyn & Bacon Sourcebook for Writing Program Administrators*, edited by Irene Ward and William J. Carpenter, 34–37. Harlow, UK: Longman.
George, Diana, ed. 1999. *Kitchen Cooks, Plate Twirlers and Troubadours: Writing Program Administrators Tell Their Stories*. Portsmouth, NH: Boynton/Cook-Heinemann.
Hesse, Doug. 1999. "The WPA as Father, Husband, Ex." In *Kitchen Cooks, Plate Twirlers and Troubadours: Writing Program Administrators Tell Their Stories*, edited by Diana George, 44–55. Portsmouth, NH: Boynton/Cook-Heinemann.
Hesse, Doug. 2013. "What Is a Personal Life?" In *A Rhetoric for Writing Program Administrators*, edited by Rita Malenczyk, 407–14. Anderson, SC: Parlor.
Holt, Mara, Leon Anderson, and Albert Rouzie. 2003. "Making Emotional Work Visible in Writing Program Administration." In *A Way to Move: Rhetorics of Emotion & Composition Studies*, edited by Dale Jacobs and Laura Micciche, 147–60. Portsmouth, NH: Boynton/Cook.
Janangelo, Joseph. 2002. "Writing Across the Curriculum: Contemplating Auteurism and Creativity in Writing Program Direction." In *The Writing Program Administrator as Theorist: Making Knowledge Work*, edited by Shirley K. Rose and Irwin Weiser, 143–56. Portsmouth, NH: Heinemann.
Lakoff, George, and Mark Johnson. 2003. *Metaphors We Live By*. Chicago: University of Chicago Press. https://doi.org/10.7208/chicago/9780226470993.001.0001.
Micciche, Laura R. 2002. "More Than a Feeling: Disappointment and WPA Work." *College English* 64 (4): 432–58. https://doi.org/10.2307/3250746.
Miller, Richard. 1999. "Critique's the Easy Part: Choice and the Scale of Relative Oppression." In *Kitchen Cooks, Plate Twirlers and Troubadours: Writing Program Administrators Tell Their Stories*, edited by Diana George, 3–13. Portsmouth, NH: Boynton/Cook-Heinemann.
Pinard, Mary. 1999. "Surviving the Honeymoon: Bliss and Anxiety in a WPA's First Year, or Appreciating the Plate Twirler's Art." In *Kitchen Cooks, Plate Twirlers and Troubadours: Writing Program Administrators Tell Their Stories*, edited by Diana George, 56–62. Portsmouth, NH: Boynton/Cook-Heinemann.
Qualley, Donna, and Elizabeth Chiseri-Strater. 2007. "Split at the Root: The Vulnerable Writing Program Administrator." *WPA: Writing Program Administration* 31 (1–2): 171–84.
Rose, Shirley K., Lisa S. Mastrangelo, and Barbara L'Eplattenier. 2013. "Directing First-Year Writing: The New Limits of Authority." *College Composition and Communication* 65 (1): 43–66.
Sledd, James. 2013. "Disciplinarity and Exploitation: Compositionists as Good Professionals." *Workplace: A Journal for Academic Labor* 7. http://louisville.edu/journal/workplace/issue7/sledd.html.
Sura, Tom, Jaclyn M. Wells, Megan Schoen, Cristyn Elder, and Dana Lynn Driscoll. 2009. "Praxis and Allies: The WPA Board Game." *WPA: Writing Program Administration* 32 (3): 75–88.
White, Edward. 2003. "Use It or Lose It: Power and the WPA." In *The Allyn & Bacon Sourcebook for Writing Program Administrators*, edited by Irene Ward and William J. Carpenter, 106–13. Harlow, UK: Longman.

4
"AN EXERCISE IN COGNITIVE DISSONANCE"
Liminal WPA Transitions

Talinn Phillips, Paul Shovlin, and Megan L. Titus

This chapter considers how the field might support liminal WPAs as they transition in and out of their administrative roles. We created the term *liminal WPA* in our 2014 article "Thinking Liminally: Exploring the (com)Promising Positions of the Liminal WPA" and identify WPAs as liminal when there is a mismatch between a WPA's institutional status and the level of responsibility that WPA holds (Phillips, Shovlin, and Titus 2014). Liminals are asked to engage in work incommensurate with their institutional status—an institutional status that marks them as impermanent and thus lacking the power senior WPAs have to do their jobs effectively. For liminals, institutional status can manifest in a variety of forms, like rank (being a graduate student, contingent faculty, contingent staff, NTT faculty, or tenure-track faculty at lower rank, such as instructor), credential (being ABD, having a degree from the "wrong field," such as an MFA directing a writing center), job title (being an interim director or being asked to do director-level duties with the job title of assistant director or graduate assistant), or compensation (receiving a minimal salary, being excluded from benefits, having a smaller budget). Thus liminals can easily embody multiple characteristics of liminality at once, like an ABD graduate student in creative writing serving as interim director of a composition program whose student status makes her ineligible for benefits. Further, inherent in this lack of institutional status is a lack of institutional permanence; thus, a liminal's work and initiatives are easily disregarded because the liminal "won't be here next year," "is just a graduate student," "doesn't really know the field," doesn't have the status to gain entry to the right meetings, and so forth. The characteristics of liminality are multiple: the bottom line is that

DOI: 10.7330/9781607326335.c004

liminal WPAs' institutional status means they lack the direct power and resources to approach the job in the same way as a senior WPA (hereafter, sWPA) would, despite performing tasks typical of an sWPA. Liminals also typically have lower salaries, fewer (if any) benefits, and minimal resources to do the job they've been given.

The title of our chapter emerges from a comment made by April, a liminal WPA and an interviewee in our study of graduate-student administrators' workloads. In describing her position, April said, "I think being a grad student in general is sort of an exercise in cognitive dissonance. So you are both a teacher and a student, you're both an administrator and a student. But even as an administrator, you have infinite amounts of power, yet you have none." April's application of the term *cognitive dissonance* to her work as a liminal WPA is apt, especially when liminals transition in and out of roles. Liminals must often adopt multiple mindsets in order to fulfill different facets of their jobs; they move between different roles and different contingents of faculty and administrators (from programmatic to university-wide), often so fast they can barely maintain focus. Liminals are "threshold people"—neither one thing nor the other, existing in a state of what Lila Naydan terms "hybridity" in her contribution to this collection—and their inability to fully inhabit the positionality of either WPA or graduate student (or contingent faculty, etc.) makes their work especially challenging.

We believe it is vital to recognize liminal WPAs' unique positionality and differing access to power if the field of writing program administration is to support the work of *all* its WPAs. The research we present in this chapter is part of a larger research project on graduate students' WPA work.[1] We certainly don't claim that the problems these participants experienced are exclusive to liminals but instead work to theorize the different ways common WPA issues impact liminals in transition. We offer strategies for liminals' success in "Thinking Liminally" (Phillips, Shovlin, and Titus 2014), but here we draw on interviews to highlight the transitional moments in the lives of four liminal WPAs—April, Christine, Emma, and Pat. We then offer recommendations to ease liminal WPAs' transitions since these transitional moments were pivotal to the overall experiences of our interviewees.

TRANSITIONING INTO WPA ROLES

For our liminal WPAs, all of whom were graduate students, transitioning into a WPA position meant taking on additional responsibility in programs in which they were already active. For example, both

Christine and Pat taught in their respective writing programs and both had applied for their WPA positions. These positions were temporary; in Christine's case, she was the acting director of composition while the director was on summer break. Pat was an assistant director for a National Writing Project (NWP) site, and his position rotated every one to two years. We identified Christine as a liminal WPA because she was serving as an interim director of a writing program while a graduate student. We identified Pat as a borderline liminal; his position seemed set up to allow him to be a liminal WPA if he wanted to be (but Pat didn't). He seemed to have a great deal of freedom in shaping his work portfolio, but Pat experienced this freedom as a significant mismatch between his expectations and the reality of the job. He felt he was being expected to do work outside his job description, sometimes beyond the number of hours he had contracted for, and with a more hands-off supervision approach than he'd expected.

Both Christine and Pat moved into their positions without significant training. This was the first WPA position for each, and neither had taken a WPA course. Both had done some work in the field already; Christine, in particular, had experience teaching and training new teachers. However, Christine "had not realized" the director would be gone for two months when she accepted the position, although she recognized she perhaps "should have," given her prior knowledge of the program. Pat also accepted his position without a full understanding of the job, noting that the job description mainly focused on "planning meetings" and "assisting and facilitating" a month-long workshop for K–12 teachers. Pat quickly found himself largely dealing with "logistical" issues, such as booking flights and hotel reservations or troubleshooting technology concerns, in addition to his duties planning the lengthy workshop and facilitating meetings. For Christine, the additional responsibilities were not a drawback, whereas for Pat they were.

Although Christine took on a significant number of added tasks, she did not perceive these tasks as cumbersome. She was largely assigned to handle low-level issues such as workshops, transfer-credit petitions, and plagiarism cases. While the director was on leave, she and Christine maintained their relationship, communicating several times a week. Thus, the sWPA was available for high-level concerns, like classroom incidents. Christine noted, "I'm still very much in contact with the director of composition, though. She's my advisor, and I talk with her probably twice a week about what's going on in the office, so she's still advising me on anything that I have questions about or dealing with anything that is very, like, explosive." Although Christine took on additional tasks, the sWPA seemed to have made sure Christine was capable of accomplishing them and made herself available to handle more volatile situations, thus protecting Christine.

In fact, Christine commented that she felt she was getting exceptional mentoring and preparation for her WPA position from the director. Even though the director was on leave, she was still in the area and able to advise Christine on complex issues. Christine observed, "I'm getting, I feel, really close advising about the job. Even though the director is not physically available, she often—I go to her house or we meet once a week anyways. So I really value her mentoring, and I really see her as a strong mentor for the WPA position." The level of mentoring and the protection provided by the director seemed to ease Christine's transition into the acting-director position, one she would only hold for two months.

Our second participant, Pat, was drawn to his position at an NWP site because of his interest in the connection between writing and place. Although he didn't have any formal WPA training, he anticipated liking the job, which he thought would allow him to build relationships with local teachers and schools. However, Pat struggled to transition successfully into this role because the job description did not match the actual workload, and he had concerns about mentoring.

Contrary to the job description, Pat was asked to do substantial logistical planning, which became a source of stress. Laughing, he recalled, "There were times when I was on the floor of the library, literally, crawling on the floor trying to plug in the right computer so that the right projector would show up on the right screen for this event. . . . I remember crawling around on the floor and thinking, 'This isn't worth it.' I think I quit shortly after that." For Pat, these logistical tasks were not quite what he had signed up for and were then doubly challenging for him as he transitioned into the role. Had they been in the job description, it might have been easier for him to accept these duties, or perhaps he would have recognized immediately that the position wasn't one he wanted.

We fully acknowledge that many WPAs must negotiate conflicting opinions from various stakeholders (self, other WPAs, departments, institutions) about their duties. Many WPAs feel compelled to take on additional tasks; however, having a higher status affords sWPAs greater agency to set the boundaries of their jobs than liminal WPAs have. In addition, more senior WPAs are better equipped to respond to or weather disadvantages workload ambiguity creates. They may be able to use their institutional authority to better educate colleagues or supervisors about the ramifications of additional duties or to negotiate additional compensation or merely gain acknowledgment in exchange for additional work. Liminal WPAs, especially those who are grad students, experience the same stressors of discovering additional duties or creating them to meet needs and so forth, but their liminal status gives them less authority to ameliorate the conditions those additional duties raise. For instance, graduate students may be seen as creating unnecessary work out of naïveté. Or, such work may be invisible to those in the department who are concerned with "real" work done by full-time staff or tenure-track faculty. Moreover, in a department that depends on graduate-student administrative positions for labor, it's likely the importance of that labor has been minimized by the very designation "graduate student." In such situations, graduate-student liminals may be doing the work of seasoned WPAs but without the institutional authority of a terminal degree, without an accurate conceptualization of the scope of the position by those supervising them, and without the personal and disciplinary experience to anticipate concerns and negotiate them effectively. Our discipline's literature doesn't serve them well either since it doesn't fully account for or explore the nature of liminal WPAs.

In addition to concerns about workload, Pat also had mixed feelings about the mentoring he received, from both peers and the director. The other assistant director was not involved with Pat's side of the work and was rarely on campus, so Pat didn't feel he could seek advice from him. And, while Pat had an excellent relationship with the director, a tenured professor, he also had reservations about frequently asking for advice. Pat said,

> I do think she helped me many times, and if I ever had a problem, I did feel like I could go to her. I don't have a dramatic story to tell about her—whatever—dismissing me or anything like that. Even so, I saw a lot of people on campus were very dependent on her . . . I could see that her time was very full, so she would make time for me, but at the same time, I almost felt guilty about going to her with my questions. I found myself trying to juggle people to consult with if I had a problem . . . because I felt bad or guilty sucking away this faculty member who I think was greatly overextended.

Here, Pat found himself in a difficult situation. Because he had a close relationship with the director and because he saw all the other work the director was asked to do, he worried about overburdening her with his questions and concerns. Pat then found himself consulting with others in order to avoid adding too much to the director's plate. Thus, when Pat felt overwhelmed or confused about his work, he often conferred with other graduate students in his office instead of the director. Perhaps if Pat hadn't felt he was adding to the director's burden, or if he'd had a consistent person to whom he could go for advice, he could have eased into the role more smoothly.

We recognize it's challenging for anyone to transition into a WPA role but argue that this move is especially fraught for liminal WPAs. While sWPAs typically have established relationships with other writing-program stakeholders, or at least a defined institutional status, liminals most likely have neither. They also lack the protection of a permanent job when implementing the kinds of politically charged changes (e.g., curriculum reform) their new jobs may require. Finally, liminals like Pat may lack the agency and authority to renegotiate workloads or set important boundaries on their work—both of which can be important elements when moving into an administrative position.

TRANSITIONING OUT OF THE LIMINAL WPA ROLE

The process of leaving WPA roles was also pivotal for liminals in our study and at times seemed to become the lens through which they viewed the rest of their WPA experiences. April and Emma had both held significant responsibility as liminal WPAs. We identified April as a liminal WPA because of her high-stakes workload (involving skills her supervisor did not possess) and extensive hours. Emma was identified as liminal for similar reasons since she was the de facto program director (while a graduate student) and actually trained the faculty member who would replace her. As April and Emma transitioned out of their positions, both made efforts to keep their programs running efficiently. The extent to which they were allowed to do this impacted their overall impressions of both the programs and the jobs.

Although April enjoyed her position maintaining her writing program's website, she felt the work was too much to do successfully *and* allow her time to write her dissertation. Instead of finishing her term, April elected to step down early. April cited her relationship with her boss and advisor as contributing significantly (and positively) to her decision. She said that although Professor X "was sad to see me go, she totally respected that and continued to work with me on my diss." April also noted that, had her relationship with her boss/advisor been weaker, "that could have been, really, a very bad position," one that could have demonstrated April's "powerlessness" in the position. However, because of her strong relationship with Professor X, April felt comfortable telling her boss she wanted to step down.

Despite the support April received during her departure from her position, she still faced challenges. April hoped to create a smooth transition for her successor but recalled, "I worked tirelessly . . . to get the server administration offloaded to people at the university who really knew how to do it. And then as soon as I left, apparently all of that stuff changed, and then the person who came after me had to do it anyway. So that was . . . probably the most stressful part." April's work to prepare the next person to ease into the role was unsuccessful, and she remarked how "stressful" that situation was. However, despite her difficulties, she still felt she was strongly supported by her boss and advisor. Although she was disappointed in the result of her work, she was not bitter about the outcome.

Perhaps April's reaction had a lot to do with her intrinsic understanding of her position as a liminal WPA. April commented that "as an administrator, you have infinite amounts of power, yet you have none" and that relationships with faculty "aren't quite collegial, but they're not quite like an undergrad student is to a faculty member, either." April captured the concept of liminality well here; she recognized she was both powerful and powerless and that her relationships with faculty weren't professor/undergrad but that she and the other faculty also weren't quite colleagues. Her understanding of her position's liminality could have contributed to how she handled events as she stepped down; she knew she had the power to make changes but little power to implement them. When those changes fell through, she understood she had little control over the situation.

Emma, on the other hand, had a much more traumatic experience transitioning out of her liminal WPA role. Emma and a colleague were assistant directors of composition who worked for an untenured faculty director. According to Emma, the director wanted to keep Emma and her colleague on for two years instead of one, and they agreed. However, halfway through Emma's tenure, the director resigned suddenly, and a new WPA took over. Emma's tenure thus required her to not only transition in and out of her WPA role but to also transition to a new WPA. She was understandably "resentful" and wondered, "Why [did the WPA leave] us in a lurch like this?"

It is strange Emma wouldn't know what triggered her supervisor's resignation. She said, "We heard through the grapevine bits and pieces. I think she was trying to be very diplomatic about it." The underlying reason for Emma's lack of knowledge may well have been her liminality. Since liminals lack institutional status, it's easy to imagine a scenario in which her supervisor thought she was protecting Emma from the truth, which Emma's "very diplomatic" comment suggests. Everyone else may have either assumed Emma knew or forgotten her existence altogether, and Emma was perhaps afraid to ask. Had Emma been a faculty member, it's far less likely she would have had no idea why a colleague had resigned. Not being informed then made Emma feel even more liminal because it was a clear marker that she had less status and was less valued. Her experience of not knowing made it more difficult for Emma to negotiate her WPA position.

That position became even more complicated because Emma's new WPA supervisor was tenured and had been a WPA (but not recently); thus, it fell to Emma and the other graduate student WPA to essentially train their new supervisor. Emma recalled she and her colleague were "very much respected by the new WPA" and that it was "almost like we were a faculty member" because of how much responsibility they were given. And they did the work well; Emma recalled that they were praised and told, "The thing would fall apart without you guys." They had a clear sense of the value they brought to the program while they held the positions.

Finally, when the second year was up and Emma and her colleague left the position, they met with the senior WPA to discuss possible replacements and a transition plan. Yet, after they rejoined their graduate cohort, Emma stated, they "basically just fell off the planet": "Nobody talked to us anymore. Nobody let us in on what was going on. Nobody told us anything. It was like this dramatic cut." Emma commented that, after all the work they had done keeping the program intact, this felt like "a slap in the face." Although Emma asked the new sWPA and graduate WPAs to involve her (and they agreed), she was never contacted again. As a result, Emma felt "some lingering bitterness."

In this collection, readers will note a common thread: the transitory nature of WPA experiences. Many WPAs are engaged in their work, find personal investment in the programs they serve, and experience loss when those positions end, regardless of the reason. Yet Emma's feelings of loss seem heightened by her liminality. Had Emma been tenure-line faculty, she likely would have spent time with the new WPA in the hall, in department meetings, and so forth, and her negative feelings might have abated. Moreover, the conditions that signaled the liminality of Emma's experience and the minimization of her position as a co-assistant graduate-student administrator likely contributed to her exclusion by the new WPAs, even if that exclusion was accidental or for Emma's "own good." For Emma, the problem was not simply experiencing loss after transitioning out of her WPA position. It was the implication that her impact was minimal, that her expertise and experience were unimportant, and that her work was not that of a real WPA but simply of an assistant.

EASING LIMINAL TRANSITIONS

As a field, we might prefer that liminal positions, which easily become exploitative, disappear. We have argued since beginning this project that economic and other forces mean such positions will persist, regardless of the field's good intentions. Indeed, the literature reveals other liminal WPAs who have similarly struggled with shifting power, identities, positions, and duties (e.g., Alexander 2002; Danko 2008; Inman 2011; McGlaun 2008), and this literature often highlights various crises that resulted in the creation of liminal positions. Brenda Helmbrecht and Connie Kendall's experiences were surrounded by "special circumstances": faculty members who took leave, directors who were literature specialists and thus relied on graduate WPAs for disciplinary expertise, and unexpected increases in workloads (Helmbrecht and Kendall 2008). These kinds of "special circumstances" echo other liminal narratives (e.g., Danko 2008; Inman 2011), signaling both the institutional pressures that lead to such positions and liminals' tendency to normalize unrealistic obligations by creating narratives about a perfect storm of emergencies. While some liminals successfully transition into and/or out of those positions, others, like Emma and Pat, may find the pressure to normalize "special circumstances" proves problematic in wrestling with their own identities as administrators and scholars.

Further, WPA experience is important for professionalization and preparation for the job market: we each believe our liminal experiences played pivotal roles in securing our current tenure-line positions. We certainly don't endorse the exploitation attached to many liminal WPA positions; however, for us, the issue is not whether such positions do or should exist but rather how to support the bodies already doing this work. Our study suggests that some of the most valuable opportunities for supporting those bodies come as those who hold those jobs transition in and out of their positions.

Liminality is transitional by nature; it suggests the overlap of statuses or identities and the attendant power and authority. Often, when the field discusses strategies for WPA work, we imply a discrete status attached to that strategy; yet, more WPAs might benefit from strategies that derive from a recognition that overlaps in roles and statuses exist and that some work falls outside the scope of the contractual position. For example, honoring liminals' requests for future involvement in the program means we cease seeing them as disposable workers with little persistent value for and interest in the program beyond their brief and poorly paid positions. This acknowledgement means operating from an understanding that such WPAs have invested *more* than the job has or "should have" required and that they may have an emotional or professional investment that deserves respect. They may be liminal WPAs, but they are doing the work of senior WPAs.

As our examples of Christine, Pat, Emma, and April show, there are clear paths to success in helping liminal WPAs transition. Based on our analysis of their experiences, we make the following recommendations to support liminal WPAs as they enter and leave their roles. Again, we discuss strategies for liminals' success more broadly in "Thinking Liminally" (Phillips, Shovlin and Titus 2014). Finally, although many of our suggestions are aimed at those with power to positively change conditions for liminals, we also have suggestions for those who identify as liminal WPAs.

Conduct an Accurate Appraisal of the Context of the Position and Program

Our research shows graduate WPA positions vary dramatically with duties, training, mentoring, authority, and so forth and often hinge on special/crisis circumstances within a department. A carefully designed and mentored graduate WPA position may be vulnerable because of staff changes, or graduate WPAs might find themselves working outside their job descriptions to direct programs. It is therefore vital for sWPAs, department heads, or others in authority to routinely initiate a reevaluation of the program and its effect on those working within it and then reassign or eliminate tasks accordingly. Such an appraisal should occur annually or when a staffing change occurs and should involve all members of the team making an honest assessment of their work. What reasons were behind the resignation? Are problems with the position likely being masked by more professionally acceptable reasons like needing to finish a dissertation or seeking a long-term position? What impact will the resignation have on colleagues—especially colleagues who are or are likely to become liminals?

For liminals themselves, we suggest asking a lot of questions. To determine the context of the position, identify the other relevant stakeholders. What faculty have been working in the program and why? What will your relationship to them be? How do different factions in the department feel about the writing program? What about the wider institution? Why are you being asked to do this work, and whose work is it? How will it be valued? Support staff, former liminal WPAs, graduate students, trusted faculty members, and folks outside the department can all be good sources of information (and may even offer widely divergent answers).

Provide Realistic and Accurate Job Descriptions

When new WPAs, regardless of rank, receive inadequate or inaccurate job descriptions, everyone loses. The three of us value our own liminal WPA experiences, *including* the ambiguity in our job descriptions. We were self-starters who liked the variety and responsibility afforded to us as liminals; however, Pat did not. He quickly felt overwhelmed and underprepared and left his position midyear. It's possible that, even with a more accurate description, Pat still would have taken the position and still would have disliked the work. Yet neither Pat, his mentor, nor the program were well served by Pat's feeling that the job was more than he'd bargained for. Clear job descriptions help potential liminals assess what is really at stake for them in accepting a WPA position and can empower them to say "this is too much." They also delineate boundaries that help nonliminal colleagues understand a liminal's role, thus making it possible for those colleagues to help enforce those boundaries and educate others about them, a task liminals may not be able to do effectively for themselves.

For liminals, it is first vital to request an accurate and thorough job description that includes duties, compensation, and expectations regarding time. They then might keep a weekly or monthly log of work and time involved, especially for additional duties, in order to make such work visible. While supervisors may not request such reports, it's still valuable to provide them. Finally, liminals might create a handbook that serves as an informal narrative job description with more detail than any job description would contain. Such a notebook prepares other liminals for the position, establishes institutional memory, and paves the way for increased communication between former and current liminal WPAs. If supervisors take an interest in these nuts and bolts, all the better.

Honor Liminals' Requests about Future Involvement in the Program

Emma's was perhaps the most disheartening of all our interviewees' stories. She was committed to her writing program and invested a great deal of time in it only to leave feeling used. Many WPAs justifiably prefer a clean break from their writing programs, and that request should certainly be honored. It's easy to abuse liminals' goodwill and to encourage them to overextend themselves. But Emma had substantial personal and professional investment in her program. She also had future WPA ambitions, despite how difficult her experience had been. These factors meant she wanted to ease out of her role slowly and support the program in smaller ways. If liminals actually request limited, ongoing involvement in the program, we do them a great disservice by promising that involvement and not following through. Emma experienced "this dramatic cut" that made her feel used and disrespected. We discuss possibilities for appropriate ongoing involvement in more detail in "'Like I'm the Man'" (Phillips, Shovlin, and Titus under review).

Respect Liminals Who Need to Walk Away
While Emma left her position because her term was up, others stepped down early because of professional concerns. Pat realized he didn't like the work and that it was causing him significant stress. April loved her job but recognized it was hampering her dissertation progress. Liminal WPA work is highly demanding and may ask more than someone is willing to give to a job that typically offers poor pay, no benefits, and no job security. Although April hated to leave her position, she realized completing her dissertation was more important. Had her supervisor been less supportive of April's difficult decision, April could have experienced damaging repercussions, like losing a vital reference for the job market. At a minimum, April might have reflected on her liminal WPA experience much more negatively if her advisor had not supported her resignation. For April, being valued as a liminal WPA included being valued during the resignation process. When liminals choose to stop being liminal, supervisors and colleagues must recognize the often untenable nature of liminal WPA work and support the liminal's decision to move on. Their departure may also signal the need for constructive critique of the position.

For liminals themselves, leaving a WPA position may be the most difficult decision they make. Liminals must balance the value of the experience for a future career with the impact on current responsibilities (like completing a dissertation or publications) and their health. Given many liminals' dedication and personal drive, they may not be the best people to assess that enough is enough. They may also overestimate the value of staying in a position or taking on additional duties. Now that we are on the other side of the job market, we often see graduate students overestimating the value of additional administrative work on their CVs at the expense of completing their dissertations or publications. Mentors are vital for helping liminals make these assessments.

Make a Concrete Plan for Mentoring
Similarly, among our participants, strong mentoring seemed to compensate for a multitude of ills. These graduate students were often willing

to do work far beyond their pay grades and/or do substantial extra work *when strong mentoring was in place*. The details of the job seemed less important than whether these liminals felt valued and supported. Consequently, we strongly urge those who employ liminals to identify mentors who can support (and even protect) liminal WPAs and provide advice as they negotiate their complicated workloads and career paths. Excellent mentorship doesn't excuse exploitation but, again, our goal is to support real people who exist in complicated situations that may not be amenable to other kinds of amelioration. If the Band-Aid of mentorship is the only Band-Aid available, then know it seems to be a powerful one. Likewise, we strongly encourage liminals to find both a *mentor* who will guide a liminal in how to do the job effectively and an *advocate* who will look out for a liminal's well-being. This advocate does not necessarily need to be someone within a liminal's program; an advocate with a different scholarly expertise could even be better suited to supporting a liminal in the face of programmatic critique.

CONCLUSION

It is far easier to offer those with power advice on how to support liminals in their transitions than it is give liminals advice on how to negotiate those transitions. The truth is that liminal transitions have the potential to be deadly, even though they weren't for us or for our participants. After months or years of doing far more than anyone should have expected, liminals may feel they risk losing all that goodwill in what may be a desperate bid to keep themselves sane and their families together. Neither we nor our participants are aware of any negative repercussions from leaving our own liminal positions, but the possibility remains. We encourage liminal readers to remember they wouldn't be successful liminal WPAs without the strong people-reading abilities that will also help them negotiate an exit. Ultimately, these suggestions will never erase liminality because they can't erase the conditions that force the creation of liminal positions. We do hope these recommendations might make liminal work and liminal transitions more manageable and productive and that they might give liminals the kind of conceptual space they need to assert the agency afforded to more privileged WPAs.

Note

1. The interviewees featured here participated in a nationwide survey on graduate students and WPA work that we conducted early in 2012 with IRB approval. The

participants all provided contact information for follow-up interviews. Megan conducted the interviews, and we coded them using Geisler's protocol for spoken data. We discuss the study and our methodology in greater detail in "(Re)Identifying the gWPA experience" (Phillips, Shovlin, and Titus 2016) and strategies for liminals' success in "Thinking Liminally: Exploring the (com)Promising Positions of the Liminal WPA" (Phillips, Shovlin and Titus 2014). Just as the larger study focused on graduate-student experiences, all participants featured here are graduate students as well. We wish to emphasize that liminal WPAs of all kinds may have similar experiences as they transition in and out of their WPA roles. It is our hope that collections such as this one will inspire more liminals to come forward and share their experiences.

References

Alexander, Bryant Keith. 2002. "Betwixt and Between: The Liminal Space of the Graduate Student as Administrative Assistant." In *Ready to Teach: Graduate Assistants Prepare for Today and Tomorrow*, edited by Will Davis, Jan Smith, and Rosslyn Smith, 16–20. Stillwater, OK: New Forums.

Danko, Nita. 2008. "Without Title: One NTT's Struggle in the TT Society." In *The Promise and Perils of Writing Program Administration*, edited by Theresa Enos and Shane Borrowman, 135–39. West Lafayette, IN: Parlor.

Helmbrecht, Brenda M., and Connie Kendall. 2008. "Graduate Students Hearing Voices: (Mis)Recognition and (Re)Definition of the jWPA Identity." In *Untenured Faculty as Writing Program Administrators*, edited by Debra Frank Dew and Alice Horning, 172–90. West Lafayette, IN: Parlor.

Inman, Joyce Olewski. 2011. "Reflections on Year One as an Almost-WPA." *WPA: Writing Program Administration* 35 (1): 149–52.

McGlaun, Sandee K. 2008. "Administering Writing Programs in the 'Betweens': A jWPA Narrative." In *Untenured Faculty as Writing Program Administrators*, edited by Debra Frank Dew and Alice Horning, 219–48. West Lafayette, IN: Parlor.

Phillips, Talinn, Paul Shovlin, and Megan Titus. 2014. "Thinking Liminally: Exploring the (com)Promising Positions of the Liminal WPA." *WPA: Writing Program Administration* 38 (1): 42–63.

Phillips, Talinn, Paul Shovlin, and Megan Titus. 2016. "(Re)Identifying the gWPA Experience." *WPA: Writing Program Administration* 40 (1): 67–89.

Phillips, Talinn, Paul Shovlin, and Megan Titus. "Like I'm 'The Man': Identifying Key Factors in Graduate Student Administrative Success." Unpublished manuscript.

SECTION 2

Identities and Subjectivities

5
DEFINING DISCIPLINARITY AT MOMENTS OF TRANSITION
The Dappled Expertise of the Multidisciplinary WPA

Andrea Scott

My research focuses on disciplinarity, but I was trained in a field skeptical of this very concept. Those of us who have chosen to make writing studies our intellectual homes after earning PhDs in literature know this move is accompanied by tensions and opportunities grounded in both lived experience and scholarship (e.g., Raymond 2008; Tokarczyk, and Papoulis 2003). Yet the official narratives of such transitions have become so settled they now obscure as much as they illuminate. As Karen Kopelson (2008) put it recently, conversion narratives of the literature-turned-composition scholar are firmly part of the field's lore, and they go something like this: "Fed up with, or not fully inspired by, literary studies, English graduate student or young professor stumbles upon rhetoric and composition, finds it—largely because of its focus on teaching—more political, pragmatic, and relevant than the former pursuit, and 'crosses over' with religious fervor" (751). Peter Elbow (2002) reproduces this narrative of transitions when he describes feeling "pleased and proud when I was drawn *away* from literature by my growing interest in writing," which allowed him to experience "enormous relief at finally feeling *useful*—as though I could make an actual difference for people" (536; emphasis in original). Likewise, Joseph Harris (2012) recounts his satisfaction in finding in composition a "style of doing English" (xvii) in which teaching was imagined as an "integral part of (and not just a kind of report on) my work as an intellectual" (xv–xvi). Versions of this narrative see composition as a "teaching subject" (to borrow Harris's term) more practical than literary studies, though no less compelling.

On the flip side of these conversion narratives we find proclamations of divorce—often told with the same fiery conviction. In this version of

DOI: 10.7330/9781607326335.c005

the story, composition's transition away from literary studies is imagined as a rite of passage. In her chair's address to the CCCC convention, Maxine Hairston (1985) famously implored compositionists to liberate themselves from the "mandarins" of English. "We will come of age and become autonomous professionals with a discipline of our own only if we can make a psychological break with the literary critics who today dominate the profession of English studies," she argued, and "no longer accept their definition of what our profession should be" (273–74). Barry Maid (2006) has made a similar claim more recently, urging writing programs to abandon their "psychological ties" to English departments, where composition still tends to be devalued as an applied discipline (107). At stake in these narratives is the desire to rectify power differentials in English studies by asserting disciplinary independence. As Maid puts it, "The problems, the rift, the disagreement, the animosity, the class warfare, the bad marriage, or the whatever between literature and composition" have "everything to do with issues of privilege, power, and economics" (93).

Both these well-known narratives pit writing and literary studies against one another in ways that are no longer constructive. By relying on metaphors of competition, they ultimately perpetuate stereotypes about both fields. Kopelson's study, for example, suggests doctoral students in rhetoric and composition are more reluctant to subscribe to the "pedagogical imperative" of the field's early converts, despite ongoing pressure from mentors, because it limits inquiry into new approaches to literacy and rhetoric. These students long for the intellectual freedom to engage in projects that may have no practical implications for teaching (757–58). Likewise, Melissa Ianetta (2010) claims that scholarship—in the aftermath of emancipation narratives—misses opportunities to explore affinities between composition and literature, giving the false impression that the "unyoking of literature from composition is well nigh complete" (53).

These emancipation narratives are still with us, but they've changed shape. One consequence of them is that they erase from view the interdisciplinary work of WPAs who have transitioned into the field. In recent years, calls to arms have been replaced by narratives of triumph, with literature and composition studies trading sides. Writing studies has long since arrived as a discipline, the story now goes, outpacing literary studies by virtually every measure—from the growing number of tenure-track jobs posted by the MLA to the increase in editorships in English studies. The institutional strength of writing studies will render the field's ur-conversion narratives obsolete, so it seems. Tenure-track positions in composition usually require terminal degrees in rhetoric and composition, which means scholars now pursue a more linear path to professionalization. English literature PhDs who discover a desire to teach writing early in their careers are perceived as having missed the boat before they set foot in graduate school—unless their doctoral programs offer a specialized track in writing studies. If literature scholars remain a source of tension in composition programs, it's because readers can sympathize with their plight: they are often, as Ianetta (2012) calls them in a recent issue of *WPA*, "literary specialists who were unable to find employment in their field of choice" and are now subjected to disciplinary norms at odds with their original training (182–83). When these same scholars teach theme-based first-year writing seminars in their fields, writing studies scholarship gently mocks them for imposing their interests on their students (Yancey, Robertson, and Taczak 2014, 3, 31), teaching vampires not writing, and violating—often unwittingly—nearly every threshold concept in writing in the process (Adler-Kassner 2012; Adler-Kassner and Wardle 2015; Downs 2013).[1]

The prevalence of this narrative has resulted in a kind of unquestioned dismissal of the multidisciplinary writing programs often led by multidisciplinary WPAs—that is, scholar-teacher-administrators formally trained in disciplines other than composition who nonetheless draw on theoretical frameworks from writing studies in their teaching, administration, and scholarship. The assumption is that such WPAs are undisciplined, discrediting the field of writing studies and impoverishing writing instruction at their institutions. The narrative is so pervasive it is often evoked as an a priori truth—which recuses even the most respected scholars from citing evidence to support their claims. In her plenary address to the Council of Writing Program Administrators, Linda Adler-Kassner (2012), a scholar whom I admire, urged WPAs to support the principled position that "writing classes focus on the study of writing within particular contexts, the values reflected in that writing, the implications of relationships between writing and values. Not vampires" (134). Implicit in this call is the assumption that theme-based first-year writing seminars do not teach these disciplinary values, focusing instead on writing as a "content-vacated, vocationally-oriented frame that undermines our credibility and our field" (134).

In *Writing Across Contexts: Transfer, Composition, and Sites of Writing*, Kathleen Blake Yancey, Liane Robertson, and Kara Taczak are equally quick to dismiss theme-based first-year writing seminars. They frame their own innovative curricular approach to FYC as an alternative to the multidisciplinary approach of what they refer to vaguely as "many elite institutions like those in the Ivy League" (Yancey, Robertson, and Taczak 2014, 3). The authors go on to list several course titles from Harvard's expository writing program and one course description from Haverford's catalog (31) as the sole evidence that "writing hardly appears" (32) in these courses designed according to "faculty interest" (31).

By not engaging with evidence from well-established multidisciplinary programs—or the scholarly conversations that situate such curricula in writing studies traditions (e.g., Brent 2005, 2013; Daniel 1998; Harris 2004; Reitmayer 2009; Sommers and Saltz 2004)—the field's current master narrative represents these programs as out of touch with the field, inculcating "skills" and arhetorical understandings of writing. In the process, the field both misses opportunities to explore common ground among curricular models and undervalues the multidisciplinary perspectives on writing cultivated in such programs. The field also writes entire institutions—like the small college—out of national conversations about writing pedagogies. According to the National Census of Writing (Gladstein and Fralix 2015), small liberal arts colleges use topic-based and WAC-based approaches to first-year writing far more often than any other curricular model—and this can be traced back to the particular cultures of writing on these campuses, where writing instruction is often viewed as the shared purview of all disciplines (Fletcher Moon 2003; Gladstein and Rossman Regaignon 2012, 98–107).

In my contribution, I reflect on the value of working multidisciplinarily as a WPA. By telling the story of my multidisciplinary status as a WPA transitioning from literary studies to writing studies and then moving from a writing program at an Ivy League to a writing center at a small liberal arts college, I highlight how different conceptions of disciplinarity can make our professional lives feel complicated for good reasons, particularly at moments of transition when they're brought into sharp relief. I intend this story to complement narratives of the affective dimensions of WPA labor (Jacobs and Micciche 2003; Micciche 2002) by introducing ways "structures of feeling"—to borrow from Raymond Williams's theory (1977)—underwrite divergent concepts of disciplinarity. If Jill Gladstein and Dara Rossman Regaignon argue in *Writing Program Administration at Small Liberal Arts Colleges* that a different structure of feeling defines the writing cultures and leadership configurations at SLACs (Gladstein and Rossman Regaignon 2012, 5–22), I'd argue there are also different structures of feeling at work in different disciplines and types of WPA work. Directing a writing center at a progressive SLAC on the West Coast feels radically different from associate directing a first-year writing seminar program at a highly selective research institution on the East Coast. Leadership configurations, institutional cultures, and the often separate discourse communities engaging in scholarship about writing centers, first-year composition, and literature shape how WPA work is enacted, framed, and understood by its practitioners. Anyone who's been to both MLA and CCCC conferences knows they can seem, for the most part, like two different worlds, even if both professional communities study writers and writing. Disciplinary differences *do* matter—within and across fields. And it's worth attending to these differences with care.

My interest in disciplinarity emerges from my experience with disciplinary contradictions. As a graduate student at the University of Chicago, I found faculty in my department tended to dismiss reflection on disciplinarity even though we were expected to enact disciplinarity in identifiable ways—in the ways we wrote, interacted, and positioned ourselves in the field. I was initially drawn to writing studies because it offers a theoretical framework for understanding these tacit expectations. Like many others, I entered graduate school feeling unprepared to do the intellectual work of the profession. As an undergraduate, I wasn't trained to understand literary studies as a *discipline*. Professors sometimes taught close reading through the lens of their scholarship, but with the exception of one class taught by a visiting professor, none of our teachers asked us to read and *do* literary criticism. In fact, we were in a sense *protected* from this professionalization by a curricular focus on imaginative and self-reflective close readings of primary sources. In graduate school, expectations shifted radically. Suddenly, we were prompted to develop bold and theoretically informed arguments about those same texts.

I stumbled upon writing studies by coincidence. My first year of graduate school, the Little Red Schoolhouse hired me to teach first-year writing in the humanities core. The Little Red Schoolhouse was well known on campus as an institution that helped graduate students learn how to write publishable articles in their fields and teach writing. That spring I underwent ten weeks of training in writing pedagogies I now know were developed largely in the 1980s (Reitmayer 2009). Looking back, this is a striking anachronism at an institution that would not have tolerated such fossilization in other fields. Despite its limitations, this first introduction to the field proved transformative because it offered a flexible heuristic for understanding scholarly discourse as a rhetorical system. It wasn't until the following year that I would begin learning how to adapt this pedagogy to writing in my discipline: I began attending biweekly workshops where graduate students—alongside junior and senior scholars—presented works in progress, giving others the gift of seeing how projects get made.

While the threshold between undergraduate and graduate studies is likely to always be what Jan H. F. Meyer and Ray Land would call a "troublesome" crossing (Meyer and Land 2006, 9), the gap between the undergraduate and graduate study of literature seems particularly pronounced. In a special issue of *Critical Inquiry* on disciplinarity, Robert Post (2009) offers an explanation for this disconnect. Post—a legal scholar—comprehensively surveyed metadisciplinary debates in literary and media studies to identify a tension between what scholars characterize as "charismatic" versus "disciplinary" forms of scholarly authority (760). Humanistic scholars are anxious about the notion of expertise, he claims, tending to "disparage scholarship that displays . . . [mere] disciplinary accomplishment" (761). Instead, they prefer arguments that distinguish themselves as "charismatic" through their resistance to adhering to disciplinary conventions. This preference has led a number of prominent scholars to describe their work as "disciplines of the imagination" (quoted in Post 2009, 760) or, as the University of Chicago's own W. J. T. Mitchell puts it, "indisciplines" that possess an "antiprofessionalism" resistant to "the institutional structures by means of which the various academic disciplines establish and extend their territorial claims" (quoted in Post 2009, 750). In other words, literary scholars seem particularly skeptical of the potentially colonizing effects of laying claim to disciplinary authority because it's perceived as limiting intellectual inquiry.

This self-perception is, of course, problematic. Even a passing glance at journals like *Profession* suggests that organizations like the MLA are hyperprofessionalized and its practitioners deeply concerned about the status of English as a discipline. Indeed, the survival of the discipline in the midst of widespread cuts to the humanities seems dependent on articulating the field's relevance. Yet Post points here to a paradoxical self-understanding that continues to operate within the field. Disciplinarity is often conflated with a stifling of creative ambition. With this conflation in mind, Post opens up questions for WPAs that invite them to empathize with their literature colleagues' skepticism toward any approach to teaching writing that seems reductive. How might class discussions and assignments be designed to cultivate the "charismatic" arguments valued by literary studies? If antiprofessionalism remains integral to the humanities' ethos, how might WPAs collaborate with faculty to develop writing pedagogies respectful of this disposition?

If literary scholars are often skeptical of debates about disciplinarity, then rhetoric and composition scholars have a strong tradition of naming and defending disciplinary authority as a means of legitimizing the field—from Janice Lauer's "Composition Studies: Dappled Discipline" to recent volumes like Linda Adler-Kassner and Elizabeth Wardle's *Naming What We Know: Threshold Concepts in Writing Studies* and Rita Malencyzk, Elizabeth Wardle, and Kathleen Yancey's *Composition, Rhetoric, and Disciplinarity: Shadows of the Past, Issues of the Moment, and Prospects for the Future* (Adler-Kassner and Wardle 2015; Lauer 1984; Malencyzk, Wardle, and Yancey 2017). Yet conceptions of disciplinarity remain opaque in the scholarly literature about WPAs, particularly for those in transition. In *A Rhetoric for Writing Program Administrators*, Malencyzk (2013) argues that we can only answer circumlocutorily the question "what *is* a WPA?" given incomplete data about the CWPA's membership and the multidisciplinary backgrounds of many WPAs—both within and without writing studies (4; emphasis in original). If disciplinary expertise is defined as consisting "not merely of a body of knowledge but also of a set of practices by which that knowledge is acquired, confirmed, implemented, preserved, and reproduced," as Post (2009) claims (751), I wonder, too, what this means for those of us navigating new WPA positions, where knowledge and practices must first be troubled in the encounter with local cultures before they can be acquired, confirmed, preserved, and reproduced in our programs and centers. Working within and across multiple disciplines in these new roles makes our professional identities more complicated—and, I'd like to argue next, perhaps more interesting.

In the past five years, I've inhabited two WPA positions—as associate director of a first-year writing seminar program at an Ivy League institution and as a writing center director at a small liberal arts college. While I was finishing my dissertation on the Cold War politics of postwar poetry in West Germany and the United States, I applied for a lecturer position in a multidisciplinary writing program. The program recruits mostly PhDs from over a dozen disciplines to teach writing seminars situated in interdisciplinary scholarly conversations in their fields. All members of the faculty undergo intensive and ongoing training in the teaching of writing and design courses to meet shared learning goals based on the WPA Outcomes Statement for First-Year Composition but emphasizing scholarly argument and research. My contract, renewable for five years, was not tenure stream, but it provided resources to conduct research and attend conferences, which helped me develop a professional identity in writing studies. Unlike most faculty members in the program who return to their home disciplines (often in tenure-track positions), I knew early on that I wanted to transition into a career in rhetoric and composition. At the same time, the curricular structure of the writing program allowed me to draw on my expertise in literary studies to teach writing seminars grounded in my doctoral research.

Two years in, I transitioned into a new role as associate director of the first-year writing seminar program. I spent the next three years educating myself about the field as much as possible. I read writing studies scholarship, followed discussions on listservs, and attended conferences and events on writing and WPA work. In retrospect, I realize I was using that time to build the subject-matter and discourse-community knowledge needed to begin participating in the field—even if my approach was admittedly ad hoc. While I was initially drawn to writing studies as a teaching subject, like many others, I began undertaking research outside the pedagogical imperative that allowed me to draw on my training as a comparatist. One of my current projects, for example, focuses on the reception of Anglo-American writing studies scholarship in Germany, Switzerland, and Austria. Without training in comparative literature—which involved extended stays in Germany, interdisciplinary inquiry into postwar educational institutions, and proficiency in research languages—I don't think I would have been able to embark on this new project.

The field doesn't yet have a language for describing such early-career WPAs in transition. The closest thing is Talinn Phillips, Paul Shovlin, and Megan Titus's notion of the "liminal WPA" (Phillips, Shovlin, and Titus 2014, 50). Yet the term doesn't capture the more positive experiences of those of us who found an intellectual home in writing studies during transitions into assistant- or associate-director positions after earning our PhDs. "Many liminals are without institutional permanence," they argue, "and therefore have little power to enact the change" initially drawing them to WPA work (54). While I didn't have the authority of a director (and would not have wanted it at that stage in my career), I didn't think of myself as liminal in my first WPA role. Unlike the under-resourced new WPAs described in their study, I viewed my choice to become an associate director as a rite of passage that would allow me to pursue the longer-term goal of directing a program or center someday. This transitional period felt less like exploitation and more like a useful apprenticeship. While I recall sometimes feeling isolated in my position because of our program's inward focus, the orientation had other benefits. I was able to develop close professional relationships with my colleagues because we were part of a shared teaching project that valued multidisciplinary scholarship.

Likewise, my position wasn't tenure track, but I had no reason to believe it wasn't permanent. A former director liked to joke that none of us had tenure, but the writing program did since it had undergone a successful external review. The university had committed significant resources to the program to ensure its operations remained sustainable. Growth was built into our annual budget projections, and our salaries were more generous than many tenured lines at other universities. More important, being well resourced helped protect good teaching and ethical labor practices. We were in the privileged position of knowing the institution would likely always be able to afford low faculty course loads (two/two) and small class sizes (twelve students maximum), which enabled us to prioritize faculty development and individualized feedback on writing. Liminal positions are not always as liminal as they seem.

In fact, multidisciplinary writing programs can empower disciplinary newcomers by offering fertile ground for exploring hybrid disciplinary identities and practices. Like nothing else, a multidisciplinary writing program gives faculty and WPAs an inside perspective into just how formative disciplinary training is to how we understand, value, and teach writing in our fields. The experience prepared me for the next transition ahead.

In the summer of 2013, I began a new position as a tenure-track director of a writing center at a SLAC. The transition from a staff WPA position to a faculty line in a writing center has been a significant change. Whereas running a writing program is like steering a large cruise ship, writing centers are a much more nimble operation; it's easier for us to fine tune and change course because we aren't locked into the academic calendar in the same way. There have been other key differences as well. I left a well-established program where my work focused largely on refining a well-oiled machine. My new position required much more curricular reinvention. Since the founding director's retirement several years prior, the position had been configured as a staff line and had lacked consistent leadership. I inherited only a handful of reports dating back a few years—and a small file cabinet of fliers and teaching materials. Everything needed to be rebuilt, so to speak, from the ground up—from creating signs for the door to developing infrastructure to support the center's new WAC-based mission. I also needed to establish a research agenda driven by my writing center work. This was a conscious decision to ensure my WPA work was in conversation with current scholarship, but it was also risky: I didn't have my dissertation to rely on as a safety net.

I found this challenge equal parts exhilarating and terrifying during my first months. But I remember feeling buoyed by the sense that my work was genuinely supported by the institution. Whereas my previous university had very clear hierarchies that made it more difficult to access institutional power, the SLAC environment was much flatter and, despite its smallness, less insular in its writing culture. Writing instruction was not located in any one program or center but was diffused across the curriculum. I marveled at how, as an assistant professor, I reported directly to the dean of faculty, who doubled as vice president of academic affairs. In regular meetings I was able to update the institution about the writing center's work and learn ways to link our initiatives to other programming on campus. The flat structure also allowed me to collaborate more easily with colleagues across offices and departments (or *field groups*, as we call them at my institution).

Here, "smallness" afforded opportunities for thinking big. Like at many SLACs, relationships form quickly and the ethos is collaborative. As a WPA, I had the kind of visibility and autonomy unimaginable within the institutional culture of my previous university. This phenomenon is described at length in Gladstein and Rossman Regaignon's *Writing Program Administration at Small Liberal Arts Colleges* (2012, 5–22). Yet it was powerful to experience on the ground.

Raymond Williams (1977) offers a language for conceptualizing such transitional experiences that are palpably felt but difficult to describe. In *Marxism and Literature*, he settles on the term "structures of feeling" to account for forms of social consciousness that are "lived, actively, in real relationships" (130) but are so emergent they are often "not yet recognized as social but taken to be private, idiosyncratic, and even isolating" (132). His attention to these "structures of experience" allows him to articulate what he calls the "affective elements of consciousness and relationships" (132)—what it *feels* like to inhabit social experience that hasn't yet been named. Gladstein and Rossman Regaignon describe how Williams's concept is useful for understanding writing cultures and WPA leadership configurations at SLACs, but the concept is also useful for describing the social feelings experienced by WPAs, particularly when they inhabit multiple disciplines and transition from one position to another—which sometimes involves migrating across subfields. In my case this transition involved the shift from writing program to writing center leadership—which felt like a radical change in professional ethos. At these moments, we may feel like our experiences are "private, idiosyncratic, and even isolating," but Williams's concept helps us see them as part of a larger social dynamic in the field.

Transitions across disciplines and the subfields within them can be landmines of contradictions. To negotiate them, I find reassuring

Ianatta's advice on how to avoid tying ourselves up in knots over inevitable tensions in our ways of seeing the world. In her critique of a commonplace in WPA mentoring scholarship—particularly the ethos of egalitarianism and self-sacrifice—she argues that WPAs perhaps unwittingly undercut their own authority when they attribute conflict to interpersonal relations (*you don't appreciate what I do!*) rather than disciplinary differences (*I'm not into Thomas Paine, so why should you be into rhetoric?*). She calls this focus on "differing intellectual commitments and institutional perspectives . . . far less emotionally exhausting—and far more generative—than thinking in terms of attending to emotional commitments—or lack thereof" to the curricular project of composition (Ianetta 2012, 183). I couldn't agree more. But my own experience tells me disciplinary allegiances are bound in strong feelings, too—and not just in WPA scholarship with its commonplace investment, Ianetta argues, in an "ethics of care" (183).

What we value is, in a sense, who we are—so it's no wonder disciplinary perspectives can feel so personal. Thinking about these perspectives as structures of feeling allows us to ask new questions. What are the structures of feeling embedded in disciplinary work? How does it *feel* to navigate different disciplinary contexts (sometimes all at once) in our professional roles? And what ideologies (disciplinary, gender, class, race, or otherwise) underwrite these social feelings, as Marc Scott addresses in his contribution to this volume?

If we dig deep enough, I suspect there are as many answers to these questions as there are WPAs. Subjectively experienced feelings have complex social contexts bound to disciplinary practices and beliefs. As I see it, the experience of inhabiting multiple disciplines is not a step backward in the field's disciplinary history but an extension of the field's roots as a "dappled discipline" with a "highly multidisciplinary cast," as Lauer famously put it in 1984 (Lauer 1984, 20). After all, being a WPA is an intellectual endeavor rife with paradoxes. When newly hired, we are often experts in our fields but novices to our institutions. Many of us have research agendas that align with our WPA roles and thus depart from our dissertations—regardless of our home fields. For junior WPAs, this disparity can make it difficult to map out linear narratives for our scholarship. Yet it also enriches the scope of our work.

Even many years down the road, I imagine I'll always *feel* like a WPA in transition in so far as this means seeking out interstices where learning and growth happen. Charles Bazerman (2011) sums it up this way: "If our research is narrow, our teaching and learning will follow on narrow paths" (10). The key to making this intellectual work sustainable at moments of transition may be, as Bazerman advises, to develop a "disciplinary core problematic" that can be investigated in depth with the help of approaches and insights from other disciplines (19). The very notion of a "disciplinary core problematic" challenges us to define our work as WPAs in radically expansive ways. Perhaps this exercise in zooming so far out to identify commonalities can help us frame scholarship that transcends some of the traditional divisions between literature and composition and between subfields like writing center scholarship and writing program administration. The latter two fields often talk past one another at separate conferences and in separate journals. A more synergetic disciplinary ethos may help us reimagine the teaching and tutoring of writing—and their administration—as the dappled purview of many disciplines.

Note
1. I am using the term *first-year writing seminars* as defined by Jill Gladstein and Dara Rossman Regaignon in *Writing Program Administration at Small Liberal Arts Colleges* (2012, 98–107).

References
Adler-Kassner, Linda. 2012. "The Companies We Keep or The Companies We Would Like to Try to Keep: Strategies and Tactics in Challenging Times." *WPA: Writing Program Administration* 36 (1): 119–40.
Adler-Kassner, Linda, and Elizabeth Wardle, eds. 2015. *Naming What We Know: Threshold Concepts and Composition Studies.* Logan: Utah State University Press.
Bazerman, Charles. 2011. "The Disciplined Interdisciplinarity of Writing Studies." *Research in the Teaching of English* 46 (1): 8–21.
Brent, Doug. 2005. "Reinventing WAC (Again): The First-Year Seminar and Academic Literacy." *College Composition and Communication* 57 (2): 253–76.
Brent, Doug. 2013. "The Research Paper and Why We Should Still Care." *WPA: Writing Program Administration* 37 (1): 33–53.
Daniel, Beth. 1998. "F-Y Comp, F-Y Seminars, and WAC: A Response." *Language and Learning Across the Disciplines* 2 (3): 69–74.
Downs, Douglas. 2013. "What Is First-Year Composition?" In *A Rhetoric for Writing Program Administrators*, edited by Rita Malenczyk, 50–63. Anderson, SC: Parlor.
Elbow, Peter. 2002. "Opinion: The Cultures of English and Composition." *College English* 64 (5): 533–46. https://doi.org/10.2307/3250752.
Fletcher Moon, Gretchen. 2003. "First-Year Writing in First-Year Seminars: Writing across the Curriculum from the Start." *WPA: Writing Program Administration* 26 (3): 105–18.
Gladstein, Jill M., and Brandon Fralix. 2015. National Census of Writing. https://writingcensus.swarthmore.edu/.
Gladstein, Jill M., and Dara Rossman Regaignon. 2012. *Writing Program Administration at Small Liberal Arts Colleges.* Anderson, SC: Parlor.
Hairston, Maxine. 1985. "Breaking Our Bonds and Reaffirming Our Connections." *College Composition and Communication* 36 (3): 272–82. https://doi.org/10.2307/357971.

Harris, Joseph. 2004. "Thinking Like a Program." *Pedagogy* 4 (3): 357–64. https://doi.org/10.1215/15314200-4-3-357.

Harris, Joseph. 2012. *A Teaching Subject: Composition Since 1966*. Logan: Utah State University Press.

Ianetta, Melissa. 2010. "Disciplinarity, Divorce, and the Displacement of Labor Issues: Rereading Histories of Composition and Literature." *College Composition and Communication* 62 (1): 53–72.

Ianetta, Melissa. 2012. "Composition, Commonplaces, and Who Cares?" *WPA: Writing Program Administrators* 35 (2): 179–83.

Jacobs, Dale, and Laura R. Micciche, eds. 2003. *A Way to Move: Rhetorics of Emotion and Composition Studies, CrossCurrents: New Perspectives in Rhetoric and Composition*. Portsmouth, NH: Boynton/Cook.

Kopelson, Karen. 2008. "Sp(l)itting Images; or, Back to the Future of (Rhetoric and?) Composition." *College Composition and Communication* 59 (4): 750–80.

Lauer, Janice. 1984. "Composition Studies: Dappled Discipline." *Rhetoric Review* 3 (1): 20–29. https://doi.org/10.1080/07350198409359074.

Maid, Barry. 2006. "In This Corner . . ." In *Composition and/or Literature: The End(s) of Education*, edited by Linda S. Bergmann and Edith M. Baker, 93–108. Urbana, IL: NCTE.

Malenczyk, Rita. 2013. "Introduction, with Some Rhetorical Terms." In *A Rhetoric for Writing Program Administrators*, edited by Rita Malenczyk, 3–8. Anderson, SC: Parlor.

Malenczyk, Rita, Elizabeth Wardle, and Kathleen Blake Yancey, eds. 2017. "Composition, Rhetoric, and Disciplinarity: Shadows of the Past, Issues of the Moment, and Prospects for the Future." Unpublished manuscript.

Meyer, Jan H. F., and Ray Land, eds. 2006. *Overcoming Barriers to Student Understanding: Threshold Concepts and Troublesome Knowledge*. New York: Routledge.

Micciche, Laura. 2002. "More Than a Feeling: Disappointment and WPA Work." *College English* 64 (4): 432–58. https://doi.org/10.2307/3250746.

Phillips, Talinn, Paul Shovlin, and Megan Titus. 2014. "Thinking Liminally: Exploring the (com)Promising Positions of the Liminal WPA." *WPA: Writing Program Administration* 38 (1): 42–64.

Post, Robert. 2009. "Debating Disciplinarity." *Critical Inquiry* 35 (4): 749–70. https://doi.org/10.1086/599580.

Raymond, Richard C. 2008. "When Writing Professors Teach Literature: Shaping Questions, Finding Answers, Effecting Change." *College Composition and Communication* 59 (3): 473–501.

Reitmayer, Morgan T. 2009. "Programs that Work(ed): Revisiting the University of Michigan, the University of Chicago, and George Mason University Programs after 20 Years." *Across the Disciplines* 6. https://wac.colostate.edu/atd/technologies/reitmeyer.cfm.

Sommers, Nancy, and Laura Saltz. 2004. "The Novice as Expert: Writing the Freshman Year." *College Composition and Communication*, special issue, *Writing Technologies and WAC* 56 (1): 124–49. https://doi.org/10.2307/4140684.

Tokarczyk, Michelle M., and Irene Papoulis, eds. 2003. *Teaching Composition/Teaching Literature: Crossing Great Divides, Studies in Composition and Rhetoric*. Bern: Peter Lang.

Williams, Raymond. 1977. *Marxism and Literature*. Oxford: Oxford University Press.

Yancey, Kathleen Blake, Liane Robertson, and Kara Taczak. 2014. *Writing across Contexts: Transfer, Composition, and Sites of Writing*. Logan: Utah State University Press.

6
THE JOYS OF WPAHOOD
Embracing Interruption in the Personal and the Professional

Kate Pantelides

The myth of the work-home divide needs to be re-imagined in our narratives and scholarship, not as a dichotomy, but as a system of reciprocal relationships that create both complexity and value.
—Loren Marquez, "Narrating Our Lives"

Conventional wisdom advises: do not make too many changes at the same time. For instance, do not move across the country *and* start a new job. Certainly, do not have a baby and start your first tenure-track job. But wisdom functions differently in the academy. When you get the job, you go to the job, wherever it is. And, particularly for WPAs, such *interruption* (as theorized by Micciche and Strickland 2013; Stenberg 2006; Strickland and Gunner 2009; Reynolds 1998) is a defining characteristic of our work. Casting aside conventional wisdom, embracing interruption, ignoring the bounds of *chronos*, trusting in *kairos*—this is how I came to be in the position of defending my dissertation, selling my house, asking my husband to leave his successful career as an attorney, and driving across the country with a six-week-old baby and a toddler to be an assistant professor and the associate director of first-year writing at a midwestern comprehensive university.

I share this narrative of the convergence of the "personal, professional, and the political" (Bizzell 1999, vii) in my transition into a new faculty and administrative role to theorize interruption as central to "femadmin" (Micciche and Strickland 2013), a feminist approach to administration. Subsequently, I hope this narrative interruption does some work in reframing what interruptions can do for us as WPAs and in expanding the possibilities for ways of "making it" (Ballif, Davis, and Mountford 2008) in composition studies.

DOI: 10.7330/9781607326335.c006

Interruption, or, as is often the case for new parents and new WPAs, jarring change, can act as a necessary "thinking [tool] for rejuvenation" (Micciche and Strickland 2013). And I'd like to suggest that we can "make it" in and through composition by making the most of transitions, embracing interruption as a way of resisting and revisioning the politically strained world of writing program administration. In this way, our personal and professional goals can be more about mindfully persisting, "becoming" (Restaino 2012), and being rather than making it by arriving at a particular destination. I situate this discussion of interruption as effective WPA practice by illustrating how in my own WPA transition I replaced my traditional desire to make it as "superparent" and "super-WPA" (hiding any challenges in balancing the personal and the professional), instead choosing to embrace my dual role of parent and WPA and actively perform parenthood in my professional role.

Although we often long for the relative stillness that comes with teaching a class for the umpteenth time and resting on our laurels, allowing roles such as parent and professional—roles often seen as competing—to interrupt each other can be productive for WPA work.

INTERRUPTION AS PRACTICE

Interruption has been central to feminist practice, and it is not a new concept for WPAs. In fact, the popular collection *The Writing Program Administrator Interrupted* came out in 2009, with the hope of "engaging" the WPA community by interrupting institutional orthodoxies (Strickland and Gunner 2009). Interruption necessitates what Laura Micciche (2011) has called "suspended agency," a pause and a rethinking/reworking of a problem or belief system (Micciche 2011, 75). For example, Marika Seigel's (2013) recent work on pregnancy manuals as technical communication extends the use of interruption. Seigel's study examines how pregnancy manuals position women as straightforward users of the prenatal healthcare system without questioning the use or structure of that system and the way it renders women subject to what is characterized as their unreliable, problematic bodies.

To interrupt this relationship, Seigel draws on Kenneth Burke's notion of piety—which is related to propriety, "an organizing principle" for social structures (Seigel 2013, 30) that suggests conventional ways of interacting within a system. For example, the pieties associated with being a "good" WPA might include being accessible and available to put out fires, adhering to the WPA Outcomes, approaching WPA work as intellectual, and so forth. The pieties for a pregnant woman might include exercising carefully and avoiding large fish and soft cheeses. In illustrating the pieties constituted by and maintained in pregnancy manuals, Seigel attempts to disrupt these connections by "making impious associations in order to affect a reorientation of sense and meaning. If these associations are intentionally impious, then they can be called planned incongruity. Perspective by incongruity creates opportunities to resist or transgress established ways of making sense and to establish new linkages and, possibly, articulations" (73). Siegel's "perspective by incongruity," in which she purposefully makes impious associations in order to interrupt an established discursive system, extends the possibilities of feminist interruption. Instead of ephemeral interruption, which might mean taking a stand or changing course, this notion of interruption is more deep-rooted and persistent. Such interruption seeks to initiate change so as to make new, ongoing connections or upset and redistribute a substructure, system, or foundation. It is this notion of interruption I hope to engage here in discussing simultaneous parenting and WPA work.

PARENTING IN THE ACADEMY: THE SPECIAL CASE OF WPAS

Scholarship on the relationship between parenting and academia suggests it is not a happy marriage. For instance, in *Women's Ways of Making It in Rhetoric and Composition,* published in 2008, the authors note, "Having children is still considered a disadvantage for women academics" (Ballif, Davis, and Mountford 2008, 179). The text draws on an extensive survey and portraits of women in the field who have done incredibly important work and who were recognized by survey respondents as those who have "made it." Regardless of the authors' insistence that making it can mean other things than being a full professor with an impressive publishing record and relative "fame" in the discipline, one particularly exalted story in the text suggests that the ways of making it in composition are closed to many. They detail the story of one woman who, when writing a book all summer in four-hour increments, once lost such track of time and the outside world that she was surprised to learn, at the persistent reminder of her cat, that she hadn't fed her pet for twelve hours. For WPA parents, such a schedule would be impossible and not necessarily enviable, and if we forget to feed those who depend on us—well, that's illegal.

Mothers with young children are the least likely to get tenure, and tenured women are significantly less likely than their male peers to be faculty parents. However, according to Mary Ann Mason, Nicholas H.

Wolfinger, and Marc Goulden, the authors of *Do Babies Matter? Gender and Family in the Ivory Tower*, things aren't quite as dire in the humanities as they are in the sciences (Mason, Wolfinger, and Goulden 2013). They explain the difference between the humanities and the sciences: "The bench sciences demand very long hours in the laboratory, a place where children are not welcome. And compared to the sciences, few scholars in the humanities depend on federal grants and the lockstep professional progress they entail" (Mason, Wolfinger, and Goulden 2013, 58). For WPAs, these disciplinary differences aren't quite so neat. Though we don't have long hours in the lab, there are real constraints placed on our time by instructor observations, TA training, face-to-face out-of-class mentoring, emergency meetings with upper-level administration (I've had more than I expected), complaints from students, equivalency requests, and semester scheduling—all with pretty specific, "lockstep" due dates and child-unfriendly spaces. Further, funding for our programs, including our staff, curriculum development, and materials, often rests squarely on our shoulders. For those of us who are jWPAs ("junior," untenured WPAs), our "professional progress" is especially tenuous (Charlton et al. 2011; Horning 2011; Schell 1998) and ultimately tied to our successful management of these long hours and uncertain budgets.

Despite the gloom and doom, however, many of us are entering into such transitions willingly, happily, and with eyes wide open (for a discussion of this shift, see Charlton et al. 2011). The problem is we just don't have many stories that discuss broader ways of making it as WPAs. Our transitions are often quiet or purposely hidden. I was especially guilty of this hiding in my initial WPA transition. Trying to deny the literal, embodied interruption to my workday of persistently using a breast pump, I often snuck into my office to do the deed. After closing and locking my door quietly, I would proceed to disrobe in my closet-like room, trying to look at pictures of my kids, trying to ignore how vulnerable and strange I felt. Listening to the labored breathing of the pump, I desperately hoped the student who promised he would stop by would be late. I crossed my fingers that my colleagues standing outside my door wouldn't knock and invite me to lunch because I wouldn't know what to say. In fact, my wonderfully supportive colleague once said, as I awkwardly tried to excuse myself from a conversation because it was time to pump, "Don't worry! Take your time. I'm a parent too. I know what you're doing in there." I smiled but stayed quiet.

In a special issue of *Composition Studies* that responds to *Women's Ways of Making it*, Loren Marquez (2011) writes that such silence isn't helpful;

instead, she explains how her "life as a mother has greatly infused [her] life in academia" (Marquez 2011, 74). I found this too, as soon as I began to embrace my transition instead of fearing or denying it. Many parents note how their concept of time at work changes drastically after having children. After my son was born, I began to see short time increments in terms of potential items I could cross off of my list. If I had fifteen minutes, that meant I could finish the writing center schedule, or work on tutor training, or finish my IRB protocol. When I had to revise an article on the eve of my daughter's birth—I fit it in between my work as a writing center coordinator, doctoral student, and parent. I have learned to make my schedule fit into the hours between 9 a.m. and 5 p.m. and between 8 p.m. and 10 p.m. because it has to. And everything somehow gets done. Or it doesn't. And life goes on.

But even more important than bending time to my will (or living at its mercy), parenting necessarily, and fruitfully, interrupts WPA work. Although such interruption is challenging because WPA schedules are somewhat less flexible than what I know of scholarly work outside admin, it usefully insists upon the distance and perspective so hard to get and so necessary for persisting (sanely) as a WPA. Since I often had to dash from an infuriating meeting (not that most of my meetings were infuriating—just that I always had to dash) to pick up my kids from daycare, there was only so long I could stew before I had to move on and suck it up. This very literal interruption meant I was not able to send an e-mail or make a call I might otherwise regret. Such distance breeds mindfulness and a reminder to *be* in the moment. I knew that once I left, I wouldn't have time or energy to focus on work: children are really effective, healthy distractions from writing programs.

However, parenting as a gendered institution (Sallee 2013) hasn't quite caught up with the *implications* of what it means for women to be in the workforce. For example, although I found frequent social support for *my* choice to parent, teach, and work as a WPA, my husband was professionally punished for, as a father, acting as the primary caretaker of our children, for following an academic woman. The partner problem/trailing spouse/dual-career predicament is well known in academia (Buzzanell 1997; Cain and Kalamaras 1993), frequently discussed in informal and professional circles, periodically (and unofficially) mused about during hiring discussions, but rarely studied. Though my husband had been on the brink of making partner at his previous law firm, having to explain the choice to stay home with our infant and move for my significantly less lucrative job was met with, let's say—some skepticism.

When he chose to opt back into full-time employment, a necessity for someone married to an assistant professor with two children, his choices were not welcomed as warmly as mine had been. As Margaret Sallee has noted in her work on professional fathers, "Men and women who violate their assigned gender roles are often eyed with suspicion" (Sallee 2013, 372). In not demonstrating the pieties of traditional husband/lawyer/patriarch, his choices didn't fit into a familiar narrative of parenting. Thus, in order to interrupt the systems that make it a "disadvantage" to be a mother in academia or a male caregiver, I consciously frame this particular way of making it in composition in terms of parenthood. Ultimately, I hope my husband's impious position, an unavoidable interruption, ultimately yields professional dividends, a rhetorical interruption. I have personally and professionally benefited from his choices and support (incredibly so).

SUPERPARENT/SUPERWPA SYNDROME: NOT DOING ANYONE ANY FAVORS

When I arrived on campus, my colleagues were warm and welcoming, but when they said, "You're so brave!," I heard, "Are you crazy?" In my hypervigilant need to appear impervious and professional, I denied all offers for babysitting and domestic-related assistance. Of course, I don't know how this refusal was perceived, but in retrospect, I was trying my best to be superparent and superWPA (I doubt I was pulling it off), trying to pretend nothing had changed though I had taken on another child, a new WPA position, and very little sleep. I stayed up later than I should have responding to e-mails, and I went to too many meetings before I was officially compensated as a WPA. While I'm not suggesting I should have let it all fall apart and shared the various details of my life with passing colleagues and students, this patriarchal notion of what woman as parent can/should be if she's doing it "right" is deeply flawed. Amy Koerber describes the problem in terms of Sarah Palin's representation of motherhood during the 2008 presidential campaign.

> Indeed one of the most troubling aspects of the brief time that Palin as vice-presidential candidate enjoyed in the media spotlight was that it perpetuated the idea of good motherhood as clean, seamless, sanitary, and, perhaps most important, as not interfering with anyone else's business. . . . Although her devoted followers touted her accomplishments as evidence that today's woman can "have it all," her many critics shuddered to think that her example would be used as further justification for why

we need not worry about issues such as parental leave, health care, and work-family balance. (Koerber 2013, 131)

Doug Hesse (1999) also describes similar pressure as connected to his roles as "Father, Husband, and Ex" and its relationship to his work as a WPA. He posits the impact of his particular subject position as preventing him from asking for help or collaborating with others: "I considered my reasons to be fairly altruistic, not colonially paternalistic in the ways that men's actions are often described, but rather practicing good fathering and husbanding as I knew it: self-reliant and taking care of others" (Hesse 1999, 49). Ultimately, Hesse concludes that this way of making it in composition wasn't sustainable, and he highlights the changes he had to make to find a better balance. Essentially, promoting the fiction of superparent is too exhausting, and it doesn't do anyone any favors in their respective transitions, be it to parenting, academia, or WPA work specifically. Regardless of their child status, WPAs often have a "do-it-all" mentality, and we often do it with a smile on our faces. But what are the implications for others if we work around the clock without compensation and without interrupting the happy picture to expose our complicity in unethical labor practices? (For further discussion of these concerns see Naydan; Phillips et al.; and Tetreault, this volume).

TRANSITIONAL WAYS OF MAKING IT

We in the current generation of jWPAs have limited but increasingly excellent models (Gabor, Neeley, and Leverenz 2008; Ghodsee and Connelly 2014; Perl 1998; Peskowitz 2008) to support us in our decision to be parents and WPAs simultaneously, and to prove that it's possible, but once we "have it all"—how can we do any of it well? The embodied realities of simultaneous parenthood and WPAhood—pumping while I wrote e-mails, noticing midway through meetings with upper-level administrators that I had spit-up on my sweater (and knowing I would wear the offending item one more time before getting it dry-cleaned)—interrupts the fantasy. Such interruption (though perhaps more literal than metaphorical in the examples provided) helps construct a "feminist discursive space" for WPAs, a "noisy banter—the kind of vibrant discussion in which feminist scholars will not fully agree, but in which the new ideas produced from the disagreement make the conversation worthwhile" (Koerber 2013, 132). Such convergence, of personal, professional, and political, is essential to confront the realities of simultaneous parenthood and WPAhood, and, important for the community at large, the pressing WPA problems of labor, assessment, and representation.

Adopting the extended notion of interruption I advocate here means we must embrace impious associations of WPA and parent to draw new lines of what these roles mean. For example, Ann-Marie Slaughter (2012) describes how, as dean of Woodrow Wilson School, she "decided that one of the advantages of being a woman in power was that I could help change the norms by deliberately talking about my children and my desire to have a balanced life." She actively performed motherhood with the purpose of making it "normal" to speak of one's children in this space. Since releasing my need to portray superparent, I too have consciously performed the roles of parent and WPA, bringing my children to professional social gatherings and not resisting when something cute they did offers a perfect example of what we're talking about in class. Such performances are, by definition, impious because the "making-it" narrative that often drives us to project superparent/superWPA suggests that we hide the cracks beneath the armor—that we impossibly carry it off. Our super power is successfully pretending that we can defy the limits of time and stress and all that is healthy without it all falling apart. Although my more honest performances initially felt uncomfortable, my conscious interruption has helped open political spaces for me and allowed me to forge relationships institutionally. Perhaps most important, many student parents have approached me with their own stories, questions, and insecurities. This sharing has been a wonderful revelation, a new, important learning opportunity for me.

In talking about my syllabus on the first day of a recent writing course, I mentioned that *I answer e-mails from nine to five, but beyond that my responses are sporadic since I have two little kids. If I'm awake at two a.m., it's because I'm dealing with babies—I'm not answering homework questions.* My students laughed, and we got on with class. Articulating this simple limit felt good, and it reflected my pedagogy: I always try to be explicit about why I do things, how assignments are crafted, and the purpose of various policies. After class, a student came up to tell me how excited she was to take the class, and how, although she had struggled in recent semesters to balance being a full-time parent, student, and technical writer, she was looking forward to working in my class. A few weeks later, I tried not to cry as she told me, sitting slumped in a chair during my office hours, that she didn't think she could make it through the semester. Exhausted, defeated, she looked at me directly and asked, "How do you do it?" I realized that, at least for her, I had sold the fiction of superparent and superWPA, and it hadn't helped. Despite my efforts to lift the curtain on the realities of my life as a WPA parent, I had pulled off the myth that, for a while at least, I had desperately tried to forward. I told her the truth: *I have an awesome, supportive partner; makeup covers my dark circles; I do yoga in my office when I start to nod off; and I try to be gentle with myself—remembering that I can't do it all.* I would like to say this honesty helped my student be successful in my class—and maybe it did. She felt comfortable enough to bring her daughter in one day when she had a childcare conflict. In previous years, I would have worried that having a child in class would interrupt the other students, and I still think it does—but my ideas about interruption have changed. Such interruption is generative. Isn't it good if "traditional" students know that being a single parent/student/breadwinner means that sometimes the various worlds must collide? Such interruption subtly and usefully calls into question the pieties discursively associated with a traditional writing classroom. My student turned in one really great paper and made some insightful comments during class, but she didn't turn in the final project and ultimately failed the course. When I e-mailed to ask if she was okay, she thanked me for my concern and for my help during the class. She had needed to prioritize her daughter, and schoolwork just didn't make it on the list at the end of the semester. She was going to take some time to reassess and then transition to a more sustainable schedule. I hope she does.

And maybe I need to revise my disappointment as well, taking into account that maybe this was *her* version of mindfully persisting, "becoming" (Restaino 2012), and being. She honestly confronted the challenge of navigating competing, seemingly incompatible, worlds, and she made a difficult choice.

CONCLUSION

As I write this, I prepare for yet another WPA transition, one that will take me to a new tenure-line position in a new state that will be more sustainable for my family. I could not have asked for a better institution than my current one or for more supportive, wonderful colleagues, but unfortunately, the realities of a dual-career family have interrupted. What would have made a difference? An active spousal-hiring assistance policy (Mason, Wolfinger, and Goulden 2013, 45)? Asking for a semester deferral for maternity leave? Who knows? But just as we are settling into the rhythm of this life, just as things are getting easy(ish), we're about to interrupt it all. And, ultimately, it doesn't matter if the interruption is good—a new baby, a new job—or bad—a family illness, a reduced salary:

all we can control is how we react to the interruption. All I have been able to do is take these interruptions as they come and use them as a reminder to slow down, to rethink, to rebalance.

On the job market, I tried to be myself, the best version of myself, but myself all the same. That meant breaking many of the pieties outlined in *Ways of Making it* (Ballif, Davis, and Mountford 2008). I wore "dangly earrings" (in case you didn't know, you're not supposed to do this), and I mentioned both my husband and children to would-be employers. My family wasn't the first and certainly not the only thing I talked about, but I wanted to be at a place where you don't have to hide pictures of children. Making it for me has always meant finding colleagues I respect, teaching engaged students, tackling WPA challenges, asking and attempting to answer relevant questions in my scholarship, and finding moments of stillness in the balance between my personal and professional responsibilities.

Though at times I've done it hesitantly, I've tried to interrupt traditional ways of making it by performing impious ways of being a mother and WPA. I hope this approach will continue to work for me, and I hope it will in some small way impact my colleagues, students, and the discourses associated with ways of making it in composition. Embracing interruption as rhetorical strategy and as administrative method, finding space for stillness and mindfulness within these interruptions, seems to me an effective way to herald change. As a parent and WPA, I've found it's the only way to function. It is often a struggle, sometimes deeply so, but it is also full of joy. And it's not superparent or superWPA syndrome to strive for joy in the professional and the personal, but it is impious. We *need* to be impious. We need to be honest. We need to be actively looking for joy and be able to recognize it when it appears, hold on to it when we can, and embrace the next interruption as mindfully as we are able.

References
Ballif, Michelle, Diane Davis, and Roxanne Mountford. 2008. *Women's Ways of Making It in Rhetoric and Composition.* New York: Routledge.
Bizzell, Patricia. 1999. Foreword to *Kitchen Cooks, Plate Twirlers and Troubadours: Writing Program Administrators Tell Their Stories,* edited by Diana George, vii–ix. Portsmouth, NH: Boynton/Cook.
Buzzanell, Patrice M. 1997. "Toward an Emotion-Based Feminist Framework for Research on Dual Career Couples." *Women & Language* 20 (2): 40–48.
Cain, Mary Ann, and George Kalamaras. 1993. "Three into an Interview Do Not Go: Negotiating the Paradoxes of Institutional Hiring Practices." *Written Communication* 10 (3): 414–19. https://doi.org/10.1177/0741088393010003005.

Charlton, Colin, Jonikka Charlton, Tarez Samra Graban, Kathleen J. Ryan, and Amy Ferdinant Stolley. 2011. *GenAdmin: Theorizing WPA Identities in the Twenty-First Century*. Anderson, SC: Parlor.
Gabor, Catherine, Stacia Dunn Neeley, and Carrie Shively Leverenz. 2008. "Mentor, May I Mother?" In *Stories of Mentoring: Theory and Practice*, edited by Michelle F. Eble and Lynee Lewis Gaillet, 98–112. West Lafayette, IN: Parlor.
Ghodsee, Kristen, and Rachel Connelly. 2014. *Professor Mommy: Finding Work-Family Balance in Academia*. Lanham, MD: Rowman & Littlefield.
Hesse, Douglas. 1999. "The WPA as Father, Husband, Ex." In *Kitchen Cooks, Plate Twirlers and Troubadours: Writing Program Administrators Tell Their Stories*, edited by Diana George, 44–55. Portsmouth, NH: Boynton/Cook.
Horning, Alice. 2011. "From the Editors." *WPA: Writing Program Administration* 37 (2): 7–10.
Koerber, Amy. 2013. *Breast or Bottle? Contemporary Controversies in Infant Feeding Policy and Practice*. Columbia: University of South Carolina Press.
Marquez, Loren. 2011. "Narrating Our Lives: Retelling Mothering and Professional Work in Composition Studies." *Composition Studies* 39 (1): 73–85.
Mason, Mary Ann, Nicolas H. Wolfinger, and Marc Goulden. 2013. *Do Babies Matter? Gender and Family in the Ivory Tower*. New Brunswick, NJ: Rutgers University Press.
Micciche, Laura R. 2011. "For Slow Agency." *WPA: Writing Program Administration* 35 (1): 73–90.
Micciche, Laura R., and Donna Strickland. 2013. "Feminist WPA Work: Beyond Oxymorons." *WPA: Writing Program Administration* 36 (2): 169–76.
Perl, Sondra. 1998. "Composing a Pleasurable Life." In *Women/Writing/Teaching*, edited by Jan Zlotnik Schmidt, 239–53. New York: SUNY Press.
Peskowitz, Miriam. 2008. Foreword to *Mama, PhD: Women Write about Motherhood and Academic Life*, edited by Elrena Evans and Caroline Grant, xi–xiv. New Brunswick, NJ: Rutgers University Press.
Restaino, Jessica. 2012. *First Semester: Graduate Students, Teaching Writing, and the Challenge of Middle Ground*. Urbana, IL.: NCTE/CCCC.
Reynolds, Nedra. 1998. "Interrupting our Way to Agency: Feminist Cultural Studies and Composition." In *Feminism and Composition: In Other Words*, edited by Susan Jarratt and Lynn Worsham, 58–73. New York: MLA.
Sallee, Margaret W. 2013. "Gender Norms and Institutional Culture: The Family-Friendly versus the Father-Friendly University." *Journal of Higher Education* 84 (3): 363–96. https://doi.org/10.1353/jhe.2013.0017.
Schell, Eileen. 1998. "Who's the Boss? The Possibilities and Pitfalls of Collaborative Administration for Untenured WPAs." *WPA: Writing Program Administration* 21 (2): 65–80.
Seigel, Marika. 2013. *Rhetoric of Pregnancy*. Chicago, IL: University of Chicago Press. https://doi.org/10.7208/chicago/9780226072074.001.0001.
Slaughter, Ann-Marie. 2012. "Why Women Still Can't Have It All." *Atlantic*, July/August. https://www.theatlantic.com/magazine/archive/2012/07/why-women-still-cant-have-it-all/309020/.
Stenberg, Shari. 2006. "Making Room for New Subjects: Feminist Interruptions of Critical Pedagogy Rhetorics." In *Teaching Rhetorica: Theory, Pedagogy, Practice*, edited by Kate Ronald and Joy S. Ritchie, 131–46. Portsmouth, NH: Boynton/Cook.
Strickland, Donna, and Jeanne Gunner. 2009. *The Writing Program Interrupted: Making Space for Critical Discourse*. Portsmouth, NH: Boynton/Cook.

7
METAPHORS WE WORK BY
New Writing Center Directors' Labor and Identities

Rebecca Jackson, Jackie Grutsch McKinney, and Nicole I. Caswell

As articles in this collection make clear, one of the biggest challenges new WPAs face is reconciling their expectations about who they will be and the roles and labor they will take up in their new positions with the identities, roles, and labor these new positions demand. The process of coming to terms with new tasks, responsibilities, bureaucracy, and professional relationships, as well as reimagining who they are as they do this work, is not completed the first week, the first month, even the first year on the job. *Process* is the operative word here: transitions take time. Researchers in career development refer to this process as the "transition curve" and point out that for people going through "significant change," moving through this phase can take up to two years (Young and Lockhart 1995).

For new writing center directors (WCDs) in particular, transitioning into a WCD position is further complicated by the (mis)conceptions and unknowns of writing center director work. Writing center and writing program administration scholarship has largely ignored writing center directors, save for a few didactic advice pieces here and there saying what directors' labor *should* be rather than documenting what it is and surveys like the one by Gary Olson and Evelyn Ashton-Jones (1988) and those that followed (Balester and McDonald 2001; Ervin 2002; Charlton 2009; Griffin, et al. 2005; Isaacs and Knight 2014) that offered much-needed stats on who was directing writing centers and what their responsibilities were. What's still largely missing, however, are rich portraits of writing center directors, the various forms of labor they engage in day to day, month to month, and year to year, and the ways in which they experience this work at various stages in their careers. A recent

DOI: 10.7330/9781607326335.c007

(and welcome) exception is Anne Ellen Geller and Harry Denny's 2013 article "Of Ladybugs, Low Status, and Loving the Job," in which they offer glimpses into writing center professionals' "lived experiences" and explore some of the potential consequences of participants' preferred labor (administration rather than scholarship) on disciplinary knowledge making and institutional presence (Geller and Denny 2013).

In 2012–2013, motivated to understand writing center directors' labor, we embarked upon a year-long qualitative study of nine new writing center directors (in their first or second year) and their work. Our study was guided by two overarching research questions: *Who is directing writing centers? What is the work of directing a writing center?* We interviewed each director several times over the course of the academic year, always asking what they had done in their jobs since the last interview, what they wanted to do but weren't able to, what significant moments or communication they'd had, and anything else they felt was important to note about their positions. In doing so, we captured their transitions into writing center work in vastly different institutional settings.

We also wanted to understand how participants experienced their labor and, as a consequence, conceptualized their work—that is, how they figured their labor in metaphorical terms. Thus, early in the first semester of interviews, we asked participants to complete the phrase *Being a writing center director is like . . .* Our participants' responses to this request were rich, intriguing, frustrating, complicated and, at times, not entirely unexpected; further, their answers cohered in a way that hinted their jobs might be similar and/or that they might be conditioned to think about their jobs in similar ways. Foremost, participants' metaphors tell us how they experienced the transition into writing center director positions—that is, what it felt like to become a writing center director and to do the work of writing center administration. Too, participants' metaphors prompt us to question the narratives available to new writing center directors and to reinvigorate the questions of writing center director identities and status.

THE STUDY

Participants were selected through a purposeful sample; we invited participants from national listservs and new writing center directors we knew personally. We chose our nine from the nearly two dozen volunteers in order to include directors at different levels (high school, community college, four-year universities), different geographical locations (United States and abroad), and different types of institutions (online college, charter school, boarding school, HBCU) and with varied credentials (BA, MA, and PhD) and experience in writing centers (several years to no previous experience) (see app. A.) We interviewed participants two to four times each semester by phone, Skype, or e-mail, based on their preferences and availability.

In this chapter, we focus on participants' metaphors for their jobs for a couple of reasons. First, though metaphors for writing centers are common (see Davis 2001; Haviland et al. 1999; Healy 1995; Owens 2008) and metaphors for writing program administrators have been explored (see George 1999), writing center directors' metaphorical conceptions of their jobs thus far remain undocumented. Second, metaphors are, as Spoel, Harris, and Henwood (2012) suggest, "a form of rhetorical action that play a significant role in how we constitute reality through our everyday language." That is, we shape metaphors, and metaphors shape us. Consequently, studying how people use metaphors—either as invited to or as naturally occurring in language—offers dual insights. We acquire keener understanding of the thing described (in our case, participants' jobs as writing center directors) as well as of the cultural and narrative playbooks that shape participants' metaphors of work. The study of metaphors—as is true for the study of narrative more generally—can help us see both the individual and the culture operating upon one another.

Our analysis of our participants' metaphors was guided by narrative theorists Jerome Bruner (1991), Susan Chase (2003), and Michael Bamberg (2006)and by George Lakoff and Mark Johnson's 2003 work on how metaphors function culturally. Key to each of these thinkers is the sense that humans craft narratives carefully, if subconsciously, to do what Chase (2003) calls "identity work." We confront often dueling impulses when we tell stories to show both that we belong to a particular group and that we have a coherent internal narrative. In our attempts to belong via the stories we tell, we are "both enabled and constrained by a range of social resources and circumstances" (Chase 2003, 65). Thus, as researchers, we listen to try to understand the story, or metaphor in this case, and what it reveals and hides. Yet we also think about how the story is functioning for the teller within a particular cultural context.

In the following section, we examine the metaphors directors used to describe how they experienced their work during the transitional phase, situating these metaphors within one of two overarching themes: directing is performative and directing is risky, unpredictable, and outside the new directors' control.

THE METAPHORS

Kerr Inkson (2004) tells us "careers are figural" (96). When we think about work, we think about the story of our work: who we are as characters, what kind of journey we're on, whom we like, whom we dislike, what kind of world we live in—ultimately, how we navigate the terrain and the people we encounter along the way. We story the present and we predict the future, even if we're not aware we're doing so. As the chart below illustrates, our participants' metaphors of work underscore what transitioning into writing center direction feels like to those in the midst of the process: one commandeers a ship, another plays a video game, one conducts an orchestra, another has her teeth pulled. Yet despite their seeming differences—how is having teeth pulled remotely similar to conducting an orchestra?—these metaphors also fall into patterns. The first is that transitioning into writing center work is performative: directors take up roles, perform duties associated with those roles, and are watched. Directing is theater. The second is that the transition phase is risky, unpredictable, and often outside a director's control. Directors must grapple with the unexpected; things threaten to fall apart.

We organize our discussion around these two patterns, although we recognize participants' metaphors also overlap. A metaphor about juggling, for example, embodies the idea that directing is risky, unpredictable, and impossible to control, but it also suggests directing is performative. When metaphors could be said to suggest both themes, we categorized by greatest emphasis but also discuss the ways in which the metaphor contains resonances of the other pattern. An example is the conductor metaphor. We argue that the metaphor places primary emphasis on directing as performative, so we discuss the metaphor within that category; however, we also talk briefly about the ways in which the metaphor implies directing is also risky and unpredictable.

Directing Is Performative

During the transition phase into writing center work, new writing center directors take up particular roles, are placed into particular roles, and find themselves in particular roles. These roles, given or chosen, known and unknown, guide and shape directors' relations (or performances) with others. Their work takes place "on stage" and is exposed to view. Because of this, Jennifer, Darya, Anthony, Allison, Katerina, and Mandy each conceptualize writing center direction as performative. Their metaphors emphasize the experience of being watched and judged: writing center directors' labor is not only public but is also

Table 7.1. Participants' metaphors

Participant	Position	Metaphor
Allison	Tenure-track faculty, public university in Southwest	Being a writing center director is "**like an orchestra director** or a conductor. That's what I want. You've got lots of different people doing lots of different things sort of on their own and your job is to make sure all those different elements come together seamlessly and beautifully."
Anthony	Full-time administrator, private college in New England	Being a writing center director is "like **conducting an orchestra**."
Darya	Full-time non-tenure-track faculty, community college in Southeast	"Being the writing center director is like, well, in my situation, it is like **wearing a bunch of different hats**. It's being the advocate for the writing center, for the writing across the curriculum, it's being the writing consultant, it's being the manager, it's being the trainer with the tutors, it's being the web designer, and . . . there's just so many things."
Isatta	Tenured (non-teaching) faculty, HBCU in South	Being a writing center director is like "**pulling teeth**. I don't know how many people really want to go to the dentist anyway. [laughs] To have a tooth pulled. It's painful, and before they even pull that tooth, they have to give you a shot. So, that's how I'm looking at the situation that I'm in right now. I have to, my shot is that I have to put the disconnecting parts of this whole puzzle out of my mind and try to work with what I know and try to bring people on board slowly with that. So, it's like pulling teeth for me, but I know that eventually the pain will heal if I continue to do what I know is right to do. The wound will go away. The problem will go away."
Jennifer	Full-time administrator, for-profit online university	"Being a writing center director is like **running a small company** sometimes. It's such an isolated sort of part of the university I feel like. I mean it's not a class, and it's not a library, so you know, it's very different and I feel like you have customers which are the students and you have employees and it's just very much like managing a business to me—a small little business that's not really like any other business in the university if you thought of every department as a business. The writing center director would be, in my world, the president and my supervisor would be the CEO and I would have to report back to the CEO and the board in order to make decisions."
Joe	Tenure-track faculty, public university in Midwest	"Being a writing center director is like, uh, the cliché of **herding cats** does seem to come to mind, but it's kind of one of those things where, maybe, after you've been **playing Tetris** for a while, and you're sort of at a high level and the blocks are falling, and you're just trying to sort of keep surviving. I think that's really what it is. It like it's just really hitting fast and furious. And these things are really coming in and having to deal with the structures that are left behind or that are not particularly great, or that have never really been thought through." "Being a writing center director is like **steering a really large ship**. You can't really move as fast as you want, necessarily. And you have to get people on board and get it all moving."

continued on next page

Table 7.1—continued

Participant	Position	Metaphor
Katerina	Full-time teacher, secondary boarding school in Eastern Europe	"Being a writing center director is like being on a **rollercoaster**. I am always scared something will not work, students or I will fail an activity, students will not come on time or to assigned tutors, etc. I don't always know where the next turn will be (what the teachers or administration will ask me to do or just ask how to do something, how our activities will work with a new group of students, etc.), and at each 'slower' point there is such a feeling of relief and happiness." "Being a writing center director is like **being a teenager**: you try to figure out what you are doing in this world/life/school/WrC; you have to prove that you are worth appreciation/understanding/being listened to/etc.; you are against someone's rules but you definitely want to set your own rules; you have to be in a 'good group'" to be heard/ valued/ appreciated." "Being a writing center coordinator is like **living through a culture shock** when at first you are excited about everything, then you see that nothing works the way YOU want and think it should be done, and then adjustment and learning to be more flexible and open-minded."
Mandy	Staff, volunteer corps member, at eastern secondary charter school	Being a writing center director "feels **like juggling**, learning how to juggle. Really difficult and a lot of work on the front end that once you start going with it, it works really well, but then you add something into the mix or you drop a ball."
Sara	Full-time administrator, public university in Midwest	Being a writing center director is "**like sailing through choppy waters**. There's plenty of enjoyable moments when you're catching sight of the view and it looks pretty nice, but there's these sort of daily, or these waves that come along periodically and threaten to upset the vessel."

easily critiqued and scrutinized. The directors are vulnerable, worried about bad reviews.

Jennifer, for example, tells us that directing an online writing center in an online for-profit institution is similar to being the president of and "running a small company." There are student "customers" and there are employees. Jennifer's supervisor is the CEO. As president, Jennifer must "report back to the CEO and the board in order to make decisions." Jennifer's metaphor emphasizes the hierarchical nature of writing center direction at her institution—not unlike the hierarchical nature of writing center direction at many nonprofit colleges and universities. Relationships exist in a formal network, and part of being an effective writing center director at her institution is knowing how to leverage that network of connections—to enact the role of president. Jennifer's metaphor suggests the highly visible (and potentially risky) nature of her work as well. Presidents don't work underneath the radar, particularly in a for-profit institution during a time of fiscal belt tightening. Jennifer's metaphor foregrounds roles, scripts, and relations but in doing so implies work as theater and, as a consequence, work as risk.

For Darya, being a writing center director at her institution is like "wearing a bunch of different hats": from writing center and WAC advocate to consultant and manager. Like Jennifer, Darya conceptualizes her labor in terms of roles she must play, although, for Darya, the nature of the role is that it is ever changing. One role morphs into another morphs into another as the situation demands. This makes sense, given that Darya is her writing center's founder: thus, at least for now, she assumes responsibility for all the roles and activities a director at an established writing center would have help with. Darya's metaphor of the director who wears several hats also tells us how Darya conceptualizes responsibility for the writing center director position in her department. Hats are accessories; they can be taken on and off, much as actors shed costumes. And in Darya's particular vision of writing center direction, the hats is to be put on and taken off, shared if you will with other faculty in her division. This isn't necessarily because Darya doesn't like directing the writing center; rather, she sees writing center administration as a collaborative endeavor, a kind of "let's trade parts and scripts" perspective that, unfortunately, is not shared by the colleagues with whom she wants to collaborate.

Both Anthony and Allison compare directing a writing center to conducting an orchestra. The writing center director is an artist of sorts, charged with making order from very different kinds of elements. The director/conductor is central—without her the orchestra does not play or, at least, does not play beautifully. At the same time, a conductor relies on the talent of others. Still, the orchestra is a reflection of the conductor's knowledge and talent, in very much the same way Allison's and Anthony's writing centers reflect their knowledge of and experience in writing centers. Allison and Anthony *represent* the orchestra, and thus there are implied risks in their metaphors of work. That is, while Allison's and Anthony's metaphors emphasize the outcome of effective (read *controlled*) writing center direction, there is potential (albeit unstated) risk to managing so many moving parts.

For Katerina, who directs a writing center at a secondary boarding school, being a writing center director is like "being a teenager" who must figure out a path for herself and do so in an environment where the only chance she'll have to be heard and respected is to get in with the "good group." Katerina experiences writing center work as a novice might, as someone with little stature in the organization who must curry favor for recognition and acceptance. This is a precarious place to be, for while Katerina has a sense of what she wants to be and do in her writing center, she understands she must follow the rules and perceives that others are watching her performance. Roles shapes relations: Katerina must act the role of novice even though she may not feel like one. Put another way, Katerina, like most teenagers, must endure a probationary period before she can be trusted with more responsibility. Her success will depend upon the groups she aligns herself with, and the work of aligning herself with them will require dexterity (and persevering through catty infighting).

What these metaphors suggest is that while the work of writing center directors is performative, the ways directors perform are not consistent across contexts. In addition, such performances are not always expected or known: that is, as individuals navigate the transition into *being* and identifying as writing center directors, they are asked to perform in ways they may or may not have expected or have experience with. Thus, some directors could be said to embody a public performance of work, while others can be said to manage the performance. Whatever new directors' knowledge or experience, the performance is left to the director to figure out on the job.

Directing is Risky, Unpredictable, and Outside Our Control

Joe, Mandy, Katerina, Sara, and Isatta offer metaphors of writing center direction as tricky business—safe, coordinated, controlled one minute, treacherous, haphazard, and out of control the next. Joe compares his job to playing the video game Tetris and playing it at a "high level [at which] the blocks are falling and you're just trying to sort of keep surviving." Likewise, Mandy compares directing a writing center to juggling. "It works really well once you get going," Mandy explains, until "you add something into the mix or you drop a ball or something like that." For Katerina (whose teenager metaphor we've already discussed), directing a writing center is also like being on a rollercoaster. The track is unpredictable, invisible to the rider but for the few feet or seconds before the next drop or curve. There is also "relief and happiness," Katerina says, but only during the "slower points," places where she might catch her breath before the next twist or plunge breaks any illusion she might have that she's in control of the ride.

Joe's, Mandy's, and Katerina's metaphors figure the lack of control these new writing center directors feel in explicit ways. That is, the metaphors they offer foreground lack of control rather than imply it: lack of control is the metaphor's featured experience. Sara's and Joe's nautical metaphors hint at the idea that directing a writing center is precarious and unpredictable in less explicit ways. Sara, for example, tells us directing a writing center is like "sailing through choppy waters." Yes, "there are plenty of enjoyable moments when you're catching sight of the view and it looks pretty nice," but there's also "these waves that come along periodically and threaten to upset the vessel." Joe says directing a writing center is like "steering a large ship" that, because of its size, just can't move as quickly as the captain might want it to. Joe, Mandy, and Katerina call attention to their jobs' harrowing pace, as well as the consequences they face if they miss the next new task thrown at them, fail to dodge the unexpected player, or (inevitably) fail to predict the next bend in the track. Sara points out the sometimes beautiful view but, like Joe and Mandy, also reminds us disaster is just one big wave away. Joe's second metaphor emphasizes that the ship he steers is moving in the right direction; it just can't get there as quickly as he (or others) might like.

For each, the choice of metaphor tells us about the specific nature and realities of their work. Joe's frenzied pace, captured in his Tetris metaphor, suggests the multiple moving parts of his job, parts he had no say in choosing. Joe has a predecessor, and the reality of inheriting this predecessor's writing center is that Joe must "deal with the structures that are left behind or that are not particularly great, or that have never really been thought through." This will take time, as Joe's ship-steering metaphor makes clear. Mandy doesn't attribute the "juggling" she must do as a writing center director to any specific cause, but her metaphor does establish how precarious such work is: add a new item to the routine—as when she is suddenly asked to add math tutoring to her workload—and you risk dropping the ball and botching the routine altogether. Katerina's roller-coaster metaphor suggests the limited line of vision writing center directors must cope with when building a writing center from the ground up. Curves and dips can't be seen; they can only be reckoned with as they arise. Relief (success) will come too. We just don't know when that will be or how long it will last. Likewise, Sara and Joe each conceptualize the hazards of captaining a big ship; there are moments of calm when one might enjoy the scenery, but movement is slow, and there's also the ever-present chance that a rogue wave might upset the smooth ride

It seems clear to us, as well, that the positions and locations Joe, Mandy, Sara, and Katerina inhabit shape the metaphors they craft to describe their work. Joe's Tetris metaphor tells us as much about his own interest in writing centers and technology as it does about his position and location in this setting—a WC/WAC director in a split appointment who receives mixed signals about his job. Mandy labors (juggles) in similarly shaky circumstances. Her job is officially authorized for only two years; in the year we interviewed her, she was waiting to hear whether her request for a third year would be granted. For Sara and Katerina, it is the sheer size of their jobs and the unknowns that attend them that cause stress: scope makes the work of directing unwieldy. So although we've focused on the ways their metaphors are similar, there are hints of how their particular contexts shape their telling.[1]

Isatta leaves us with arguably the most disturbing conceptualization of directing a writing center—a vision of work that isn't just risky, but painful, isn't just unpredictable, but unwanted. She tells us that being a writing center director is like having a tooth pulled. Isatta's metaphor is interesting on a number of levels but particularly in the way she imagines her role in relation to others and the situation she's in. Directing and the responsibilities associated with it have been foisted on her without her consent. She did not ask to be named the writing center director; rather, she was told to do it. There are two stages to the suffering Isatta endures. The first—the shot—involves getting her brain around the complex pieces of the puzzle she has been tasked to put together. Isatta must draw upon her knowledge and her relational skills to do this. The reward comes when the tooth is pulled: the pain subsides and the wound begins to heal. In Isatta's case, the end result will be worth the pain—"we'll be better than we are right now"—although there is a hint of skepticism about how smoothly the process will go. "We'll be better than we are right now" Isatta tells us, not necessarily because "being better" is the foregone conclusion to hard work. Rather, Isatta and her faculty will "be better" because they "have to be." If it isn't so, we hear, it will be made so.

Participants' metaphors frame the "unknown" aspects of work with which new writing center directors must contend. Regardless of planning or educational background, individuals transitioning into writing center director positions must learn to navigate work about which they have learned very little and that is also out of their control. Put another way, new directors find themselves facing the (almost) impossible task of having to invent the known from what is not or can't be known. To say this work is difficult (or treacherous or unwieldy) is an understatement.

CONCLUSION

We asked directors again in their final interviews to complete the same statement about what a directing a writing center is like. Their answers, for the most part, stayed the same. Most participants remembered what they said at the beginning of the study year, and there were a few laughs as they thought about what their metaphors implied—the danger, the overwhelming nature of it all, the art. We find their metaphors telling because they dramatize how the directors feel about their work and how much they feel they have a handle on that work. Participants' metaphors are the stories they offer about their transitions. Though space constraints mean we cannot offer here full-color portraits of how each of our participants labored throughout their year, we do think this close look at how they conceptualize their work metaphorically is telling and offers a counterbalance to the largely quantitative previous research on writing center director identity. We do not just ask how positions are configured; we ask how the positions are lived during the early transition from school to job, and we pay attention to how the labor is storied.

These metaphors paint writing center director labor as perilous and tenuous. The directors feel pressure, have their hands full, and feel as if they work in front of an audience. Juggling, Tetris playing, ship steering, business operating, and orchestra conducting are exhilarating and exhausting—not tasks one can maintain indefinitely. And yet, many times in the transcripts, participants spoke with excitement and pride about their work. Many saw that they made a difference in their settings, and they talked eagerly about how they achieved goals they set for their work. So, why are their metaphors, largely, for lack of a better word, so *negative*?

To conclude, we offer a few thoughts on this. First, the way in which the metaphors overlap with one another signals to us that the labor in which these new directors engage is similar and, more than that, *feels* similar across their varied contexts and even with their different backgrounds. Directing a writing center is hard; it is complicated. In the transition phase, directing a writing center is particularly hard and particularly complicated because previous roles and previous assumptions often don't align with new WCDs' lived realities. Since our participants were all new, it is not surprising they felt challenged by their new jobs and, as the metaphors suggest, skeptical about being able to keep up. This is to say we believe the ways the directors story their work accurately describe their lived, "felt" experiences.

Moreover, the ways in which their metaphors cohere also suggest to us the possibility that participants were influenced to think about their work in particular ways by the networks of writing center professionals to which they are exposed. Especially in early anecdotal accounts of writing center directors within the scholarship, labor was storied as Sisyphean, as too much, as too hard, and as likely doomed to failure (or as Olson and Ashton-Jones [1988] would have it—writing center directors have identity crises). Narrative theorists suggest we tell stories not just to report but also to signal belonging. These new directors were talking to us, writing center researchers, in the context of a writing center labor study, and as such they may have (subconsciously) felt compelled to tell a story that resembled internalized disciplinary narratives. They might be likely to see and experience their work as difficult, or to primarily express the work as difficult, because the scholarship sets that expectation. Thus, we must wonder what other stories can be told about directing a writing center that signal belonging? And how do or how might writing center directors take up such narratives at pivotal moments in their careers?

Given these possibilities, we think those transitioning into writing center director positions can take a few points from this study. First is that no matter how strong the director's preparation—whether a PhD in rhetoric and composition, a dissertation in writing center studies, coursework in administration, years of writing center experience—or confidence going into their job, each had to learn to negotiate the system in which they worked. They learned quickly that they could not control everything or foresee what was coming next, that the feeling they were judged on their every move was at times overwhelming, and that the work itself was sometimes painful and disappointing. These things do not mean the work is not worth doing, but that, perhaps, future directors are fed particularly sunny disciplinary ideas about their autonomy and their preparation that works against them during their first years. Second, we suspect many directors told us stories about their struggles in their work that they did not tell their supervisors (which is fair, since often they struggled with their supervisors). However, we encourage new directors to document their labor carefully and strategically voice concerns about their roles to peers and supervisors within their institution. Especially when positions are brand new within institutions, no one on campus understands what the directors do or knows whether the working conditions are fair.

Finally, for those who craft writing center director positions or evaluate writing center directors, we suggest careful and ongoing consideration of job expectations. Here, we are speaking directly to our writing program director peers, as we imagine them to be our closest advocates: our study of nine new directors in wildly different institutional contexts reveals some degree of hopelessness and despair across the board. Perhaps because writing center directors' labor has been so poorly documented beyond quantitative stats, expectations placed on new directors are sometimes unsustainable. In fact, just two years out from our study, only five of the nine are still in their roles as writing center directors. Moreover, the struggles of the directors in their second year on the job were strikingly similar to those in their first year; the period of care and concern should extend beyond the first few weeks into the first few years the director is on the job to mirror what we know about how long transitions take. We hope this study can stand as the first of many empirically grounded cautionary tales about the cost of ignoring the labor and lived experience of those who transition into roles as new writing center directors.

APPENDIX: PARTICIPANT MATRIX

	Institution type	*Location*	*Position type*	*Year on job*	*Academic background*
Allison	Public university	Southwest (US)	Tenure-track faculty	Second (first year tenure-track)	PhD rhetoric and composition
Anthony	Private college	New England (US)	Full-time administrative	Second	PhD rhetoric and composition
Darya	Community college	South (US)	Full-time faculty	First	Master's in TESOL
Isatta	Historically black college	Southeast (US)	Tenured faculty	First as director (sixth year on job)	PhD rhetoric and professional communication
Jennifer	For profit	Online (US)	Full-time administrative	First	Master's in English (medieval literature)
Joe	Public university	Upper-Midwest (US)	Tenure-track faculty	First	PhD rhetoric and composition
Katerina	Secondary boarding school	Eastern Europe	Teacher	First	Master's in TESOL; master's in teaching English
Mandy	Secondary public charter school	Mid-Atlantic (US)	Program associate through a volunteer corps	Second (first year writing center)	Bachelors of arts in English and math
Sara	Public university	Midwest (US)	Full-time administrative	First	PhD literary studies

Note

1. We didn't notice, however, that the differences in their metaphors correlated with their types of institution, backgrounds, credentials, or previous experiences.

References

Balester, Valerie, and James McDonald. 2001. "A View of Status and Working Conditions: Relations Between Writing Program and Writing Center Directors." *WPA: Writing Program Administration* 24 (3): 59–82.

Bamberg, Michael. 2006. "Stories: Big or Small: Why Do We Care?" *Narrative Inquiry* 16 (1): 139–47. https://doi.org/10.1075/ni.16.1.18bam.

Bruner, Jerome. 1991. "Self-Making and World-Making." *Journal of Aesthetic Education* 25 (1): 67–78. https://doi.org/10.2307/3333092.

Charlton, Jonikka. 2009. "The Future of WPA Professionalization: A 2007 Survey." *Praxis* 7 (1). http://www.praxisuwc.com/charlton-71.

Chase, Susan. 2003. "Taking Narrative Seriously: Consequences for Method and Theory in Interview Studies." In *Turning Points in Qualitative Research*, edited by Yvonna Lincoln and Norman Denzin, 273–94. New York: Alta Mira.

Davis, Jeffery. 2001. "Pitching a Tent, Welcoming a Traveler, and Moving On: Toward a Nomadic View of the Writing Center." *Writing Lab Newsletter* 25 (10): 12–15.

Ervin, Christopher. 2002. "The Writing Centers Research Project Survey Results, AY 2000–2001." *Writing Lab Newsletter* 27 (1): 1–4.

Geller, Anne Ellen, and Harry Denny. 2013. "Of Ladybugs, Low Status, and Loving the Job: Writing Center Professionals Navigating Their Careers." *Writing Center Journal* 33 (1): 96–129.

George, Diana, ed. 1999. *Kitchen Cooks, Plate Twirlers and Troubadours: Writing Program Administrators Tell Their Tales*. Portsmouth, NH: Boynton/Cook.

Griffin, Jo Ann, Daniel Keller, Iswari Pandey, Anne-Marie Pedersen, and Carolyn Skinner. 2005. *Local Practices, Institutional Positions: Results from the 2003–2004 WCRP National Survey of Writing Centers*. Writing Centers Research Project. http://coldfusion.louisville.edu/webs/a-s/wcrp/reports/analysis/WCRPSurvey03-04.html.

Haviland, Carol Peterson, Sherry Green, Barbara Kime Shields, and M. Todd Harper. 1999. "Neither Missionaries nor Colonists nor Handmaidens: What Writing Tutors Can Teach WAC Faculty about Inquiry." In *Writing Centers and Writing Across the Curriculum Programs: Building Interdisciplinary Partnerships*, edited by Robert Barnett and Jacob S. Blumner, 45–58. Westport, CT: Greenwood.

Healy, Dave. 1995. "In the Temple of the Familiar: The Writing Center as Church." In *Writing Center Perspectives*, edited by Bryon Stay, Christina Murphy, and Eric Hobson, 12–15. Emmitsburg, MD: National Writing Centers Association.

Inkson, Kerr. 2004. "Images of Career: Nine Key Metaphors." *Journal of Vocational Behavior* 65 (1): 96–111. https://doi.org/10.1016/S0001-8791(03)00053-8.

Isaacs, Emily, and Melinda Knight. 2014. "A Bird's Eye View of Writing Centers: Institutional Infrastructure, Scope, and Programmatic Issues, Reported Practices." *WPA: Writing Program Administration* 37 (2): 35–67.

Lakoff, George, and Mark Johnson. 2003. *Metaphors We Live By*. Chicago, IL: University of Chicago Press. https://doi.org/10.7208/chicago/9780226470993.001.0001.

Olson, Gary A., and Evelyn Ashton-Jones. 1988. "Writing Center Directors: The Search for Professional Status." *WPA: Writing Program Administration* 12 (1–2): 19–28.

Owens, Derek. 2008. "Hideaways and Hangouts, Public Squares and Performance Sites: New Metaphors for Writing Center Design." In *Creative Approaches to Writing Center Work*, edited by Kevin Dvorak and Shanti Bruce, 71–84. Cresskill, NJ: Hampton.

Spoel, Philippa, Roma Harris, and Flis Henwood. 2012. "Healthy Living: Metaphors We Eat By." *Present Tense* 2 (2). http://www.presenttensejournal.org/volume-2/healthy-living-metaphors-we-eat-by/.

Young, Alison, and Terry Lockhart. 1995. *A Cycle of Change: The Transition Curve*. Cranfield School of Management. http://www.ucd.ie/t4cms/Transition%20Curve%20Cranfield%20Article.pdf.

8
GET OFFA MY LAWN!
Generational Challenges of WPAs in Transition

Beth Huber

Published in 2005, "The Progress of Generations," written by Anthony Baker, Karen Bishop, Suellyn Duffey, Jeanne Gunner, and Shelley Reid, attempts to outline the shifting landscape WPAs faced nearly three decades after their professional organization was formed at the 1976 MLA convention. The stories are told by five administrators who have transferred the baton from or to another WPA and who describe the transitions in pedagogy and institutional pressures over time. The authors conclude that "perhaps WPA agency does depend on our recognizing the moments that allow for the undermining of paradigmatic 'common sense.' But in these moments that are also spaces in time, each WPA is carrying the professional DNA of earlier generations" (Baker et al. 2005, 55). Simply put, every WPA carries the past into the present and then waits patiently for their moment to create the future.

One more generation has passed and another has begun since "Progress" was written. Four generations in, and the "professional DNA" chain is longer and significantly more complex. The shifting ground under our discipline (professionalization as one example) has made generational transitions even more challenging. Current WPAs may, quite literally, have nothing in common with their predecessors; they may be on a completely different definitional plane. In other words, it may not just be the movement of time and space that is complicating a new WPA's agency. Instead, it may be the *stuff* surrounding time and space.

THIS IS MY HOUSE

We all own our tiny slice of the world. We've built it (or it has built us) from the *stuff* of the generation we were born into, educated from, and

DOI: 10.7330/9781607326335.c008

are in service to.[1] My stuff is different from my father's and daughter's stuff, though we are members of a single genetic line. My father, for example, was taught to obey authority; I was taught to question it and my daughter to obliterate it. Authority hasn't changed, but the stuff around it has. Our stuff creates our worldview, and our worldview creates our stuff. Our vision of what things (and people) are made of and how they work follows us from our homes and into our schools, relationships, and careers. In the case of WPAs, when we're *in charge*, the stuff of stuff becomes really important. Am I built from an ability to enforce the rules, or is my DNA more inclined to break those rules? And what do I do with my stuff when someone else's stuff starts taking over the rooms? It *is* my house after all.

Every WPA begins their service with a vision for the writing program grounded in theory and supported with pedagogy. Each future administrator has been in a doctoral (or master's) program—often fairly recently—that helped form that vision and construct that pedagogy. As the next WPA takes the reigns from the former, so too the fresh vision, grounded in the newest research, takes over from the last. Further, as time passes (WPAs frequently serve multiple years), the next administrator is often a generation apart. Amidst the transition, the WPA on their way out is sometimes left feeling the culture shock of the unfamiliar or the near betrayal of having one's coveted vision shown to be outdated at best or ineffective at worst. Likewise, the WPA on their way in must engage with ideas from the past, be they from the former WPA or, even more challenging, from the institution as a whole. As Baker et al. suggest, the "time-based metaphor of *generations* elides crucial local contexts" (Baker et al. 2005, 32). In short, we come into our positions and quickly find that the stuff of self and place must inevitably collide. For the program to move forward, then, we must realize "the importance of seizing the 'right institutional kairotic moment' in any WPA's tenure [as] a crucial component of exercising positive institutional change " (Shaw, Winter, and Huot 2009, 164). The right stuff for the right time.

The generational push-and-pulls that occur as new WPAs bring fresh visions to their writing programs create important conversations about stuff. In these transitional moments, we not only learn about ourselves as individual teachers and scholars, but we also shed light on the rich history of our discipline as a whole as it has moved from one "right" way to teach writing to another "better right" way. We understand that each of us could not have created our vision without the existence of the preceding visions, yet we find that old visions must often die to make way for the new. We are, simultaneously, standing on the shoulders of giants and ghosts.[2]

THIS IS MY LAWN

I was the third of four WPAs serving Western Carolina University (NC) over the last twenty-five years. We are all from different generations (in age) and carry that generational stuff. Each of us, with the exception of our current WPA, served seven years in the job, putting our hearts and philosophical/pedagogical worldview into every decision made. And we've all felt the frustration (or perhaps relief) as our vision has been challenged and changed. I have heard stories of my predecessor's struggles to change what was a current-traditional-based program into an expressivist/liberatory-based one. Years later, I found myself battling an institutional generation gap from a social epistemic stance. Then recently, I watched as our current WPA was so challenged by a systemic worldview determined to revive the "right way" of the past that his own vision for progress could scarcely take shape. As we four began to recount those transition narratives, the stories of our giants and ghosts, I realized our struggles paralleled the national professionalization of WPAs as compositionists progressed from being "academic serfs" to "professor's wives" to scholars who also direct to WPA scholars.[3] Further, our stories mirror pedagogical chronologies like those James Berlin lays out in his attempt to ascribe worldview categories for writing and their relative influence within the academy.

Berlin, in his 1982 "Contemporary Composition: The Major Pedagogical Theories" and the companion 1988 update "Rhetoric and Ideology in the Writing Classroom," overlays then-current pedagogical styles with the ways a teacher makes sense of the world (their stuff) and lands on four categories: classical rhetoric (Aristotelian); positivist rhetoric (current traditional); neo-Platonic (expressionist) rhetoric; and new rhetoric (social epistemic):[4]

> Classical Rhetoric considers truth to be located in the rational operation of the mind, Positivist Rhetoric in the correct perception of the sense impressions, and Neo-Platonic Rhetoric within the individual, attainable only through an internal apprehension. In each case knowledge is a commodity situated in a permanent location, a repository to which the individual goes to be enlightened. For the New Rhetoric, knowledge is not simply a static entity available for retrieval. Truth is dynamic and dialectical, the result of a process involving the interaction of opposing elements. (Berlin 1982, 773–74)

A teacher's worldview (and, therefore, pedagogy) could be rational, scientific, personal, or situational/relativist, and that "choice" likely depends upon when they were educated. As new theories developed—say, for example, the introduction of personal expression in the 1960s—young teachers embraced fresh ideas. Further, when those young teachers became older WPAs, their ideas became programmatic. So, while all four pedagogical categories were still being practiced in composition classrooms in the late 1980s, there was a sort of popularity quotient for each. For example, Aristotelian pedagogy was "far from" a "dominant force" and often masqueraded as current traditionalism (Berlin 1982, 767, 769). Genuine current traditionalists were starting to clear the buildings after holding classrooms hostage for the better part of century (Fulkerson 1979, 344). Expressionist pedagogy, after the Dartmouth Conference of 1967, increased in popularity every year through the late 1970s and was still going strong. And the new rhetoric was, as its name implied, new; the very purpose of Berlin's articles was to advocate for this new rhetoric. All of this is to suggest not only categories but also a timeline.[5] Composition's common pedagogies were generational.

With this in mind, let me briefly introduce you to four WPAs of WCU. I'm first providing a certain biographical context to aid in a wider understanding of my argument.[6] Thereafter, I'll dig into the importance of the transitions that have taken place between us. Elizabeth Addison (pers. comm., April 27, 2015) was born in 1947 in Oak Ridge, Tennessee, which was a city full of scientists and engineers from the Manhattan Project. When Elizabeth took over our writing program in 1992, she had an MA in literature and no experience in directing a composition program. But she was the wife of a tenured literature professor who had a reasonable understanding of classical rhetoric. Close enough. She would have her PhD in literature from Duke before she handed over the reins of FYC.

Though born and eventually ending up in North Carolina—the southern-belle drawl is nearly trademarked—Marsha Lee Baker (pers. comm., May 18, 2015) moved frequently with her career-air-force father and spent her early school years in Tokyo, Japan. She is most known for her lived philosophy of nonviolence and liberatory pedagogy. Marsha Lee was specifically hired in 1997 to direct FYC and was the university's first composition and rhetoric PhD—received from the University of North Carolina, Greensboro. She officially took over from Elizabeth in 1999.

I arrived at Western Carolina University, which is nestled in the tiny mountain town of Cullowhee, in 2004 after forty-one years of midwestern, big-city living. My mom was in politics; my dad was a preacher. Given this history, my singular focus in life has been the study of power and ethics in the creation of perceived reality. I was hired to direct the program in 2005.

Nathan (Nate) Kreuter (pers. comm., May 14, 2015) is a young man, which already makes him different from the rest of us in oh-so-many ways. He was born in 1980 in the small mountain town of Buchanan, Virginia, and was hired in 2010. Nate was not hired with an imminent administrative position hanging over his newly PhD-ed head. Instead, we were overrun with comp/rhet graduate students in our recently formed emphasis and needed a top-notch teacher/researcher. Nate's UT-Austin credentials, as well as his tech-savvy youthfulness, made him the obvious choice. Nate eventually took on WPA duties in the fall of 2013.

There were two years during which the four of us occupied the halls of WCU at the same time: the scientist, the expressivist, the relativist, and the techie—the academy's version of the Breakfast Club. We spanned four generations and four cultures. We had four different piles of stuff. As is true with all generational shifts, it is in the moment the piles collide for the first time that the most important transitions occur.

GET OFFA MY LAWN!

This is how it begins: "Congratulations (*your name here*), you're hired!"

Perhaps the biggest challenge of a new WPA is navigating the question of why you're being hired in the first place.[7] Why does the university think you're there? What does the department, and even the soon-to-be-former WPA, expect you're going to do versus what they *tell you* they want you to do? Most important, what do you think your charge is? Are you there to create a program, change a program, or merely keep the thing going? Or are you in your office just minding your own business when all of a sudden—bam!—you're now running the writing program?

Whether we are hired fresh or promoted from within, we all have some sort of interview process. They read our carefully worded CV. We read their mission statement written during the Nixon administration. During multiple conversations, it's likely we're told what will be expected from us when we take over. But these dialogues are oftentimes inadequate, incomplete, or downright incorrect. I don't think this problem is a matter of disingenuousness on one side or a lack of preparation on the other but is, rather, mismatched worldviews. When there is not just a mutual misunderstanding of our practical duties but a misunderstanding of vision, the transition, for everyone, becomes a slow and painful journey.

Revisiting Berlin here can help us see how this kind of philosophical miscommunication can be problematic for WPA transitions. The hiring committee at Generic University scouts for someone to manage the composition program after criticism from the campus community that "our students can't write." These outside stakeholders are concerned that "our students need grammar help" (current traditional). The department agrees that "our students require instruction in invention, persuasion, and research" (Aristotelian). Writing faculty are on board with the idea that "our students need help finding their unique voices" (expressionist). The brand-new WPA is totally ready to "help our students think critically about the world in all its contexts and power structures" (social epistemic). If you're that WPA, you've already lost because while *your* students are making assessable progress, *their* students still "can't write." As you transition into your new position, then, you must not only provide vision but also navigate re-vision (without letting the irony make you surly). Meanwhile, the next doctoral candidate waits in the wings wondering, "Why aren't your students also analyzing the Twitterverse?" Remember, too, that since these philosophical shifts tend to be generational shifts—movement through time—we must add to this transitional complexity an element of respect for those who came before you. Now, you are not only misinterpreting the vision, you're being rude about it.

To understand the generational implications of these shifts in pedagogical vision and professionalism, a more complete discussion of WCU's four WPA "beginnings" is in order. When we four began to tell our transition stories, we realized much of what we thought about each other—incompetence, stubbornness, or even insubordination—was really an inability to understand each other's beginning contexts.

Elizabeth was not hired to be a WPA. Though the FYC sequence had been in existence for a number of years, there was no WPA since there was no established *program*. The decisions were made by the department chair and other senior faculty (all literature people) and were then *managed* by the FYC director. So, for example, there was already a preexisting guide to composition (called the "Freshmen Manual") which included a common syllabus based on current-traditionalist pedagogy straight from the *Harbrace College Handbook*. Since Elizabeth had no experience in composition-program direction, her charge upon taking over was pretty clear: stay on the well-worn path. She recounts, "It was all very prescriptive . . . I'm not really a revolutionary, I guess."

What Elizabeth doesn't realize is that, in a time of nationally shifting pedagogy and professionalization, this literature MA did manage a minirevolution, first by forcing a shift to a more Aristotelian mindset—"We really drilled invention and arrangement strategies"—and second by requiring that students spend one class per week on computers.[8] Of course, they spent that time doing invention and organization exercises on a computer program designed for such a thing, but it was still significant progress. Since Elizabeth was one of the literature folk, therefore not particularly threatening, these shifts were seamless. More important, by adding an element of professionalization to her work through giving a definition beyond grammar to composition, Elizabeth made it possible for the department to imagine it might need someone who specialized in the field for their next hire.

So, when Marsha Lee was hired, everyone was on the same page, right? Not so much. While the department was ready to establish a composition program with a professional at its helm, it was not necessarily ready to embrace a new vision. Baker et al. describe the challenges of new WPAs attempting to professionalize a long-standing writing program and conclude that "those of us in WPA positions invariably find ourselves adjusting principles, practices, and perhaps our own philosophies to fit a particular set of institutional conditions and constraints" (Baker et al. 2005, 41):

> Thus while the WPA must try to redefine the new position to professionalize it, he cannot define that position far from standards accepted at the institution, nor describe it without the language that has been locally institutionalized, nor entirely expect the institution to validate and uphold the progress he defines. (Baker et al. 2005, 35)

Being from the next generation of composition and rhetoric scholars, those who trained during the expressionist movement, Marsha Lee came to WCU with three programmatic and pedagogical goals: "collaboration, conversation, and human connection." Her first order of business was to establish a committee of composition faculty of all ranks to make decisions and set policies. Next, she set about undoing the product-oriented and genre-based pedagogies of the past in favor of more "authentic student writing rather than school writing." As she describes it, it was a "liberatory pedagogy." Or as Elizabeth puts it, "[It was] all so touchy-feely . . . too loose. There didn't seem to be any rules."

Rules versus freedom—a clash not of people or personalities but of generational worldviews. One can almost imagine a "long hair" confronting a "suit" with the complaint, "You're killing my vibe, man!" and getting the response, "Kids these days have no respect!" In one regard, the charge is true. While expressionism and Freire-ism did throw out the rules of the past, guidelines were still established to conform to a different vision. To understand the new rules, however, one had to understand the new reality. That understanding did not occur during Marsha Lee's first year as WPA, leaving both sides with hurt feelings over a perceived lack of respect. As Freire began to replace Harbrace, the former FYC decision makers just assumed Marsha Lee Baker couldn't possibly be a competent administrator.

That's where this transition story takes a bit of a turn. During her second year, Marsha Lee was summoned to a faculty meeting called specifically to determine whether or not their new WPA knew what she was doing. Interestingly, the questions asked of Marsha Lee's faculty were not overtly pedagogical but rather were focused on the appropriateness of her management style. The senior faculty didn't understand the vision; therefore, they didn't understand the methods used to achieve that vision. And Marsha Lee was left without the expectation that the institution would "validate and uphold the progress [she] define[d]" (Baker et al. 2005, 35). When FYC faculty refused to confirm her incompetence, senior faculty finally left Marsha Lee alone to fight for a pedagogy that, frankly, they never fully accepted.

In retrospect, Marsha Lee believes the department thought they wanted a program when they actually wanted another manager. Regardless, this story has a happy ending because Marsha Lee ended a seven-year run as WPA with a solid, professionalized program and the respect of the entire faculty. She won the fight to convert all adjunct positions to full time (with benefits), expanded departmental definitions of rhetoric, and encouraged faculty to work together to connect to students. When challenged, the new vision eventually provided its own solution: collaboration, communication, and human connection.

I was blissfully unaware of the trials my predecessor had gone through until our recent interview. Therefore, I naively assumed my role as WPA with all guns blazing. While Marsha Lee was a lover, I was a fighter. While she was all about communication and collaboration, I was a one-woman wrecking crew, fixing the injustices, real or imagined, I saw everywhere I went. Marsha Lee had left me with a solid, professional program, so there was little in-house work to do. I made a few substantive pedagogical changes to ground us solidly in the social epistemic and changed our two-semester sequence to a two-year sequence under the newly named Writing, Rhetoric, and Critical Studies program. I created digital-assessment procedures and made other minor tweaks here and there. But that was the easy stuff. Unfortunately for me, all the injustices I saw were above me.

If you've followed my argument thus far, this is the next generational step. As we move from expressionism to the new rhetoric, we are reminded that truth is "the result of a process involving the interaction of opposing elements" (Berlin 1982, 774) and an understanding of power structures. Since I began college during the height of new rhetoric, I was trained and more than ready to oppose some elements. Pretty much any element. As Marsha Lee accurately informed me, "Your weakness was that you were always overreacting to stuff." Consequently, the transition between Marsha Lee and me frequently consisted of the words, "Perhaps you ought to take a step back and breathe for a second." Sometimes I did; more often I did not.

Our discipline's move toward professionalization ended up becoming the most important and frustrating aspect of my work as a WPA. It became not only my transition story but also the transition story of my department and the university as a whole. In 1998, the CWPA approved Evaluating the Intellectual Work of Writing Administration, which argued that WPA work can be "seen as scholarly work and therefore subject to the same kinds of evaluation as other forms of disciplinary production" and is therefore "worthy of tenure and promotion when it advances and enacts disciplinary knowledge" (Council of Writing Program Administrators 2002, 499). When I was hired in 2004, I was told WCU was transitioning to the Boyer model of scholarship in its tenure decisions, and the strong implication was that my work as administrator would be valued accordingly. In short, I was hired to be a professional WPA. In new-rhetorical terms, the absolutist, positivist truths of the past were being reevaluated, and traditional power dynamics were shifting.

So, I worked tirelessly to create a scholarly paper trail for every move I made as WPA. I connected every possible aspect of our program pedagogy to a larger public purpose. We got high marks from students and the department, and because I was constantly showcasing our successes, the program also became a pedagogical model for some other departments in the university and a few community colleges and high schools. The drive to make my scholarly work public (according to Boyer definitions) created concrete ties between our program's work and the larger university community. In one respect, my goal was selfish; I needed to make sure I got tenure. In another respect, I also felt a zealous political drive to prove the scholarly worth of our discipline to those who had long thought not only that "anyone can teach writing" but that "anyone can direct a writing program."

Apparently, *anyone can*, in fact, direct a writing program. Despite the university's commitment to Boyer, a change in our departmental tenure document that specifically accounted for the CWPA protocols, and extremely favorable ratings from outside reviewers, my tenure and promotion vote was split at all three levels. I got tenure by one vote and lost promotion by a mile. But I caused a Boyer fight in the university that persists to this day. Therefore, one of the first things I said to Nate after he was hired was, "Don't trust Boyer. Just publish as many academic articles as you can." Three steps forward; one step back. I had to make my new vision a ghost so it wouldn't haunt Nate in his future.

Fortunately, Nate had no immediate need to worry about whether his WPA work would be valued because he wasn't hired to directly take over the program. Following my tenure challenges, the department agreed he should be given as many years as possible to focus on *traditional* scholarship before stepping in, and he did just that. So, unlike most new WPAs, Nate was in great scholarly shape when he assumed his position. He also agrees I left him with a pretty solid, albeit not perfect, program. The three WPAs in whose footsteps he would follow had already advanced the program through three major shifts in worldview. The vision, for the time being, was stable. Nate wouldn't have to be in constant disaster mode. When I asked him what his goals had been upon taking over the WRCS program, Nate replied, "Don't hit icebergs."

Truthfully, Nate did not hit any icebergs. The icebergs hit him. In an almost surreal return to the worldviews of the past, and after years of progressive reforms, higher education in North Carolina came under a conservative attack that seemed to trickle down (pun intended) into every aspect of university life, including composition pedagogy and practice. Lawmakers were publicly promoting Ayn Rand as a higher education ideal, and so-called liberal centers and programs were being targeted for closure.[9] So, whereas Elizabeth had needed to shift the vision of a few English faculty, and Marsha Lee had to transform the worldview of a department, and I had to battle a university system, Nate would have to push back against a whole state. I suspect this is the reality for many current WPAs across the country.[10]

During the five years prior to Nate's becoming WPA, North Carolina lawmakers cut higher education funding by nearly 15 percent per student, eliminated many hundreds of faculty positions, and raised classroom caps (Oliff et al. 2013). Additional cuts are expected in the next two-plus years. While the greater percentage of cuts to WCU occurred during the final years of my administration, the consequences were just starting to be felt as Nate came on board. A total of twenty WRCS faculty contracts were not renewed; we lost fifteen in just one year. Class caps were raised from twenty to twenty-four. Yet, during that same time frame, the first-year student population, all of whom were required to take our two-course sequence, increased by 12.5 percent (*The Reporter* 2009; Western Carolina University 2014). In other words, we had far fewer teachers teaching far more students.

As cuts squeeze administrators, priorities get set and worldviews become transparent and set in stone. Since all the vision in this case belonged to lawmakers, all Nate could do was put out fires. There was little room or time for a vision of his own. So, in his first years as WPA, Nate has had to contend with a giant backlog of students who couldn't get into required composition classes; an administration looking to potentially ease the load by floating the idea of paring down the requirements to one course; an incredibly overworked and underpaid faculty barely keeping their heads above water; and a growing number of international and/or otherwise underprepared writers who had zero services available to them. And one cranky senior faculty member who believed Nate was too young to be in charge of anything.

THIS IS OUR HOUSE

When asked what his vision for our program will eventually be, if and when he is left to put down the water bucket, Nate describes a faculty at work reevaluating and revising the definitions of a rhetoric grown too comfortable: "Do we even know what we mean when we say 'critical thinking' or 'process'?" He also sees adding complexity to our views about the sites of writing by expanding our connection to the digital world. This vision is what one would expect from the next generation. It's what I expect from this moment in time.

It's true none of us made it easy on the person who followed in our footsteps. We were each trying to be giants while terrified we were becoming ghosts. We saw each other as too touchy feely or too prescriptive, too hot headed or too practical. But on reflection, our transition challenges were not rooted in personalities. They were rooted in the stuff of time. Moments of transition offer us choices: follow the rules, ignore them, or obliterate them. But those moments also tell us stories about who we are individually and as a discipline; they tell us how we've gone from serf to scholar and how we can avoid becoming serfs again. Each of us four WPAs tried, in our own way, to tell our story to the ones before and after. Follow the rules. Don't be so combative. Do as I say, not as I did.

It's tempting to suggest the lesson here should be about listening as an act of learning what not to do. But had any of us "listened," our program and profession would not be where it is today. Instead, we should listen to each other's stories about stuff so we know how to build on that foundation. Some visions must wait for time to catch up. Our successes, on the other hand, rest in our abilities to push the envelope just enough. After all, it's *our* house.

Notes

1. *Stuff:* (1) the materials of which something is made (noun); (2) to cram full (verb); (3) a fraudulent vote (verb). Given the generational influence of child-rearing practices, religious and academic education, sociocultural contexts, and media, I believe all three definitions apply.
2. I take this metaphor partially from "The Progress of Generations" by Anthony Baker et al. (2005).
3. For a detailed history of various aspects of composition professionalization, see Sharon Crowley's *Composition in the University* (Crowley 1998), Robert Connors's *Composition-Rhetoric: Backgrounds, Theory, and Pedagogy* (Connors 1997), and, more recently, Colin Charlton et al.'s *GenAdmin: Theorizing WPA Identities in the Twenty-First Century* (Charlton et al.2011).
4. Berlin later adds cognitive psychology and ties it to the positivist world view. See also Berlin's history of writing pedagogy in *Rhetoric and Reality: Writing Instruction in American Colleges, 1900–1985* (Berlin 1987).
5. I do not suggest, nor does Berlin, that these are the only four ways to envision composition pedagogy. I do agree with Berlin, however, that these categories are useful for talking about ways of seeing the world. Further, these categories correspond nicely to historical movements that spawned similar shifts in worldview. See, for example, Richard Ohmann's *English in America* (Ohmann 1976).
6. Each of the WPAs identified herein agreed to be interviewed and gave permission for this project to be written.
7. Shaw, Winter, and Huot (2009), as well as Baker et al. (2005), touch briefly on this issue as part of the confusion during WPA transitions.
8. Hugh Burns's *Stimulating Rhetorical Invention in English Composition through Computer-Assisted Instruction* (Burns 1979), the first dissertation on computers and composition, had just been published a little over a decade earlier, so the idea was still very new, particularly for a small mountain college.
9. For a complete accounting of the conservative changes to higher education in North Carolina, see Jedediah Purdy's (2015) "Ayn Rand Comes to U.N.C." or Zoe Carpenter's (2015) "How a Right-Wing Political Machine is Dismantling Higher Education in North Carolina."
10. In fact, state systems like those of Wisconsin and Louisiana, to name just a few, have been coming under what Saul Newton (*Milwaukee Wisconsin Journal Sentinel*, June 10, 2015) calls an "ideologically motivated attack" from state governments since 2010. In each case, higher education funding has been slashed, to the detriment of the system as a whole.

References

Baker, Anthony, Karen Bishop, Suellyn Duffey, Jeanne Gunner, Rich Miller, and Shelley Reid. 2005. "The Progress of Generations." *WPA: Writing Program Administration* 29 (1–2): 31–57. http://wpacouncil.org/archives/29n1-2/29n1-2-Baker-etal.pdf.

Berlin, James. 1982. "Contemporary Composition: The Major Pedagogical Theories." *College English* 44 (8): 765–77. https://doi.org/10.2307/377329.

Berlin, James. 1987. *Rhetoric and Reality: Writing Instruction in American Colleges, 1900–1985.* Carbondale: Southern Illinois University Press.

Berlin, James. 1988. "Rhetoric and Ideology in the Writing Class." *College English* 50 (5): 477–94. https://doi.org/10.2307/377477.

Burns, Hugh. 1979. *Stimulating Rhetorical Invention in English Composition through Computer-Assisted Instruction*. PhD diss., University of Texas at Austin. Computer Microfilm International.

Carpenter, Zoe. 2015. "How a Right-Wing Political Machine is Dismantling Higher Education in North Carolina." *Nation*, June 8. https://www.thenation.com/article/how-right-wing-political-machine-dismantling-higher-education-north-carolina/.

Charlton, Colin et al. 2011. *GenAdmin: Theorizing WPA Identities in the Twenty First Century*. Anderson, SC: Parlor.

Connors, Robert J. 1997. *Composition-Rhetoric: Backgrounds, Theory, and Pedagogy*. Pittsburgh, PA: University of Pittsburgh Press.

Council of Writing Program Administrators. 2002. Evaluating the Intellectual Work of Writing Administration. Appendix in *The Writing Program Administrator's Resource*, edited by Stuart C. Brown, Theresa Enos, and Catherine Chaput, 499–517. Mahwah, NJ: Lawrence Erlbaum.

Crowley, Sharon. 1998. *Composition in the University: Historical and Polemical Essays*. Pittsburgh, PA: University of Pittsburgh Press.

Fulkerson, Richard. 1979. "Four Philosophies of Composition." *College Composition and Communication* 30 (4): 343–48. https://doi.org/10.2307/356707.

Ohmann, Richard. 1976. *English in America: A Radical View of the Profession*. Middletown, CT: Wesleyan University Press.

Oliff, Phil, Vincent Palacios, Ingrid Johnson, and Michael Leachman. 2013. "Recent Deep State Higher Education Cuts May Harm Students and the Economy for Years to Come." Center on Budget and Policy Priorities. http://www.cbpp.org/research/recent-deep-state-higher-education-cuts-may-harm-students-and-the-economy-for-years-to-come.

Purdy, Jedediah. 2015. "Ayn Rand Comes to U.N.C." *New Yorker*, March 19. http://www.newyorker.com/news-desk/new-politics-at-the-university-of-north-carolina.

The Reporter. 2009. "WCU Student Enrollment Tops 9,400 to Set Record." Western Carolina University. Accessed June 28, 2015. http://thereporter.wcu.edu/2009/09/wcu-student-enrollment-tops-9400-to-set-new-record/.

Shaw, Margaret, Gerry Winter, and Brian Huot. 2009. "Analyzing Narratives of Change in a Writing Program." In *The Writing Program Interrupted: Making Space for Critical Discourse*, edited by Donna Strickland and Jeanne Gunner, 155–65. Portsmouth, NH: Boynton/Cook.

Western Carolina University. 2014. "Enrollment at WCU Hits Another All-Time Record High." http://news-prod.wcu.edu/2014/09/wcu-enrollment-hits-10382-for-another-record-year/.

9
PERFORMANCE ATTRIBUTION AND ADMINISTRATIVE (UN)BECOMING
Learning to Fail While Trying to Fly

Steven J. Corbett

> *If you want to be a complete human being, if you want to be genuine and hold the fullness of life in your heart, then failure is an opportunity to get curious about what is going on and listen to the storylines. Don't buy the ones that blame it on everybody else, and don't buy the storylines that blame it on yourself, either.*
> —Pema Chödrön, "How to Fail: Advice for Leaning into the Unknown"

Rachel Hodin reports on thirty-five people who failed or were miserably rejected before becoming famous in their fields and professions (Hodin 2013). Some of these notable "failures"?

- Thomas Edison was fired from Western Union for an acid-spilling accident that occurred while conducting an experiment he should not have been conducting on the job.
- Abraham Lincoln entered the army as a captain and left a private. He also tried to start several businesses before becoming president, all of which failed.
- Vincent van Gogh only sold one painting during his lifetime, and that was to a friend for very little money.
- Steven Spielberg applied to, and was rejected three times from, the UCLA School of Theater, Film and Television.
- Michael Jordan was cut from his high-school basketball team.
- Stephen King's first book, *Carrie*, was rejected thirty times.

In all my journeys toward writing program administrator (WPA) professional roles, I've made plenty of deliberate choices to toe the line, to conform. I've made conscientious choices in my attempts to *avoid failure* by studying and performing more "expert," "smart" communicative moves

DOI: 10.7330/9781607326335.c009

that would not shock the minds and memories of my various audiences. I've tried my best to act in ways becoming a budding administrator-teacher-scholar. But I've also prepared myself to fail at making everyone love me and need to hire me or want to work with me.

Looking back, I now try to understand—as best I can—when to attribute my performance shortcomings to events I could control or to circumstances I had little or no agency in.

Current discussions of transfer research in writing studies and learning theory (Bransford, Brown, and Cocking 2000; Elon University 2013; Donahue 2012; Driscoll and Wells 2012; Wardle 2012; Yancey, Robertson, and Taczak 2014) acknowledge that coping with *failure* is an important part of learning. But to date, few scholars in our field have committed focused attention to the importance of learning from failure (for notable exceptions, see Brooke and Carr 2015; Carr 2013). While elsewhere colleagues and I have treated the notion of performance failure through the lenses of queer theory (Corbett and LaFrance forthcoming), imposter syndrome (Corbett and Decker 2012), and grading practices (Babb and Corbett 2016) my goal in this essay is to bring the concept of failure to the forefront of discussions about WPAs in transition. Drawing on research in knowledge transfer and productive failure—particularly discussions of discourse communities and individual dispositions in transferable identity performances—and my own experiences as a WPA, this essay synthesizes theory and lived experience in order to highlight why coming to terms with and learning from failure is an important, even necessary, part of the training and professional work of the WPA.

I begin this essay reviewing current research on knowledge transfer in writing studies, building toward a knowledge-transfer-inspired, performance-failure-informed analytical frame. I draw especially on current work in knowledge transfer in writing studies from the 2012 special issue of *Composition Forum*, "Writing and Transfer" (Weisser, Ballif, and Wardle), and from Kathleen Blake Yancey, Liane Robertson, and Kara Taczak in *Writing across Contexts* (Yancey, Robertson, and Taczak 2014). I extend and complicate current notions of transfer and failure by factoring in attribution theory (Babb and Corbett 2016; Driscoll and Wells 2012; Turner 2007) and performance theories from Erving Goffman (1959; 1967; 1981). I move on to narrate ways I've purposefully chosen to "succeed" or "fail" on the road toward becoming a good WPA, sometimes opting for what I believe to be my full understanding and consent in my own WPA (un)becoming processes and performances. I scrutinize these "critical incidents" (Yancey, Robertson and Taczak 2014) through the lens of my failure-friendly, attribution-theory performance frame. My hope is that sharing my experiences in honest, critically self-reflective ways might offer future WPAs (and coaches of future WPAs) concepts and strategies for using failure and attribution theory as potentially productive rather than destructive performance lenses.

(ATTRIBUTING AND LEARNING FROM) FAILURE *IS* AN OPTION: DISCOURSE COMMUNITIES, KNOWLEDGE TRANSFER, AND THE PERFORMANCE OF SELF

We use the term *discourse community* with neophytes to reassure them that learning to perform effectively in a particular academic context will take time and focused effort (see, for example, Bizzell 1992; Bruffee 1999; Swales 1990). With this conceptual nudge, we can think about learning the many facets of becoming a WPA as more than the rote act of reading a "how-to" guide. Learning to become a successful WPA is a larger and more difficult process than simply working hard, getting a job, working harder, and getting tenure. Becoming a good WPA is a process of coming into one's own within a group of interlocutors who share not only similar interests but also similar values. Joining the professional conversations of WPA work, then, is as much a process of socialization into unwritten norms and community standards as it is a matter of simply becoming aware of the formal conventions active within that protean community. It is a gradual process of learning to temper our attitudes and actions in relation to our colleagues.

But while writing studies' interest in learning theory and discourse communities, especially in terms of knowledge transfer, is commendable and can add to conversations involving failure and the attribution of failed performances, the field still has much to learn about how to coach potential WPAs toward a stronger understanding of these often difficult and sometimes emotionally charged experiences. What does it mean to "fail" as a WPA? Does a WPA fail at an R1 research institution if they devote too little time to research but execute successful programmatic or campus-wide curricular reforms or changes? Who exactly gets to define failure or success, and what assessment mechanisms determine when a WPA has succeeded: students, teachers, department chairs, deans, tenure committees, other WPAs, promotion and tenure documents and guidelines (including departmental laws and bylaws)? Given all these—sometimes competing and divergent—variables, is the quest toward becoming a successful WPA really just an overdetermined game for the lucky who just happen to be at the right place at the right time?

Or are there some things we—as students of the becoming-a-successful-WPA game—can all learn about what it means to learn from failed performances and transitions? Is there some way to think proactively, as well as reflectively, about the many variables we can attribute to successful WPA performances and transitions?

If we seek to account for ways to synthesize theories of failed and successful knowledge transfer—the *transitioning* of knowledge from one situation to another (if you will)—with theories of identity performance, we might inch toward realizing a more robust lens with which to analyze the vagaries of learning to become a successful WPA. The recently articulated studies of transfer by Yancey, Robertson, and Taczak (2014)—especially their notion of "critical incidents"—offer a useful place to start in relation to failure, attribution theory, and discourse communities. The authors define a critical incident as "a situation where efforts either do not succeed at all or succeed only minimally" (120). They illustrate this concept through the extended study of Rick, a first-year physics and astrophysics major, who struggled to write about science for a general audience in his writing course, then failed to write an acceptable lab report for his chemistry professor based on what he learned from writing about science for a more general audience. In short, Rick's struggles between two discourse communities involved complicated trial-and-error negotiations among genre, audience, prior knowledge, and his own developing self-efficacy and motivation (cf. Anson 2015). Ultimately, Rick learned to make moments of failure opportunities for growth and improvement. He came to "identify failure as a learning experience rather than a judgment . . . an opportunity for learning rather than defeat" (135). Revisiting and reconsidering the attributive role of discourse communities plays its part in our quest for a robust frame for learning to use failure in productive ways (see Beaufort 2012; Donahue 2012 for complementary critiques of discourse communities and transfer). What other variables do we need to consider, though, as we continue to construct this failure-friendly frame? How do we proceed when theories of discourse community begin to fail to fully account for all possible attribution variables of failed performances?

While the concept of discourse communities can account for a lot of the sociorhetorical reasons we might experience a critical incident during a transitional period, we must also consider more personalistic and individualistic attribution variables. Dana Driscoll and Jennifer Wells argue that individual dispositions—like motivation, values, self-efficacy, and self-regulation—must be accounted for much more in transfer research (Driscoll and Wells 2012). Important to note, this attention would bring the *Framework for Success in Postsecondary Writing* (2011) "habits of mind" to center stage for our developing failure-friendly analytical frame. Turning our lens toward the personal and individual might nudge us to ask different types of attribution questions regarding Rick's critical incidents. Could there have been personal reasons that caused some of the initial trouble Rick had in negotiating in and between writing for the discourse communities of first-year composition and his science courses? Too many commitments like a job, family, or illness might have played a part. Simple lack of motivation and effort may have been a culprit. Neglect of any of the *Framework's* (2011) habits of mind—curiosity, openness, engagement, persistence, creativity, flexibility, responsibility, and/or metacognition—may have contributed just as much to Rick's critical incidents as forces outside his individual dispositions.

A concept Driscoll and Wells (2012) touch on in their disposition theorizing is the theory of attribution, a theory that can help us begin to make connections between individual agency and motivation and the outside force of discourse communities. Simply put, attribution theory deals with how much control a person believes they have over a situation, how much the cause of success or failure is a result of their own actions versus circumstances beyond their control (harking back to the Pema Chödrön, blame-game-storylines quote that opens this essay, which is taken from a comment posted to *Tricyle: The Buddhist Review* blog on May 11, 2015).

So, it would make good sense, as we continue our analytical-frame-building quest, to carefully consider and attribute the effects of both the forces that might lie outside our control, the vagaries of discourse communities, and those that might be located closer within the grasp of individual control and self-regulation. Elizabeth Wardle believes we might do better to do away with the overused term "transfer" altogether, replacing it with the term "creative repurposing" (Wardle 2012). She argues that she has repeatedly encountered students (like Rick) who can repurpose their prior knowledge when confronted with ill-structured problem situations. But Wardle also articulates, "In contrast, I also see students who cannot or will not solve an ill-structured rhetorical problem and who, instead, repeatedly and in the face of obvious failure, keep trying to solve ill-structured problems by bringing what they already know to bear and applying it with no attempt to repurpose, explore, or create. This can happen even with advanced students" (see Anson 2016). Drawing on Pierre Bourdieu's concept of "habitus," Wardle (2012) speculates that perhaps fields themselves play a major part, and warrant attribution for, inculcating students with problem-solving attitudes and dispositions at the expense of problem-exploring dispositions. Wardle believes this dichotomy forces students into a "psychological double-bind" that can result in confusion and failure.

In many ways, then, during his academic transitions, Rick was understandably facing both immense sociorhetorical as well as psychorhetorical forces. He was doing his best to negotiate problem situations in the quest to survive those critical incidents, and the accompanying chance of a failed performance, we all must inevitably face. Just because we (as advanced students of the academy) make our ways successfully into the discourse community of WPAs—publishing and presenting our fair share in/at recognized and suitable venues and performing service to the field—does that automatically confer success? Can a WPA be successfully working toward building a national reputation as an accomplished, respected voice in the field and yet still fail at their own institution based on expectations and standards laid out by others?

Finally, and to further complicate this analytical frame, we would do well to remember the eminently quotable Erving Goffman's words from *The Presentation of Self in Everyday Life*: "We must be prepared to see that the impression of reality fostered by a performance is a delicate, fragile thing that can be shattered by a very minor mishap" (Goffman 1959, 56). Goffman suggests the ways in which sociorhetorical actors, rather than simply "attempting to achieve certain ends by acceptable means," also "can attempt to achieve the impression that they are achieving certain ends by acceptable means" (250). Elsewhere, in the later work *Forms of Talk*, Goffman (1981) analyzes the consequences of failure to execute a successful performance. He explains how the very awareness and prospect of social control is a powerful means of social control, causing social actors to usually initiate remedial action. And if they don't self-regulate toward more (seemingly) appropriate performances, sooner or later, others will "remind" them to do so (199). The plurality, often ambiguity, of attributing control lends itself to the drama of human communication—including failed transitional performances—and adds yet another layer to the many variables that can help us make sense of the following personal critical incident I share and scrutinize in the rest of this essay.

CRITICAL INCIDENT: ATTRIBUTING FAILURE TO "FIT" WITH FORMER INSTITUTION

*Elation. Success. Made it through the multiple exam*ination *performances of the job-search process, and first tenure-track job accomplished in a pretty good location! But little did I know this was really just the beginning of a new set of* transitional challenges. I worked even harder and (I thought) smarter than I ever had as a graduate student helping direct writing programs at the University of Washington (U-Dubb). But . . .

"Once more into the breach, dear friends, once more" (Shakespeare 3.1.2).

I soon found myself in a tug-of-war between my goals and visions of a teacher-scholar and the expectations of who my new institution wanted me to (un)be. Coming out of an R1, and trained to highly value scholarship and creative activity (which I came to deeply enjoy), I struggled with the transition to present myself as—above all—a great teacher and local-service-oriented colleague. I held tightly to my goals and visions, continuing on what I saw as an R1-level research agenda, while trying my best to also meet my department's 4/4 teaching and service expectations.

In my first couple of years as co-coordinator of the composition program, I played my part in our composition-by-committee administrative structure. I initially received two course releases to do all the scheduling, help with interviewing and hiring, and help lead faculty development. I also worked closely with the WAC program in initiating and organizing a very popular Practical Pedagogy workshop series that offered two or three forty-five-minute gatherings per term focused on writing pedagogy.

My first-year review went very well, so I assumed I was on the right track, transitioning smoothly, toward success. I decided to continue with my ambitious research agenda, something I truly loved and believed also made me a better WPA and teacher. I even told two senior colleagues in a perhaps regrettable burst of passion, "I want to show everyone that I can teach in a 4/4 system and still out-publish them all!"

Arrogance. Hubris.

Failed "fit."

(Un)becoming performance of self . . . I must take my share of the blame . . .

As you can probably imagine, it did not take too long before, despite all my goals and efforts to succeed on all fronts, my new discourse community began to gradually, yet persistently, chip away at my notion of a teacher-scholar. In my second-year review, the chair and committee began to express some "concerns" about my teaching and admin work. The chair began to claim I did not listen to my colleagues enough. The committee began to suggest I was perhaps focusing on my scholarship so much that my teaching must be suffering somehow. These claims were made in stark contrast to the evidence in my files, which offered the portrait of a colleague with a sound pedagogical philosophy well-liked by his students and doing his share of service and admin work for the department and composition program.

So, in order to attempt to accommodate my assessor-and-judger colleagues, I actually pulled back on my publication and presentation agenda. Voila, my third-year review saw me somehow "bouncing back" from the disappointing second year.

Yet there were still lingering vague issues of my somewhat questionable communication skills and pedagogical methods and methodologies. While I had renewed hope, I still felt on edge, precarious, insecure. I was still very much on transitional, tenure-track "probation."

I began to see my performances as a perfect castle of cards that—with each presentation I delivered and every new publication—I just kept destabilizing. And as the paper castle became more and more unstable, I found myself pulling further and further away, diverging further from what I felt they wanted me to (un)become.

Strangely, by the end of my third year, my fellow comp-by-committee colleagues decided it might be a good idea to have one acknowledged director of composition. All signs pointed toward me, and the committee (including the chair of English) unanimously voted me in as director. "Wow," I thought, "This must mean I am okay now." But perhaps I got a little too cocky, a little too ambitious . . .

At about the same time, the director-of-WAC position was becoming available. I approached the committee with the idea of my taking on that role as well, perhaps with a codirector. Since I had been doing so much collaborative work between the WAC and comp programs, it made good sense. Everyone on the committee thought (at least they expressed it openly) that was a good idea—except the chair of English. The next thing I knew, the previous director of WAC (whom I had initially asked to consider being cochair with me) and another colleague were announced as codirectors of the WAC program. Later, in my big fourth-year review, the one just before what would have been the year of my bid for tenure and promotion, the chair decided to argue (in a five-page polemic) for why my contract should not be renewed. Despite a different verdict from the departmental P and T committee, the support of several faculty colleagues, and my own best counterarguments, the dean and provost (who, by the way, no longer work at that institution either) went lockstep with the chair's decision.

Arrogance. Hubris.

Failed "fit."

(Un)becoming performance of self . . . they must take their share of the blame . . .

Despite garnering strong support from students and several faculty colleagues, performing more than my share of service to the institution, and even winning a distinguished university teaching award, I could not ultimately be who they wanted me to be. Even though I had anonymous surveys proving that the composition faculty (all part-time adjuncts) overwhelmingly believed me to be an "excellent" director, I could not ultimately be who they wanted me to (un)be. I came to attribute much of what they demanded as too much control and kneel-and-kiss-the-ring and not enough freedom and let-me-be-me.

And I came to a point, finally, at which I could not bend any further. Nor could they . . .

And the walls came tumbling down.

DIAGNOSING A CRITICAL INCIDENT: ATTRIBUTING (UN)BECOMING ATTITUDE AND ACTION

There are no easy answers to explain away this critical incident. Despite my, especially initial, desire to transition into and perform well in this discourse community, several complex factors began to erode even my early desires and dispositions to succeed. In contrast to my experiences as a teacher and administrator at U-Dubb primarily with rhetoric and composition specialists, at the institution where the critical incident happened, I was in the thrall of mostly literature specialists in an English department. While I believed my actions and performances were representative of the field of writing studies, I felt the ways I was being asked to sway my teaching and research often flew in the face of what I considered the values of our field (e.g., by my second-year review, I was beginning to receive formal criticism for my extensive use of guided peer review and response, small-group conferences, teaching with and about technology and digital media, and teaching with student texts. Still worse, in the eyes of my assessor-and-judger departmental colleagues, I was encouraging fellow teachers to practice or consider adopting these pedagogical methods and methodologies.) Rather than have the salutary and beneficial presence and influence of mentors who cared about me and took pains to help me succeed, I felt instead that many of my colleagues were actually working against me to undermine my credibility and image—especially the person I reported directly to, the chair of English. And the more I felt this way, the more I purposefully distanced myself and resisted their control. Could I have proved more open and persistent in my efforts to conform to their image of what I should (un)be? Probably. Would it have been worth it, in the long run, to defer my resistance just long enough to earn tenure and then securely ease back into my true vision of a teacher-scholar in our field? Maybe.

But there were a couple of attributable circumstances working against my transition long before I even applied to the position in the first place. For one, the faculty member I was "replacing" had similarly traveled a rough road toward success. She had also been a very productive scholar who assumed control of both the comp and WAC programs. Luckily for her, however, she had a different chair, one much more sympathetic to her cause. In fact, during my campus visit, the chair of the hiring committee told me point blank that I reminded them a lot of that former colleague, and that resemblance caused them more than some concern. In effect, then, another attributable variable in my overall failed transitional performance was that (all along) I was attempting to remedy or redefine a *preexisting* breach. As Goffman (1981) writes, "Remedial rituals tend to be dialogic in character. Once such a remedy is provided, the provider typically requires some response from recipients so that he can be sure his message has been correctly received and is deemed adequate, effectively redefining the breach" (199–200). I knew I was performing in the shadow of my predecessor. Subsequently, above all else, I needed to let my assessors and judgers know that I would be different. That I had much more to give on the local level, that I could remedy and redefine the breach. And yet history, in several ways, ultimately seemed to unapologetically repeat itself . . .

Another attributable culprit that has plagued me (and, historically, many like me) points back to Wardle (2012) and her use of Bourdieuean habitus. While Wardle offers a useful frame in terms of the dispositions of fields, in relation to individual dispositions she may have left out an important factor. Linking more closely with Driscoll and Wells's (2012) theorizing of dispositions, I come from a working-class background, experienced a dysfunctional and abusive home life growing up, and was a high-school dropout until returning as a nontraditional student at the age of twenty-seven. To this day I bear the sociorhetorical marks of my habitus in some ways, like a visible tattoo. Like so many nontraditional, nonmainstream, Othered individuals I've encountered (people with disabilities, people of color, LGBTQ people), I've tried my best to "overcome" this unfortunate upbringing when it comes to more formal academic communicative performances. I therefore often find myself in situations in which I can attribute my success to my nontraditional dispositions—when I work with people who either have similar habitus and dispositions *or who understand*—and just as many situations in which I cannot—in more formal communicative situations in which my listeners do not know (or maybe don't care) about my identity.

But in so many complex and, in some still unresolved, ways, I ended up sort of giving up on my former institution, and I have to point the attribution finger directly at the person I see in the mirror every day. Even though I really loved working with the students (who were actually more like me in terms of habitus than most of the students I had encountered at U-Dubb) and I got along with and worked well with several of my closest colleagues, I lost the motivation to continue trying to make it work. Goffman (1967) posits that at such moments, while it is typically understood that the person whose self has been threatened should be ashamed, "by the standards of the little social system maintained through the interaction, the discreditor is just as guilty as the person he discredits—sometimes more so, for, if he has been posing as a tactful man, in destroying another's image he destroys his own" (106).

Perhaps while *exploring* and trying to *solve* this problem situation, I had actually *found* a problem—a notion supported by creativity theorists (Feldman, Csikszentmihalyi, and Gardner 1994, 138–41) and developmental psychologists (Bruner 1966, 157–59). I began to lose focus on and conviction in the portrait of my former institution I had so diligently begun to paint at the start. And even the trust and belonging I had developed with several individuals who advocated for me and tried to help me get on the "right" track could not ultimately help me remedy this critical incident. For me, the members of my discourse community who had the most direct control over my future at that institution[1] had shown their true colors, and I had shown them mine. In my attempts to gain control and remedy this problem-exploring situation, in attempting to revisit and revise my failed performances, I gathered together and danced with all my dispositional habits of mind—openness, engagement, persistence, flexibility, responsibility, creativity, and metacognition. But it proved not enough . . .

And it was time we both decided to quit each other.

CODA: A RETROSPECT AND PROSPECT

I continue my quest for some sort of golden mean, some sort of universal presentation of self that will not shatter the expectations of the discourse communities I hope to join, while at the same time not selling out my own identity and sense of self. Being a WPA—like being a cyclist, nature lover, or dog lover—is a part of my identity in the way Colin Charlton et al. (2011) and Rupiper Taggart (this volume) express: once a WPA, in many ways, always a WPA. If I were to offer any cautionary advice to future WPAs and those preparing future WPAs, or to those looking to transition from WPA at one institution to another, I'd include:

- Carefully consider and pay attention to signs of any previous unhappiness with the former WPA(s). Looking back, it probably would have been wise to really think carefully about why the search committee was so concerned about my seeming so like the previous WPA (whom I admired very much then, and now). If I still truly wanted to fit/transition in, I might have actively sought advice on more becoming ways to act.
- Time may be on our side. Since this critical incident, I've heard similar cautionary tales from several respected and successful colleagues, colleagues whose names you might or might not be surprised to hear. Let's listen to our stories of failed performances and add any useful advice to our failure-friendly, attribution-negotiating bag of transitional strategies.

- Let's prepare ourselves to play the never-ending identity game that is the negotiation of attribution (and, granted, misattribution) between individual dispositions and discourse communities. As we sort through the forces of inner and outer control, especially during pivotal transition periods, let's ask ourselves what we are willing to compromise and what we must hold tightly to as best we can. Looking back, for example, I've asked myself whether or not I should have slowed down on my publication and presentation activity the way I did after that shocking second-year review.

As internal and external forces pull endlessly on us, let's ask ourselves what sort of person we want to be and, if it's important to us, how we want to contribute to and perhaps work toward leaving our mark on society. In a wonderful retrospective essay, sixty-five-year-old professor of human development at Cornell, Robert Sternberg (2015), offers poignant advice in terms of things to consider prioritizing now before it's too late. Among such sage admonishments as put family first, take care of your health, and save as much money as you can, he urges us to try to consider the gravity of who we are: "Once you start to sell out your integrity as a professional and even as a person, the slope becomes slippery. In the short run, you sometimes will pay for being true to yourself. In the long run, you will be glad you maintained your integrity. When you look back from age 65, you will only take pride in having lived up to your own expectations."

People like Rick (from Yancey, Robertson and Taczak's 2014 study) and I can draw more than a little cold comfort from the fact that we are in the good company of Edison, Lincoln, van Gogh, Spielberg, Jordan, King, (and . . . ?) in our efforts to turn moments of failure into learning opportunities. Will I ultimately end up succeeding or failing to (un)become a successful WPA, one who can look back on my performances and choices with pride and dignity? Only, and soon enough, time will tell . . .

Note

1. While I've attempted to construct an analytical frame that takes into account both social and personal factors, another useful frame to consider—one that angles more towards material working conditions and institutional attribution—is institutional ethnography (see, for example, LaFrance and Nicolas 2012; Smith 2005).

References

Anson, Chris M. 2015. "Crossing Thresholds: What's to Know about Writing across the Curriculum?" In *Naming What We Know: Threshold Concepts of Writing Studies*, edited by Linda Adler-Kassner and Elizabeth Wardle, 203–19. Logan: Utah State University Press. https://doi.org/10.7330/9780874219906.c0013.

Anson, Chris M. 2016. "The Pop Warner Chronicles: A Case Study in Contextual Adaptation and the Transfer of Writing Ability." *College Composition and Communication* 67 (4): 518–49.

Babb, Jacob, and Steven J. Corbett. 2016. "From Zero to Sixty: A Survey of College Writing Teachers' Grading Practices and the Affect of Failed Performance." *Composition Forum* 34. http://compositionforum.com/issue/34/zero-sixty.php.

Beaufort, Anne. 2012. "*College Writing and Beyond*: Five Years Later." *Composition Forum* 26. http://compositionforum.com/issue/26/college-writing-beyond.php.

Bizzell, Patricia. 1992. *Academic Discourse and Critical Consciousness*. Pittsburgh, PA: University of Pittsburgh Press.

Bransford, John D., Ann L. Brown, and Rodney R. Cocking, eds. 2000. *How People Learn: Brain, Mind, Experience, and School*. Washington, DC: National Academy Press.

Brooke, Collin, and Allison Carr. 2015. "Failure Can Be an Important Part of Writing Development." In *Naming What We Know: Threshold Concepts of Writing Studies*, edited by Linda Adler-Kassner and Elizabeth Wardle, 62–64. Logan: Utah State University Press.

Bruffee, Kenneth A. 1999. *Collaborative Learning: Higher Education, Interdependence, and the Authority of Knowledge*. 2nd ed. Baltimore, MD: John Hopkins University Press.

Bruner, Jerome S. 1966. *Toward a Theory of Instruction*. Cambridge, MA: Harvard University Press.

Carr, Allison. 2013. "In Support of Failure." *Composition Forum* 27. http://compositionforum.com/issue/27/failure.php.

Charlton, Colin, Jonnika Charlton, Tarez Samra Graban, Kathleen J. Ryan, and Amy Ferdinandt Stolley. 2011. *GenAdmin: Theorizing WPA Identities in the Twenty-First Century*. Anderson, SC: Parlor.

Corbett, Steven J., and Teagan E. Decker. 2012. "Imposters, Performers, Professionals II." *Inside Higher Ed*, October 17. https://www.insidehighered.com/advice/2012/10/17/essay-feeling-impostor-academic-job-hunt.

Corbett, Steven J., and Michelle LaFrance. Forthcoming. "Discourse Community Fail! Choices in Success/Failure in Graduate-Level Writing Development." In *Graduate Writing across the Disciplines: Identifying, Teaching, Supporting*, edited by Trixie Smith. Fort Collins, CO: WAC Clearinghouse and Parlor.

Donahue, Christian. 2012. "Transfer, Portability, Generalization: (How) Does Composition Expertise 'Carry'?" In *Exploring Composition Studies: Sites, Issues, and Perspectives*, edited by Kelly Ritter and Paul Kei Matsuda, 145–66. Logan: Utah State University Press.

Driscoll, Dana Lynn, and Jennifer Wells. 2012. "Beyond Knowledge and Skills: Writing Transfer and the Role of Student Dispositions in and beyond the Writing Classroom." *Composition Forum* 26. http://compositionforum.com/issue/26/beyond-knowledge-skills.php.

Elon University Center for Engaged Learning. 2013. "Critical Transitions: Writing and the Question of Transfer." http://www.centerforengagedlearning.org/critical-transitions-writing-and-the-question-of-transfer/

Feldman, David Henry, Mihaly Csikszentmihalyi, and Howard Gardner. 1994. *Changing the World: A Framework for the Study of Creativity*. Westport, CT: Praeger.

Goffman, Erving. 1959. *The Presentation of Self in Everyday Life*. New York: Doubleday.

Goffman, Erving. 1967. *Interaction Ritual: Essays on Face-to-Face Behavior*. New York: Random House.

Goffman, Erving. 1981. *Forms of Talk*. Philadelphia, PA: University of Pennsylvania Press.

Hodin, Rachel. 2013. "35 Famous People Who Were Painfully Rejected before Making It Big." Thought Catalogue. http://thoughtcatalog.com/rachel-hodin/2013/10/35-famous-people-who-were-painfully-rejected-before-making-it-big/.

LaFrance, Michelle, and Melissa Nicolas. 2012. "Institutional Ethnography as Materialist Framework for Writing Program Research and the Faculty-Staff Work Standpoints Project." *College Composition and Communication* 64 (1): 130–50.

Shakespeare, William. 1993. *Henry V.* In *The Tech.* Cambridge: Massachusetts Institute of Technology; http://shakespeare.mit.edu/henryv/index.html, accessed July 4, 2016.
Smith, Dorothy E. 2005. *Institutional Ethnography: A Sociology for People.* Oxford: AltaMira.
Sternberg, Robert J. 2015. "Career Advice from an Oldish Not-Quite Geezer." *Chronicle of Higher Education,* May 26. http://chronicle.com/article/Career-Advice-From-an-Oldish/230335/.
Swales, John M. 1990. *Genre Analysis: English in Academic and Research Settings.* Cambridge: Cambridge University Press.
Turner, Jonathan H. 2007. *Human Emotions: A Sociological Theory.* New York: Routledge.
Wardle, Elizabeth. 2012. "Creative Repurposing for Expansive Learning: Considering 'Problem-Exploring' and 'Answer-Getting' Dispositions in Individuals and Fields." *Composition Forum* 26. http://compositionforum.com/issue/26/creative-repurposing.php.
Weisser, Christian, Michelle Ballif, and Elizabeth Wardle, eds. 2012. "Writing and Transfer." Special issue, *Composition Forum* 26. http://compositionforum.com/issue/26/from-the-editors.php.
Yancey, Kathleen Blake, Liane Robertson, and Kara Taczak. 2014. *Writing across Contexts: Transfer, Composition, and Sites of Writing.* Logan: Utah State University Press.

10
RESEEING THE WPA SKILL SET
GenAdmins Transitioning from WPA to University Pedagogical Leadership

Amy Rupiper Taggart[*]

For a time, I missed being a WPA, in the way that you miss a family, the bustle to get ready, the seasonal routines, the identity that complements and defines you.
—Doug Hesse, "Not Even Joint Custody"

GENADMIN AND TRANSITIONS

In the groundbreaking book *GenAdmin: Theorizing WPA Identities in the Twenty-First Century*, Colin Charlton, Jonnika Charlton, Tarez Graban, Kathleen Ryan, and Amy Stolley suggest that many of those who have been trained to be WPAs[1] never stop seeing themselves as WPAs: the identity is more durable than the position (Charlton et al. 2011). Not all in the field and doing the work see themselves as GenAdmin, as Sarah Stanley makes clear in her contribution to this collection. Yet my experience reflects, adds to, and even complicates the theory of flexible, evolving GenAdmin identity from the vantage point of the advanced-career WPA. This chapter extends and adds to that argument and the theorizing of the WPA identity by examining how advanced WPAs may move *through* that position, situated in the discipline of rhetoric and composition, and *into* other campus pedagogical positions—directors of centers of teaching and learning, general education, honors programs, and campus-wide assessment—with an eye to identity and when transitions take us by surprise or our path takes an unexpected direction. I argue that the GenAdmin identity not only leads us to transport our expertise from context to context in positive ways but that it can also cause distress or identity crisis when we are not doing the work or not recognized for that expertise. And my experience further highlights something that may seem obvious: WPA preparation, like most

DOI: 10.7330/9781607326335.c010

preparation in higher education, is ongoing, not at all ending when the PhD is issued, nor when tenure is achieved.

WPAs train and retrain as they stretch to new administrative positions, and these experiences cross-pollinate, enhancing both writing program and other administration.

If we are to help graduate students think about the long path, help midcareer academics think about evolving vocational directions, and help those who are making the move into these adjacent positions prepare for their transitions, issues of advanced career identity and transitional resources will be important to examine in our scholarship; there are implications for professional development and evaluation, as well as for our theories of professionalization and leadership. Further, when incidents out of our control lead us to no longer do this particular work, we must be able to reflect on the broader skill and knowledge sets we possess and their relevance in other institutional spaces. Look around the WPA network; there is evidence that writing-program work allows people to transition into other locations in higher education. This chapter works to identify some possible paths, potentially transferrable skills and knowledge, identity-related pitfalls we are likely to experience in transition, and ways to cope with abrupt shifts in direction.

Autoethnography: Life Happens

When writing specialists identify as GenAdmin, whether we call it that or not, even life crises cannot stop us from seeing the world through those eyes. In 2012, the year I was diagnosed with breast cancer before age forty, I was a tenured professor who had participated in shaping a writing program in her pretenure years as part of a first-year English committee and as WPA "in waiting." That period of preparation was an ideal way to transition from graduate student with some gWPA (graduate WPA)[2] experience, as it gave me leadership opportunity with minimal responsibility. Just prior to tenure, then, I comfortably took over the running of that program; because I had helped shape it, it already felt like one I "owned" on some level and understood and agreed with philosophically. I completed my WPA workshop[3] far later than is typical (the majority of participants in my workshop were brand new to WPA work, most freshly out of graduate school), which meant rather than boot camp, it felt like just-in-time professional development. My pre-WPA preparation is a story of coming in a rather ideal way to official WPA work. Instead of being *the* writing specialist in charge of a writing program from day one, I had gradual preparation and participation with other writing specialists in the department. I know that is not the story for most WPAs. However, my health crisis was something else; I didn't neatly plan an exit but was forced out of this position. I never expected I wouldn't choose when to stop serving as WPA.

Fortunately, while traumatic, breast cancer is not typically a life- or career-ending diagnosis, and it was not for me. But it had the side effect of pushing me out of the work I had so long prepared to do, and had done, well before I intended to quit doing that work. My generous department chair at the time (a former WPA himself) made it possible for me, within the modified-duties policy of our campus, to step out of directing the program, and he got permission to hire a one-year professor of practice for the WPA job, with the idea that the position should later become a tenure-line position. This generous and resourceful work on his part allowed me to focus on treatment and recovery while doing other kinds of work when I could (including supporting the professor of practice). And the possibility of hiring a tenure-line WPA meant an additional faculty member in the department at a time when we otherwise would not have received a new line.

But I felt unseated and tetherless. If not a WPA, what was my contribution to my department and campus? It may seem ridiculous that these questions even crossed my mind given that program administration was never my entire job, nor had I always done it formally, but life crises such as serious disease likely bring many of us to ask existential questions, and my experience of a feeling of loss confirms the GenAdmin identity. I didn't think of myself as *only* a WPA, but I had come to see WPA as a key feature of my scholarly and professional identity, and my work life had the rhythms of that identity. Such is the nature of forced, unanticipated (all?) transitions. They are unsettling. Writing such transition stories may be important, then, because we cannot and will not experience all transitions. The stories can help us become aware of a wider range of WPA contingencies. And part of the value of this story, I hope, is that it helps augment these new conversations about administration as a scholarly identity, not just service work or the work of those who are not "serious scholars." Those who develop as WPA scholars in the GenAdmin fashion integrate the work into our interlinked teaching, researching, and leadership identities.

The ways I started to navigate and answer the identity questions raised by this experience are, I think, relevant to thinking about a whole host of issues related to WPA transitions: What is there beyond WPA work? What can WPAs bring to broader campus contexts? What kinds of strengths and limitations are there in the WPA outlook? And what losses might we experience in transition? Susan McLeod's lucid "Moving Up the Administrative Ladder" chapter in *The Writing Program Administrator's Resource* offers much practical guidance in response to questions such as these, some of which I echo here (McLeod 2002); it is essential reading for those interested in doing the good work of administration (rather than seeing it as purely a "dark side"). But beyond that practical advice, less has been said about identity, skill, limitation, and loss in transition.

Identities and Roles

Implicit in this collection on transitions is that WPA identities matter and that WPA roles shift and morph over time. I don't think this movement is unique to WPA experience; rather, it is part of human experience to be ever changing. Regardless, or perhaps precisely because of this, identity in transition in the WPA context is worth study. Christopher Burnham and Susanne Green offer insight into a few of the reasons identity is worthy of our attention: they suggest that "we play many roles, and each involves, if not a discrete identity, at least a thread within the whole cloth of our identities. With all that we do, the cloth tatters, threads unravel. So we believe identity deserves close attention, although it has been largely overlooked within WPA literature" (Burnham and Green 2009, 175). This global argument suggests things fall apart when we play so many roles and do not examine our sense of self in relation to others, the programs we lead, and our environment. Burnham and Green go further, suggesting identity rises up in our activities, from assessment to classroom teaching to professional disciplinary-level activity. Without some attention turning to identity, then, they suggest, we cut out a piece of our understanding of all dimensions of our work. And because they suggest identity and ethos are the same ("We go so far as to equate identity and *ethos*"), from a rhetorical perspective, it would be deeply strange not to consider identity when we talk about WPA transitions (Burnham and Green 2009, 177).

My forced transition encouraged me to look around, to consider how much I felt my scholarly and professional identity was connected to WPA and other campus-level work I had been involved in as a result of having led the faculty senate on my campus. That first year, while I was undergoing treatment, I channeled my remaining energies into supporting the professor-of-practice WPA as she jumped into the work under very short time constraints. That mentorship experience was a way to stay in the role, a way to start letting go, and, frankly, a way to not "be sick" all the time. Perhaps I overstepped at times. Perhaps she didn't feel allowed at times to do what she wanted, as I offered her materials for teacher preparation, assessment, and workshops. But she never let on if that was the case; she was always gracious about what I offered. Interestingly, this experience of not quite being ready to let go had its mirror in my work with the person who had directed general education before me, and I hope it made me more sensitive to his possible sense of loss and transition.

The position I later moved into, director of general education, was in a sense a new position on my campus, though a dedicated faculty member from history had done the work for decades as chair of the general education committee and then as an add-on to his work as director of accreditation, assessment, and academic advising. A previous provost had run an internal search for the position before I was promoted to professor and very near the time I served a three-year term in faculty-senate leadership. While I was encouraged to apply then, I balked because I didn't feel the timing was right. The position was initially not funded, but when it was reopened a year or two later with minimal funding, I was in a very different place: I had more distance from the senate work, the security of full professorship, and an action-oriented pedagogical leadership mindset[4] without a clear outlet. I was fortunate that general education work looked to me like a sensible analogue to and extension of running a general education writing program. Both involve supporting teachers in achieving shared goals and objectives and conducting program-level assessment, and both require institutional savvy and collaborative and organizational skills, among other similarities.

There are many opportunities in higher education for administration, including some that bring together the strands of teaching, learning, and administration. For those of us interested in continuing to think about how to scale up instruction beyond our own classrooms, connect curriculum, and professionally develop other teachers, a few logical outlets for our creative, leadership, and scholarly work include the leadership of general education programs, centers for teaching and learning, honors programs, and campus-wide assessment, as well as working in vice-provost positions related to academic affairs. These are all pathways former WPAs have transitioned to successfully: for example, Doug Hesse has directed the writing program at the University of Denver, led the field's national organizations (CCCC and NCTE), and directed an honors program, a center for the advancement of teaching, and a graduate program. But these pathways are not just for the field's luminaries: every campus, regardless of size or type, needs pedagogical leadership. Rhetoric and composition, because of its valuing of the scholarship of teaching and learning (SoTL), has prepared its professionals to provide such leadership more than have other disciplines that keep pedagogical scholarship and preparation for administration on the fringes. This is not to say former WPAs are the only appropriately trained professionals for these positions; rather, it is to acknowledge that some of our training is advantageous and gives us intellectual and administrative access points to adjacent or advanced leadership positions.

DISCIPLINARY AND ROLE AFFORDANCES: WHAT CAN WPAS BRING TO BROADER CAMPUS CONTEXTS?

What, then, are some of those intellectual and administrative access points that emerge from our discipline-specific training and that it may be helpful to deliberately develop? While a comprehensive list could be long, I highlight here some of those I am drawing on in my own transition and that WPA scholarship further affirms: pragmatism, a disciplinary sense of moral charge, rhetorical sensitivity, and a heightened valuing of teaching and learning.

Pragmatism

Donald Bushman's argument that WPAs are pragmatist scholars, engaging in action and reflection to create change in writing programs, resonates with and is echoed in other WPA and composition studies scholarship such as Burnham and Green's discussion of WPA identity and Linda Flower's (2008) use of Cornel West's prophetic pragmatist philosophy to examine literacy work and its rootedness in action. Part of the skill-and-knowledge set that seems to transfer with us is this belief (for many of us) that action followed by reflection in a Deweyan sense builds knowledge but also contributes to change. The attitude that our work is less service and more social science shifts the focus to knowledge building and the positive experimentation that is program direction. We research best practices and our local contexts, discovering intersections between local data and those national best practices, and then make changes and recommendations on the basis of that research. We then test the results of those changes through assessment, stakeholder surveys, and even institutional critique (Porter et al. 2000). All researchers might be capable of conducting this kind of research, but WPAs are experienced in thinking about the nature of program-level, curricular "experimentation." Our published scholarship exemplifies this orientation: see Rose and Weiser's excellent collection *The Writing Program Administrator as Researcher* for examples such as Betty Bamberg's chapter on using research to resolve conflicts between teaching and assessment (Bamberg 1999). In my current work with general education, I started just as a new proposed model was nearing completion by the Core Undergraduate Learning Experience (CULE) committee. They had surveyed stakeholders, drawn on National Survey of Student Engagement (NSSE) data, and looked to evidence-based practices that might inform the revised curriculum. I was able to quickly build on that work as we considered the long vision: how assessment might work to confirm effectiveness and lead to refinement where necessary. Having developed program focus as a writing program administrator and having used assessment to test that program's success meant I required less training to participate in similar conversations in this new role.

Perhaps this orientation toward pragmatism is the reason I have long been drawn to Donald Schön's examination of reflective practitioners in a range of professional fields. He suggests that this reflective action, repeated over time and with the myriad tools of a profession, leads to expertise (Schön 1983). It builds the professional's schema and intellectual toolkits for responding even to unfamiliar problems. Clearly, we are not alone as professionals in active reflexivity. However, WPAs' attention to rhetoric and contingent, contextual action disciplines us to increased attention when navigating complex, nondisciplinary situations and addressing multidisciplinary audiences.

Disciplinary "Moral Charge"

Related to this pragmatic-change orientation is what Bob Connors calls compositionists' "open and almost ingenuous desire to *do some good in the world*" (Connors 1989, 237; emphasis in original). He continues, "Composition teachers and composition researchers from early on have felt a moral charge that goes far beyond mere aesthetics: instill the literacy, transfer the power, solve the problem" (Connors 1989, 237). Charlton and his colleagues might call this the "active hope" they see as an ethics for the WPA rooted in critical reflection and "praxis" (Charlton et al. 2011, 172–78): a pragmatic hopefulness. That combination of a desire to advocate for and work with those who aren't powerful has implications for pedagogical work across campus, as we tend to advocate for better conditions for teacher labor and for broader, more democratic access to resources and ultimately success for students.

This outlook also sometimes means we aren't as involved and invested in our own research agendas as exclusively as we are invested in the research that will lead to this kind of doing good and change. That kind of research benefits from interdisciplinary and collaborative teams of the types formed at the university level. For instance, in my new position, I have found colleagues in the Office of Institutional Research and in the Office of Teaching and Learning, among other locations, and have been fortunate to join them on writing grants for improved STEM teaching on my campus. I could shy from this activity because of its STEM focus, but I perceive it as "doing good" for general education pedagogy that will have spillover across the institution, particularly in the case of institutional transformation grants and workshops offered to all, not just STEM, teachers. After our Gateways-ND team received the 2.6-million-dollar NSF grant to transform STEM teaching and learning, a parallel team of non-STEM faculty led by me wrote a campus grant that would give access to the same professional-development opportunities for faculty outside STEM and ensure both cohorts benefit from the cross-pollination. Budget cuts stopped that grant from being funded, yet having had the conversation allowed us at the Office of Teaching and Learning to fund non-STEM faculty for cohort two. My hope that working with multidisciplinary faculty on improved teaching would make general education better on the campus led me to take a risk on work I might have considered "not my area."

Rhetoricity

I see rhetoric and writing as tools especially suited to administrative work. Most WPAs are trained to see the rhetoric around us, to listen more closely, even to the degree that we understand listening as rhetorical (Ratcliffe 2006). David Schwalm talks about the WPA's power of persuasion in the sense that when one has "responsibility and no authority," one must "learn to get things done without authority" (Schwalm 2002, 132).

The principle can be intensified in campus-wide work, as I found when the campus Core Undergraduate Learning Experience committee, including me, tried to convince colleagues across the disciplines that the time had come for general education reform and that the outcomes-based QUEST model developed by the committee over a more than five-year process of research and debate would likely yield better results than our current model. The committee had a charge from a previous provost and from the faculty senators in service five years prior, and I had the title of general education director, yet we had little more than our powers of persuasion to try to move this work forward. That model jumped its first hurdle, garnering a vote of support from the faculty senate, but the experience of having no money and no supervisory authority was at least familiar, and I knew going into the venture that the work would be challenging, would take time, and would require social capital. We used the tools of open dialogue, presentations of what we viewed as compelling data, and some one-to-one conversations to try to mitigate understandable fear and resistance. This model process stalled because of state-level policy, but relative openness in the campus conversation means if the policy is changed, we can continue to move forward.

Ratcliffe's notion of the openness of rhetorical listening is an action I am practicing. My colleagues from many disciplines can help me to understand the constraints and affordances of their varied contexts as I, and others, try to support curricular change. For example, when a colleague who was apparently a vocal opponent of the curriculum-revision process and possibly of the model itself seemed to approach me with hostility via e-mail, I first balked at engaging in the discussion. But in time, I did meet with her and tried to hear through the anger what might be key insights for improvement. Her perspective that course approvals should not be granted by a committee of faculty untrained in the discipline out of which the course emerges resonated with other discussions I had had with faculty and leaders on campus about our campus's tendency to have faculty committees for compliance (review, evaluation, approval) rather than a more decentralized model of control. The questions she raised may become key to the structure of processes going forward.

Valuing Teaching

I won't linger long on this point, as it seems obvious. Composition as a discipline was built from the challenges of teaching writing. It has transcended its early, almost exclusive, focus on pedagogy, but the discipline remains rich in pedagogical research. That disciplinary training means writing program administrators have made pedagogical questions central to their work, and that expertise is largely unmatched in other disciplines outside education. In my case, nearly my entire scholarly career has focused on pedagogy and the scholarship of teaching and learning. I was able to specialize in composition pedagogy as a graduate student, it was seen as a valid research agenda by hiring committees in English departments, it counted for promotion and tenure, and it counted again for promotion to full professor. Even a coauthored textbook counted. Again, I acknowledge that not all English departments count things in exactly the same ways, but my story is possible, and that I am not alone in this focus suggests writing studies fosters pedagogical expertise. There are many fields in which this long focus would not be supported. And the long focus means I've been able to develop an expertise rather than making SoTL a sideline to other "more important" disciplinary work.

THE OVERALL ORIENTATION

In his comparison of faculty and administrative orientations as he situates the WPA, David Schwalm reveals what he sees to be the WPA difference. He claims that "the fundamental differences [between faculty and administrators], then, are these: faculty tend to be critical, analytical, open-ended, focused, self-centered, and uncompromising; administrators tend to be synthetic, goal oriented, comprehensive in their views, open to compromise—often confused with being wishy-washy, valueless, and arbitrary" (Schwalm 2002, 128). And the WPA often stands between these two spaces as what Schwalm terms a "quasi-administrator . . . viewed by faculty as an administrator and by administrators as a faculty member" (Schwalm 2002, 127). Schwalm's argument is that WPAs are uniquely qualified to transition to upper administration because they have greater knowledge of the institutional infrastructure than do most faculty, often know the education literature, have built relationships with key people on campus (such as registrars), are good at persuasion instead of top-down decision making, are comfortable or at least experienced with compromise, and have empathy for typically disenfranchised campus groups and individuals, a cluster of qualities he summarizes as "knowledge, friends, persuasion, and empathy" (Schwalm 2002, 133–34).

All of these resonate with my own experience. Beyond my pedagogical research agenda, I've built relevant knowledge by participating in state-level discipline-group meetings that helped me to understand issues such as transfer and shared outcomes other faculty may not have to consider much. At those same discipline-group meetings, I was introduced to Schwalm's friends outside the institution but within the system, some of whom turned out to be my colleagues on the state-level General Education Council. Serving as WPA meant I knew many of those registration and records friends, who helped with enrollment management, course scheduling, and the like. I also knew the math colleagues who dealt with similar gateway general education course issues, such as placement, who now participate with me on campus GE committees. Persuasion is the tool of the quasi-administrator with no budget and no supervisory oversight. And empathy means, for instance, I genuinely care that several of my colleagues were upset at the prospect of removing a required science lab from the proposed general education model early in the process.

LIMITATION AND LOSS

While, echoing Schwalm, I advance a largely positive argument here about what WPAs can bring to the university pedagogical context as administrators and campus leaders, I would be remiss to leave out some discussion of the limits of our preparation for this work and the losses experienced in transition. Virginia Anderson and Susan Romano's collection, *Culture Shock and the Practice of the Profession: Training the Next Wave in Rhetoric and Composition*, suggests that the transition from graduate student to professional, including the dramatic graduate-student-to-WPA transition, is often an experience of culture shock (Anderson and Romano 2005). The training graduate students get often just doesn't match up with the varied contextual constraints and demands of professional work in higher education. It's important that we, as preparers of those graduate students, help them build foundations for the first critical transitions. I concur. But the idea that after one gets a job, the transitions are all smooth, easy, and naturally flowing from previous experience and training is a pipe dream.

Each professional transition comes with a new set of culture shocks, even when one stays at a single institution. I'm a clear example of this, as I have stayed at the same campus for thirteen years, working as a faculty member, WPA, presiding officer of the faculty senate, director of general education, and associate director of the Office of Teaching and Learning (an evolution of the previous position). Each role, each job came with culture shocks having to do with role, scope of the work, and disciplinary or discourse-community differences.

As WPA, I felt the increased responsibility of the administrator, someone to whom others looked for guidance about their own classrooms and someone to whom students came with concerns, the "quasi-administrator" status changes Schwalm discusses as a "loss of innocence" (Schwalm 2002, 129). In that role, the scope of the work had to expand beyond my own research and teaching, and I had to accept pragmatic rather than closer-to-ideal solutions.

In leading the faculty senate, the culture shock had primarily to do with finally understanding campus governance, both its possibilities and its dark corners, another loss of innocence. Where before policy had impacted my work largely without my awareness, now I knew how to change it. This role was more service than administration, but it bore many of the hallmarks of moving from and through WPA work into adjacent experiences.

A culture shock I experienced as I moved into general education work was that colleagues on campus saw me as an administrator, even though I had no budget and no supervisory authority. I felt less like an administrator in some ways than when I was a WPA but was treated more like one. My "administrator" status made me seem to some like an opponent or antagonist. I have had to learn both that I cannot just be a faculty member ally and how to continue to be trusted. A key moment on that path involved a campus colleague's shift from antagonism to at least momentary trust. Upon presentation of the new general education model, this colleague pressed, berated, inquired, and was visibly angry. He was one of the scientists concerned that the loss of the lab would diminish education at our institution. He was also concerned that science was being slighted in the new model, as the shift to outcomes meant disciplines weren't structurally assigned a set number of credits. But because he was heard, among other voices, and the lab added back in and more credits assigned under understanding science, he stopped me as I passed him one day and expressed surprise and relief that anyone would actually listen and change in response.

As I moved into the Office of Teaching and Learning, the cultural territory shifted again, making my purview more about sharing of expertise and directing of particular projects and less about bureaucratic involvement. The down side is a loss of a clear focus (general education) and an unsureness about my continued role in general education on the campus. Though shifting institutional territory makes for unsteady footing, continuing good work supporting teaching and learning, whatever the space and title, provides professional grounding.

Beyond the culture shock and rejiggering of identities in the eyes of colleagues, much of this transdisciplinary campus work divides the minds and labor of those who do it even more than the typical teaching-research-service load does. While directing general education is connected to teaching when I provide professional-development opportunities to teachers, connected to service when I run committee meetings, and can be connected to research when I conduct studies that lead to publications about general education and assessment, it is also administration. Work-life balance and the distribution of load are persistent challenges in academic work. Taking on additional or next-level responsibility means a rebalancing of that load.

Others likely strike the balance far better than I have, but a key for me as my work has shifted and changed year to year for the last six to seven years has been a statement of mutual expectation (SME), used widely at North Carolina State University and recommended to me by Chris Anson at the WPA workshop. The statement of mutual expectation is akin to an annual negotiated contract, an expression of goals by the academic and signed and agreed to as appropriate by the immediate supervisor. Each year, in the late summer, I review my goals for the academic year. I adjust the percentages of work where appropriate (when there are course reassignments, for instance), list the teaching I am assigned, and list those scholarly tasks I'm working on and where I expect them to be, realistically, by the end of the academic year. These are estimates, and as long as I make significant progress on most of my goals, my annual reviews are good. This statement is not just a protection; it is an opportunity for me to assess what I'm supposed to accomplish each year and to have discussions if the load has gotten too heavy. I prioritize a bit more than if my job description were nebulously large and the same every year. There is no end to service work for those who are competent and open to it. Protecting ourselves is one of the important issues in taking on administrative work, particularly when not in a full-time administrative position. The SME also seems to provide me some agency to develop my professional identity—to resee myself and to re-present my evolving professional profile to others—through the priorities set there.

In Doug Hesse's brief discussion of his life as an "ex-WPA," he talks about a then-recent move into directing the Center for the Advancement of Teaching at Illinois State, and he claims "most days . . . I feel split" (Hesse 2005, 503). His split is not the balance of load issue I previously discussed but another split it's important for us to discuss as a potential loss when transitioning out of WPA work and into work outside English: the sidelining of disciplinary affiliation. Hesse talks about being careful, after he made this move, not to get too involved in reading the WPA listserv or in other disciplinary business, about reading the sources useful to administrators, about even moving out of his departmental office. Moving may mean new beginnings, but it is also fraught with losses. Disciplinary connection is still very important to me, which is one reason I have never applied for a full-time, eleven- or twelve-month, 100 percent administrator's position. I am loathe to lose my connections to the physical space of the department and the intellectual space of the field. The bargain I've had to strike means I must deal with job-balance issues that, frankly, lead me to question often whether the piling on is worth it. Others might be better prepared to let go and would then have more focused work each day, not juggling multiple graduate students, departmental committees, and courses with university-level leadership, committees, and professional retooling. I'm simply not ready to put my discipline to the side (yet).

TAKING STOCK AND *EXPECTING* TRANSITION

Based on a casual survey on the WPA listserv, Susan McLeod wisely offers this advice to WPAs thinking of advancing to other administrative jobs: "Take stock of what you already know and the skills you have already developed" (McLeod 2002, 118). This chapter attempts to add to our field's taking stock in anticipation of the transitions that inevitably happen across a career, some more and some less abruptly. Individually we bear these strengths and limitations, gains and losses, in differing measures. Yet articulating what some of our discipline-specific tendencies are by virtue of our typical training and discourse-community values may help us more quickly revise our CVs, write letters, interview successfully, and interact with our colleagues in other disciplines. When we talk about transitions, we often talk about them as planned, anticipated, and on our own schedules, or at very least we don't often talk about the myriad constraints on choice and planning. But an ever-increasing attitude and some habits of readiness can serve us well as we see ourselves as evolving members of a generation of writing program administrator-teacher-scholars. And we may need a term even newer than GenAdmin as more than one generation sees itself as adminischolars. Perhaps this identity is not so much generational as it is a new scholarly paradigm for writing program administrators.

Notes

* Editors' note: Amy Rupiper Taggart passed away in 2017 after a battle with cancer. The editors assumed the responsibilities of copyediting and proofreading her chapter. Any errors should be taken as our fault, not hers. We edited as lightly and respectfully as we could, especially since Amy's chapter addresses her diagnosis.

1. While there are key differences among WPA roles, such as directing first-year writing programs and upper-division programs, WAC/WID programs, and writing centers, I think there are enough similarities to refer to them here as WPA experiences relevant to transferring to other campus leadership, particularly leadership connected to pedagogy and curriculum.

2. See Brenda Helmbrecht and Connie Kendall's 2007 chapter "Graduate Students Hearing Voices: (Mis)Recognition and (Re)Definition of the jWPA Identity" for a critique of the use of gWPAs. While my experience was useful and professionalizing, I recognize there might be abuses in "using" graduate students to run significant components of writing programs.

3. Joining the disciplinary chorus, I highly recommend the WPA workshops for new WPAs. Chris Anson and Carol Rutz were exemplary guides for the workshop I attended, as I am sure are others each year.
4. I use the term *pedagogical leadership mindset* (as contrasted with, for instance *curricular leadership*) as a broad umbrella for a range of work focused on some level on leadership for improved teaching and learning. Even work on curriculum has as its objective improvement of teaching and learning. Pedagogy is thus, to me, not just what happens in the single classroom because if it were, education would be very fragmented.

References

Anderson, Virginia, and Susan Romano. 2005. *Culture Shock and the Practice of Profession: Training the Next Wave in Rhetoric and Composition*. New York: Hampton.

Bamberg, Betty. 1999. "Conflicts between Teaching and Assessing Writing: Using Program-Based Research to Resolve Pedagogical and Ethical Dilemmas." In *The Writing Program Administrator as Researcher: Inquiry in Action and Reflection*, edited by Shirley K. Rose and Irwin Weiser, 28–39. Portsmouth, NH: Boynton/Cook.

Burnham, Christopher, and Susanne Green. 2009. "WPAs and Identity: Sounding the Depths." In *The Writing Program Interrupted: Making Space for Critical Discourse*, edited by Donna Strickland and Jeanne Gunner, 175–85. Portsmouth, NH: Heinemann.

Charlton, Colin, Jonnika Charlton, Tarez Samra Graban, Kathleen J. Ryan, and Amy Ferdinandt Stolley. 2011. *GenAdmin: Theorizing WPA Identities in the Twenty-First Century*. Anderson, SC: Parlor.

Connors, Robert J. 1989. "Rhetorical History as a Component of Composition Studies." *Rhetoric Review* 7 (2): 230–40. https://doi.org/10.1080/07350198909388858.

Flower, Linda. 2008. *Community Literacy and the Rhetoric of Public Engagement*. Carbondale: Southern Illinois University Press.

Helmbrecht, Brenda M., and Connie Kendall. 2007. "Graduate Students Hearing Voices: (Mis)Recognition and (Re)Definition of the jWPA Identity." In *Untenured Faculty as Writing Program Administrators: Institutional Practices and Politics*, edited by Debra Frank Dew and Alice Horning, 172–88. West Lafayette, IN: Parlor.

Hesse, Douglas. 2005. "Not Even Joint Custody: Notes from an Ex-WPA." *College Composition and Communication* 56 (3): 501–7.

McLeod, Susan H. 2002. "Moving up the Administrative Ladder." In *The Writing Program Administrator's Resource: A Guide to Reflective Institutional Practice*, edited by Stuart Brown and Theresa Enos, 113–24. Mahwah, NJ: Erlbaum.

Porter, James E., Patricia Sullivan, Stuart Blythe, Jeffrey T. Grabill, and Libby Miles. 2000. "Institutional Critique: A Rhetorical Methodology for Change." *College Composition and Communication* 51 (4): 610–42.

Ratcliffe, Krista. 2006. *Rhetorical Listening: Identification, Gender, Whiteness*. Carbondale: Southern Illinois University Press.

Schön, Donald. 1983. *The Reflective Practitioner: How Professionals Think in Action*. New York: Basic Books.

Schwalm, David. 2002. "Writing Program Administration as Preparation for an Administrative Career." In *The Writing Program Administrator's Resource: A Guide to Reflective Institutional Practice*, edited by Stuart Brown and Theresa Enos, 125–35. Mahwah, NJ: Erlbaum.

SECTION 3

Collaborations and Dialogues

11
"YOU SAY GOODBYE, I SAY HELLO"
Transitions as Two Programs Consolidate

Letizia Guglielmo and Beth Daniell

In their call for proposals, the editors of this volume used the words *unstable* and *fraught* to characterize transitions into and out of writing program administration, terms that call up Ed White's descriptions of "what we abhor" in WPA work (White 1991, 5). Transitions into and out of the position create anxiety not only for the transitioning WPAs but also for instructors over whose lives WPAs have influence. In our case, transition was exacerbated by the consolidation of our university, Kennesaw State (KSU), with Southern Polytechnic State University (SPSU). Announced in the fall of 2013 by the Board of Regents of the University System of Georgia, the consolidation and its ensuing process heightened the stress of every area of the university, including so-called normal transitions. Our contribution to this volume recounts our experiences throughout this process and illustrates for readers what it can look like—and feel like—to move out of final and into first administrative positions against the backdrop of campus-wide confusion and instability. We explain how we negotiated the unexpected subject positions—the "betweens," as both Nedra Reynolds and Sandee K. McGlaun describe them—transitions of this kind may create for WPAs (McGlaun 2007; Reynolds 1993).

Indeed, the more we have considered our experiences as out-going and in-coming WPAs during the consolidation, the more we have come to see what happened as struggles for identities. In *Identity and Agency in Cultural Worlds*, authors Dorothy Holland, Debra Skinner, William Lachicotte, and Carol Cain define identity as "a concept that figuratively combines the intimate or personal world with the collective space of cultural forms and social relations" (Holland et al. 1998, 5), and they argue that identities "are unfinished and in process" (Holland et al. 1998,

DOI: 10.7330/9781607326335.c011

vii). Anyone leaving or moving into a WPA position is aware of an identity that is "in progress." Because identities "happen in social practice" (Holland et al. 1998, vii) against changing conditions, they are "improvised . . . from the cultural resources at hand" according to Holland and her coauthors (4). When the transitions take place in the midst of the consolidation of two universities, the cultural resources at hand may be unfamiliar. Drawing on both Vygotsky and Bakhtin, Holland and her colleagues claim identity is both developmental and dialogic (Holland et al. 1998, 8). No doubt, our transitions out of and into the WPA position at KSU would require some modifications in the identities of both of us. But consolidation served as a threat to the identities of writing teachers, particularly, we think, those on the SPSU campus, and perhaps also to that of the program we had led for some years.

UNIVERSITY CONSOLIDATIONS IN GEORGIA

Research on mergers in higher education, which are typically motivated by financial challenges at one or both institutions, indicates this process can be understandably difficult and disruptive on many levels. Although described as failing most often at the proposal stage, if not sooner (Fain 2012), mergers—or *consolidations*, as they are alternately termed—have become all the rage within the state of Georgia since 2009, when "13 of the state's 33 state technical colleges . . . bec[ame] six" (Technical College System of Georgia 2008). Soon after, the Board of Regents announced four mergers within the University System of Georgia, stating that "the purpose of campus consolidation is to increase the system's overall effectiveness in creating a more educated Georgia" (Board of Regents 2015, 2). The consolidation of KSU and SPSU would become the fifth of these mergers but not the last. The process throughout the university system has been described as "the nation's most aggressive and high-profile campus consolidation program" (Zalaznik 2015). As rhetoricians, we know word choice matters. The term *merger* was consistently used to describe the process within the technical college system yet not within the university system. Reflecting on his experience as university president in one of the previous university consolidations in Georgia, Riccardo Azziz distinguishes mergers from consolidations, noting the benefits and challenges of each.

- Merging may ease issues around lines of authority and branding but can marginalize the absorbed entity and reduce incentive for the dominant partner to embrace transformative change.

- Consolidation can create something new and better but risks alienating constituents from both university communities and introduces added complexities in management, branding, and identity. (Azziz, *Huffington Post*, October 21, 2013)

Our experience suggests that the KSU-SPSU consolidation seems to fit the description of merger since it was the first in which a new university name was not created (the name Kennesaw State University was retained) and since the size of SPSU, one-fourth that of KSU at the time, made SPSU faculty vulnerable to feeling "absorbed" in the process. We surmise that because our SPSU colleagues also saw this process as a merger, they perceived threats to the identities they had formed to fit the campus conditions there. Not surprisingly, following the announcement of the consolidation, the SPSU faculty and student body responded with anger.

UNDERSTANDING INSTITUTIONAL CONTEXTS

Originally established in 1948 as a two-year program whose purpose was to prepare veterans for Georgia Tech, SPSU, known for a while as Southern Tech, had had various locations in and around Atlanta. In 1970 it became a four-year college located in Marietta, focusing primarily on the practicalities of engineering and architecture. SPSU was a school of just over six thousand with a clear sense of mission and community, and no one at SPSU—not faculty, not students—wanted to merge with KSU. Frankly, no one at KSU wanted this, either. But the decision came down from the Chancellor and the Board of Regents, all appointed by Republican governors, whose *raison d'être* seems to be cutting spending for education. At Kennesaw, the initial announcement of the consolidation felt somewhat like business as usual because KSU has a long history of rapid change and shifting ground.

If KSU ever had a clear mission, it was lost and reshaped and reshaped again in the rapid growth. Established as a two-year college in 1963, Kennesaw State became a four-year college in 1976 and a university in 1997. By the time Letizia joined the English department in 2001, the university's enrollment was over thirteen thousand students. When Beth arrived three years later, the student population was about sixteen thousand. The English department was responsible, as it continues to be today, for three general education requirements—two semesters of first-year composition and one semester of sophomore literature. In the early years, all faculty taught these courses and were grateful for a course in the major from time to time. But without consistent funding for full-time tenure-track positions, and with a burgeoning student body, the English department, like many departments across the university, began to employ a significant and constantly growing number of part-time faculty to teach first-year writing. Thus it was that an acting vice president suggested full-time instructor positions for English; teaching focused, these lines were created in order to address this growth. The ten hires over two years that the English department was allotted were supposed to solve what was perceived as the "composition problem."

OUR STORIES, SEPARATELY AND TOGETHER

Letizia

For me, work—as well as my professional identity—at KSU has always been shaped by continuous change. Following the completion of an MA in English, I was hired as one of those full-time instructors and assigned five sections of general education courses each semester. The supposition was that during our sixth year, we would be eligible for review for promotion, which could elevate us to the rank of assistant professor; at that point, we would be on the tenure track. At the beginning of our ninth year, we would be eligible for tenure review. Then two years later, during our eleventh year, if we made it that long, we'd be eligible for yet another review and promotion to associate professor. For those without the PhD, associate professor would be the highest rank available. I don't think the upper administrators who originally made the decision to create the instructor track expected anyone to remain in this unusual position long term.

Just surviving this "plan" would require regular modifications of anyone's identity, and my own identify underwent some dramatic changes. By the time I was eligible for tenure review at the beginning of my ninth year in 2009, I had completed the PhD, despite little official support. After the PhD and promotion to assistant professor, and even before, I worked hard to make myself an asset to the department. I volunteered for committees, applied for grants, developed new courses, taught online and in the graduate program, affiliated with the gender and women's studies program, and took advantage of numerous publishing opportunities. The uncertainty associated with the position, the lack of the terminal degree in the early years, the changing expectations for tenure and promotion reviews in tandem with university growth, and the fact that there was no precedent for these reviews for someone in a position like mine may have made me anxious and even a bit paranoid. Change like this requires an individual to reassess her identity periodically and can have other effects when departments, like ours, grow so large they become impossible for one person to chair.

The one part of my work that has remained constant since the beginning has been my work in first-year writing. In the early years, my 5/5 and then 5/4 teaching load often consisted exclusively of first-year writing courses. My doctoral work in rhetoric and composition included a dissertation on online first-year writing courses. Even as I began to teach upper-division and graduate writing courses, I remained active in the collaborative work of the composition committee. I also developed expertise in writing program administration through both graduate course work and scholarship. Beth knew about this interest and encouraged it.

Beth

From what I have been able to piece together, for a long time there had been no need for a composition director at KSU because the English department was still small enough that everything could be run out of the chair's office. Since the teachers of first-year writing had originally been tenured or tenure-track faculty, there had been little guidance about pedagogy. This continued with the hiring of part-time faculty and the instructors, even though faculty with expertise in rhet/comp had led workshops on teaching writing from time to time. The growing numbers of students in the major and in the MA in professional writing required more and more faculty time, and it became apparent that the ten instructors would be unable to solve "the composition problem."

As the university approached fifteen thousand students, the old model in English became unsustainable, and the department suffered something of an implosion. Much of the controversy focused on the chair; another issue, raised by some of the women faculty, was scheduling by cronyism. Some tenured faculty began to see the instructors as part of the chair's power base; the instructors, already insecure in their vaguely defined positions, felt the hostility. One solution was to hire a composition director. Arriving in the summer of 2004, I found the chair had been relieved of her duties by the dean and the dean had then been relieved of hers. This situation required immediate adjustments in the identity I had imagined for myself at Kennesaw.

Thus it was that I walked into a department administration comprised of an interim chair and the assistant to the chair (the scheduler) but with no job description for the composition director. Truth be told, I hadn't asked the questions I should have during the interviews because

I saw this position as my chance to get back home to Atlanta. I wish I'd read Chris Blankenship's chapter in this volume, especially his frank discussion about how race and gender play out in negotiations. But I did push on the money, figuring I would straighten out the rest later on.

And I did, with my WPA experience and with help from the instructors. During graduate school, I served as the assistant director in a very large FYC program, and then later, on the tenure track, I did a stint as an associate director. With a job change, tenure, and promotion, I became the comp director at Clemson and then later at the University of Alabama. At both places, my chief responsibility had been to train the TAs to teach first-year writing. With all this on my CV, I had confidence that I could manage at Kennesaw.

The adjustment for me was seeing myself less as professor of graduate students and more as supervisor/support/resource for teachers with advanced degrees. Though at first the instructors were understandably wary of the new position and of a new person, we began to work collaboratively to develop a coherent writing program. During the first three years, the composition committee and I worked together to write guidelines for both ENGL 1101 and 1102, pared down a textbook list from nearly one hundred titles, and planned an in-house conference and other faculty-development activities. Later, we devised policies on attendance and technology, and then, with leadership from two of our teachers, we instituted a writing contest. All this work relied on collaboration, cooperation, and trust. The composition-committee meetings became a kind of continuous professional development that, I am happy to say, "avoid[ed] devaluing lore" and allowed both experienced and novice teachers to share and to learn together (Hansen 1995, 32). Believing as, Rita Malenczyk explains, "that WPA work . . . is grounded in research and scholarship and is ultimately intellectual and pedagogical rather than managerial" (Malenczyk 2001, 18), I worked with instructors to produce scholarship (see Daniell et al. 2008) and encouraged them to extend these conversations beyond our campus (see Davis and Stewart 2011).

As the number of first-year students and teachers increased, so did my responsibilities. The one thing that did *not* increase was support. I was told time and again that while such-and-such was a good idea, it could not be funded. Professional development required creativity. As the major grew, the tenured and tenure-track faculty disappeared from FYC altogether. A new dean gave us two full-time lecturer lines. In subsequent years, we filled more lecturer positions, up to a total of about twenty. I participated in the interview process and read the lecturers' voluminous student evaluations in order to respond to their annual-review documents. I welcomed the extra work because the lecturers were, generally, excellent teachers who lent stability and continuity to the program. As the responsibilities increased, the identity I had constructed for myself of the cultural materials at hand had to be modified.

Starting in 2004 at least, enrollment in FYC averaged an increase of about 5 percent each year, and the money for the extra teachers generally came mid-July. By 2011, university enrollment exceeded twenty-two thousand, and my position required additional interaction with an even larger number of teachers and students. After intense work on an assessment of first-year writing I knew to be flawed because there was no money for outside readers, my stress level was exacerbated by guilt. I was dead on my feet. In fact, the cardiologist asked whether the symptoms I was experiencing came from some undue stress in my life in August and September. Yes, I said, from trying to find teachers for the first-year classes in English at KSU. Recognizing all the work I had been doing as WPA as well as director of the WAC program for the college, I approached the chair about an assistant-director-of-composition position. After some discussion, he and I talked with Letizia, who had been serving as online and technology coordinator for the department and had always been one of my go-to people in terms of technology. Because I knew Letizia had read widely on WPA work, I was confident her qualifications would be an asset to the program.

Letizia was a lifesaver: she wrote drafts of proposals for faculty-development workshops; she worked with lecturers on technological innovations and then planned panels for SAMLA; she turned our first-year writing contest into a book to be used by the next year's classes; she served as a sounding board for ideas and an editor for my memos. The partnership we developed shifted my identity once again.

With the composition program working better than ever, I began to contemplate retirement and its timing. Shortly after, however, pressure mounted, but now from the department rather than from the writing program. Tensions began to show between the tenured/tenure-track writing faculty and the tenured/tenure-track literature faculty. Because I had worked in English departments for my whole career, none of this, after thirty-three years, was surprising. What was different this time was my impatience with the condescension toward, and dismissal of, the rhetoric faculty.

That's when I realized that at my age and with my years of service, I didn't have put up with this. Though I considered leaving immediately, I realized almost all the knowledge about the composition program was in my head, not in anyone else's and not on paper for someone else to read. I decided to stay one more year, giving the department fair warning. The WPA part of my identity was so deeply engrained in me that abandoning the FYC program midyear seemed impossible.

TRANSITIONING IN CONSOLIDATION

Even though we had worked with constant change for years, neither of us was prepared for what happened next. About the time Beth decided she would retire at the end of the following academic year, giving the department plenty of time to plan for a national search, the Board of Regents announced the consolidation with SPSU. Even in a stable environment, Beth's transition out of the WPA position would be disruptive. As the first official WPA in the English department at KSU, Beth had spent eleven years engaging in "macrolevel teaching" (Gebhardt 2002, 35) and working to establish a community of writing teachers among an ever-growing and diverse group of contingent faculty.

So now it wasn't just the transition from Beth as WPA to another person; the more complicated goal became figuring out the future of two composition programs from two very different universities. What was of most concern to us was the identity of our writing program. Then we discovered the WPA on the SPSU campus had exactly the same concern. Writing programs don't simply have identities; those identities develop over time using the cultural resources unique to a particular campus, and the cultural resources were about to change. Almost immediately, Beth and the composition director from Southern Poly began talking, finding their backgrounds in rhet/comp similar. Though they agreed fundamentally about composition, they were unable to make definite plans because decisions about larger structures for the composition program were on hold. Along the way, the interdisciplinary English department at SPSU decided to propose remaining a separate department within the College of Humanities and Social Sciences. Because the future of the interdisciplinary department had not been determined, the dean was unwilling to consider the possibilities in the plan the two WPAs collaborated on for first-year composition within the consolidated university.

Since Beth was retiring and the composition director on the other campus said she was unwilling to direct a combined program serving nearly six thousand students, it was clear a search still would be necessary. The following fall a search committee was formed and an ad written, but forward movement stopped there. A year following the initial announcement of the consolidation, one decision at the dean's level was made, however: the national search for a composition director would be postponed until after new structures were in place, and Letizia would serve as the interim composition director.

Beth

Because the ad had not been posted, I suspected this decision. So while I was not surprised, I was hurt that neither the dean nor the chair offered the courtesy of even mentioning it to me—talk about a blow to my identity. I was glad Letizia had accepted the interim post because that would ensure continuity, and preserving the strengths of our program was important to me. Letizia had told me privately some months earlier that she would not apply to be my replacement. She had, she said on that occasion, seen too much of the perils of administration and too much dissention between our department and the interdisciplinary department on the other campus. I didn't blame her for not wanting my job; though I was still invested in the composition program and its future, all I could see was chaos and upheaval. I knew with certainty that for a number of professional and personal reasons, the following summer would be the right time to leave.

Letizia

When the dean decided to call off the search in order to buy some time to work through consolidation, I was approached about an interim position because I had worked most closely with Beth and had a long history with the program. It was clear that first-year composition made up a significant part of my identity at KSU because of that long history and because of the professional-development activities I had been a part of both as a teacher and as the assistant director. Yet my professional identity also included teaching in the graduate and gender and women's studies programs, mentoring undergraduate and graduate students on research projects, and maintaining an active research agenda of my own. The interim position surely would require that I shift attention away from some of those activities and toward first-year composition exclusively. Although I hesitated in accepting the position, especially because Beth was not included in these discussions, I believed, perhaps naïvely, that negotiating for the position might allow me to force a few decisions, including decisions about the administrative structure of the composition program as part of the new university. For example, it was not yet clear to me whether the new university would include two composition programs administered by two WPAs on two campuses—one in English on our campus and one in the rebranded interdisciplinary department on the Marietta campus—or whether the program would be housed in English with one director but offering the same courses to students on both campuses.

The interim position, while not ideal, would allow Beth and me to work closely up to the moment of the transition—still eight months in the future—in a way that would not have been possible had we completed the national search and made a hire from outside for the following academic year. Since I was tenured and had thirteen years of experience with the composition program at KSU, I also felt I had the knowledge to define the position in a way that would work for me and for the program—or to walk away if that became necessary (see Horning 2007, 45–47; White 1991;). I agreed to take the interim position for twelve months as the director of one program on two campuses with an assistant director (yet to be appointed) on each campus.

MORE CHANGES

When the universities officially merged in January 2015 with much of the real work of consolidation remaining, Beth and Letizia began a series of meetings with the WPA on the Marietta campus to plan for composition at the New U, as the president had come to term this new entity. The VP for general education asked Beth for an assessment plan before the semester's end. Assuming our Marietta colleague would remain as the assistant composition director on that campus, we discussed a long list of issues—pedagogy, administrative structure, the composition committee, curricula for both 1101 and 1102, assessment. When the Marietta WPA suggested that our common purpose was nicely summed up in the new WPA Outcomes Statement, which her program had adopted, we knew we had it. Beth presented the statement to the Kennesaw composition committee, demonstrating that there was nothing in that statement that wasn't in the guidelines we had written ten years before. Then using the Outcomes as the basis, the three of us worked on an assessment plan that turned out to be more sophisticated than the General Education Council wanted, requiring some downward modification. For the first time, we were told the provost would pay for a few independent readers. We were feeling good that we could administer a legitimate assessment of our agreed-upon outcomes.

But more changes were in store. The WPA on the other campus chose to remain a member of the rebranded interdisciplinary department.

Since the composition program would be housed in English and the dean had declared a moratorium on joint appointments, our Marietta colleague could no longer be affiliated with the composition program. The result for the Marietta composition faculty was confusion and uncertainty. We also felt the effects of this decision because, as we realized, we had been counting on her to smooth the way with composition faculty on the Marietta campus. At this point everyone's identity was in flux, including our own.

ATTENDING TO EMOTIONS

Despite our attempts at careful planning in this time of transition, we were less prepared for the roles the consolidation seemed to create for the two of us. Although at the start of spring semester we were technically operating as a single university, separate academic calendars, class schedules that did not overlap, and courses already scheduled through summer 2015 made operating as one department, much less as one composition program, nearly impossible. Eight full-time faculty from the Marietta campus officially joined the English department and the composition program, yet their teaching schedules on a separate campus made participation in department and program meetings difficult, certainly not an auspicious way for "new" faculty to begin to identify with another community of teachers. In her essay on place and WPA work, Kathleen J. Ryan explains, "Knowing our place and developing a sense of responsibility to it gives us a shared context for communicating with others, enabling our abilities to listen, talk, and learn" (Ryan 2012, 89). But the two places had not in actuality become one place. In our case, because we were now required to be working together through decisions outside our control despite still being physically separate, all of us experienced "the kinds of gaps in communication and understanding that occur when a strong sense of location and an awareness of the connections and patterns among members of a university community are not fully present" (Ryan 2012, 84). As WPAs closely associated with the Kennesaw campus, the two of us did not fully understand our new colleagues' loss of place.

Because the WPA is often the most accessible administrator for many composition faculty, and because all our new colleagues would be teaching general education courses exclusively, as WPAs we were drawn into the center of consolidation anxiety. Compounding this anxiety and our shifting identities were the ongoing discussions about upper-division professional-writing courses at the New U, discussions in which we were both involved. As a member of the subcommittee charged with eliminating overlap in curriculum between the two English departments early in the consolidation process, Letizia found that experience revealed more details to be worked out than reasonably possible in the time allotted. Because faculty had to argue for their courses and programs, the work became increasingly contentious, and new tensions appeared between the two faculties. Having to compartmentalize our feelings about those consolidation negotiations—tied very closely to our professional and scholarly identities—while facilitating the composition's program's transition was taxing for both of us.

With no decision about how the department would deliver services on the Marietta campus, including whether we would in fact have an assistant director on that campus, uncertainties remained and fears increased. Indeed, almost every day one or both of us found e-mail asking how things would work on the Marietta campus; these were questions we could not answer. Because the budget for AY 15–16 was still in process, the dean was still unwilling to make decisions on these and other matters. The uncertainty was anxiety making for the two of us and for a good number of composition faculty who, within two or three days of the consolidation announcement, had asked Beth whether the consolidation meant they would lose their jobs. But the uncertainty was even greater for the Marietta faculty, who felt the most disruptive effects of the consolidation. Waiting for decisions exacerbated their fear and anxiety. As institutions of higher education are driven to make decisions based on efficiency rather than on traditions of self-governance, disruptive situations like ours will increasingly become the norm, according to Philip Altbach writing about trends in higher education in the twenty-first century (Altbach 2011, 28).

In our context, despite the fact that the consolidation was intended to streamline programs and make the two campuses *more* efficient, the results were anything but. In a paper on mergers in higher education, Kristen Koontz argues that the planning necessary for successful consolidation is seldom part of the mix and that expected monetary savings often turn out to be mythical (Koontz 2009). In fact, an *Inside Higher Education* article reports on several consolidations that were called off because careful planning showed the mergers would be too expensive (Woodhouse 2015). Throughout the transition process, we saw no sign of any previous planning for the consolidation, and our suggestions and requests were met with polite *thank-you*'s but with no follow-up. While expensive new signage went up and replacement computer programs appeared, the KSU consolidation continued seemingly oblivious to precedent elsewhere and chaos locally.

What we discovered in the midst of this ongoing process was that the anxiety raised numerous other issues related to the teaching of writing, issues that further complicated the WPA transition. During the spring semester, for example, the unhappiness began to focus on the writing center (WC). Although decisions about the writing center for the two-campus university did not directly involve the two of us, given the KSU Writing Center's independent administrative structure, its close relationship with first-year composition meant we were included in the discussions. Impassioned e-mails from the Marietta campus proliferated defending the teacher staffing of the WC on that campus. Proposals for a single WC with two sites were revised any number of times in an attempt to reach consensus, but similar to the WPA structure, the process was slow and decisions postponed. Though we had both vowed not to become involved in the electronic WC debate, Beth finally did reject, on the basis of her experience at Clemson, the argument that the other campus's STEM students required a writing center staffing plan different from that on the Kennesaw campus. In one e-mail, one Marietta colleague stated that she felt "colonized." Both of us were aware that the Marietta faculty felt marginalized, but the word "colonized" implied a willful occupation. We found that comment offensive since we had not asked for this merger any more than the Marietta faculty had and we had no control over decisions made or not made by upper administrators. With distance, of course, we can see her feelings were legitimate. And although we resisted being identified with administrative structures responsible for those decisions, that resistance also made us unaware of our own privilege.

According to the Koontz paper, the impact of institutional mergers on faculty and staff seems to follow Kubler-Ross's stages of death and dying—denial, bargaining, anger, and sadness before arriving, finally, at acceptance. The grief, she says, arises because individuals "are stripped of their identity, traditions, and long-established practices" (Koontz 2009, 24). In *Identity and Agency*, the authors say traditions and established practices are components of identity; thus, the loss of a particular identity seems to require grief almost by definition (Holland et al. 1998). Koontz (2009) also tells us that other components of consolidation grief include nostalgia and confusion, which we also observed in our Marietta colleagues and in ourselves. We understand this response intellectually, of course; nonetheless, certain comments and attitudes still hurt because we both believed we were doing our best to smooth over the process in our small area. We tried to remember we were not experiencing a loss of identity in the way our Marietta colleagues were because of our affiliation with the larger institution and our experience with the ongoing change endemic to that institution.

What we learned from working with English colleagues at SPSU on the upper-division courses is that the sort of bureaucracy Kennesaw faculty was used to, the specific procedures regarding curriculum development and shared governance we had learned to follow as a result of constant and tremendous growth, seemed to have been less formal on the other, much smaller campus. Perhaps decisions at SPSU had been announced quickly because that campus did not have the levels of hierarchy that existed at Kennesaw. We believe this unfamiliarity contributed to the anxiety. We—all of us on the Kennesaw campus—have never known anything except growth and change, typically announced from the top. We know problems do get solved at KSU, though often at the very last minute. We tried to share our experiences so colleagues on the Marietta campus would understand how things work at KSU and would know that as soon we knew of a decision, they would know it, too. And yet we both have been positioned by our new colleagues as having control over these decisions, the kind of power often assumed to reside with WPAs (George 1999, xiii). The transition, which we, two consummate problem solvers, had hoped would go smoothly was and actually continues to be rockier than we wanted it to be.

Despite all this, we have confidence in our composition program's tradition of collaboration and of coming to consensus on policy issues after everyone has been heard. Letizia would, as interim WPA, continue the practice of listening to the voices of all who teach in the composition program on both campuses. Yet we realize this commitment must be demonstrated over time, not just stated once or twice or even three times. Writing about the difficulty of effecting change with upper administration regarding the exploitation of part-time faculty, Kristine Hansen says, "Perhaps the best explanation for the unethical treatment these teachers are subjected to is that they are known personally only to their students and to the WPA who hires and supervises their work" (Hansen 1995, 37). Although our new colleagues were not part-time faculty, it appeared to fall on the two of us as WPAs in transition to, as Hansen puts it, "return the gaze of these teachers" (Hansen 1995, 37). What may have been an easier transition as a result of our successful collaboration became much more difficult during the consolidation because issues and responsibilities arose that had not previously been part of our work. The identities we had constructed as part of the composition program at KSU were reshaped by the consolidation in ways we had not expected. Because we were an outgoing WPA and an incoming interim

WPA, it was not always clear to us who should respond to these issues and anxieties, but what did become clear is that decisions that should have been made at higher levels were not made, leaving all of us uncertain. McGlaun's comments regarding the "betweens" of WPA work, the "liminal, shifting space," seem fitting for our situation, as we were cast into and out of often competing subject positions by our colleagues (McGlaun 2007, 220–21, 229). We both worked to show we welcomed our new colleagues, and we tried to offer reassurance. But who, we asked in that overlap semester, should respond to misinformation and rumors?

Because of our work together over time in the program, as colleagues in the department and as coauthors on previous projects, we felt comfortable negotiating these responses and talking about them openly. Because of the trust and respect we'd developed, we did not waste time quibbling over who should say what to whom and when. While much of this trust and respect is the result of our personal relationship, it is also a fundamental part of the composition program Beth worked to build over her eleven years at KSU. Beth often has said that leading composition meetings was like teaching a graduate seminar, with information shared, ideas debated, plans modified, and compromises effected, all based in custom and in theory. As the same teaching schedule applies on both campuses, it will be easier, we hope, for composition faculty to meet together and for those relationships to develop with our Marietta colleagues, for shared social practices to shape new identities (Holland, Skinner, Lachicotte, and Cain 1998, vii).

In this chapter, we have shared the experience of our transitions—in the midst of consolidation—and, we hope we have shown, our professional relationship, forged out of common values about writing and pedagogy, our mutual commitment to decentered administrative practices, and our dedication to both professional and personal respect and honesty. "When WPA work is viewed as intellectual inquiry," Gaillet and Guglielmo (2010) argue, "writing programs have the potential to become powerful institutional systems that foreground the localized collaborative work of writing teachers, researchers, administrators, and students within (and outside) the university" (54). This commitment to inquiry and to the intellectual contributions of all who teach in a writing program can allow WPAs to navigate change, growth, and transition, even though sometimes this may mean serving as apologist for upper administration, and sometimes it may mean allowing others the time and space to work through their changing identities. What we have come to see is that in a composition program, the WPA serves as mediator between the teachers in the program and higher administrators but that this part of the WPA's identity can be disrupted when the WPA has little power to make big decisions during times of transition.

POSTSCRIPT

Beth had hoped to leave Letizia with a clear administrative plan for the following year because she knew how much of the WPA's time the day-to-day work can take. But this was not to be. When she left, some of the things that had been promised to Letizia had yet not come about. Beth moved from the chaos at KSU to the chaos of renovating an old condo closer to the city. The difference was she could see an end to the painting, installing, and repairing. She now has time to write without interruption and to go out to lunch with her friends.

When she took up her administrative duties in July, Letizia found over fifty uncovered sections between the two campuses and hired fourteen new full-time limited-term faculty. Following the WPA transition, no assistant director position was created for the Marietta campus for 2015–16. Hence, Letizia worked on two campuses, with inadequate office space for Marietta faculty and no dedicated administrative support on that campus. The WPA search was again postponed even before the academic year began because of the priority of the chair search. Letizia was offered the position for a second year, but this time she declined. The interim position was then offered to a lecturer who was more than qualified but who was, nevertheless, untenured.

Both Beth and Letizia agree with Shirley Rose (2012), who has explained that you don't have to be an official WPA to maintain a WPA identity.

References

Altbach, Phillip G. 2011. "Patterns of Higher Education Development." In *American Higher Education in the Twenty-first Century: Social, Political, and Economic Challenges*, edited by Phillip G. Altbach, Patricia J. Gumport, and Robert O. Berndahl, 15–36. Baltimore, MD: Johns Hopkins University Press.

Board of Regents of the University System of Georgia (BOR). 2015. *Recommended Consolidations*. http://www.usg.edu/docs/consolidations.pdf.

Daniell, Beth, Laura Davis, Linda Stewart, and Ellen Taber. 2008. "The In-house Conference: A Strategy for Disrupting Order and Shifting Identities." *Pedagogy* 8 (3): 447–65. https://doi.org/10.1215/15314200-2008-005.

Davis, Laura, and Linda Stewart, eds. 2011. *Teachers as Avatars: English Studies in the Digital Age*. Cresskill, NJ: Hampton.

Fain, Paul. 2012. "Major Mergers in Georgia." *Inside Higher Ed*, January 6. https://www.insidehighered.com/news/2012/01/06/georgia-university-system-proposes-consolidation-8-campuses.

Gaillet, Lynée Lewis, and Letizia Guglielmo. 2010. "Collaborative Writing Administration as Intellectual Inquiry." In *Performing Feminism and Administration in Rhetoric and Composition Studies*, edited by Krista Ratcliffe and Rebecca Rickly, 53–66. Cresskill, NJ: Hampton.

Gebhardt, Richard. 2002. "Administration as Focus for Understanding the Teaching of Writing." In *The Allyn and Bacon Sourcebook for Writing Program Administrators*, edited by Irene Ward and William J. Carpenter, 23–33. New York: Longman.

George, Diana. 1999. Introduction to *Kitchen Cooks, Plate Twirlers and Troubadours: Writing Program Administrators Tell Their Stories*, edited by Diana George, xi–xiv. Plymouth, NH: Boynton/Cook.

Hansen, Kristine. 1995. "Face to Face with Part-Timers: Ethics and Professionalization of Writing Faculties." In *Resituating Writing: Constructing and Administering Writing Programs*, edited by Joseph Janangelo and Kristine Hansen, 23–45. Portsmouth, NH: Boynton/Cook.

Holland, Dorothy, Debra Skinner, William Lachicotte, and Carol Cain. 1998. *Identity and Agency in Cultural Worlds*. Cambridge, MA: Harvard University Press.

Horning, Alice. 2007. "Ethics and the jWPA." In *Untenured Faculty as Writing Program Administrators*, edited by Debra Frank Dew and Alice Horning, 40–57. West Lafayette, IN: Parlor.

Koontz, Kristen. 2009. "The Impact of Mergers in Higher Education on Employees and Organizational Culture." Research paper submitted for the MS in applied psychology, U of Wisconsin–Stout. http://www2.uwstout.edu/content/lib/thesis/2009/2009 koontzk.pdf.

Malenczyk, Rita. 2001. "Fighting Across the Curriculum: The WPA Joins the AAUP." *WPA: Writing Program Administration* 24 (3): 11–23.

McGlaun, Sandee K. 2007. "Administering Writing Programs in the 'Betweens': A jWPA Narrative." In *Untenured Faculty as Writing Program Administrators*, edited by Debra Frank Dew and Alice Horning, 219–48. West Lafayette, IN: Parlor.

Reynolds, Nedra. 1993. "*Ethos* as Location: New Sites for Understanding Discursive Authority." *Rhetoric Review* 11 (2): 325–38. https://doi.org/10.1080/0735019930 9389009.

Rose, Shirley. 2012. "Review: The WPA Within: WPA Identities and Implications for Gradate Education in Rhetoric and Composition." *College English* 75 (2): 218–30.

Ryan, Kathleen J. 2012. "Thinking Ecologically: Rhetorical Ecological Feminist Agency and Writing Program Administration." *WPA: Writing Program Administration* 36 (1): 74–94.

Technical College System of Georgia (TCSG). 2008. "TCSG State Board Reaffirms Technical College Merger Plan." https://tcsg.edu/press_detail.php?press_id=118.

White, Edward M. 1991. "Use It or Lose It: Power and the WPA." *WPA: Writing Program Administration* 15 (1–2): 3–12.

Woodhouse, Kellie. 2015. "Anatomy of Failed Merger." *Inside Higher Ed*, August 5. https://www.insidehighered.com/news/2015/08/05/college-merger-negotiations-are-long-and-complicated.

Zalaznik, Matt. 2015. "Georgia Leads College Consolidation Movement." University Business. http://www.universitybusiness.com/article/georgia-leads-college-consolidation-movement.

12

COMMAND AND COLLABORATION
Leading as a New WPA

Laura J. Davies

At the beginning of my second year as the WPA at the United States Air Force Academy (USAFA), the USAFA superintendent retired, yet he remained in charge of USAFA until the official change-of-command ceremony. In this ceremony, the outgoing superintendent, a three-star lieutenant general, handed an American flag to the Air Force Chief of Staff. Then, the Air Force Chief of Staff turned to the incoming superintendent, another three-star general. She stepped forward, took hold of the flag, and assumed command. In front of her, the base airmen, officers, and four thousand cadets stood at attention in the blazing Colorado sunlight.

The change-of-command ceremony, the military's public display of the transfer of power, happens at every level of the military chain of command. The transfer of power from one commander to the next happens at the moment the flag is passed from one person to the next, as the unit's flag is the symbol of the commander's authority and presence. The way the change-of-command ceremony is constructed ensures there is never a moment without clear leadership: at all times, every person in the unit knows who is in charge. The outgoing and the incoming commanders stand next to each other, symbolic of mutual trust and respect. The outgoing commander freely relinquishes their power, and the incoming commander willingly accepts the command. Finally, the surrender, transfer, and acceptance of command are public, witnessed and sanctioned by others. The US military's change of command is solemn, logical, and reasonable: this is no *Game of Thrones* with clashing kings and Battles of the Trident.

As a civilian professor and WPA at USAFA, I witnessed many of these change-of-command ceremonies. These ceremonies prompted me to think about the differences between how these two realms—the academy and the military—handle transitions in leadership. Specifically,

DOI: 10.7330/9781607326335.c012

these ceremonies made me realize that incoming WPAs rarely participate in public ceremonies that acknowledge and legitimize them as the new leader of a program. Sometimes, WPA transitions can be sudden, contested, and emotionally charged. My experience as the new WPA at the United States Air Force Academy also drove me to consider how the rhetoric and theories of command could be useful for transitioning WPAs. Our field has theorized and described the relationship between WPAs and power (Howard 1993; White 1991), and some of this scholarship is related to transition (Phelps 1995), yet there is not adequate attention to the wide range of leadership theories a new WPA can rely on during a time of transition. In this essay, I explore two of these leadership theories, the concepts of collaboration and command, and argue that they are both useful, positive, and even complementary leadership strategies for transitioning WPAs. I use my experiences as the new WPA at the United States Air Force Academy as well as the scholarship about WPA transition and power by Louise Wetherbee Phelps to explain the tensions and possibilities in each approach.

Though the importance of collaboration in WPA work is well established, there is no research yet that discusses what role military command theory could play in WPA work, especially during the critical transition years. I believe part of the reason we are reluctant to discuss administrative work in terms of command is the militaristic connotation of the term *command*: on the surface, command brings to mind images of top-down, patriarchal, and authoritative power. However, different institutional contexts require different leadership strategies. Solely relying on a collaborative leadership model may not be in the best interest of a writing program's teachers or students. I am not suggesting new WPAs should abandon collaboration as a viable strategy for periods of transition. Rather, I argue that transitioning WPAs would benefit from a serious consideration of alternative styles of leadership such as command theory. In this essay, I argue that theories of command and collaboration are far more complicated and complementary than they may seem. In times of transition, WPAs could benefit from thinking of themselves as both collaborator and commander.

THEORIES OF COLLABORATION AND COMMAND FOR TRANSITIONING WPAS

Collaboration is not a new theory in WPA work. With its connections to feminist theory and feminist pedagogy, collaboration's decentering, democratic nature is comfortable and familiar to many writing teachers and WPAs. Collaborative administration is a useful and productive way to ensure multiple stakeholders and voices are heard when making programmatic, curricular, and personnel decisions. Writing programs are often unique, multitiered administrative structures that extend both horizontally (through first-year writing programs) and vertically (through WAC initiatives) throughout an institution, and these sprawling systems can benefit from diffused leadership. WPA scholarship has consistently shown the benefits of collaborative administrative structures. Collaborative administrative structures allow people to share administrative tasks and responsibilities, freeing up faculty to teach and do research, and invite participation from many constituencies within the writing program (Cambridge and McClelland 1995; Meeks and Huit 1998). In many ways, collaboration is an attractive model for transitioning WPAs: collaborative models encourage discussion, and a new WPA can ask for advice and learn about the institutional context and politics through conversations with other stakeholders inside and outside the writing program.

However, there are risks to collaborative administration for transitioning WPAs. First, a WPA who is new to the institution or even just new to the WPA role may not know whom to listen to and whom to trust. Second, as Eileen E. Schell points out, for an untenured WPA, giving up "the traditional authority role" can undermine that WPA's tenure and promotion case (Schell 1998, 69). Especially in cases in which an untenured WPA is relying on their administrative work to count as scholarship in their tenure review, dispersing those administrative tasks among various people may dilute on paper the amount of work the WPA is responsible for. Third, collaborative administrative structures are fragile, as explained by Susanmarie Harrington, Steve Fox, and Tere Molindar Hogue using their experiences as members of a ten-person Writing Coordinating Committee. They point out a major problem with collaborative models of administration, which is the tendency for groups of people to drift toward consensus as a way to avoid disagreements, choosing "silence over conflict" (Harrington, Fox, and Hogue 1998, 60). They also describe how the lack of clear authority in a collaborative administrative model, especially one as large as their ten-member committee, can contribute to slow communication and questions of who has the authority to speak for the program, especially to people outside the program (Harrington, Fox, and Hogue 1998, 63).

Contributing to these risks is the absence of alternative models of leadership for transitioning WPAs. Collaborative leadership and administration is often an assumed, unchallenged good within WPA scholarship.

As Chris M. Anson and Richard Jewell attest, "good" writing programs "create a climate in which people of all ranks and employment categories work together in a spirit of cooperation and collaboration" (Anson and Jewell 2000, 71). Laura R. Micciche's advocacy for "slow agency" in WPA work also presumes that a collaborative decision-making process, involving as many stakeholders as possible, is a sustainable, healthy, and good administrative practice (Micciche 2011, 80).

Part of the reason for collaboration's dominance as an administrative theory can be traced to the advent of WPA theories and scholarship in the 1980s that, as Jeanne Gunner explains, were a critical response to hierarchal and patriarchal structures within the academy. Gunner's (2002) taxonomy of collaborative models of writing program administration demonstrate the wide diversity of these cooperative structures, from programs in which directors rotate in and out of the WPA position to others who have faculty and/or non-tenure-track administrators and instructors dividing and sharing administrative responsibilities. Gunner explains collaborative administration as an alternative to a hypothetical model of WPA work in which a single director has "total authority over faculty, curriculum, and program policies" (Gunner 2002, 257). Earlier, in her 1994 article "Decentering the WPA," Gunner claims concentrating power in a single WPA can lead to oppressive leadership that ignores the needs and the desires of the teachers within a writing program: "The WPA-centric administrative model, in which a tenured WPA controls the writing program, has a troublingly anti-democratic cast and potential" (Gunner 1994, 9). Gunner's critique of a single writing program administrator aligns with other critiques of power discussed in WPA scholarship (Bousquet 2002; Harris 2000; Kinney 2009; Sledd 2001). These critiques and subsequent analyses of the benefits of collaborative administration seem to suggest that WPAs who hold authority alone act primarily for themselves, not others. Phelps makes a similar argument when she questions why WPAs so often equate power with corruption. The problematic premise in these arguments against a solitary WPA— or one that might choose to make a decision without a long, collaborative process—is that a solitary WPA ignores the perspectives of others, resulting in a narrow-minded or unethical decision. The solution these scholars offer for this potential problem is to unreservedly promote a model of writing program administration that strictly relies on cooperative decision making.

An alternative to a collaborative model of administration—in which authority is diffused among several individuals—is an administrative model based in command theory. This model is distinct from the solitary-WPA model currently present at many institutions today. WPAs often find themselves the solitary WPA by default: they may be the only composition or writing studies scholar in an English department, or their position or program may have been designed so they are the sole administrator or faculty member who has the responsibility of a first-year writing program, writing-across-the-curriculum program, and/or writing center. As opposed to a solitary WPA, command is a leadership model that deliberately concentrates power in one decision maker, not because no one else wants to do WPA work but because this model results in effective, smart, and ethical administrative decisions. Command theory, although its military overtones may seem incongruous with the goals and values of the academy, presents a different, positive view of the benefits of concentrating power in one decision maker than do the portraits of problematic authority found in WPA scholarship.

According to military leadership theories, explained below in further depth, commanders are not dictatorial, self-interested autocrats. Rather, commanders have an ethical responsibility to use their expertise and authority proactively toward a particular purpose. Also, good commanders do not make decisions in a vacuum. Instead, commanders depend on the counsel and advice of others, including those who hold lower rank than they do, and are held accountable for the well-being of all within their command.

In my previous research on writing program administration, I cannot remember a single reference to command as a potential administrative style. When scholars use military terms to describe administrative work, as Edward M. White (1991) does, they package those terms with caveats and apologies. Military terms and frames of reference, it seems, don't become us academics. I speculate this uneasy relationship with the military is rooted in our society's ever-growing civilian/military divide (Fleming 2010). Yet in dismissing the military, we miss an opportunity to understand administrative work through different frames.

There is a crucial distinction between the military command theory I am advocating and what Schell defines as a "might and right" leadership style, in which the WPA holds power individually and "the WPA's power and authority emerges from his or her position as a powerful director with tenure in a hierarchal administrative framework" (Schell 1998, 66). Schell cites White's aggressive, masculinist "use it or lose it" maxim about power as a manifestation of this leadership style (Schell 1998, 67; White 1991, 3). What I learned about command during my time at USAFA, though, was different than this might-and-right approach.

Command theory, grounded in military science, strategy, and history, is something other than this strict top-down hierarchal representation of power. Instead, what I saw enacted at USAFA was an interdependent system in which people had clearly defined roles and responsibilities and depended on one another. The chain of command fits together like a set of Matryoshka nesting dolls: at every level, there is a commander who has authority over others yet is also led by someone of higher rank. This authority is always visible and publicly recognized. Commanders' uniform insignia mark their higher rank, and the members of their units greet them with salutes and by standing at attention. The position of the commander depends on a certain rhetorical acuity. A commander is not only charged with the responsibility of leading a mission but also with communicating that mission in a way "so prescient, sound, and fully conveyed to subordinates that it would allow the commander to leave the battlefield before the battle commences, with no adverse effect upon the outcome" (Builder, Bankes, and Nordin 1999, iii). Clearly, the work of WPAs is far different from the work of the battlefield, but command theory's emphasis on clear communication is applicable for transitioning WPAs, who cannot and should not micromanage every writing classroom but also need to be confident in their ability to convey a vision for their new writing program.

Command is as much about creativity and problem solving as it is about control (Builder, Bankes, and Nordin 1999, xii). In order to successfully determine a course of action in multivariable situations apt to change rapidly, the commander who is driven by *concepts* rather than *control* must have up-to-date "situational awareness" and "prior concepts of impending operations" on which to base decisions (Builder, Bankes, and Nordin 1999, xv). I argue that there are compelling parallels between this element of command theory and the widely held belief among WPAs that administration is scholarship. Writing program administrators must have "prior concepts" (theoretical and practical knowledge of writing theory and pedagogy) and "situational awareness" (an understanding of their institution, faculty, and students) in order to design dynamic writing programs.

Commanders willingly accept power and authority. They are in charge of their units. They sign off on decisions, ensure they are followed, and take ownership of the consequences. As the US Army Command Policy states, "Commanders are responsible for everything their command does or fails to do" (US Army 2014, 6). Most important, though, for this discussion of command in reference to WPA leadership, is the responsibility commanders have to their people. Commanders must make certain their people (and their families) are safely housed, are adequately fed, and have access to the healthcare, education, and all other resources they might need. In this way, a commander embodies the "caretaker" role that might be attributed to a feminist, collaborative model of leadership (Schell 1998). Furthermore, a good commander cannot act alone. Commanders depend on the insight and expertise of others because without these, their decisions are fraught. Commanders must listen well, understand the rhetorical (or tactical) situation, think creatively and expansively, seek out advice, and take the risk of action over inaction in rapidly changing circumstances (Builder, Bankes, and Nordin 1999).

My point here is not that command is a flawless administrative theory, or that concentrating power in the WPA position is preferable to a collaborative administrative model. It is not difficult to find historical and modern-day accounts of how military commanders have used their power to abuse and manipulate their subordinates as well as purposefully exploit others, deceive the public, and waste resources. Moreover, it is true that a command model of leadership works in the military because it is supported by military law, discipline, and regulations, structures civilian academic institutions do not (and should not) have. Furthermore, I do not believe transitioning WPAs would benefit if they completely abandoned collaboration in favor of command. Rather, I am arguing that WPAs, especially transitioning WPAs, might find themselves with institutional constraints or rhetorical situations that call for leadership strategies other than collaboration, and for those situations, military command theories might offer a useful model WPAs can adapt for their circumstances.

I think it is important to point out that no model of leadership—collaboration or command—is perfect. They are models, to be used well or poorly. Both concepts of command and collaboration are far more complicated than they may seem, and together they can be complementary and useful leadership theories for WPAs to rely on during times of transition. In the next section, I describe how two WPAs relied on a combination of command and collaboration strategies to enact curricular change at their new institutions. The first example focuses on Louise Wetherbee Phelps's first few years as the WPA in the new Syracuse University Writing Program. The second example is my own, as the new WPA at USAFA. I use these two examples to explore how WPAs can simultaneously rely on command and collaboration leadership strategies in order to make necessary curricular changes in their transitioning years.

TWO ACCOUNTS OF WPA COMMAND AND COLLABORATION
1. "Becoming a Warrior" as a New WPA

In her essay "Becoming a Warrior: Lessons of the Feminist Workplace," Louise Wetherbee Phelps describes her transitional years as the WPA for the Syracuse University Writing Program (Phelps 1995). Her essay is a powerful testament to what she describes as "the triple burden created for the woman leader in composition by the intertwinings of power with gender, teaching, and writing" (Phelps 1995, 297). In her search for a positive theory of feminist leadership, she moves between snippets of remembered conversations with colleagues and administrators, descriptions of the curricular revisions she led in her first few years as the WPA, and analyses of feminist theories and their usefulness and limitations for women writing program administrators.

Phelps explains that when she became the director of the Syracuse University Writing Program in 1986—an independent writing program created through a top-down administrative decision—she did not have a model available to her about how she, as a woman, a teacher, and a compositionist (all feminized identities), could accept and use the institutional power invested in her administrative position. What she noticed was the "killer dichotomy" presented in scholarship that seemed to ask WPAs to choose between embracing completely collaborative power or accepting a problematic hierarchal power structure that was already in place without challenging or disrupting it (Phelps 1995, 320). Early on in her WPA work at Syracuse, Phelps explains, she chose to reject this dichotomy. Phelps argues that power is not antithetical to feminist principles. Rather, she uses the essay to "construct a more adequately complex and nuanced feminism," one in which feminist power can be productive, generative, and expansive, allowing for both a strong executive leader and a distributed and collaborative authority (Phelps 1995, 300). Phelps does not choose between collaboration or command: she embraces both.

Many of the teachers in the new Syracuse University Writing Program—both part-time instructors and English department teaching assistants—had been teaching at Syracuse in the old freshman English program before Phelps arrived on campus in 1986. The freshman English program was physically and theoretically pushed to the margins in the Syracuse University English Department, housed in a separate building and constructed as "teacher-proof" curriculum, with instructors given little to no flexibility in how to design and teach their courses. The devaluation of composition (and its instructors) within the Syracuse University English Department was a major reason the two

Council of Writing Program Administrators consultant-evaluators who visited Syracuse in 1984 recommended creating a stand-alone writing program outside the English department, a recommendation taken up by the Syracuse University administration (Gates et al. 1985). Phelps seized on the opportunity to legitimize and authorize the teachers in the Syracuse University Writing Program. Instead of imposing a new curriculum, Phelps turned to the teachers. She explains, "Despite my inexperience as an administrator, I assumed that the single most critical factor in the success of a programmatic enterprise is smart, dedicated people: faculty and staff who are intellectually and morally engaged in working for shared goals" (1995, 308). She asked the teachers to collaborate with her, the other tenure-track faculty in the program, and each other to "invent curriculum together" (Phelps 1995, 309).

On the surface, this decentering move of creating curriculum with the teachers enacts a collaborative model of leadership. Phelps invited multiple perspectives into the conversation, drew on the diverse strengths of the program's members, and was willing to have a messy, slow, yet dynamic process. However, the process wasn't completely democratic. Phelps explains that the members of the writing program worked together in "asymmetrical power relations"—people held different degrees of power and responsibility (Phelps 1995, 323). In the writing program, she saw herself as the unapologetic leader. Her role, she explains, was in "orchestrating the activity of a teaching community," and she asserted her authority by writing programmatic documents that set out the theoretical principles of the new writing program, by publishing director newsletters and statements, and by giving speeches at the writing program's annual spring conferences. These public manifestations of Phelps's leadership—of her command—did not sit well with some of the instructors and faculty in her program. They did not, Phelps explains, want any whiff of a hierarchal structure in the writing program. Rather, they imagined the director as a position virtually void of real authority, as the "first among equals" (Phelps 1995, 296).

Phelps rejects the idea of collaborative utopia: a writing program is a workplace, and workplaces, like all human organizations, are not utopias. Phelps explains that in her leadership decisions, she "assumed that inequalities of power as well as of hierarchy are inevitable in any large social organization, patriarchal or otherwise." (Phelps 1995, 320). Inequality—differences in rank, title, and expertise—is part of human reality, and Phelps questions whether a WPA should fight against this inequality. She asks, could these differences be useful? Authority within a writing program, Phelps points out, results in increased responsibility and discipline: those who are authorized to develop their own curriculum are responsible for its consequences; those who are authorized to make administrative budget and personnel decisions must accept the rippling ramifications of those decisions. As Phelps explains, not everyone wants the burdens that emerge from increased power and authority (Phelps 1995, 317–318). Phelps argues, "An increase in authority, voice, and autonomy is not an unqualified good in and of itself" (Phelps 1995, 312). An increase in authority means greater accountability, and as Phelps explains, the responsibilities of this authority can be frightening (Phelps 1995, 328).

Though Phelps draws on military frames of reference in her essay (as she explores the positive connotations of "becoming a warrior"), she does not specifically refer to command. Nonetheless, her description of power and how she led the Syracuse University Writing Program during her transitional years hearken to basic principles of command. She asserted her director role in public, both in her public speeches and in the writing she published in the program, to the greater university community, and in writing studies scholarship. Phelps made executive decisions about the theoretical foundations of the new required composition sequence, composing and signing off on new course descriptions and frameworks. Yet, she did this curricular work by relying on the insights of composition theory and the expertise of the instructors in the program, who had vast local knowledge of teaching at Syracuse. Finally, she took care of her people. She leveraged curricular development as a way to professionalize the program's instructors, which allowed her to advocate for better positions, pay, and working conditions for her instructors (Davies 2013; Lipson and Voorheis 2000). Though she never named what she did as *command* or called herself a *commander*, I believe her actions—assuming authority, looking out for the professional needs of those within her program, and relying on the advice of others—are all examples of Phelps acting as a commander.

Taking on a command role was not easy, Phelps explains. At times, it was "painful," lonely, isolating work (Phelps 1995, 299). I imagine one reason Phelps was able to resist the arguments for complete, democratic collaborative authority that rose up from within her program was her position as a tenured WPA. During her negotiations with Syracuse, before accepting the job to direct the university's new writing program, Phelps successfully argued she could not direct a university-wide writing program without the same authority as a department chair. Prior to coming to Syracuse, Phelps spent six years as a tenure-track faculty member: she was no new jWPA kid on the block.

Phelps deliberately asserted her authority in a commander-like way during her transitional years as a WPA. As I read about her early years at Syracuse, I'm struck by the differences between her experience and my own at USAFA. She carved out space to command in an environment that expected collaboration; I tried to collaborate in a structure that expected command.

2. "We Don't Do Pilots"

When I was hired as an assistant professor of English at USAFA in 2012, I knew I'd be teaching writing, but I did not know I would be taking over the direction of the academy's required first-year writing course. Looking back, I realize how shortsighted I was: though neither the term *director* nor *writing program administration* appeared in the job ad, I was entering a literature-heavy department with only one other writing studies scholar, who was there only temporarily as an endowed chair. In my interviews, I was never asked for my administrative philosophy (as with other jWPA positions I had applied for), and through the interview process, no one on the search committee nor in the department queried me about issues I thought central to administration, namely professional development for writing teachers, assessment, and first-year writing outcomes and curriculum. These were the cues I had expected for a job with significant administrative duties.

In October of my first semester, my chair, an Air Force colonel, asked me to meet with her in her office. The mountain air was snappy and crisp, the aspens were turning yellow, and I was beginning to feel a bit settled in my first tenure-track faculty position. My learning curve was steep. Not only did I feel the whiplash most new assistant professors feel, suddenly transformed from doctoral candidate to faculty member, but I also became quickly schooled on military life and culture, such as duty hours from 8 a.m. to 4 p.m. and identifying uniform insignia at a distance. Most of the faculty members at USAFA are either active-duty military officers, there for a two- to three-year tour of duty, or retired officers. I, on the other hand, was what the academy (and the US Congress, who has some authority over the composition of military academies' faculty) called a *pure civilian*: a civilian academic with no prior military experience (Keller et al. 2013). At the all-faculty dean's calls, my pink shirt stood out in an auditorium of blue; only about 16 percent of the faculty at the United States Air Force Academy are "pure civilians," and less than half of these are women (Keller et al. 2013, 10).

My chair and I sat in her sixth-floor corner office, overlooking the parade field. She explained that in the spring, she wanted me to direct the academy's first-year writing course. Part of my administration would be developing a new first-year writing curriculum that would be adopted department-wide in the spring. This assignment was a surprise to me. I did some quick mental calculation—only ten weeks until the spring semester began. My graduate coursework and dissertation research on writing program administration did not prepare me for this moment.

"How about I develop a pilot course," I started, "and I can try it out in the spring, and then . . ."

"We don't do pilots," she stopped me. "We make changes. That's why we hired you."

As I walked out of her office, I was both eager and worried. I had always imagined myself as a WPA, but I had thought that role was a few years away. I didn't feel ready to do that work. My graduate program was housed within an independent writing program, and there, the value and integrity of composition and rhetoric were never questioned, and the hallways buzzed with the talk of teaching and writing. In contrast, my colleagues at USAFA had a well-meaning yet reductive understanding of what the teaching of writing entailed. The first-year writing curriculum was vintage current-traditionalist, and each day of the semester was scripted. Most of the instructors who were assigned to teach first-year writing were first-time teachers, junior military officers who had earned their master's degrees in a military-efficient eleven to eighteen months. They were slogging through a 4/4 load with two preps, both first-year writing and a sophomore required literature course. These teachers were grasping at straws for classroom activities or assignments that could help them survive the forty class sessions of the semester.

What buoyed me, though, was my chair's utmost confidence in my ability to "make changes." The flag was in my hands. In contrast to the gridlock I had heard plagues academia—the slow, politically charged battles over programmatic changes that can take years—this snappy decisiveness and unwavering belief in my newly minted "expertise" was refreshing, though a bit unsettling.

At the next department meeting in early November, my chair announced the change of command: in the spring semester, which started the first week of January, there'd be a new curriculum, new texts, and a new director—me.

A captain raised his hand. He diplomatically nodded toward me, agreed that the switch would be good. "But," he pointed out. "I just figured out this course. Can't we make the change next year? We'd have the whole summer then."

His concern made sense to me, but before I could speak, my chair spoke. "No," she answered. It will be a lot of work, "but we're changing now."

He didn't object. After the meeting, I went to his office. The junior officers were drowning in grading and teaching prep, he told me, but the decision of his chair (and commander) was clear: the curricular revision would be made, top down, and rolled out in January.

As I walked back to my office, I realized I was part of the military's web of hierarchy. I was both commander, given what seemed to be carte blanche authority to change and lead a whole writing program, and commanded, told to make extensive changes to the current curriculum over the reservations of the teachers in my program.

I didn't like it. It was more power than I wanted. More important, I felt the power invested in me undermined the authority of the teachers, and I needed the instructors to have authority in order to take ownership of their teaching and the curriculum. The model of curricular development I was comfortable with, the one I saw modeled in my PhD program at Syracuse, was collaborative and experimental. I learned through Louise Wetherbee Phelps's example and scholarship that the teachers are the most important resource a writing program has. Teachers, working together in a reflective teaching community, should invent curriculum. A WPA can and should set an overarching theoretical vision for that curriculum, but a WPA is not the writing program. The teachers are.

And so, in my direction of the academy's first-year writing course over the next eighteen months, I tried to nurture collaboration by planting the seeds of a teaching community. I emphasized shared outcomes instead of shared texts, which contradicted the cookie-cutter approach the academy took to its required English courses. Department lore said a previous chair had stated that his ideal curriculum had identical sections of a course: on a given day, every section, regardless of instructor, would discuss the same passage from the same text with the same set of discussion questions. I tried to find the sweet spot between structure and freedom by sharing my ideas, reflections, and assignments with the first-year writing instructors and encouraging them to use my materials as jumping-off points. Too often, though, the instructors worked to replicate what I was doing in my courses. Instead of holding grade-norming sessions, I asked the instructors to read snippets of composition theory, and we talked together over lunch about how those ideas could work in our writing classes at the Air Force Academy. One of my first-year instructors read about the flipped classroom model and asked me if she could try it in her classes. "Go for it," I said, and the next semester, she was abuzz with ideas, her enthusiasm contagious. Although I was in command, I did not act in a vacuum. Like good commanders, I relied on the experiences, insights, and passions of my teachers to shape the curriculum.

The day my USAFA chair invited me to command marked a critical shift in how I understood the responsibilities of the WPA position. My chair rejected my idea for a pilot course because in her eyes, I was the expert, the newly minted PhD, and therefore I had the authority to make this change without a trial period. Her call for a top-down curricular revision challenged me in a good way. The command role she placed me in helped me learn how to accept power, take ownership of my authority, share my disciplinary expertise with people outside my field, and name and defend what I know about writing, learning, and teaching both to the people within my department and to the officers and professors in other departments. Instead of abdicating authority over the goals for the first-year writing course, I took charge and set a direction for our program-wide curricular conversations. My responsibility as a WPA—even as a new WPA unfamiliar with the institution and military culture in general—was to be a leader and use my knowledge and experience to lay a solid foundation for a stronger, theory- and research-based first-year writing program.

CONCLUSION

What is important about these two examples is that they show command and collaboration are both useful leadership strategies for transitioning WPAs. Furthermore, both Louise Wetherbee Phelps's explanation of her first years as the WPA at the Syracuse University Writing Program and my experience as the new WPA at USAFA demonstrate that command and collaboration are not diametrically opposed leadership theories. Collaboration invites people to come to the table and make a personal and professional investment in their writing program, which can result in better curriculum and stronger teaching communities. Command gives a WPA the power to make public statements, set visions, and direct changes. Military command theory also emphasizes a commander's fundamental identification with and responsibility toward the people they are in charge of. In a writing program, those people include a program's teachers, administrative staff, campus community, and students. Commanders need their people, lead their people, provide for their people, and take responsibility for their people.

As transitioning WPAs become more established in their programs, they become more nuanced in their administrative choices. It becomes clearer, with time and a greater attunement to context, whether a WPA should approach a problem more as a collaborator or as a commander. Once Phelps had established a coherent vision for the new Syracuse University Writing Program, her administrative style shifted. The teachers gradually had more agency and power in decisions about curriculum, professional development, and professional evaluation. Likewise, once I had a better understanding of how military units like my department at the United States Air Force Academy functioned, I felt more comfortable in the commander role: naming what I knew as a scholar in rhetoric and composition and arguing for particular pedagogical approaches in the first-year writing classroom. Transitioning WPAs don't have to choose between acting as a commander or as a collaborator. Using collaborative theory and command theory together can be a rhetorically savvy and effective administrative strategy.

References

Anson, Chris M., and Richard Jewell. 2000. "Shadows of the Mountain." In *Moving a Mountain: Transforming the Role of Contingent Faculty in Composition Studies and Higher Education*, edited by Eileen Schell and Patricia Lambert Stock, 47–75. Urbana, IL: NCTE.

Bousquet, Marc. 2002. "Composition as Management Science: Toward a University without a WPA." *JAC* 22 (3): 493–526.

Builder, Carl H., Steven C. Bankes, and Richard Nordin. 1999. *Command Concepts: A Theory Derived from the Practice of Command and Control*. Santa Monica, CA: RAND Corporation.

Cambridge, Barbara L., and Ben W. McClelland. 1995. "From Icon to Partner: Repositioning the Writing Program Administrator." In *Resituating Writing: Constructing and Administering Writing Programs*, edited by Joseph Janangelo and Kristine Hansen, 151–59. Boston, MA: Boynton/Cook-Heinemann.

Davies, Laura J. 2013. "Taking the Long View: Investigating the History of a Writing Program's Teacher Evaluation System." *WPA: Writing Program Administration* 37 (1): 81–111.

Fleming, Bruce. 2010. "Bridging the Military-Civilian Divide." *Yale Review* 98 (2): 1–21. https://doi.org/10.1111/j.1467-9736.2010.00596.x.

Gates, Robert, et al. 1985. *Final Report of the Ad Hoc Committee to Review Writing Instruction*. Syracuse, NY: Syracuse University.

Gunner, Jeanne. 1994. "Decentering the WPA." *WPA: Writing Program Administration* 18 (1–2): 8–15.

Gunner, Jeanne. 2002. "Collaborative Administration." In *The Writing Program Administrator's Resource: A Guide to Reflective Institutional Practice*, edited by Stuart C. Brown and Theresa Enos, 253–62. Mahwah, NJ: Lawrence Erlbaum.

Harrington, Susanmarie, Steve Fox, and Tere Molinder Hogue. 1998. "Power, Partnership, and Negotiations: The Limits of Collaboration." *WPA: Writing Program Administration* 21 (2–3): 52–64.

Harris, Joseph. 2000. "Meet the New Boss, Same as the Old Boss: Class Consciousness in Composition." *College Composition and Communication* 52 (1): 43–68. https://doi.org/10.2307/358543.

Howard, Rebecca Moore. 1993. "Power Revisited; Or, How We Became a Department." *WPA: Writing Program Administration* 16 (3): 37–49.

Keller, Kirsten M., Nelson Lim, Lisa M. Harrington, Kevin O'Neill, and Abigail Haddad. 2013. *The Mix of Military and Civilian Faculty at the United States Air Force Academy: Finding a Sustainable Balance for Enduring Success.* Santa Monica, CA: RAND Corporation.

Kinney, Kelly. 2009. "Fellowship for the Ring: A Defense of Critical Administration in the Corporate University." *WPA: Writing Program Administration* 32 (3): 37–48.

Lipson, Carol, and Molly Voorheis. 2000. "The Material and the Cultural as Interconnected Texts: Revising Material Conditions for Part-Time Faculty at Syracuse University." In *Moving a Mountain: Transforming the Role of Contingent Faculty in Composition Studies and Higher Education,* edited by Eileen Schell and Patricia Lambert Stock, 107–31. Urbana, IL: NCTE.

Meeks, Lynn, and Christine Huit. 1998. "A Co-Mentoring Model of Administration." *WPA: Writing Program Administration* 21 (2–3): 9–22.

Micciche, Laura R. 2011. "For Slow Agency." *WPA: Writing Program Administration* 35 (1): 73–90.

Phelps, Louise Wetherbee. 1995. "Becoming a Warrior: Lessons of the Feminist Workplace." In *Feminine Principles and Women's Experience in American Composition and Rhetoric,* edited by Louise Wetherbee Phelps and Janet Emig, 289–339. Pittsburgh, PA: University of Pittsburgh Press.

Schell, Eileen E. 1998. "Who's the Boss? The Possibilities and Pitfalls of Collaborative Administration for Untenured WPAs." *WPA: Writing Program Administration* 21 (2–3): 65–80.

Sledd, James. 2001. "On Buying In and Selling Out: A Note for Bosses Old and New." *College Composition and Communication* 53 (1): 146–48. https://doi.org/10.2307/359066.

US Army, 2014. *Army Command Policy: Army Regulation 600-20.* Headquarters, Department of the Army, Washington, DC. http://gordon.army.mil/sharp/downloads/Army_Command_Policy_AR_600-20.pdf.

White, Edward M. 1991. "Use It or Lose It: Power and the WPA." *WPA: Writing Program Administration* 15 (1–2): 3–12.

13
THE COLLABORATIVE WPA
Bringing a Writing Center Ethos to WAC

Tereza Joy Kramer, Jaquelyn Davis,
Holland Enke, and Reyna Olegario

When I began my current position, I perceived it as intriguing and daunting: unlike the writing center I'd directed before, this new program would serve both students and faculty; there were expectations for writing-across-the-curriculum workshops, curricular guidance, and support for individual faculty. I reasoned it should be possible to create both a student writing center and WAC program for faculty because my new school was smaller than my previous university. However, rising to the double challenge proved to be too much, and I found myself turning to the students I was mentoring as writing advisers to help me serve not only students but also faculty; as a result, the student writing advisers helped me envision and, eventually, even collaboratively lead our faculty development. My commitment to service learning certainly has factored into the evolution of our Center for Writing Across The Curriculum (CWAC), as I emphasize we are all learning and serving together and as I'm continually trying to live up to that ideal. Reflecting across the five years of building CWAC, I am realizing both how much our program has grown and how much I have evolved as a WPA—transitions that would have been far less dramatic without our dual mission and certainly without the dynamic of student leaders journeying with me. This has been a gradual journey not so much of letting go of the reins as of multiplying them: widening the stagecoach driver's seat to take advantage of more knowledges and perspectives and helping all of us—me included—never stop learning.

In this spirit, the writing of this chapter is as collaborative as our daily work, incorporating the perspectives of multiple voices within CWAC: me (Tereza), the WPA; Jaquelyn, a lead adviser; Reyna, a graduate

DOI: 10.7330/9781607326335.c013

student and former lead adviser; and Holland, a veteran writing adviser and writing-circle facilitator. We explore ways my coleadership with students has facilitated my transition and helped me figure out what the program needs, and we reflect upon how this narrative speaks to WPA work in a broad sense.

There have been many scholarly debates about the place of a WPA on campus. Take writing centers, for instance: in the introduction to their anthology *Marginal Words, Marginal Work?*, William Macauley and Nicholas Mauriello acknowledge that "marginalization and struggling against it" are practically a given in writing center work (Macauley and Mauriello 2007, xiii). More broadly, marginalization is often described as applying to all writing programs and those who lead them. WPAs must run their programs while also wrangling with campus politics. Upper administration is "often thought to be an uncaring and distant threat," forever misunderstanding WPA work and poised to cut budgets at a moment's notice (Weiser 2013, 252). And English departments, which often house WPAs and their programs, can be antagonistic at worst and indifferent at best, with rhetoric and composition languishing at the bottom of the political and social scale. Melissa Ianetta (2013) notes that "a focus on the acrimony of literature-composition relations has long been the definitional quality to rhetoric and composition's representations of the English department" (365). Not only is the writing program marginalized, but the WPA is also sometimes cast on the fringe, doing work that supposedly no one else wants to do. The WPA is praised in ways that confirm the role of subsidiary faculty, such as, "Thank god you are working with these students" (Geller et al. 2007, 131). And colleagues sometimes undervalue the research of WPAs, leaving them "adrift" as scholars in a department (Ianetta 2013, 362). WPAs can be rendered, either in fact or by perception, powerless.

Macauley and Mauriello (2007) and Ianetta (2013) suggest that open communication can be a way of empowering WPAs and building understanding among departments. Ianetta argues that as WPAs we must work to "hear beyond the stereotypes we've helped to perpetuate . . . and to see our colleagues for who they are and to help them listen to our proposals—and to hear what they say in return" (Ianetta 2013, 369). What I have found is that coleading with students makes open communication with my colleagues more possible. My credibility benefits from my close relationship and platform sharing with well-trained student leaders; I am perceived not as a removed administrator but rather as a hands-on teacher and mentor who does significant researching and presenting with students. Another interesting discovery has been the power of student testimonies: because faculty enjoy watching insightful students present and generally want students to do well, faculty tend to be open to receiving wisdom through the perspective of student leaders. Furthermore, involving students in faculty-development workshops makes it easier for us faculty to collaborate among ourselves—it's as though the dynamic conversation spurred by student input opens a safe space for dynamic conversation among colleagues.

I have been witnessing an interesting result of this platform sharing: not only can our CWAC offer more and therefore be more involved across campus, but the visibility and appreciation for what we're doing also seems to increase proportionally to the degree of my willingness to share power. Inviting students to help teach faculty can be risky: what if a writing adviser were to blurt out advice I was not in agreement with? Interestingly, that pretty much never happens—it's almost as though the more I let go, the more in accord we all are.

This reality works against the narrative of marginalization that shadows some WPA practice and scholarship. Bringing an ethos of student-centered dialogue characteristic of writing centers into WAC support for faculty opens doors and allows for the WPA to be viewed as integrally connected to students and faculty peers across the college. For the field of writing program administration, this is a critical identity shift, one that transforms the representation of WPA from isolated and undervalued to essential and respected.

~

Back in graduate school, my mentor Jane Cogie introduced me to, among other scholarship, Michele Eodice's (2003) "Breathing Lessons, or Collaboration is. . . ." I credit the perspectives of Cogie and Eodice for having influenced me over the years far more than I could have predicted—informing my evolution as a WPA and undergirding my current practices. As I learned from Cogie, one-to-one sessions in the writing center privilege dialogue as a conversation of equal exchange, in which listening is just as valuable as speaking and no voice is inherently privileged. Such conversations require a great deal of holding back: the best conversationalists draw out ideas from those with whom they speak rather than dominating them. I suspect that because of this grounding, I connected easily with Eodice's explications, particularly her idea of a collaborative ethos that flourishes in writing centers and empowers peers. I have always been confused, however, that the same ethos that makes one-to-one work with students so impactful is often left behind in other aspects of WPAship. As Eodice writes, "Although we seem to recognize these activities when they fall within our own brick and mortar or electronic environments, we often fail to carry them beyond—to our offices, committees, programs, and faculty who could learn from us" (116). I cannot agree more with Eodice that there is no reason our writing center ethos should not be carried beyond our work with students and into our broader WAC efforts, allowing for the same impacts among faculty. I define our CWAC version of this ethos as collaborative service learning: all of us—students with students, faculty with faculty, and students and faculty together—are serving each other and learning from each other. My own WPA journey continues to evolve through the attempt to apply this ethos.

It certainly did not begin here. In my first position after graduate school—directing a writing center at a midsized public university—I operated from what in hindsight I would call an *authoritarian stance* since I did all the planning, hiring, and training. Toward the end of that experience, however, I had learned to relax somewhat and begin sharing some responsibilities with the students I was mentoring.

By the time I was hired to create CWAC at Saint Mary's College of California, in 2011, I felt ready to embrace the liberal arts institution's emphasis on peer dialogue, community engagement, and collaborative learning. I started by setting up the student services first, building a writing center similar to the one at my previous university. I thought I had it down—had figured out what did and didn't work well—and therefore could bring forward only the most successful aspects of what I had created before, including limited collaboration with lead student writing advisers. And that's what I did, for about the first year or so, and it did work at Saint Mary's as well, in many of the same ways. But despite my rhetoric of collaboration and mutual learning, I realized I actually was more of a teacher than a collaborator with the student writing advisers, even the lead advisers. I was developing all the writing resources, I was doing all the hiring and mentoring of new writing advisers, and I was the sole designer of training pedagogy and projects—all just as I had been at my previous campus. This was partly justifiable since I was again building a program and the students were not yet steeped in writing pedagogy and practice. But it is equally true that I didn't really know another way.

Realizing how much I could partner with others has taken some time and experimentation. It was when I turned toward creating other services, such as student writing workshops and faculty-development support, that my approach began to shift significantly, although I did not fully realize this shift until the call came out for this *WPAs in Transition* collection and I stepped back to think about my transition. At first I viewed it through the lens of transitioning our program, but I was encouraged to reflect on the transition of my own identity, my own growth, within the role of leading our CWAC.

~

At Saint Mary's, the need for a combined WAC and writing center program had been heightened by a campus-wide faculty decision to design a new core curriculum that views writing across the college as an interwoven whole, including the existing two semesters of first-year composition and four Great Books seminars, plus the addition of new writing-in-the-disciplines courses. To fulfill the WID requirement, each department develops and proposes a course, which is then taught by professors of that discipline. I arrived at Saint Mary's just in time for the start of WID course development and joined the new Core Curriculum Habits of Mind Working Group, which reviews WID applications. I drafted our WID parameters and assisted departments in developing their WID courses. My responsibilities also include faculty-development workshops and individual consultations, campus-wide writing research and assessment, and teaching two courses a year. A study by Jill M. Gladstein and Dara Rossman Regaignon reveals that a dual WPA configuration—WAC and writing center leadership—is uncommon, particularly outside small liberal arts colleges (Gladstein and Rossman Regaignon 2012). While Saint Mary's College is a comprehensive university that offers graduate degrees, it is a liberal arts institution with only about 2,750 undergraduate and 1,250 graduate students.

Gladstein and Rossman Regaignon, in discussing the inherent dangers and potentialities of a dual WPA, write, "It is possible to see this configuration as necessarily burdened and isolated, but it is important to also recognize that solo administrators have enormous leeway to design and implement initiatives in the hybrid space between the curriculum- and student-centered domains" (Gladstein and Rossman Regaignon 2012, 52). The fact that I serve both students and faculty has benefits in terms of perception: my dual position prevents marginalization that might result from directing only student writing support, which can be misperceived as off to the side of curricular life. I believe it is the hybridity of CWAC's faculty and student services that empowers me to innovate more effectively and integrate into campus endeavors. And while it is possible to become burdened by the dual workload, our collaborative approach makes doable the implementation of more initiatives than I could carry out or even think of on my own.

Moving beyond the student writing center to accomplish the slew of other responsibilities required of my position, including faculty development and whole-class workshops for students in WID courses, was no easy task, and I sometimes felt like the person "who serves as 'all things writing'" (Gladstein and Rossman Regaignon 2012, 51). Realizing I could not do everything single-handedly, however, caused me to try involving the student writing advisers more fully. During our first year of CWAC, there was a graduate-student writing adviser who had previous teaching experience, so I chose him to collaborate with me; because of his background, he was the only student I even considered coleading with. I invited him to copresent writing workshops for education graduate students based on topics I had devised in concert with the education faculty. At the time, I was not thinking this collaboration could possibly be the first of many such with student advisers. But he did such a good job that I expanded my thinking and, by the second year, had begun identifying other student leaders on staff, even undergraduates, and gingerly extending them opportunities for creating and presenting writing workshops, particularly since requests for workshops were increasing as our college's new writing-in-the-disciplines undergraduate courses were coming on line. At first, I created the workshops and the student advisers presented alongside me, but as time progressed and demand kept growing, I started in some cases to only mentor them so they could present the workshops in student pairs. I was developing trust in the students because they proved themselves worthy; besides, they often knew more about certain disciplines than I did—these workshop situations, I realized, had turned into opportunities not only for the writing advisers to learn pedagogy but also for me to learn more about their disciplines. Now, I hire new writing advisers with their disciplinary backgrounds specifically in mind, considering their potential to work with other students from their discipline as well as to help me guide the faculty who are folding writing to learn into upper-division courses.

Our collaborative workshops continued to grow in frequency because of continued growth in demand, such that during our fourth year of CWAC, we led thirty-nine workshops, each tailored to the writing of a particular course. Each time, I was involved in organizing and helping design the workshops. And each time, it was an interesting balancing act for me as WPA: I knew I should not lean back and do nothing, and I found myself repeatedly figuring out how much to be involved. For students presenting for the first time, I was more hands on, helping them develop materials and coaching them on presenting skills; for students who already had impressed me with their presentations, I generally gave them only initial guidelines, made myself available as they developed materials, and gave them feedback on their practice run-throughs. All of this amounted, ultimately, to the bulk of the work being done by students, most of whom were undergraduates. While responding to so many workshop requests by myself could have become a burden or, frankly, been impossible, choosing instead to privilege collaboration has allowed CWAC to deliver quite a lot of support across campus.

When students are given the opportunity to solve problems, we all begin to see ourselves as more capable of doing so. Such collaborations give the writing advisers professional experience and give faculty members opportunities to learn from the student leaders who enter classrooms to teach writing workshops. For example, one veteran adviser, a premed student, suggested she work with her chemistry professor to create workshops for chemistry majors writing lab abstracts. I gave her an enthusiastic go-ahead, and she conferred with her chemistry professor to develop the workshop and handouts, which I merely looked over and provided suggestions for; then, she and I trained other student advisers to help her present the workshops, as there were several sections of the chemistry lab. Throughout all this, several student advisers and I were learning details about the writing situation of chemists that we could use when working with other science writers and faculty. This experience of collaboration and learning mirrors our philosophy for one-to-one student sessions: both writers at the table are eager to experiment, discover, and learn from each other. Each of the student writing advisers has unique expertise and perspective that add to mine, and through all our exceptional moments and our stumbles, their leadership styles inform my own. By embracing collaboration, we have broadened the potential for learning for all involved, including me. I am reflecting now that none of this transition—this relaxing and opening of my leadership style—could have occurred as the result of my dictating instructions.

~

Working closely with students to develop whole-class workshops for WID and other courses has occurred in tandem with, and was perhaps fostered by, heightened collaborations between the students and me within the center itself. There are some aspects of our program that have made it easy—perhaps necessary—for me to collaborate and learn with students. For instance, I was not given a separate office, which was a good thing. At my former institution, my working in a private office, even though it was near the center, created a division between the student staff and me and reified my stance as authority. In CWAC, my desk occupies a corner of the open center, signaling that I myself belong in the everyday mix of center activity.

Another situation was the quandary over what to call our center's student employees. Rather than making an executive decision, I called a meeting of my first student staff to discuss their job title. I shared with them scholarship in the field about terms such as *tutor* and *consultant*. We did freewriting and we brainstormed together on the whiteboard, all the while making liberal use of dictionaries and thesauri. After a couple of hours, we all settled on the title *writing adviser*. This collective decision making could have turned out badly: what if I had disagreed with their ideas? And in fact, this title was not what I would have declared had I made the decision on my own. But through our discussion and our explorations of their interpretations and perceptions of each potential choice, we together became sold on the term we ended up with. This early opportunity in my new center to experiment with transparency and authority sharing helped me feel safer about gradually widening that metaphoric stagecoach driver's seat.

The evolution of our collaborative practice also has been influenced greatly by the particular writing advisers I've promoted to lead advisers, including Jaq and Reyna. As our center grew and diversified, I turned more and more to lead advisers to help with or even take over things I had been doing by myself. They repeatedly earned my trust, which allowed me to expand how much I trusted them with. At this point, lead advisers are fully involved in mentoring new writing advisers. The leads, in fact, currently do the bulk of the observations of their new peers. And I now seek their advice as I'm deciding which applicants to hire. During our weekly meeting—affectionately dubbed the Leads Think Tank—we together plan staff workshops and discuss which of the advisers need what sort of support for their sessions, research projects, conference presentations, or writing workshops. All the students I work with, but most especially these lead advisers, have evolved into sounding boards I rely upon more and more. They are teaching me how to be a better manager, understated leader, and teacher. This doesn't mean there isn't a hierarchy. I am most certainly the director, but the authority is more spread out. And interestingly, it seems that the more the responsibility is dispersed, the more—not less—I feel connected, and the more it seems all of us are on the same page. I have come to believe that when each person embraces leadership, we each can more fully benefit those around us. When the four of us coauthors discussed this phenomenon, we decided collaboration is part of both the cause and the result. We also realized we couldn't think of much I do strictly by myself anymore.

~

The dual nature of my position has led me to stumble upon other ways as well to bring students into my work. For example, when I established a WAC advisory board, I invited not only faculty and administrators to become members but also a student writing adviser. Reyna, then a lead adviser, held that position for two years. She became a sounding board not just for me but for all the faculty on the board. It quickly became apparent how critical her perspective was to our considerations—inviting Reyna into the conversations gave my colleagues and me the unique insights of a student with experience working with peer student writers on various assignments, the insights of someone very much an expert on writing at Saint Mary's in her own right. Although I easily could have chosen to serve as the only "expert" at the table (I am the WPA, after all), I chose instead to bring another voice in with me, trusting Reyna's input would help all of us arrive at deeper understandings. This writing center ethos in action emphasizes that I am not the isolated expert; in fact, far from it. Faculty peers and students alike carry with them their own sets of expertise, and my role as a WPA is strengthened and expanded when I choose to let their expertise be revealed.

Like the collaborative ethos I bring to my work with students, and surely thanks to the influence of scholars such as Cogie, Eodice, Macauley, and Mauriello, peer collaboration is always in the forefront of my intentions for my work with faculty. I try to carry out the suggestion of Anne Ellen Geller, Michele Eodice, Frankie Condon, Meg Carroll, and Elizabeth Boquet, in their concluding chapter of *The Everyday Writing Center*, to create "opportunities for us to teach and for others to learn the value of the ways we think and work within the writing center and how these approaches might enrich our colleagues' teaching and learning lives as well as the institution" (Geller et al. 2007, 129). During a writing center session, the writing adviser listens and tries to draw out the ideas of the other student, affirms when the writer is uncertain yet on the right track, and suggests strategies that might be helpful. This approach is similar to the way I advise my peers one to one in developing their writing-intensive courses, and the way I facilitate faculty workshops: I begin by soliciting everyone's questions or concerns, just as a writing center session begins by negotiating what to work on; I share resources and guide discussion, encouraging everyone to contribute; as necessary, I direct the conversation to best practices; and I make sure to touch back on each concern expressed at the start. Throughout all the individual and group faculty conversations, I get to learn more about the writing of diverse disciplines, and I engage in dynamic dialogues that increase my own and my peers' repertoire of ways to teach students to write as disciplinary experts, thanks to everyone's contributions.

I also cultivate partnerships with other programs on campus. From the start, all our faculty-development sessions have been cosponsored by CWAC, the Habits of Mind Working Group, and, depending on the session topic, other programs as well. And as of last year, the Office of Faculty Development has joined in as another cosponsor, wrapping the WID roundtables into that office's annual menu of programs.

During my first year of WID faculty workshops, I myself proposed, led, and created materials for all three of the roundtables each semester. The next year, I began inviting colleagues to lead some of the workshops with me; I found such coleadership to be much more generative for me and to also allow our workshops to cover a broader range of ideas. This past year, I did none of the WID roundtables by myself but instead collaboratively designed and led each of them with peers. I won't pretend that sharing leadership is always easy. I certainly have struggled at times with knowing how much to control the situation and how much to sit back, especially when I thought I had the best solution to offer or the deepest background in the field of writing pedagogy. And I have sometimes responded by giving less than I should. Through these experiences, I have learned to not hold back my ideas out of fear of offending others but rather to offer them in the context of putting all our ideas on the table. This approach seems to be working better. I am grateful for the opportunity to learn—in terms of both ideas and leadership style—through working side by side with colleagues.

Over the past year, in addition to coleading with faculty, I have been calling on student writing advisers to help present our faculty-development workshops. For instance, during a recent roundtable on using reflective writing to facilitate transfer of knowledge, I asked four student writing advisers to participate in two ways: during the initial portion—presentation of information—the students offered testimonials about times they transferred knowledge and how they did so; then, during the small-group-workshop portion, a student sat at each table, adding a student perspective to the discussion of how to design reflective writing assignments.

Thus, faculty, administrators, and students are involved in or at least familiar with both the student and faculty endeavors of CWAC. I find that the more I ask students and faculty to join in both the learning and the decision making, the more our program's collaborative approach is embraced and respected, and the more CWAC becomes involved across campus. I have observed that faculty seem open to listening to ideas presented by students, sometimes even more so than when the same ideas are explained by peers. I'll speculate that it may be more possible to agree with students because there's no potential for intellectual competition. Or perhaps the reason is simply that faculty are sympathetic to student presenters and enjoy witnessing students perform well.

Including the perspective of students broadens the perception of me as WPA: I am viewed as someone who understands, honors, and encourages student voices.

In the early stages of writing our chapter, I mentioned to my coauthors that faculty initiatives and student writing centers tend to be separate programs, and they raised their eyebrows in surprise. It all seems like a natural fit for CWAC, with neither aspect of the program independent of nor a subsidiary of the other. That said, we're still working toward our goal of hybridity, and I'm continually looking for ways to grow as a more collaborative WPA. One realm in which collaboration could improve is in resource development and sharing. Student writing advisers interview professors and create handouts about writing conventions in each discipline, but this process is only marginally collaborative, as it establishes the professor as the expert who offers information to the student writing adviser. I'm hoping we can make the creation and sharing of writing resources among faculty and students more fluid and helpful. I believe encouraging a greater degree of dialogue could result in new ideas for us and perhaps for the field of WPA work.

Currently, most CWAC dialogues with faculty occur through me, either as the direct contact or the facilitator. We need to consider ways to dissolve this boundary and encourage my colleagues to follow in my steps of transition, applying a writing center ethos to their professor identity. We could do more to encourage faculty to enter into sessions with student writing advisers, for instance. Encouragingly, an economics professor recently came to CWAC to revise a writing-project prompt he was preparing to assign in an upper-division course, and he worked with an undergraduate writing adviser on the assignment over the course of several one-to-one sessions. These types of collaborations between faculty and students are promising.

~

One of CWAC's programs that epitomizes collaborative leadership and that, I have realized, works against marginalization is our writing-circles course for students of all disciplines. I had been asked to develop a partial-credit course for students writing in the Great Books seminars; in doing so, I privileged my writing center background and created a course made up of weekly small-group workshops in which a facilitator guides students to peer review each other's work. The initial circles were successful, so we expanded the course offering to students writing in all disciplines (Kramer 2016, 24). Most of the facilitators are adjunct writing instructors. But because of high demand, just as in the case of student writing workshops, I turned to veteran student writing advisers, including Holland,

Jaq, and Reyna, to facilitate some circles. This development has resulted in instructors and students participating together in trainings and periodic meetings to discuss pedagogy, share stories of what is working, and confer on ways to turn around problematic circles. While I develop the learning goals and hire facilitators, we all contribute and listen to ideas, learning while serving. Student writing advisers who facilitate circles have a particular opportunity to grow multidimensionally, as they lead their student peers and also lead right alongside instructors. The adjuncts and I learn from each other and the student writing advisers, who offer valuable insider perspectives on student writers' struggles. Thus, the circles program crosses disciplinary boundaries and relies upon collaborative discussion—upon equally valued contributions—both within each small group of students and within our team of facilitators.

Professors whose students enroll in circles are fully aware that either an instructor or a student writing adviser will be working with their students, and the professors seem interested in collaborating with all facilitators equally. Some professors participate in our planning process. One kinesiology professor, for instance, offers a writing-process schedule for her students' circles. The professor realizes facilitators may have their own plans that would be equally beneficial, and she also understands her collaboration is welcomed. Offering a proposed schedule and leaving the implementation up to each facilitator—instructor or student writing adviser—illustrates the trust a combined WAC/writing center program can foster. This trust was further illustrated the other day when Holland, who is facilitating a kinesiology circle, happened to see the kinesiology professor in the campus art museum; they chatted about the professor's suggested schedule, including how well it might work and how it could be improved upon. This chance meeting was an opportunity for Holland to speak with the professor one to one and peer to peer. It is possible that chatting with a student leader about one's course feels more comfortable—lower stakes—than conferring with the WPA, but I don't see this possibility as a negative thing. Such an atmosphere of confidence in writing advisers affirms the entirety of the advisers' work through CWAC, and it speaks to the trust faculty have in my guidance of these student leaders. Faculty respect and appreciate that I am ultimately the WPA, and when they talk to student leaders about courses, they know the students will seek my advice and share their conversations with me. Furthermore, faculty know the student leaders I mentor will receive the support and expertise they need to work with fellow students. This confidence only adds to the positive perception of my WPA identity across campus.

A significant example of the evolution of my role as WPA occurred when I was invited to host a meeting of the Northern California-Nevada Writing Program Administrators affiliate. In choosing to accept, I decided to schedule this gathering to coincide with one of our WID faculty roundtables, and I secured the cosponsorship of four programs on our campus. If we had hosted this affiliate gathering earlier, I would not have thought to privilege such a high degree of collaboration—among NCN-WPA affiliate members, Saint Mary's faculty, and student leaders—which now seems natural because of the transition of my role and of CWAC.

For our campus-presentation portion in the morning of the affiliate gathering, I invited Holland, Jaq, Reyna, two other students, and an adjunct circle facilitator to present collaborative research—yet again, students were copresenting with and for faculty. Then, in the afternoon, the visiting affiliate members participated with Saint Mary's faculty in a WID roundtable on informal writing, the highlight of which was sharing in small groups the practices of diverse disciplines and, thanks to the WPA visitors, across diverse campuses. The tone of the entire event was congenial, which increased its productivity. I believe the high degree of congeniality and openness during the afternoon discussion arose naturally because we had begun the day with a presentation that was low stakes for the audience because the presenters were amazing students.

The response from both local and visiting faculty was abundant and positive. One visiting WPA, H. Brooke Hessler, e-mailed me a letter on October 15, 2015, expressing her appreciation for the opportunity to collaborate with Saint Mary's faculty as well as with her WPA peers. She further reflected that the event gave my Saint Mary's colleagues a window into the field of writing program administration (pers. comm.). Hessler went on to say this about the students: "I was so delighted to know that your presenters included undergraduates. It spoke volumes about your program and the extent to which students at all levels are true partners, not just novice employees. You knew their audience would be supportive. . . . We cared about their findings and listened keenly for their insights. . . . The meeting was multidimensional" (pers. comm.). The gathering's multidimensionality mirrored what we hope to manifest throughout our CWAC work. Hessler's comments also point to how student involvement helps legitimize our program's work and increase my WPA credibility. The more I allow others to hold reins alongside me, the less the possibility for marginalization of me or of CWAC.

While our program and my role as WPA are still evolving, some consequences of these changes are already clear: WAC is not a fringe program to which faculty pay mere lip service, and the writing center is not disenfranchised as merely a place faculty send poor writers; the support of student writers and faculty coincide productively. As Carolyn Peterson Haviland, Carolyn M. Fye, and Richard Colby report, connecting a writing center with WAC can "enact the interdisciplinary nature of writing and thus its role as crossing rather than maintaining traditional disciplinary boundaries" (Haviland, Fye, and Colby 2001, 89). This has certainly been the case at Saint Mary's, although the boundary crossing is occurring not just across disciplines but across traditional lines of authority: my colleagues, my students, and I are crossing boundaries together and learning along with each other. This is not to say I don't direct or teach. I share best practices that enable us to collaborate effectively, but I am continually learning how to listen and when to offer guidance—when to lead by facilitating discussion and when by sharing knowledge and experience. Paralleling the flattening of authority is not chaos but rather a collective, mostly cohesive authority. This sense of collective authority offers an important expansion of the sometimes marginalized WPA identity: if the field of writing program administration is to move beyond understanding itself as a fringe discipline, the integration of WPA work across the curriculum and collaborative platform sharing among WPAs, other faculty, and students leaders are critical steps.

In the spirit of Eodice's "Breathing Lessons, *or Collaboration is . . .*," I feel every day that I am "work[ing] toward boundarylessness, even with the knowledge that these actions will never be fully accomplished, completed" (Eodice 2003, 129). I am always trying to negotiate where the boundary does and doesn't lie. In writing center sessions, the most effective moments are when writing advisers pause and allow their peer writers to discover and grow. Similarly, for a WPA, powerful impacts are made possible through the act of strategically and collaboratively letting go.

References

Eodice, Michele. 2003. "Breathing Lessons, *or Collaboration is. . ..*" In *The Center Will Hold: Critical Perspectives on Writing Center Scholarship*, edited by Michael A. Pemberton and Joyce Kinkead, 114–29. Logan: Utah State University Press.
Geller, Anne Ellen, Michele Eodice, Frankie Condon, Meg Carroll, and Elizabeth Boquet. 2007. *The Everyday Writing Center: A Community of Practice*. Logan: Utah State University Press.
Gladstein, Jill M., and Dara Rossman Regaignon. 2012. *Writing Program Administration at Small Liberal Arts Colleges*. Anderson, SC: Parlor.
Haviland, Carolyn Peterson, Carmen M. Fye, and Richard Colby. 2001. "The Politics of Administrative and Physical Location." In *The Politics of Writing Centers*, edited by Jane Nelson and Kathy Evertz, 85–98. Portsmouth, NH: Heinemann.

Ianetta, Melissa. 2013. "What Is an English Department?" In *A Rhetoric of Writing Program Administrators*, edited by Rita Malenczyk, 359–70. Anderson, SC: Parlor.

Kramer, Tereza. 2016. "'Writing Circles': Combining Peer Review, Commitment, and Gentle Guidance." *WLN: A Journal of Writing Center Scholarship* 40 (7–8): 20–27.

Macauley, William J., and Nicholas Mauriello. 2007. "An Invitation to the 'Ongoing Conversation.'" In *Marginal Words, Marginal Work? Tutoring the Academy in the Work of Writing Centers*, edited by William J. Macauley and Nicholas Mauriello, xiii–xvi. Cresskill, NJ: Hampton.

Weiser, Irwin. 2013. "What Are The Administration and The Budget? (And Why Are We Talking about Them Together?)." In *A Rhetoric of Writing Program Administrators*, edited by Rita Malenczyk, 252–64. Anderson, SC: Parlor.

14
THERE AND BACK AGAIN, SORT OF
Returning as WPA (and Preparing to Leave)

Chris Warnick

British continuing education researchers Trevor Hussey and Patrick Smith define transitions as "significant change[s] in a student's life, self-concept and learning: a shift from one state of understanding, development and maturity to another. . . . Some may be planned while others emerge; some will be predicted while others are not" (Hussey and Smith 2010, 156). Drawing on this understanding of transitions, Hussey and Smith theorize that one way to address changes in higher education brought on by increased access is to redesign curricula and assessments so they meet students' needs at important moments of transition. For instance, they recommend increasing the number of formative assessments and revisiting the academic calendar so students are not confronted right away with transitions for which they are likely unprepared (161–62). Such changes are beneficial, they argue, because "the process of successful transition needs careful and successful management over the whole length of the degree programme" (159).

Hussey and Smith's ideas about students' transitions, and the management of these transitions, relate to my situation as someone who has recently returned to program administration. After years of serving in an ill-defined and uncompensated administrative job and a short period of performing no official administrative work, I am almost two years into coordinating this same institution's first-year writing program, this time in an official manner with clear responsibilities and compensation. Returning to WPA work after having left it for a time has significantly changed my life and sense of identity, for both good and bad. Being able to perform administrative work with support has improved my teaching, as I now have a better sense of our program as a whole and how my pedagogy fits within it, but the greater administrative responsibilities

DOI: 10.7330/9781607326335.c014

have moved my scholarship further away from the historical work I was trained in and make me question my scholarly identity. While my transition back into administration was planned, it resulted in transitions I did not expect, as I will explain in more detail later. Most important, returning to administration has made me more aware that transitions occur repeatedly and that one of the challenges of being a WPA is to successfully manage the push and pull of these multiple transitions.

This chapter tells my story of returning to make two broader points about writing program administration. The first is that WPAs, like the students Hussey and Smith discuss, make multiple transitions throughout their careers—a point that seems obvious but is somewhat obscured by the narratives told about program administration. For instance, many of the narratives included in popular collections such as *The Promise and Perils of Writing Program Administration* (Enos and Borrowman 2008) and *Kitchen Cooks, Plate Twirlers and Troubadours* (George 1999) emphasize beginnings, whether in narratives about new or about experienced WPAs (see, for example, Enchelmayer 2008; Fulwiler 2008; Penard 1999). Other narratives stress leaving an administrative position or life after being a WPA (Hesse 2005; Hodges 2008; Weaver 2008). As recent research makes clear, the narratives we tell have consequences, whether the stories are about attitudes toward junior WPA work (Charlton et al. 2011; Stolley 2015) or the field's knowledge about the experiences of WPAs of color (Craig 2016). In the situation I write about here, narratives' emphasis on either starting or leaving an administrative position may obscure for current and future WPAs the transitions that happen between beginning and exiting, leaving them unprepared for these changes.

The second point this essay makes, following Hussey and Smith, is that these multiple transitions must be managed for WPAs to be successful. I theorize literacy brokering, a concept borrowed from new literacy studies, as a professional identity that can help WPAs negotiate and prepare for these multiple transitions. According to Deborah Brandt (1998), literacy brokers, who are "neither rich nor powerful enough to sponsor literacy on [their] own terms" (183), act as go-betweens in literacy exchanges. Literacy brokers "bridge linguistic, cultural, and textual divides for others" (Perry 2009, 256). These definitions of literacy brokering describe the situation many WPAs face, especially at institutions such as mine, where tenured faculty in literature and other areas teach first-year writing and where the department chair makes final decisions about hiring, transfer credit, and other matters. We stand between literacy's buyers and sellers, the departmental or university administration and faculty, when we make hiring recommendations but lack the power to hire faculty on our own. We stand between a different set of buyers and sellers, students and the admissions office, when negotiating transfer and placement policy. We bridge linguistic, cultural, and textual divides when we train new faculty or run writing-across-the-curriculum workshops.

The remainder of this essay develops these two points by focusing on key transitions that occurred to this point in my administrative career: returning to coordinate the program in an official capacity and transitioning into my second year as coordinator with more experience and training. I also briefly touch on an important future transition I have begun planning for: namely, my exit. To substantiate my claims about the literacy broker as a viable identity for WPAs at times of transition, I explain how the values involved in literacy brokering helped me find solutions to problems I faced at these moments of transition. This essay contributes to recent scholarship connecting writing program administration and literacy studies, including research by Linda Adler-Kassner (2008), who argues that questions about students' literacies are at the center of writing program administration (27), and Elizabeth Boquet (2015), who draws on Brandt's notion of literacy sponsorship to reflect on her "institutional literacy biography" (95). Most important, my aim is to provide new and experienced WPAs across institutional contexts with a strategy they can use to construct identities that allow them to successfully negotiate the varied transitions they face.

RETURNING TO A NEW WPA ROLE

This section recounts my version of the institutional history leading up to the position I currently occupy, which contextualizes my departure from and return to program administration. In addition, it draws on Ligia Mihut's (2014) research on literacy brokering, particularly her idea of interruption, to propose one way the metaphor of literacy brokering can assist WPAs in transition, especially WPAs entering institutions where program administration is new or WPAs negotiating transitions that have emotional consequences. Being able to leverage in a productive way the emotional labor involved in writing administration is crucial because, as Laura Micciche (2007) observes, "WPAs find themselves immersed daily in anger, frustration, and disappointment" (74). As the experience I write about here illustrates, the metaphor of literacy brokering can be a powerful tool to help WPAs negotiate the emotions involved in crucial transitions.

Even though I recently became my department's inaugural first-year writing coordinator, this transition marked a return to WPA work since I had served as a quasi-WPA after joining the college as an assistant professor ten years ago. (For clarity's sake, I refer to my current position as coordinator and my previous position as committee chair.) For six years, I served on the department's First-Year Writing Committee, which made major changes during the time I served on it. We overhauled the required first-year writing curriculum, cutting it from two semesters to one and revising it from a writing-about-literature curriculum to one focused on academic discourse. We toughened our placement policy, raising the AP score required for exemption and eliminating a previous policy that allowed students to earn writing credit for AP literature exam scores. We designed a staff syllabus for new faculty, began conducting authentic program assessment, and successfully proposed and implemented a number of other initiatives, including a faculty mentoring program and student writing awards. Yet despite all these gains, as committee chair I served in a quasi-WPA capacity, or what David Schwalm (2008) would call a "task" rather than a "position" (10) because, in addition to there being no compensation for this work, the job's official responsibilities and reporting structure were not defined.

In many respects, though, there was a lot that was new about the WPA role I returned to as coordinator. First and foremost was that I was now occupying an actual position, which included a stipend, travel funding, a course reassignment, and official responsibilities. With this new title and compensation came powers and responsibilities I did not have before: observing adjunct faculty's teaching, interviewing prospective adjunct faculty, making hiring recommendations to the department chair, coordinating with stakeholders across campus. I was also at a new place in my career when I began as coordinator, having earned tenure and been away from WPA work for two years. So while I was confident stepping back into WPA work given my prior experience, I was also reminded of Heraclitus's famous words, "No man ever steps into the same river twice."

For me, the most significant issue at stake when I returned was how to negotiate the history that led to the coordinator role being created. Part of this negotiation had to do with my own personal experiences with this history as well as the belief that, as Shirley Rose (2013) expresses it, "a WPA will always need to understand the past of his or her writing program in order to make good decisions about leading the program in its future direction" (241). The department debated whether to have an official WPA off and on for over eleven years before finally approving the coordinator role I now occupy. The duration of this debate, combined with my sense that not everyone was on board despite the unanimous vote, gave me the impression I would need to deal with some unresolved history when I transitioned into my first year as coordinator. I had an advantage because I had participated in some of this history, but I was unsure how to win over silent skeptics since the conversation about hiring an official WPA began before I was hired. As someone who in graduate school specialized in archival histories of writing pedagogy, I was acutely aware I was missing information about the debate's beginnings, a key piece of the puzzle that would allow me to align my values with those who might remain on the fence about a WPA.

Fortunately, colleagues shared with me committee reports, meeting minutes, and other documents that shed light on the department's early efforts to hire a WPA. According to these records, the debate started when the department crafted the job description for the tenure-track line in composition and rhetoric I would eventually inhabit. The original draft of the advertisement simply asked for a comp/rhet PhD to teach first-year and advanced composition. A tenured literature specialist suggested the advertisement be revised to explicitly ask for a writing program administrator. For reasons not entirely clear, the motion was not approved; however, this debate about the job advertisement led the department to hold a series of meetings over the next year to discuss the possibility of creating a formal WPA position. These meetings began with the Freshman English Committee (as the department's writing committee was then called) proposing the department appoint a director who would conduct ongoing faculty development, carry out program assessments, and review syllabi and teaching portfolios. The proposal further suggested that the director earn two course releases per semester (teaching a 2/2 load), a summer stipend, and additional travel funds. After being debated and revised for a year, the proposal failed due to concerns over workload, administrative oversight, and the lack of a program to oversee. Course releases were hard to come by at the time, so a two-course release per semester was read by some as exorbitant. Faculty additionally argued that there was no actual program for a director to oversee since the department had two loosely defined required writing courses. The most widespread concern, though, seemed to be administrative oversight. The particular phrase that comes up over and over again in e-mails and other documents is the director "turning into a monster."

Transitioning into my first year as coordinator, I also realized some of the history I needed to deal with was my own. In other words, the debate within the department I was privy to left me with unresolved personal issues necessary for me to address if I hoped to do my job well. For one, after earning tenure, I stopped volunteering to serve as committee chair. By refusing to continue as quasi-WPA, I hoped to kick-start efforts in the department to formalize a WPA position; however, I prepared myself for the painful process of watching what gains the program had made recede or languish, as it was likely the future chair of the committee would not be a composition specialist. The gamble paid off in that the department did soon afterwards formalize the position, but the conversation began awkwardly. For instance, another composition specialist and I were inadvertently not included in an e-mail chain about formally proposing a coordinator, so the first time we saw the proposal was a few days before a department meeting. We felt blindsided because we assumed we would be consulted beforehand given our status as disciplinary experts and because we were the most likely candidates for the position. During the meeting, we found ourselves in the awkward position of speaking against the proposal as written because it was vague about the coordinator's responsibilities, powers, and qualifications. This miscommunication, among other factors, prompted one of my composition colleagues, who is also among my best friends as well as someone I collaborate with on research, to leave and take a job elsewhere.

I was personally devastated by my friend's departure, and I was mad that the debate within the department had grown toxic enough that it had led to my colleague's leaving. Despite this, I decided to help the committee rewrite the proposal and eventually put my name up for coordinator because I derive a lot of meaning from administrative work and wanted to accomplish the work I set out to do when I first joined the department. I still harbored a great deal of anger, though, while simultaneously feeling guilty, as if my decision to stay on was a betrayal of my friend. Although I did not yet know how to deal with these emotions, I knew I would need to get beyond them to successfully transition to becoming coordinator.

Approaching my professional identity in terms of literacy brokering is what eventually helped me address the challenge of managing my emotions. Ligia Mihut's research illustrates the complex role emotions play in literacy brokering. In her interviews with literacy brokers who help Romanian immigrants navigate the US citizenship process, Mihut observes how these literacy brokers are emotionally invested in their work, which is evident in the affective language they use to describe particular cases and experiences. However, Mihut (2014) interprets such emotion

> as a moment of interruption; it is not marked by an external gesture or an actual intervention of help, yet it represents a significant point of

institutional critique. Generally and most of the times, there is no room for "help" in a court proceeding. But sometimes there are moments of empathy similar to [a literacy broker's] feeling (bad) for and with his clients. While these moments do not dismantle the institutional structure, they do offer points of critique. They also profess that brokers are more than instruments, even in an institutional context that regiments people's discursive practices through patterns of communication. (68–69)

This perspective of emotion as critical interruption Mihut offers here helped me manage my feelings of anger and guilt to a point at which I was eventually able to work with the department on moving into the coordinator job and making important improvements to the program in my first year. For instance, immediately after the department meeting where I learned my colleague and I were mistakenly not included in the committee's discussion about the initial coordinator proposal, I met with the department chair and told him we as a department needed to resolve the emotional toll of this meeting before we could move on. It was clear to me during this conversation that the chair wanted nothing to do with a resolution process—and understandably so. Department meetings are not designed to produce catharsis. Thus, I no longer outwardly expressed my feelings about how the debate played out to anyone who would listen; instead, I used my anger about a lack of transparency to successfully recommend adjunct representation be added to the First-Year Writing Committee's work. While this move did not "dismantle the institutional structure," it moved the program one step further while also allowing me to deal productively with the emotions that remained from the department's debate to appoint a coordinator.

BECOMING A SOPHOMORE-YEAR WPA AND PREPARING TO LEAVE

Seeing my administrative self as a literacy broker has additionally helped me negotiate unexpected transitions after my first year on the job and prepare for future transitions important for the program's and my own well-being. What has made literacy brokering such a valuable metaphor for me to live by in these situations is that it keeps me focused on the stakeholders' interests rather than my own. It reminds me that my job as WPA is to "bridge linguistic, cultural, and textual divides for others" (Perry 2009, 256), not to serve my own interests. As I discuss in this section, this attitude has smoothed my transition into becoming a more experienced WPA in my second year, a time when it has been particularly tempting to prioritize my own agenda. It has also prompted me to begin preparing now for exiting the job responsibly.

At the time of this writing, I am starting my second year as coordinator, which has been a time of unexpected transitions. I recently returned from the four-day CWPA summer workshop for new WPAs, which profoundly transformed my administrative knowledge and practices. Before attending the workshop, I struggled to communicate with deans and other administrators higher up the chain, but the skills the workshop taught me about identifying stakeholders' values, aligning the program's values with those of stakeholders, and framing messages gave me the confidence I had previously been missing. The workshop taught me how to construct a clear and manageable action plan, which I had not yet done because I had been too focused on managing the everyday issues that came up—resolving complaints, evaluating transfer credit, and so on. In short, I saw myself as a novice during my first year as coordinator, but now I feel as if I have shed this novice label. I have even had the chance to try out this now more experienced administrative self on others, having recently used the communication practices I learned in the workshop to discuss our writing courses with the honors dean, in the process gaining an unexpected ally in our writing-across-the-curriculum efforts.

I get the sense that my chair and the department similarly no longer see me as a novice because I am getting pressure to make significant changes to the program now. For the past three years, we have been conducting writing assessment as part of the college's broader outcomes assessment of general education. The results from these assessments consistently reveal that students perform below expectations when it comes to articulating clear analytical arguments and integrating sources, two of our general education goals. Understandably, faculty, members of the assessment committee, and other stakeholders have asked me to begin making big changes that could improve students' scores: to revise the outcomes, to rewrite the "signature assignment" used in the assessment, and to revise the staff syllabus to correspond with changes made to the signature assignment. Part of my new, more confident, post-CWPA-workshop self was tempted to begin doing this work myself—retooling the curriculum around a writing-about-writing pedagogy, for example—since it would be easier and the department seems to be giving me the green light.

After the lengthy debate to create the coordinator position, I did not expect the chair and other stakeholders within the department to begin giving me such free rein. Thinking as a literacy broker, though, I knew if I took the freedom offered me, not only would whatever assessment and curriculum reforms I made fail, but my transition from novice to more experienced WPA would likely fail as well. Assessment results would likely stagnate or worsen since faculty would still be responsible for delivering a curriculum they did not help develop; increased frustration over these results would likely erode whatever new authority I had gained after my first year. Armed with this insight, I instead persuaded the chair and others who wanted change right away to conduct a year-long research project and series of workshops, using dynamic criteria mapping (Broad 2003), to determine what we as a department truly value and to collectively revise our outcomes, assignments, and rubric based on these values.

Having left and returned to different WPA positions at the same institution, I am more mindful about a transition I will have to face again in the future: leaving the position when the time comes. When I stopped volunteering for committee service the first time around, I was thinking in part about the program, but I mostly stepped down for my own self-preservation, which I tell myself was the right decision at the time. But I realize I want to avoid leaving in a similar fashion this time around since the program will hopefully be in a much better place and the consequences of an abrupt departure could be more consequential. From reading narratives of ex-WPAs, I also worry about experiencing the very understandable trauma and sense of loss that can come from stepping down. Elizabeth Hodges (2008), for instance, writes that after twelve years of administrative work, the chair's decision to not appoint her as director caused her to feel as if "someone very close ha[d] died. And to be honest," she admits, "Parts of me ha[d]" (236). Another concern I have about exiting, when the time comes, is how to avoid leaving behind a program strongly associated with me personally, thus compromising the sustainability of the program and making the new coordinator's transition that much more difficult.

Although I have not yet worked out the exact moves I will make to avoid this problem, this is another transition I expect the metaphor of literacy brokering to help me think through. As Hodges (2008) points out in her narrative about not being appointed director, "I believe that such a context coupled with too much sense of identity as a designated holder of knowledge about teaching writing can be dangerous" (236). This insight is what I see as the chief value of the literacy-brokering metaphor: it prevents me from letting that part of me who is a writing expert take over my identity. Thinking of myself less as the go-to writing person on campus, and more as someone who assists with figuring out the values about writing campus wide and how these values align with broader cultural values about writing, will allow our program to run as a "community of practice" made up of individuals with different viewpoints "engaged in the generative process of producing [our] own future" (Lave and Wenger 1991, 57–8). Building such a community will allow me to avoid the danger Hodges writes about, better ensure the program's sustainability, and manage my identity.

While the narratives in this chapter are, to some extent, specific to my institutional context, the transitions described here are ones most WPAs, no matter their context, face. All WPAs confront the histories of their writing programs as they enter. All WPAs, provided they are in the job long enough, move from being the new or interim WPA to the experienced WPA. As Margaret Weaver (2008) bravely writes, all WPAs will at one point leave: "WPAs are always faced with the risk of becoming ex-WPAs—even if we consider ourselves 'lifers'" (287). How WPAs face these transitions differs across contexts, of course. But WPAs, just like our students, must successfully negotiate the multiple transitions that occur throughout their careers. The metaphor of literacy brokering is important because it brings together the field's values about literacy with its best practices concerning administration and furthermore provides a metaphor other WPAs can draw from to construct identities that help them successfully manage the multiple transitions they face now and in the future.

References

Adler-Kassner, Linda. 2008. *The Activist WPA: Changing Stories about Writing and Writers.* Logan: Utah State University Press.

Boquet, Elizabeth. 2015. "What Remains and What Sustains: Companions in Mission, Colleagues in Action, WPAs for Life." *WPA: Writing Program Administration* 39 (1): 94–108.

Brandt, Deborah. 1998. "Sponsors of Literacy." *College Composition and Communication* 49 (2): 165–85. https://doi.org/10.2307/358929.

Broad, Bob. 2003. *What We Really Value: Beyond Rubrics in Teaching and Assessing Writing.* Logan: Utah State University Press.

Charlton, Colin, Jonikka Charlton, Tarez Samra Graban, Kathleen J. Ryan, and Amy Ferdinandt Stolley. 2011. *GenAdmin: Theorizing WPA Identities in the Twenty-First Century.* Anderson, SC: Parlor.

Craig, Sherri. 2016. "A Story-less Generation: Emergent WPAs of Color and the Loss of Identity through Absent Narratives." *WPA: Writing Program Administration* 39 (2): 16–20.

Enchelmayer, Ernest J. 2008. "Sharing WPA Perils as Pearls of Wisdom." In *The Promise and Perils of Writing Program Administration*, edited by Theresa Enos and Shane Borrowman, 49–57. Anderson, SC: Parlor.

Enos, Theresa, and Shane Borrowman, eds. 2008. *The Promise and Perils of Writing Program Administration.* Anderson, SC: Parlor.

Fulwiler, Megan. 2008. "Notes from a New WPA." In *The Promise and Perils of Writing Program Administration*, edited by Theresa Enos and Shane Borrowman, 92–101. Anderson, SC: Parlor.

George, Diana. 1999. *Kitchen Cooks, Plate Twirlers and Troubadours: Writing Program Administrators Tell Their Stories*. Portsmouth, NH: Boynton/Cook.

Hesse, Doug. 2005. "Not Even Joint Custody: Notes from an Ex-WPA." *College Composition and Communication* 56 (3): 501–7.

Hodges, Elizabeth. 2008. "At the Pleasure of the Chair: A Cautionary Tale from the Private Side of a Public Story." In *The Promise and Perils of Writing Program Administration*, edited by Theresa Enos and Shane Borrowman, 225–37. Anderson, SC: Parlor.

Hussey, Trevor, and Patrick Smith. 2010. "Transitions in Higher Education." *Innovations in Education and Teaching International* 47 (2): 155–64. https://doi.org/10.1080/14703 291003718893.

Lave, Jean, and Etienne Wenger. 1991. *Situated Learning: Legitimate Peripheral Participation*. Cambridge, MA: Cambridge University Press. https://doi.org/10.1017/CBO97805 11815355.

Micciche, Laura R. 2007. *Doing Emotion: Rhetoric, Writing, Teaching*. Portsmouth, NH: Heinemann.

Mihut, Ligia. 2014. "Literacy Brokers and the Emotional Work of Mediation." *Literacy in Composition Studies* 2 (1): 57–79. doi:http://dx.doi.org/10.21623%2F1.2.1.4.

Penard, Mary. 1999. "Surviving the Honeymoon: Bliss and Anxiety in a WPA's First Year, or Appreciating the Plate Twirler's Art." In *Kitchen Cooks, Plate Twirlers and Troubadours: Writing Program Administrators Tell Their Stories*, edited by Diana George, 56–62. Portsmouth, NH: Heinemann.

Perry, Kristen H. 2009. "Genres, Contexts, and Literacy Practices: Literacy Brokering Among Sudanese Refugee Families." *Reading Research Quarterly* 44 (3): 256–76. https://doi.org/10.1598/RRQ.44.3.2.

Rose, Shirley K. 2013. "What Is Writing Program History?" In *A Rhetoric for Writing Program Administrators*, edited by Rita Malenczyk, 239–51. Anderson, SC: Parlor.

Schwalm, David. 2008. "The Writing Program (Administrator) in Context: Where Am I, and Can I Still Behave Like a Faculty Member?" In *The Longman Sourcebook for Writing Program Administrators*, edited by Irene Ward and William J. Carpenter, 9–22. New York: Pearson.

Stolley, Amy Ferdinandt. 2015. "Narratives, Administrative Identity, and the Early Career WPA." *WPA: Writing Program Administration* 39 (1): 18–31.

Weaver, Margaret E. 2008. "Identity Theft of a Writing Center Director: The New Art of Academic Punishment." In *The Promise and Perils of Writing Program Administration*, edited by Theresa Enos and Shane Borrowman, 273–89. Anderson, SC: Parlor.

SECTION 4

Disruption and Activism

15
REVOLVING DOORS AND SETTLED LOCKS
Staying Put in an Undesirable Place

Sarah Stanley

The field of writing program administration has changed drastically in the last twenty years. The collaborative book *GenAdmin* voices a twenty-first-century philosophy in which one can think and act like a WPA with or without the job title (Charlton et al. 2011). Rather than "earning" or being "deemed" WPA, graduate students now choose to identify with the act of WPA-ing, an act removed from institutional locale or material conditions. This growth means more supply to fit more demand, an economy that enables choice about where one *does* WPA, and for how long. The authors assert that GenAdmin, as a philosophy, is a "twenty-first century" response to earlier WPA scholarship. In their rereading of the field's history, they frame earlier scholarship preceding them as "lore," showing the reader how the construct of the strategic agent, acting alone, operates in a binary discourse of hero/victim.

Having neither learned nor fully acquired the literacy of a WPA, I tell my stories of transition from outside the discourse of GenAdmin. I turn toward these hero/victim narratives of the WPA, finding critiques of the narrative's representation compelling and the storying familiar, meanwhile also finding the "old guard" mapping generally onto my experiences (Charlton et al. 2011, 38). Now, thanks to GenAdmin theory, my material positioning *outside* the WPA discussion helps me make a contribution to the field's scholarship, as my outsiderness prompts me to notice a focal point—the role of place in our careers. Whether we stay or go can detract from cultivating writers and writing in places that need it. I wish to encourage, as others have, the radical nature of staying put—because electing to try, acquire, and learn impacts places, and writing may only truly "flourish" when the WPA is trusted (Charlton et al. 2011, 194–99).

DOI: 10.7330/9781607326335.c015

REVOLVING DOORS

> *The reality is that the very best WPAs often move ahead in the power structure at their institutions, becoming department chairs, deans, provosts, directors of honors programs, and so on. Hence the position of WPA may be a revolving door. At my school, we have found ourselves several times without a writing program director as promotions drew our good people away to other jobs. We have had to, sometimes for an entire year, foist the job off on either vulnerable tenure-track faculty or lecturers who were marginally prepared for the task.*
> —Christine Hult, "Politics Redux"

Hult's (1995) "revolving door" (51) connects two locations: a horizon for the exiting WPA, as Hult assumes upward mobility, and, for the replacement, a temporary burden or trap. On the opportunity horizon, since Hult's foreshadowing of the discipline's "revolving door," the idea of a WPA has risen in notoriety. As Cristyn L. Elder, Megan Schoen, and Ryan Skinnell point out, "Greater numbers of rhetoric and composition graduates are being produced every year, thereby reducing the 'everyone has to do it' nature of the job" (Elder, Schoen, and Skinnell 2014, 14). As professionalization in the forms of dissertations, graduate courses, and WPA scholarship grows, more and more WPA transportable expertise becomes attractive, especially to those institutions already in the know. Joseph Harris reflects the burden-trap view of the WPA office in certain locales when he balances his argument about institutional conditions mattering: "And I also suspect that there may be many situations, many programs, that it might be better *not* to step into" (Charlton et al. 2011, 208) That is, some doors you want to stay away from.

To decide where *not* to step is a provocative caveat. In Harris's comment, I note how the legitimacy this discourse has constructed for the field also creates a role for a WPA with market power to select location and determine what places and institutions they end up at, and that legitimacy necessarily marks some places, institutions, and students as undesirable. For example, after I said yes to the job in Fairbanks, Alaska, as the director of composition, I received plenty of advice from experienced colleagues, including new ones I met through the title itself. In these dialogues, I came away with a couple of observations, including hints that I might have chosen a toxic environment; that I should not remain in my position for more than five years max; and that my first attempt should be to get a WPA evaluator report. We were able to secure a WPA evaluator report, and this institutional document is an example of the larger organizational effects coming about directly because of the professional WPA field. However, the advice to not stay more than five years still resonates, as I took the position in a state where teacher turnover in rural areas especially is a serious problem.

Occasional turnover can be a sign of healthy renewal in a place; however, a pattern of administrative turnover for the WPA position carries unintended consequences for a place's people. If leaving happens sporadically and occasionally, people and places can recover. However, when early exits become a pattern in a place, the effects of each early exit are negative and far from temporary for the people left behind. As WPAs, we should actively resist the idea of becoming the "jet-setter academic" or the "tenure-track temp admin" who uses one place to reach another. If motivation is to create change, how can we work toward change with one foot out the door, looking for opportunities elsewhere?

While much empirical organizational research has identified factors in a new faculty member's "intent to leave," a qualitative study in the *Journal of Higher Education* applied sensemaking theory to learn more about the specific explanations circulating at a research institution (O'Meara, Lounder, and Campbell 2014). A place is left because there is a better place, a heaven; or, a place is left because the place they work is hell. Such explanations connect to a prestige hierarchy in higher education, and these "status and prestige orientations" were found to be more frequently referenced as influencing early departure from the perspective of the people left behind, more so than proximity to family, for example. As Kerry-Ann O'Meara, Andrew Lounder, and Corbin M. Campbell argue, reasoning based on prestige or status can displace institutional responsibility to retain faculty. One such organizational story is the exit story, particularly the exit of a colleague from an undesirable institution. Regarding faculty departure, the authors state that "the ways in which individuals will seek to understand departure will be nested in their own professional identity and experienced contexts" (O'Meara, Lounder, and Campbell 2014, 609).

At the same time, such reasoning can "absolve the university and the administrator of any responsibility for faculty departure. Both explanations are framed such that the faculty member's decision to leave is interpreted as independent of the quality of work climate, leadership, mentoring, or any other environmental factors shown to influence faculty departure and other key faculty outcomes such as productivity and satisfaction" (O'Meara, Lounder, and Campbell 2014, 628). I point out this analytical finding to complicate my argument for staying put in an undesirable place. How can the field, and we, as people who live the tenets of our field, apply the radical nature of staying put in a manner that does not, in turn, make the position of WPA a doormat rather than one that stops a revolving door?

MAKING SENSE OF DOORS

A WPA transition—a door—is an opportunity for place-based storytelling, or "sensemaking" in a place (O'Meara, Lounder, and Campbell 2014). Micciche entails a door metaphor when she examines the materiality of James Berlin's doorstop, currently in use in her WPA office at the University of Cincinnati (Micciche 2011, 30–31). Doors are transitions. They can be open, closed, slightly ajar, locked, removed, or forced open. Since doors enable locational transitions, they are an apt symbol for how our postmodern identities participate in locational choices. I choose the door because a door is a situational, emplaced image (Middleton et al. 2015). While a door certainly *can* facilitate a crossing over, often, a door is locked.

Any professional who is privileged to decide where they step will ultimately not bring about institutional change for students *any*where, only *some*where. Recognizing this power, I find the idea of "sensibility," as Matthew Heard (2012) explains, a rhetorical concept in step with ethos; sensibility "describes a constant, focused attention to the decisions that we make and the consequences that these decisions generate" (Heard 2012, 38). Karl Wieck (1995) theorizes the rhetorical action of sensemaking, stating that "it is literally just what it says it is" (Wieck 1995, 16). Weick develops seven properties of sensemaking, and they begin with identity construction. This process is explained through the image of the mirror, and the experiences in which a person notices their self-reflection in the interactions with social others who impart judgment can "affect individual interpretations and actions, which can then diffuse and have much larger organizational effects" (Wieck 1995, 22).

Next, I offer my story of transition as a narrative of drawing from door imagery. I offer this WPA literacy narrative to motivate more graduate students to not only theorize the WPA activist discourse but to also apply it: choose undesirable places and commit to them as a career move, all the while as you engage with and build community. I believe in curricular change to make room for opportunities to professionalize, whatever the field. Yet, I was not aware of the WPA identity when I took the job. Perhaps had I been, I might not have stayed because I would have interpreted my experiences through the lens of a professional discourse that would have prompted me to look elsewhere for my career.

CLOSED DOORS

> December 2009. I remember being in my western Massachusetts apartment when I called my family in Kansas with the news I had a phone interview scheduled for the first day I'd be back to visit during winter break. Their first question: "Is it closer to us than Massachusetts?"
> "Well no . . . it's further . . ."

My father, with whom I'd discussed many of my prospective applications, interrupted: "Is it Fairbanks?"

It was Fairbanks. The job was an administrative role—director of composition. "Don't worry, I won't get it," I remember repeating to my family at each stage of the process—the application, the phone interview, the campus visit.

The teaching demonstration for the job, which I performed in February, was to a packed room. Along with students, there was a hiring committee of five, as well as whoever else wished to attend. I had asked for the course syllabus and the agenda for the day, reflecting an ethical position I hold still: students are not guinea pigs for a job-search candidate to use and exploit as an audience. The graduate-student teacher's readings were just as removed from the classroom I'd envisioned as I'd soon feel inside that classroom as a white woman in a fancy interview blazer, seeking buy-in from students in rugged brown Carhartt pants. My demo included these instructions: Listen to one another's stories of Alaska life, then retell another's story to some other student. Rather than just repeating it, translate the story—first in a picture, then in a metaphor. Share the end results with all of us.

Stories emerged: about healing soldiers in Afghanistan, an eagle knocking a young man off a motorcycle, a moose trapping a young woman in a car for so long she fell asleep. I could really listen to these stories, and the class was able to engage through their resulting images and metaphors.

I was told my teaching got me the job. Two Alaska Native students had shared what they drew in response to the lesson; these students hadn't previously said a word in the class. I asked about the middle-aged man who'd challenged me directly, who wanted me to tell him what I thought he should learn and our explicit purpose. In fact, the committee said, they particularly liked how open and comfortable I was in response. Our students can be challenging, they said. And further, more students had participated than was typical; the demo's increased attention simply led to more engagement than usual.

As I recounted my teaching story to friends, I began to construct more reasons to want the job in Alaska: I had found my teaching edge there and would become a better instructor. Here was a compelling reason to move so far away—I wished to grow as a teacher in a land of extremes, where people can be humbled by adventures they experience, or read about in the paper, or hear from students. Certainly no place is easy, but Fairbanks could be formative.

March. Our car slowed, exiting the New York turnpike, heading toward Buffalo for a visit with friends. I reached for my phone to help navigate and noticed a missed call. A message from UAF's interim dean of CLA, and later my colleague in the English department, with a job offer. My heart beat faster—*How could this be? What should I say? How would I say no?*

"Don't mention it, okay?" I asked my boyfriend. I said I thought it would be a distraction from our weekend. I didn't want to anticipate a stereotypical, what-if talk about Alaska. More honestly, I didn't want to think about whether I was qualified or ready for such administrative responsibilities; about how Nate might not want to go along; about how I feared loneliness; about how this decision might continue to haunt me either way. I felt overwhelmed. I felt guilty for applying for the job in the first place.

By the end of the weekend, we began to discuss it. We agreed, eventually, that it was a unique opportunity: why not? We shipped a few things and packed the car with the rest. We would begin our move six weeks before my contract date, needing to arrange, on the way, our wedding in Kansas, a return flight to Massachusetts to defend my dissertation, and a family funeral; these were times of significant transition.

April. In the haste of finishing my teacher-research dissertation, I wrote an e-mail as a quick reply to the existing composition director at UAF, who'd forwarded me a request from the graduate-student teachers. The e-mail is an artifact I saved for direction. I needed the dialogue in order to capture my vision, and it was also the only chance before starting the job for me to articulate a vision for myself as an administrator. I remember writing this—I was sitting at my kitchen table and it was a rainy afternoon.

> . . . As to your questions, there will be no more requirements/restrictions in my first year. It is really important for me to learn from what's happening already and observe as many classes as I can and think about things prior to "implementing" change. So, I'm going to do the best job I can next semester working with what is already happening. Order the book you want, though, you might consider the cost for students (as in is this something that you could just order more of, so that there would be used copies around for them). My long-term goal is for a local curriculum. One of the first things I want to do is start a curriculum committee where this will be our goal. If any of these current TAs are excited to be a part of "change" they should join the committee!

. . . I will be pushing for a lot of teacher reflection, a constant awareness and attention to different styles of learning and being in a classroom, and also, from my experience teaching, ways to think about constructing teacher authority in a manner that enhances student learning but also helps the new teachers negotiate alongside their students in the choices they make with writing.

July–August. Nate drove us through Canada, to Fairbanks. Having left an early career in publishing to teach a few courses in technical writing as an adjunct teacher for the UAF English department, he used his extra time him to make some of the furniture for our home and to strengthen his cooking skills. He decided to pursue another degree using tuition benefits from my job. These decisions, in part, allowed me the time I needed to experience the successes and failures that continued to give my life meaning.

SETTLED LOCKS

> *I remember that room was always well-lit, warm, and welcoming when I entered from those dark, Arctic days and heard the steady hum of involved discussions. That writing center, entrusted to me for three years because no one else wanted it, flourished because it was staffed by graduate students who already trusted themselves as writers.*
> —Wendy Bishop "Writing from the Tips of Our Tongues"

Wendy Bishop was the University of Alaska Fairbanks's first WPA—a graduate-student WPA in fact. I imagine she entered through the same door I did. My office is also in the writing center, still staffed by graduate students who identify as writers. But now, thirty years later, I'm searching for signs of her work, not unlike the way James Berlin's doorstop has motivated Laura Micciche (Micciche 2011, 30–31). Since Bishop's exit from the University of Alaska Fairbanks almost thirty years ago,[1] the school's writing vision had not changed. The field of writing administration, however, has changed drastically. I find a few references to Fairbanks in several essays and articles by Bishop and references to her collaborative visionary work in Florida (Bishop and Crossley 1996). Yet, I note the gap between 1989 and 2010, the year I was hired.

In the two decades before my hire, UAF's English department had made some concessions to make the WPA position more attractive, recognizing that, from the perspective of an institution like this one, the job market for a WPA was more competitive than it was for a specialist in literature. Meanwhile, I'd spent my time in a doctoral program in composition and rhetoric studying language ideologies and sentence-level choices. I showed a range of programmatic experience on my CV, including curricular design, collaborating on and teaching a basic writing curriculum, the scoring of placement essays, service on a diversity committee, and work as a research assistant to organize a conference on diversity and assessment; however, at the same time, I had no WPA coursework or formal training in administration in graduate school. I followed the advice from mentors to "cast a wide net" and applied for seventy jobs. I was an ABD candidate applying for an assistant/associate position directing composition at the flagship research institution of the University of Alaska system. I shared my programmatic experience in a cover letter responding to the job description. For a school that hadn't had writing expertise on its faculty for a decade, I imagine my placement, assessment, diversity, and grammar dissertation were appealing. I had, unknowingly, crafted a cover letter HR liked. So did the hiring committee. But I, a graduate student on the job market without administrative experience, was in disbelief. I wasn't trying to be dishonest, but the job search ended up with a mutual fit of applicant and place—neither living up to the job's potential.

Bishop's legacy is now an unlocked office door, unlocked for functional and metaphorical reasons. I leave my office door unlocked even when I'm not in my office. Occasionally, I arrive on campus to find my door is locked because someone else locked it. Sometimes I may be found outside my office, gently twisting and working the key to unlock the door to access the office. The building has settled, and the lock tells that story.

An office door is itself a daily opportunity to enable or to disable interaction and dialogue. Even with an open-door policy, people may slow roll a knock to announce an interruption since entering the office space means the person who sits in the office and the person who enters are both in need of something. The knock offers respect and recognition of a relationship. Recognizing "your door" and how you use it matters.

I learned about Bishop's impact during my first week in the job, when Carolyn, one of Bishop's former graduate students and now a long-time adjunct teacher, entered through my slightly open office door with a placement-policy question. A year later, after I had been asked to serve on the General Education Revitalization Committee, a colleague walked through that same door and slapped a thick bound document down on my desk—*thought you might find this interesting, I'd like it back, it's my only copy.* The thick document read, "Proposal for a Writing across the Curriculum Program at the University of Alaska, Fairbanks. Wendy S. Bishop. 1989."

Our department admin walked into my office and stated "I never saw her in winter boots." "Winter boots," I learned, was a sensemaking phrase applied to the third composition and rhetoric scholar who took the title of director of composition. "I see, but that was ten years ago." I learned the search that ended with my 2010 hire was the third attempt in three years. The year before, the search failed when no candidate agreed to the terms. A candidate the previous year had accepted the job to reverse course. Years before that, the position was rotated from newly hired esteemed colleague to newly hired esteemed colleague. Those years of failed searches were led by a capable, passionate person, not tenure track, who mentored graduate students but who also had vision that the position was not sustainable in the way it was being valued—as an afterthought, a role someone needed to play in the largest department in the college.

The term *winter boots* connects to other experiences I had, such as when I was given feedback about the coat I wore, or when I risked not appealing to the person who might use the office after me when I painted my office bright yellow. One aspect of story in an organization is that a story "enables people to talk about absent things and to connect them to present things in the interest of meaning" (Wieck 1995, 129). The politics of English had played out in Fairbanks in such a way that only one position in composition and rhetoric was available in a midsized English department. With a range of jobs to choose from, people highly qualified in writing program administration would likely not choose this, an isolated job in an isolated place. In such an atmosphere, attitudes can circulate about why people are here, why they stay, and what forces are contributing to their decisions. The organizational sensemaking about my identity amounts to more than these superficial observations and instead reveals deep issues of trust and even complex emotions of abandonment, the underbelly of community.

DOOR OPEN

> *I know that I need someone with more experience to help me pick the best books and to curb what might be an overly facile application of what I am learning. But I do believe that I need to make a start.*
> —Wendy Bishop, "Writing Is/and Therapy"

Right now, six years into my tenure-track position at the University of Alaska Fairbanks as director of university writing, I'm also proud to be a working part of a new local project aiming to grow 750 pounds of food for use in our downtown soup kitchen. Gardening is on my mind, and in my fingernails. So if our writing program is a garden, the director is more cultivator than harvester, and in this metaphor, I find motivation to persist (see Bishop 1988). In times of crisis, innovation can emerge, but it first needs cultivated ground. So I work to enrich the soil for future "flourishing" (Charlton et al. 2011), with further help from colleagues, graduate students, administrators, and fellow gardeners. My decision to occupy my role at the University of Alaska Fairbanks means not only that I now identify as a writing program administrator but also that I can engage with my location as a volunteer, a board member, and an activist. The practices I apply in this position are also present in my nonprofit work, as they are in my play at first base on my summer softball team. Where I fit within the field's conversations about the WPA as a position, pretenure or without graduate training, matters, but perhaps less than it does to where my feet hit the ground and the establishment of some roots. The WPA should be committed personally and professionally to where they live. Choosing a place to live, to settle, and to learn impacts whether or not writing studies can be a strategic means toward improving people's lives.

Doors are coparticipants in a WPA career because they enable locational boundaries. "Don't let the door hit you on your way out" is a rude expression people use in reference to quick departures. Being left in a place, rather than being the one who left, is also a position from which to theorize career transitions. And, given that the effect of writing program administrative turnover on the people and places left behind has only received parenthetical attention in WPA scholarship, from the perspective of the institution, an early exit from a WPA position prompts situated talk in which stories are exchanged about reasons that person left (Hult 1995)—narratives that continue to shape the place, despite a new person in that role. From the perspective of the leaver, personal reasons for leaving or for staying should always be among other considerations—including the reality that people are affected by whether or not you stay, as well as by the reasons you leave. My goal here has been to prompt deeper consideration of the reasons one has for committing to a WPA position because these reasons are as important as reasons for leaving.

Zooming out from my position within WPA discourse and briefly assuming a macroperspective, while GenAdmin philosophy foregrounds the harmful pretenure patronizing of the field, in the background are the disciplinary attitudes of places where such work is needed—places where new people struggle with settled locks. Consider Robin Gallaher's (2014) conclusion "that only-composition-scholar WPA positions have been considered undesirable and sometimes even viewed as a drain on efforts to professionalize writing program administration" (Gallaher 2014, 81). In fact, Gallaher's categorization of the "only-composition-scholar WPA position" from her dissertation at Indiana University of Pennsylvania provides descriptive, inclusive terminology for my own choices, as Gallaher works to capture institutional context. To further Gallaher's observations about trends in the field for a moment, we should reflect on how we might be unintentionally constructing tiers for graduate programs. Graduate students who are eager to work toward institutional change and social justice, no matter where they end up (thanks to people in institutions willing to provide them with the possibility doing such work), may appear "less than" or somehow evidence of the problem of the field's ongoing interest in burdening our scholarship with arguments about professionalization and legitimacy. So, while the GenAdmin argument generates many doors of opportunity for graduate students interested in WPA work, many doors will remain closed. What lies behind the revolving doors, where the views of people and places is intermittent because one may enter for a very short time? What about the students in these "undesirable" places? If we can critique students as being "undesirable" by any logic, isn't it inevitable we do the same for places and institutions? What about the work we do with administrators, students, and colleagues—graduate and undergraduate—who create an engaged, or problematic, infrastructure?

Marc Bousquet's (2002) critique of the so-called heroic WPA informs my argument. I'm focusing my critique on an organizational sensibility that encourages transition rather than staying put. I do so to put the focus on a particular kind of transformational discourse that follows or remains with these transitions. So, while I embrace working toward a "university without a WPA," I do not embrace a university without access to critical pedagogical literacy—and often this access comes to undesirable places by way of people. For example, as Tim Peeples (1999) explains, "Faculty are to some extent subject (products and producers) of disciplinary conversations" (Peeples 1999, 157). As products and producers, we need to reflect more about how GenAdmin discourse is enabled through our personal decisions about where we live and for how long. One of the consequences of the decision to switch jobs is the inability to see long-term change whether in students, colleagues, programs, and institutions. Feeding into a discourse of constant transition can overlook the productive relationships and needed sense of stability that can come out of staying in one place, making the argument for staying put a needed one in the context of disciplinary conversations about moving into and out of positions.

Note

1. In working on this article, I have determined that Bishop was committed to staying in Alaska, but the timing was not right. To put it diplomatically, it also reads as if she wanted to stay, but when she had completed her PhD, Alaska wasn't looking to hire her full time. Alaska made a big mistake.

References

Bishop, Wendy. 1988. "Teaching Undergraduate Creative Writing: Myths, Mentors, and Metaphors." *Journal of Teaching Writing* 7 (1): 83–102.

Bishop, Wendy. 1993. "Writing Is/and Therapy? Raising Questions about Writing Classrooms and Writing Program Administration." *Journal of Advanced Composition* 13 (2): 503–16.

Bishop, Wendy, and Gay Lynn Crossley. 1996. "How to Tell a Story of Stopping: The Complexities of Narrating a WPA's Experience." *WPA: Writing Program Administration* 19 (3): 70–79.

Bousquet, Marc. 2002. "Composition as Management Science: Toward a University without a WPA." *Journal of Advanced Composition* 22 (3): 493–526.

Charlton, Colin, Jonikka Charlton, Tarez Samra Graban, Kathleen J. Ryan, and Amy Ferdinandt Stolley. 2011. *GenAdmin: Theorizing WPA Identities in the Twenty-First Century*. Anderson, SC: Parlor.

Elder, Cristyn L., Megan Schoen, and Ryan Skinnell. 2014. "Strengthening Graduate Student Preparation for WPA Work." *WPA: Writing Program Administration* 37 (2): 13–35.

Gallaher, Robin. 2014. "On Being an Island: A Grounded Theory Study of Being a WPA and the Only Composition Scholar at an Institution." *Theses and dissertations (All)*. 925. http://knowledge.library.iup.edu/etd/925.

Heard, Matthew. 2012. "Cultivating Sensibility in Writing Program Administration." *WPA: Writing Program Administration* 35 (2): 38–54.

Hult, Christine. 1995. "Politics Redux: The Organization and Administration of Writing Programs." *WPA: Writing Program Administration* 18 (2): 44–52.

Micciche, Laura. 2011. "For Slow Agency." *WPA: Writing Program Administration* 35 (1): 73–90.

Middleton, Michael, Aaron Hess, Danielle Endres, and Samantha Senda-Cook. 2015. *Participatory Critical Rhetoric: Theoretical and Methodological Foundations for Studying Rhetoric in Situ*. Lanham, MD: Lexington Books.

O'Meara, KerryAnn, Andrew Lounder, and Corbin M. Campbell. 2014. "To Heaven or Hell: Sensemaking about Why Faculty Leave." *Journal of Higher Education* 85 (5): 603–32. https://doi.org/10.1353/jhe.2014.0027.

Peeples, Tim. 1999. "'Seeing' the WPA With/Through Postmodern Mapping." In *The Writing Program Administrator as Researcher*, edited by Shirley Rose and Irwin Weiser, 153–67. Portsmouth, NH: Boynton Cook.

Wieck, Karl E. 1995. *Sensemaking in Organizations*. Thousand Oaks, CA: SAGE.

16
CONNECTION, COMMUNITY, AND IDENTITY
Writing Programs and WPAs at the Community College

Mark Blaauw-Hara and Cheri Lemieux Spiegel

While WPA positions can be complex in any institution, some of these complexities are heightened at the community college. For one thing, there is little consensus about what community college writing programs should look like. Jeffrey Klausman (2008) has suggested that rather than a cohesive writing program, many community colleges have "classes loosely related by too-often unspoken and, most likely, conflicting assumptions about aims, means, and purposes" (239). For example, Janangelo and Klausman (2012) did not find "a consistent underlying theoretical frame" in any of the six community college writing programs they studied (135), and other scholars have also found that even when individual community colleges have cohesive writing programs, they tend to be institution specific and greatly differ from those at other colleges (Raines 1990; Taylor 2009). In addition, as Tim Taylor (2009) points out, community college WPAs are "largely invisible" to the larger WPA world (120), a situation that can leave new community college WPAs feeling as though they have to craft their position from whole cloth.

Ideally, a new WPA at any level transitions into a community of practice (CoP): a robust group of professionals—in this case, experienced WPAs—bound together by shared practices and understandings in which the more experienced members mentor and support those new to the community (Lave and Wenger 1991). CoPs exist in many workplaces and disciplines: Jean Lave and Etienne Wenger studied midwives and quartermasters, while others have studied health professionals (Nemec and LaMaster 2014) or the military (Kilner 2002; Stephens 2011). A number of scholars have applied the CoP framework to academe, noting the value faculty (especially newer faculty) find in peer connection and mentorship (e.g., Rees and Shaw 2014; Sherer, Shea, and Kristensen 2003). In the context of WPAs, newer WPAs might receive mentoring on an individual level as well as through participation in conferences or reading and publishing in professional journals. Gradually, new WPAs grow more confident and connected to the larger WPA community, eventually mentoring other WPAs themselves.

Part of our argument is that this transition happens more readily (though admittedly not without challenges) with university-level WPAs and is more difficult to achieve at the community college. One difficulty is that most WPA scholarship focuses on university settings while community college WPAs have jobs that are "significantly different" from their university peers (Klausman 2008, 238). A community college WPA might have many of the same duties as a WPA at a university—for example, to head up curricular decisions, schedule and staff writing courses, and hold departmental training sessions and meetings. However, the two institutions differ significantly; WPAs at the community college have roles and pressures that differ from those of their university counterparts. While all WPA work is contextually driven and differences are apparent even within various kinds of four-year institutions, WPA work at the community college is often further complicated by the fact that it is frequently not called writing program administration at all: WPAs are frequently department chairs, associate deans, or coordinators. As a result, some two-year college leaders might not readily self-identify as WPAs despite the fact that their work is deeply situated in the coordination of writing courses and the faculty who teach those courses.

Community college WPAs also have a difficult time accessing the experiences and scholarship of others like themselves. Christie Toth (2014) notes that only a small percentage of two-year college faculty attend professional conferences. In addition, there is often little to no support or recognition for research or scholarship (Miller et al. 2004, 30; Twombly and Townsend 2008; Two-Year College Association 2011). Consequently, such faculty *produce* (i.e., publish or otherwise distribute) little research, which conventionally is seen as the discovery and dissemination of new knowledge (Two-Year College Association 2011, 9), in part because of the ways in which they are evaluated and recognized within their institutions. These factors contribute to the invisibility of the two-year college WPA to both fellow community college WPAs and to the larger WPA CoP. All the above factors serve as powerful barriers to community college WPAs who might greatly benefit from participation within the larger WPA CoP.

However, we think the benefits of WPA-community membership are reason enough to try and surmount the barriers. This chapter provides a history of our own experiences as community college WPAs. It traces not only our transitions into and out of our local positions but also our transitions into the larger WPA CoP. In addition to describing our own professional growth as WPAs and our experiences effecting change in our programs, we illustrate how engagement with the larger WPA community can support those transitioning into WPA roles at community colleges. We rely on our narratives, which bear striking similarities despite the differences between our institutions. We have organized the chapter into four major sections that focus on transitions:

1. our first few years on the job as newly minted faculty with fresh MAs;
2. our struggles to take up leadership roles while remaining largely disconnected from the wider WPA community;
3. our growing connections to the wider community; and
4. our largely successful transitions into the WPA role with more informed understandings of what that role could be.

While we hesitate to claim our experiences are representative of all community college WPAs, we hope our respective stories can provide a window into some of the challenges and successes possible at the community college. Although there has been (and continues to be) scholarship done on teaching in the two-year college, what it means to be a community college WPA is still largely unexamined, and we hope our experiences can further this area of research.

TRANSITION ONE: STARTS (AND FITS) AS NEW FACULTY

Mark

I was hired into my current position in 2000, when I was twenty-five years old. The job title was *writing program coordinator*, and while I no longer have the job description, I remember that the main duties were to develop an assessment program, teach, and perform some vague administrative duties. The department had three other full-time faculty and around twenty part timers. The vibe was generally positive, both among faculty and toward the students. Collegiality was highly valued (the school is in the Midwest, after all). There was also very much a sense of live and let live as far as curricular decisions went: while we shared ideas and frustrations, there was little desire for a shared curriculum and an undercurrent of skepticism toward the idea. I shared these reservations—I certainly didn't want anyone telling me how to teach, and I felt it would be disrespectful and invasive to insist on a particular set of essays or to mandate a common text. Also, I questioned my own ability to lead in this sense: who was I to tell someone who had been teaching English nearly as long as I had been alive to change their textbook, or to suggest that a class built around the personal narrative or the study of literature might not be the best choice for first-year composition?

My master's program at Arizona State had prepared me well in terms of current scholarship, but the community college writing program was quite different from the program I came from at ASU. Of course, it was much smaller. For another thing, the students we taught came from a different academic background and had more diverse goals than at ASU; here, half of any FYC class would be made up of students who were pursuing one- or two-year occupational degrees. But the department was different, too. The tensions I had grown accustomed to in a university English department between composition and literature, creative writing and linguistics, did not exist. Everyone taught composition, and most of us also taught literature or creative writing. (No one taught linguistics.) There were no TAs who were teaching composition while on their way to something else; instead, there were part-time faculty who already had advanced degrees, many of whom had taught for a long time.

In addition, I was the first WPA the school had ever had. This meant there was nothing established in terms of job conditions and responsibilities, and there were few precedents to draw from at other community colleges. When I started, the job had loose curricular responsibilities for the writing courses but no budget and no oversight over staffing or scheduling. On one hand the situation was very positive: I got to do the "fun" parts of the job that had to do with teaching and learning, while I did not have to deal with those aspects which tend to cause WPAs the most stress. However, the vagueness of the position lent its own stress to my job.

Cheri

My story also begins with an ambitious twenty-something. I was hired full time into my department in August 2007, one month after my twenty-fourth birthday. Unlike Mark, I was not hired into a WPA position. In fact, my campus did not (and arguably still does not) have an official writing program administrator. Instead, I was brought on to be one of nearly thirty full-time faculty whose teaching load (5/5) accounted for a majority of their job responsibilities.

I felt well prepared for the position. I had a strong community of both formal and informal mentors throughout my master's preparation at Virginia Tech. I even completed a graduate certificate program, preparing the future professoriate, through which I learned a great deal about various kinds of institutions within the academy and major issues within the terrain of higher education. But I was still far more green than I cared to or, perhaps more important, knew to admit.

My new department did not resemble the university from which I came: it consisted almost entirely of full-time faculty who held master's degrees and doctoral degrees in literature, creative writing, or education (including some degrees in community college teaching). It would take me some time to understand the implications of these differences. Our campus department, which formed in the late 1960s, was one where people enjoyed working and were quite loyal to the college. As a result, they stayed with the college for long periods, often their entire careers. In fact, between the mid-1970s and 1999, the department only hired one new full-time faculty member.

When I arrived in 2007, a majority of the faculty who first helped forge the identity of the department were still active within it. As such, they had years of experience and insight to share with the junior faculty member who joined them. Unfortunately, I wasn't always ready to listen. I made assumptions about how theoretically (un)informed my colleagues were and privileged the experiences of my university mentors. This point of friction is where my story begins but, thankfully, not where it ends. The story of how I transitioned into leadership within the department and how that position evolved into a WPA is, in large part, predicated on the ways in which I had to evolve in terms of my own understanding of myself, my department's history, our field, and the ways of knowing within our discipline.

TRANSITION TWO: LEARNING WHAT TO DO AND WHO TO BE
Mark

Sometimes the WPA is portrayed as the sole voice of reason amidst a cacophony of competing and ill-informed colleagues; sometimes the WPA is a crusader advocating to a corrupt administration on behalf of students and marginalized faculty. None of this was the case at my school. I had supportive colleagues and administrators. The problem was that no one (including me) had a firm idea of what the writing program should look like and what a WPA should do. Developing an assessment program was in the job description, so that's where I started. Before I arrived, the English faculty had decided to base the assessment program on that of another community college in the state. The process we ended up with was effective from an institutional standpoint but extremely work intensive. The actual mechanics of getting final student portfolios read and scored were too byzantine to discuss here, but they involved my driving boxes of portfolios to extension campuses, coming up with codes to designate instructors so no one knew who had taught the students whose work they were reading, debating about whether portfolios could be taken home or had to be read on campus, and the like. And I wasn't the only one doing the work: every instructor had to read twice as many sections of portfolios as their current load of writing courses. This was back-breaking work—sometimes nearly literally, as instructors carried box after box of portfolios to and from quiet locations around campus to do their readings.

Few of us actually liked the program, but we had invested so much time and effort getting it into place that I do not think we felt we could stop. Running the assessment program began to take up most of my job. I felt like a manager who had the job of checking boxes and moving materials and personnel around. After seven years, I felt disheartened and out of ideas, and I stepped down. The position was assumed by one of my colleagues, who did the best she could for a year or two, and then she, too, stepped down. No one else stepped up.

My experience was similar to the one Darci Thoune describes at a small university in Wisconsin (Thoune 2011). Like me, Thoune was the first WPA at her school, and like me, she had supportive colleagues who nonetheless had an uncertain grasp of what a WPA's role should be. Thoune notes that her excellent graduate and postgraduate educations still left her "underprepared for what it meant to work in a department that had no established guidelines, expectations, or history of a WPA" (Thoune 2011, 156). This context is strikingly similar to what Cheri and I both felt as new faculty leaders in departments with no history of WPAs. Thoune realized far quicker than me that her position ran the risk of becoming merely managerial, and her department's culture of "hands-off" curricular autonomy had contributed to wildly divergent course materials within sections of the same writing classes, making it difficult for her to draw together a cohesive writing program. For Thoune, change came when she attended her first CWPA conference, where she connected with other WPAs and came away inspired and full of new ideas.

I wish I had done something similar, but I did not avail myself of the larger WPA community. I remember that period as a time of frenzied activity—learning to teach and hold a full-time job, parenting a young family, and making "adult" decisions such as when to get the propane tank filled and whether to buy a house. There just didn't seem to be enough time for the things I had to do, let alone time for "luxuries" like flying to another city to attend a conference. There was also the pressure of teaching four sections each semester and feeling as though taking half a week off to attend a conference would put me too far behind. In addition, there wasn't any money—the college guaranteed $500 a year for professional development, and anything else required competing with other faculty and staff for a share of a relatively small pot of funds. We certainly didn't have extra money at home.

Whatever the reasons, the professional disengagement I felt during that time is shared by many faculty and WPAs at the community college. As we noted in the introduction to this chapter, Christie Toth writes that engagement of two-year college English faculty in disciplinary professional organizations is quite low (Toth 2014). Her best estimates suggest that fewer than 7 percent of US community college English faculty attended any NCTE-affiliated conference between 2009 and 2011. Toth made this estimate despite the qualitative data she gathered that suggested that, like Thoune, two-year college faculty find participation in professional organizations to be rewarding and professionally inspiring.

As I think back on this time, I'm struck by how ill at ease I was in the position. I wasn't able to lay claim to it in some fundamental way—I could do the job, but I did not own it. As Rita Malenczyk notes, a degree in rhetoric and composition "is not exactly a stay against self-doubt" (Malenczyk 2012, 185). Malenczyk writes that many WPAs—especially new ones—struggle not only with how to get other people to see them as qualified but also with how to see themselves that way. I did not have the comfort in the role to trust my instincts, and I constantly worried that the work I was doing was imperfect. Again, some of this was youth. I really didn't have a lot of experience to draw from, and as the youngest faculty member in the entire college, I felt I had to constantly prove I knew what I was talking about.

I am convinced that a more experienced WPA mentor would have helped immensely. Even reading WPA scholarship would have shown me that many WPAs struggle with insecurity and the feeling that their jobs have devolved into the most basic managerial components. Yet I did none of this, and as a result, I suffered alone.

Cheri

During my first few years, I enjoyed my position greatly but often found myself stepping into conflict with my colleagues or chafing at the circumstances I observed regarding our composition sequence. I discovered exactly what Klausman (2008) characterizes as typical in departments wherein no formal writing program exists: we had course-content summaries that guided classes, but individual approaches to the two-course sequence varied widely. There was a kind of departmental lore about what the first course accomplished in relationship to the second, but that story was hardly told by the course objectives.

By fall 2010, I was serving in a number of college leadership roles, and my dean approached me about stepping into the program-head position (essentially the part-time faculty coordinator). When I agreed to take the position, I was at once struck by how little release time was awarded for this task. In this new administrative role, I would teach seven courses a year (with release from only three). I didn't see how I could get everything done. I now had, with very limited preparation, more than seventy part-time faculty to supervise. I immediately came face to face with complex labor concerns I felt ill equipped to address.

What I soon observed and heard from our part-time faculty reflected much of what Klausman (2010) found in his own survey of adjunct faculty at his institution. He reported that "adjunct faculty feel marginalized on their own campuses and are somewhat to very resentful at teaching so much of a program's courses while receiving so little in terms of pay and benefits" (Klausman 2010, 363). The working conditions at my campus certainly gave our part-time faculty cause for this resentment. During one of my first weeks in the position, I participated in what we call "Keep and Cancel." This event required me to call several part-time faculty, just one week before their classes began, to inform them that their classes had to be cancelled for low enrollment or reassigned to a full-time faculty member so they could make their load. Call after call, part-time folks, many of whom I had not yet met in person, reacted to the unfortunate news regarding a drastic, overnight shift in their employment, often speaking harshly to me or, at times, crying on the other end of the line. Although I could recognize the injustices in our labor practices, I felt powerless.

As I settled into my position as program head, I was firmly committed not only to doing right by the part-time faculty but to helping all the faculty, full and part time, come together to develop and teach within a more cohesive writing program. I felt I had a productive lens through which to view our writing courses and was listening more carefully to the perspectives my colleagues brought to those courses as well. However, I began to recognize my inexperience and lack of preparation.

TRANSITION THREE: CONNECTING TO THE COMMUNITY OF PRACTICE
Both

In 2010, both of us started a doctoral program at Old Dominion University. ODU offered a relatively new low-residency PhD that would allow us to keep our jobs while working on the degree. Both of us hoped a greater connection to scholarship would help us be better teachers and benefit our writing programs. Mark had begun to feel stagnant in his job and yearned for the kind of deep discussion of thorny concepts he remembered from graduate school. Cheri was looking for new ways to address the issues she saw in her own program and role. Both of us focused our coursework on rhetoric and writing pedagogy, working extensively with Louise Wetherbee Phelps, who had recently accepted a position in the program. Louise's deep knowledge of writing program administration and her history of serving as a peer consultant for writing programs in the United States and Canada inspired us, and when she offered to teach an independent study in writing program administration for both of us, we leapt at the chance.

Through our readings and conversations, we began to realize WPA could be a role of vision and activism, not just one of basic management. Several readings, such as Karl Weick's 1995 "Organizational Design as Improvisation" and Phelps's 2003 "Administration as a Design Art," emphasized the continual, often chaotic nature of writing-program design (Phelps 2003; Weick 1995). Mark realized his feelings of confusion and inadequacy during his tenure as WPA thus far stemmed in large part from his erroneous thinking that if he only understood the situation better, he could get it "right" and be done with it. However, Mark started to understand that successful writing programs were in continual flux and that a successful administrator was always engaged in change, working not toward the "right" but toward the "better."

Both of us also took heart in discovering how universal the challenges we faced really were. David E. Schwalm's 2002 "The Writing Program (Administrator) in Context: Where Am I, and Can I Still Behave Like a Faculty Member?" in particular helped Cheri resee the administrative role she was in (Schwalm 2002). She began to self-identify more as an administrator and to recognize the ways in which her focus needed to evolve to be more institutionally minded than it had been. Schwalm's chapter helped her determine what information about her institution she needed to be an effective administrator. Cheri began to develop the ability to articulate what she didn't know and to devise plans to collect that information. For example, after reading Gregory Glau's 2002 "Hard

Work and Hard Data," she came to realize how little she really knew about statistical analysis or how to use data to bolster her arguments (Glau 2002). She realized a sounder knowledge of data and how to use it would help her advocate for her own writing program, and she took a course in statistics for education the following semester.

Together we discussed the implications of administering writing programs that relied heavily on part-time faculty. Mark had been frustrated and demoralized by his inability to affect the material conditions of the adjuncts in his college's writing program. In addition to discussing potential arguments to improve adjunct pay and working conditions, we explored other nonmonetary ways to improve their treatment—for example, ways to help adjunct faculty integrate into the decisions of the department, develop their backgrounds in current scholarship, and share their best practices. Mark came up with an idea about how he could use a proposed revision of the developmental-course sequence to advocate for funded professional development for adjunct faculty and how he might involve adjuncts in a new revision of the capstone writing course. Cheri walked away from these discussions prepared to bolster a professional-development program that would help part-time faculty develop the skills and experience they would need to be competitive on the job market, both at her institution and beyond. We both came to understand that while a certain amount of nuts-and-bolts management was always a part of the WPA's job, there was potential for much more. We began to see how our respective writing programs could grow under the right leadership—and we even thought we might be right for the roles.

The course and Louise's mentorship led both of us to engage more fully with the larger WPA CoP as well. We started reading the WPA journal and attending CWPA and CCCC more regularly, presenting as well as listening to other, more experienced members of the community. Both of us ran for (and received) seats on the CWPA Executive Board, in part to represent the perspective of two-year college WPAs. We wrote and published more, and we collaborated formally and informally with other teacher-scholars in community colleges. Not only did we learn practical things; we grew to think of ourselves as legitimate members of the WPA community.

TRANSITION FOUR: NEW STARTS AND BETTER FITS
Mark
The three years since I started my second tenure as WPA have been eventful. The developmental-writing sequence is now streamlined, and we have fully implemented the accelerated learning program (ALP)

we adapted from the one developed at the Community College of Baltimore County. Students now complete our developmental sequence in much higher numbers than before, and the model has resulted in increased student performance and retention in the college-level classes as well. We have incorporated more professional writing into our college-level courses based on data about the degrees our students are pursuing, and we've used the results of a writing-in-the-disciplines study I did to fine-tune the types of essays we assign and our research requirements. Currently, we are experimenting with learning communities in our second-semester college-writing course, as well as developing sections targeted toward certain disciplines (health, criminal justice, early-childhood education, psychology, political science, etc.) in hopes of increasing the transfer from writing courses to disciplinary writing. We have also begun working with interested faculty in other disciplines to support their use of writing in their content courses.

We still do assessment, but our current model is light-years away from the exhausting model of the past. Now, we use assessment in a more targeted way to help us make key decisions about the writing program. For example, when we were deciding whether to scale up the ALP program, we assessed how well students in ALP sections wrote compared to those in traditional developmental sections, as well as how well the ALP students wrote compared to those in college-level sections. This model has made our assessment process manageable, fluid, and, most important, relevant to the actual key decisions of the writing program.

There has also been progress on the professionalization front. I was able to implement the ideas I came up with in the WPA class to use curricular revisions as a rationale for funding adjunct professional development. In addition, I have devoted time in our semester meetings to discussions of current scholarship, and I have asked a number of adjunct faculty to share some of their best teaching techniques with the group in a conference-like format. Many faculty have told me these gestures have not only helped them feel as though their teaching has improved but also feel more connected to the department.

Although I would love to take credit for these successes, the majority of the ideas for these innovations came from elsewhere. As I noted earlier in this piece, during my first tenure as WPA, I was only tenuously connected to the larger academic community. I rarely attended conferences or read journals, and the writing I did seldom connected to my job. I didn't realize it at the time, but I had cut myself off from most sources of new ideas. Little wonder, then, that under my leadership, the writing program was stuck in a spiral of repetition and stasis.

I came to understand others were dealing with similar challenges; some had come up with solutions I realized I could adapt to my context. In addition to gaining practical ideas, connecting with the larger WPA community through conferences and writing provided me with a sense of place and emotional belonging. I had been considering a shift to full-time administration, but I attended a CWPA conference and had an epiphany: these were my people. Similarly to Thoune, I came away inspired and connected, and I felt as if I knew not only what I could do at my school but why my school needed a WPA and how I was a good fit for the position.

And shockingly, at least to me, I started to have fun. As Lynn Bloom (2002) points out, writing program administration can—and should be—fun. She turned up several ways many WPAs enjoy the job, from getting to work with (and mentor) students and other faculty, to forming a vibrant community that cares about writing, to problem solving, to being recognized as an on-campus writing expert who can consult with other faculty in the disciplines. I feel all of that. I am excited and invested in the things we're trying.

Cheri

As I completed my degree, I started to rethink my own characterization of how we might transition into a vibrant, well-organized writing program. It became clear to me that a writing program within my context should be a collaborative effort engaged in by the full- and part-time faculty at my institution to facilitate the design, development, implementation, and assessment of writing instruction. Since the department already had a formalized assessment and I was responsible for overseeing 70 percent of the writing faculty, I decided I would focus my attention on implementation and development. I revised the process through which part-time faculty would be evaluated and encouraged active participation in the observation process on the part of full-time faculty. I rebranded the adjunct resource committee we had (which was initially designed to help support new part-time faculty) as *the composition resource group*, a group dedicated to facilitating professional-development opportunities to support all teachers of writing and to systematically target areas of interest identified by the department assessment. I made a monthly composition discussion group (which discussed articles from the field's journal, including *TETYC*) a central part of that initiative. I watched as attendance at events grew and full-time and part-time faculty stepped up to design and facilitate new workshops. Somewhere along the way, folks outside the institution started to refer to me as the WPA at my institution. At first I corrected them, indicating that I was only the program head of English adjuncts. However, as I started to evolve in my own understanding of my institution's WPA structure, I stopped resisting this description. Not long after, my title was changed to assistant dean of composition.

In May 2016, after five and a half years, I stepped down. I am no longer the assistant dean. However, because of how I have come to see the WPA CoP and writing program administration at my college, I don't think I'll ever fully transition out of being a WPA. I will always be a WPA because I will always have some claim to the way my collaborative department designs, implements, develops, and assesses the writing courses within my context. However, as I step away from the more formal position, I am turning my focus to the greater two-year college WPA community and looking for ways I might support those within the WPA CoP and encourage more two-year faculty to find a place for themselves within this community.

CONCLUSION

Writing about our transitions has led us to realize several things. One is how green we both were when we entered our jobs—partly because of our youth and partly because we were so new to the context of the community college. We came out of our master's programs full of knowledge about rhetoric and composition but with a conspicuous lack of real-world experience. Working with other faculty was hard in many ways, including negotiating how to give and take ideas about teaching and writing. We worried about stepping on toes, and we were certainly too invested in thinking we knew the right ways of doing things.

Also, neither of us knew how to connect our knowledge of the discipline to the larger questions of building a cohesive writing program. In fact, writing programs didn't exist at either of our schools—at least in the ways advocated for by Janangelo and Klausman (2012) and others. But part of the problem was that our training had been at universities, and we really didn't know what a community college writing program could (or should) look like. Nor did we know what a WPA at a community college looked like, or what, exactly, such a person's job should be.

The solution for both of us was connection. Plugging in to more experienced WPAs—in our doctoral programs, in the scholarship, and at the CWPA conference—helped us see a larger context for WPA work. We began to see how our previous tasks, while important in their way, were not ends in themselves but were parts of a whole we needed to develop at our schools. Our connections outside our colleges helped us learn what successful writing programs might look like, and this growing appreciation for connectedness helped us both reach out to our local colleagues and build programs that worked in our own individual contexts.

Our programs are very different; our jobs and titles are different, too. Yet, both of us have managed to help our schools develop much more cohesive programs, we have grown in our identities as WPAs, and we have discovered the importance of approaching WPA work as a CoP. In many ways, by engaging this greater community, we discovered something similar to what Andrea A. Lunsford and Lisa Ede point to as the result of their years of collaboration with one another. They explain, "As we wrote together, we discovered a new voice, one that was part Lisa, part Andrea, part all our other interlocutors, sources, and friends, and part something else, something *together*" (Lunsford and Ede, 2012, 4). We needed to find our own "something *together*" to navigate the complex demands of our leadership roles.

Other faculty—especially at the community college—are surely struggling with how to draw their writing courses together into a cohesive program, how to build on the talents of the faculty teaching those courses, and yes, how to accomplish the more managerial tasks like scheduling, budget, and assessment. Precedents at universities are certainly helpful, but the community college is its own environment. We encourage such faculty to reach out and connect, certainly within their own departments but also by writing, reading, and attending conferences. Connections with other faculty in leadership positions at community colleges—especially with other WPAs—can provide practical and emotional support that will lead to stronger writing programs and sustainable WPA working conditions.

References

Bloom, Lynn Z. 2002. "Are We Having Fun Yet? Necessity, Creativity, and Writing Program Administration." *WPA: Writing Program Administration* 26 (1–2): 57–70.

Glau, Gregory R. 2002. "Hard Work and Hard Data: Using Statistics to Help Your Program." In *The Writing Program Administrator's Resource*, edited by Stuart C. Brown and Theresa Enos, 291–302. Mahwah, NJ: Lawrence Erlbaum.

Janangelo, Joseph, and Jeffrey Klausman. 2012. "Rendering the Idea of a Writing Program: A Look at Six Two-Year Colleges." *Teaching English in the Two-Year College* 40 (2): 131–44.

Kilner, Peter. 2002. "Transforming Army Learning through Communities of Practice." *Military Review* 82 (2): 21–27.

Klausman, Jeffrey. 2008. "Mapping the Terrain: The Two-Year College Writing Program Administrator." *Teaching English in the Two-Year College* 35 (3): 238–51.

Klausman, Jeffrey. 2010. "Not Just a Matter of Fairness: Adjunct Faculty and Writing Programs in Two-Year Colleges." *Teaching English in the Two-Year College* 37 (4): 363–71.

Lave, Jean, and Etienne Wenger. 1991. *Situated Learning: Legitimate Peripheral Participation*. Cambridge, UK: Cambridge University Press. https://doi.org/10.1017/CBO9780511815355.

Lunsford, Andrea A., and Lisa S. Ede. 2012. *Writing Together: Collaboration in Theory and Practice, a Critical Sourcebook*. Boston: Bedford/St. Martins.

Malenczyk, Rita. 2012. "Kitchen Cooks, Plate Twirlers, and Posers; or, The I's Have It." *WPA: Writing Program Administration* 35 (2): 184–89.

Miller, Susan Kay, Shelley Rodrigo, Veronica Pantoja, and Duane Roen. 2004. "Institutional Models for Engaging Faculty in the Scholarship of Teaching and Learning." *Teaching English in the Two-Year College* 32 (1): 30–38.

Nemec, Patricia B., and Stephen LaMaster. 2014. "Education and Training Column: Communities of Practice." *Psychiatric Rehabilitation Journal* 37 (4): 336–38. https://doi.org/10.1037/prj0000081.

Phelps, Louise Wetherbee. 2003. "Administration as a Design Art." Keynote address, Council of Writing Program Administrators Conference, Grand Rapids, MI, July.

Raines, Helon Howell. 1990. "Is There a Writing Program in This College? Two Hundred and Thirty-Six Two-Year Schools Respond." *College Composition and Communication* 41 (2): 151–67. https://doi.org/10.2307/358154.

Rees, Amanda, and Kimberly Shaw. 2014. "Peer Mentoring Communities of Practice for Early and Mid-Career Faculty: Broad Benefits from a Research-Oriented Female Peer Mentoring Group." *Journal of Faculty Development* 28 (2): 5–17.

Schwalm, David E. 2002. "Writing Program Administration as Preparation for an Administrative Career." In *The Writing Program Administrator's Resource*, edited by Stuart C. Brown and Theresa Enos, 125–35. Mahwah, NJ: Lawrence Erlbaum.

Sherer, Pamela D., Timothy P. Shea, and Eric Kristensen. 2003. "Online Communities of Practice: A Catalyst for Faculty Development." *Innovative Higher Education* 27 (3): 183–94. https://doi.org/10.1023/A:1022355226924.

Stephens, Jennifer Gray. 2011. "Rethinking Marine Corps Training." *U.S. Naval Institute Proceedings* 137 (11): 75–77.

Taylor, Tim. 2009. "Writing Program Administration at the Two-Year College: Ghosts in the Machine." *WPA: Writing Program Administration* 32 (3): 120–39.

Thoune, Darci L. 2011. "The Pleasures and Perils of Being First." *WPA: Writing Program Administration* 35 (1): 156–59.

Toth, Christie. 2014. "Unmeasured Engagement: Two-Year College English Faculty and Disciplinary Professional Organizations." *Teaching English in the Two-Year College* 41 (4): 335–53.

Two-Year College English Association. 2011. "Research and Scholarship in the Two-Year College." *Teaching English in the Two-Year College* 39 (1): 7–28.

Twombly, Susan, and Barbara K. Townsend. 2008. "Community College Faculty: What We Know and Need to Know." *Community College Review* 36 (1): 5–24. https://doi.org/10.1177/0091552108319538.

Weick, Karl. 1995. "Organizational Design as Improvisation." In *Organizational Change and Redesign: Ideas and Insights for Improving Performance*, edited by George P. Huber and William H. Glick, 346–80. New York: Oxford University Press.

17
FOSTERING ETHICAL TRANSITIONS
Creating Community as Writing Program Administrators

Bradley Smith and Kerri K. Morris

We were both hired in the midst of seismic change at Governors State University. GSU had been since 1969 a senior university, offering upper-division courses and graduate programs only. Two critical events have shaped much of our local work in writing studies. First, in 2009 the Higher Learning Commission required that GSU develop general education (GE) outcomes, which it had never before needed as a senior institution. Second, GSU began the transformation into a four-year university, admitting its first freshman class in fall 2014, under the leadership of President Elaine Maimon. These events spurred a calendar change from trimesters to semesters, the first campus-wide conversation about GE outcomes and their assessment, extensive program development, substantial hiring, and construction of the first residence halls. Kerri was the first English hire in 2011. In the midst of these changes, she was tasked with serving as "Coordinator of Composition and Rhetoric campus-wide," according to the job ad. Brad was hired in 2013, the second of the rhetoric and composition specialists in the department. Changes of this magnitude foster a dynamic environment for conversation, planning, and creating, as well as opportunities for crisis and conflict. Though we are well aware of things we got wrong, we are also confident we made good choices. Our intentional choices about how to transition into and out of the writing-coordinator position are at the heart of our story. We have worked together and individually to create a rhetorical space where a group of first-year writing teachers can develop into a community able to take rhetorical action.

While there have always been smart, dedicated, and successful writing instructors and rhetorical theorists working at GSU, when we arrived there was very little in the way of a shared institutional or programmatic

DOI: 10.7330/9781607326335.c017

vision for what freshman composition should be. Our transitions into and out of our WPA roles in our short time here have been defined by our efforts to find our place in the narrative of writing instruction at GSU. Above all, the work of transitioning has been marked by our efforts to establish curricular and pedagogical common ground—principles for teaching first-year writing that will thread together the disparate group of teachers tasked with teaching in a new first-year writing (FYW) program (all of them full-time faculty)—by fostering ethical and rhetorical choices.

As our first freshmen arrived on campus, it became apparent that our emerging FYW community does share some values. Two dominate: we are committed to meeting students where they are and to promoting transfer. Shared values are essential, but they are not enough. As we worked to establish a community of first-year writing, teachers we learned we also needed a way to create opportunities for dynamic exchanges about our vision, a place where faculty could tell their stories. The importance of storytelling to framing writing program administration in both national and local contexts is made clear by Linda Adler-Kassner (2008, 40). She concludes that values and framing are integrally linked to the work of writing program administration, and she suggests that WPAs wishing to employ such methods in their work must consider three actions: first, identify important values for the writing program; second, find others with those values; third, create frames based on those values (Adler-Kassner 2008, 103). Continuing this work, Adler-Kassner and O'Neill (2010) show frames draw on "cultural values and creat[e] structures for understanding reality, defin[e] common sense, and produc[e] cultural narratives" (40). This means the frames we use and the stories we tell are linked in important ways. Through this organizational practice, a community is formed around a group of people with shared values and principles. This group uses their values as a way to reframe a particular issue and to shape the stories told in a particular way (Adler-Kassner 2008, 108). In the analysis of our own story, we have alighted on an intertwined conceptual metaphor to define our work, *discourse is space/rhetorical action is position*, which has helped us frame our collaborative efforts in building a writing-program community and has served as the common ground for our conversations. Informing our efforts at creating this community is the story of our shared transitions into and out of the WPA roles we fulfill. We have learned that a dynamic and rhetorically active community begins with us. We serve as a model for the program as a whole. By foregrounding our rhetorical agency (Werder 2000), we have discovered shared values that work in congruence with diverse approaches to teaching our writing courses. This balance between an organized, framed, and focused community (Adler-Kassner 2008) and an acknowledgment that community is diverse, multiple, and material (Harris 2001; Wiley 2001) has helped us theorize our approach to constructing a functioning and healthy writing program.

THE FIRST TRANSITION: KERRI'S STORY

As mentioned above, I was hired, according to the job ad, to be the campus-wide composition coordinator. Part of the ad read as follows: "The successful candidate will serve as Coordinator of Composition and Rhetoric campus-wide, including the assumption of leadership roles in some or all of the following: Composition and Rhetoric curriculum; WAC/WI initiatives; university assessment goals related to writing and general education; adjunct recruitment and training; and the development of a graduate degree program in writing."

The reality of the job when I arrived on campus, however, was very different. I did not have the title *coordinator of composition*. The position had never existed at GSU and under the administrative framework of the institution was not feasible. FYW did not yet exist, WAC initiatives had never been approved by the faculty senate and had not been coordinated by a WPA for several years, assessment of writing had begun before GE outcomes had been written, and the need for a graduate program in writing was unclear. The leadership I was to provide was not clearly articulated, nor was the campus broadly aware of it. From one perspective, the situation was confusing and worrying. From another, however, it was an exciting time for programs to be built from the ground up.

It took a short time to realize one person could not fill all these roles, be a creator and long-term administrator of three major initiatives—FYW, WAC, and a graduate program in writing—all while working without a mandate or a title. Even if all three were established programs, it seemed less than ideal to have one person at the helm. With regard to leadership, I'm committed to shared roles, and I knew we would be hiring several new folks. It made sense to think of those new hires as leaders. Despite this commitment, however, I was on campus for two years before hiring for the FYW and GE programs began in English. Both FYW and WAC demanded immediate attention, and I triaged the graduate program.

From the beginning, I knew I wanted to lead WAC. My heart has always been there, and my leadership qualities are more suited to grassroots and service-oriented work. I love teaching writing, especially first-year writers, and I have focused my teaching career on GE courses, but I am less inclined toward being WPA of FYW and am less equipped to provide this leadership long term. My plan, then, was to hire colleagues who were both prepared and interested in such leadership. Over the two years before Brad was hired, in preparation for our transition, I sought to create a WAC director position and a WPA position that were listed separately on my official workload and to build a composition curriculum suited to our first-year students. My intention was to ensure the two roles had clear definitions and boundaries so when the time came, the work could be divided easily and appropriate course releases made available. The WAC director reports directly to the provost and is the aspect of the original job description that is campus-wide. In contrast, the director of FYW is housed in English, works collaboratively with the English-program coordinator, and reports to the division chair. As a tenured member of the faculty, I was in a strong position to assertively influence these job descriptions, to push back against a tendency to want to wrap them all up in one job associated with one person, which potentially had less release time to support the work. For instance, separating the jobs made it more difficult for an administrator to offer 1½ course releases for one role and 1½ for the other. It's easy to give one person 3 course releases and harder to give two people 1½ each.

This sort of attention to administrative detail has required persistence and some courage, but it has been essential to how I've understood my role as the "senior" comp/rhetoric person in our program. My role has been to clear the way so we could begin building. The building of the first-year writing program has been more challenging for me, however, in no small part because I never envisioned filling the WPA role for a long period of time. Henry Johnstone's 1981 work has helped me frame these choices in a productive way. From Johnstone, I have come to think of both the WAC and WPA work I do as rhetorical work. We build programs through discourse and persuasion, through the consideration of shared values and local contexts. The foundation of rhetorical work, according to Johnstone, is that it remains rhetorical (1981, 309–310). That is, it remains in flux. We and our decisions remain open to change. Johnstone also, however, reminds me of the importance of resoluteness. We have a "duty" to ourselves to be open, and we have a duty to ourselves to be resolute while we treat others with gentleness and compassion (Johnstone 1981, 310).

Participating in the curricular work became more rewarding with this frame, and it was also more naturally rhetorical. I was resolute that our students should be able to write in FYW and throughout the curriculum as well as in their public lives outside the university. I sought to establish a curriculum focused on transferability, a writing-about-writing first-year sequence. My commitment to this approach was easy to argue for in the first discursive space I occupied, which was GSU's General Education Task Force. The task force was a dynamic community of open and creative colleagues. I was immediately included in the conversation and seen as having something unique and valuable to contribute. Serving on this committee was a singular experience for me, a model for ethical rhetorical exchange, empowered by campus leaders, fueled by new and veteran voices, intent only on building a sound and original general education curriculum. This place and this community grew up quite naturally around shared values. Writing was at the heart of our conversations and ended up being at the heart of our curriculum. This committee's work strengthened my commitment to writing about writing as the theoretical basis for first-year composition as well as my commitment to WAC.

By the time Brad was hired in 2013 as an assistant professor of English, we had already successfully submitted the syllabi for Writing Studies 1 and 2 to both the university and statewide curriculum committees for approval. Once he was on campus, I would have loved that he immediately assume the role of composition coordinator. He was less eager. As an untenured faculty member he was resolute in wanting to wait for any official role. As I reflected later, I realized it would have been unfair to Brad and, frankly, odd to expect him to move into overseeing a program I had just assembled but had never lived with. I needed to inhabit this curriculum and help others see it as I had imagined it while adhering to the principle of openness. Serving as an actual WPA in the program I had built was part of being resolute.

In addition, Brad was always deeply involved in the composition program, both in administrative and pedagogical ways. Instead of being the coordinator, he served alongside all our colleagues, using a curriculum I had developed before he arrived, and he could struggle and grapple with the difficulties the curriculum posed without representing it himself. He was in a position to guide faculty to a place where rhetorical action could happen.

AN EXTENDED TRANSITION: BRAD'S STORY

I was wary of becoming a jWPA at a new institution even though I see writing program administration as one of my primary scholarly interests, and I genuinely enjoy the work. I knew it would be risky because I had little knowledge of the institutional culture, and I would be managing this enormous task on an accelerated tenure clock. It was also clear from my interview and my early dealings on campus that the WPA position was still as of yet mostly undefined, despite Kerri's efforts. I knew if I took the position I would be struggling to earn tenure with a heavy administrative workload and without a historical precedent or codified system for evaluating and rewarding that work. Could I effectively carry out these duties while also excelling in the traditional measures of teaching, scholarship, and service? Just asking the question revealed to me I would be taking a huge risk if I immediately stepped into the WPA role. For these reasons, I opted to wait until after tenure and lend my help and expertise where I could without officially adopting an administrative role. As part of my extended transition, I led workshops on teaching first-year writing; I developed a new bridge curriculum for underprepared freshmen; I became an active member of the Composition Steering Committee; and I helped Kerri think through particularly tricky tasks, like scheduling and interpreting performance data from our first cohort of freshmen.

When I joined the faculty at GSU, it was clear to me that the program Kerri had put in place was theoretically sound. However, when theory meets practice for the first time, the necessity for revision is inevitable. Such was the case in our writing program's first year. Designing and leading workshops helped form positive relationships with my colleagues and positioned me as an expert on the new first-year writing curriculum. So it was natural (planned, even) that my new colleagues would come to me for advice and guidance while teaching the courses. This was particularly true when things did not go as expected during the first semester. With so many new variables to account for (lack of institutional context for a freshman class, new courses never before taught at GSU, a new writing program recently formed, a complex and innovative curriculum), a rough first semester was inevitable.

With this in mind, I decided to make some major changes in the spring in the way I motivated students to succeed. As part of this new set of strategies, I decided to use a grading contract, based on models created by Peter Elbow and Asao Inoue, to shift the emphasis away from performance and onto the habits of successful college students and writers. When I started at GSU, I had opted not to use contracts, though I had used them in the past. One primary reason was that during professional-development meetings, Kerri stressed the importance of having specific assignment guidelines and grade weights based on her dealings with the Illinois Articulation Initiative (IAI), a curriculum committee tasked with setting standards for transfer credit throughout the state. Needless to say, grading contracts changed the notion of weights awarded for each particular assignment.

Despite the deterrents, the problems I experienced during the fall semester necessitated a new approach. The practice seemed particularly suited for the problems I had encountered, and my sense was that using contracts would not contradict the spirit of our articulation agreement. Essentially, the course, the assignments, and the general scaffolding were the same. All that had changed was the way I motivated students to succeed.

As I prepared my syllabus for Writing Studies 2, I received an e-mail from a colleague, who was also preparing to teach the course, asking for advice. He had heard rumors about what it was like to teach this particular group of students. When asked how I planned to address these problems, I told him about my plan to adopt grading contracts. He expressed interest in the idea, so I sent him some materials about contracts, along with some other course materials I had created for the spring. As our dialogue continued, my colleague called attention to the inconsistency between Kerri's messaging about grading and the use of grading contracts. He asked me about it in an e-mail: "One quick question: have you gotten any feedback from anyone about whether the grading contract is IAI-compatible? I had gotten the impression that the relative assignment weights/point totals were pretty hard and fast." As Kerri mentioned, it was planned that I would help faculty in this way—to help them consider how they might succeed while teaching the first-year writing courses. Yet I found this conversation positioned me awkwardly in relation to the writing program under Kerri's direction. When choosing to use a grading contract, I never intended to influence other faculty to implement the practice. And furthermore, even if I thought instituting contracts was the right decision for the program, the decision wouldn't be mine to make. I found I was directly influencing pedagogical practices in a way that contradicted Kerri's official writing program policies. I couldn't help but feel guilty. Despite this guilt, I strongly believed using contracts was an appropriate response to the struggles students had during the fall, and I couldn't begrudge my colleague's arriving at that same conclusion—especially based on a discussion of my pedagogical practices.

My position in the discursive space of the writing program, as someone who is transitioning into the WPA role, means this conflict occurs repeatedly when I discuss with colleagues the use of particular textbooks, portfolios, specific assignments, and so forth. It highlights the tension we have discussed above between a framed program and a diverse community. Because I am transitioning in and out of the WPA position, this tension raises important questions while I work to balance my administrative and teaching/collegial roles.

- When considering my own pedagogical practices, how do I balance my beliefs about what's best for students with what's expected by the program?
- When discussing pedagogy with colleagues, how do I balance the competing subjectivities of being an advocate for the program, a pedagogical resource for faculty, and a supportive colleague?
- When working with Kerri, how do I make clear these competing subjectivities in a way that is honest and forthright so I am not undermining her attempts at creating a coherent writing program?

The answers to these questions grow out of contextualized and dialectic exchanges, creating a writing program that is a negotiated and dynamic rhetorical space (Qualley and Chiseri-Strater 2007, 175–76). This negotiation means my interactions with colleagues lead me to strike a balance among an adherence to Kerri's vision for the writing program; attention to my own pedagogical theories, style, and strengths; and respect for the intellectual curiosity and pedagogical theories of my colleagues. In my discussions with colleagues, I must keep these questions in mind and negotiate contextualized answers that will work pragmatically for the instructor, for me, and for the program. This negotiation means we are all searching for our own rhetorical positions in the discursive landscape of first-year composition pedagogy. To achieve the desired programmatic cohesion, those positions must be relative to the WPA's official position.

While struggling to answer the questions posed above, I crafted a response to my colleague's e-mail—as much as a way to think through the dilemma as to respond to his question about grading contracts. In it, I justified the use of contracts based on what I saw as the limits of IAI's authority, the pedagogical value of grading contracts, and academic freedom. However, I qualified what I wrote by relating it to official program policies, making it clear we should defer to Kerri's judgment for a program-wide policy. In the exchange, I offered pedagogical advice while working to enact Carmen Werder's (2000) call for rhetorical agency, in which pedagogical decisions are made through dialectic interactions between colleagues. Perhaps the result is not what Kerri would envision for the program, nor what I expected to occur, but the collaborative work that comprises the process creates something new and unexpected that, I argue, strengthens the way first-year writing is taught and the way we colleagues work together to shape the first-year writing program. This approach, in which I balance policy with pedagogy and pragmatics, serves as a bridge that brings faculty together.

INTENTIONAL TRANSITIONS MEAN COLLABORATIVE WPAS

Our collaborative work on the administrative duties of the writing program means our subjectivities shift according to the situation. As Kerri's story illustrates, even as she was building a place where the program could grow, she was thinking about the transition out of the coordinator role. Likewise, Brad's story illustrates moments in which he has taken on administrative roles while working to remain separate from the official position. So, we have always been transitioning in and out. The intentional transition, however, posed several problems for us. What are our roles in the program? To what extent is it Brad's responsibility to reinforce the official program position, and to what extent is he a fellow traveler with faculty colleagues who have some freedom to roam and find their own place in the broader discursive landscape? While the transitions have been intentional, our roles have evolved as we have continued to work together on administrative tasks.

As we have said, it was important for us to build a community, but Suellyn Duffey (2007) reminds us that just because an entire faculty teaches composition does not mean there is a disciplinary culture of rhetoric and composition (65–66). Certainly the culture of our department is congenial to rhetoric and composition. However, the disciplinary ideals at the core of the writing-about-writing curriculum are unfamiliar and discomfiting for some, which serves as a reminder that a group of faculty teaching composition is not necessarily a community with a shared discourse and pedagogical goals.

Thus, we needed to build a first-year composition community, a rhetorical location, with its own identity that would draw from the community of faculty in the English department yet foreground their distinctiveness, even though, in our case, the two communities overlap completely. We argue that they are distinct communities, not because the faculty are different but because of the distinctive discursive, disciplinary, and pedagogical features each community has—a place where specific rhetorical actions are located in the discursive landscape.

Because the writing program draws faculty from different subdisciplines of English, the writing program is a community nested in overlapping discourse communities, each of which is tacitly in competition for controlling the framing narrative of first-year writing's pedagogical context. Adler-Kassner (2008) calls for a writing program as a community that is organized, focused, and framed. Framing, when executed successfully, tacitly discourages competing discourses from controlling the group narrative. Resolving this tension in our formative work allows an appropriate system of values and morals to begin to inform the work of teaching writing. When the tension between these two concepts of community (diverse, multiple, material and organized, focused, framed) are considered, it necessitates an approach to community building that is conducive to programmatic cohesion but that also allows for continual rhetorical work, as characterized by Johnstone (1981), among community members—members who bring to bear a number of competing interests that are always in tension: competing discursive frames, institutional policy, programmatic vision, and individual pedagogical practices, to name a few. As we worked together, we intentionally formed a model for ethical interaction based on Adler-Kassner's notion of community: "The WPA's agenda, in other words, becomes *mobilizing others around their interests*, not mobilizing others around *her* interests" (Adler-Kassner 2008, 106).

Werder (2000) sets the stage for how this mobilization can occur by defining the WPA "not only as an individual position, but as a site—a space where rhetorical agency is fostered," where rhetoric is viewed as persuasion in cooperative terms rather than in strictly agonistic terms (12). The notion of creating rhetorical agency within a writing program, which Werder (2000) defines as "the potential for effecting change based on the extent to which the collective resources, titles, and expertise of a particular situation are made available for the individual and common good" (12), is at the center of her argument. Werder works to "promote a professional ethos that pays close attention to moral judgement, one that highlights our association with a rhetorical ability to make judgements based on a sound ethical system" (7). For Werder, this ethical system is centered on a relationship of mutual agency rather than control, formulated around a "dialectic interplay between actors" (11–12).

Werder's focus on rhetorical agency offers the mechanics for how such a community can function—how it can be multiple and disparate but also organized and framed. Yet the balance implied in this task is tricky since WPAs are responsible for setting the frame in motion that will guide and give shape to the interests of faculty teaching in the program. Without this guiding voice (or voices), alternative and undesirable frames have an opportunity to control what the writing program is to become. The exact processes enacted by different WPAs at different institutions vary, as does the level of programmatic coherence necessary to achieve curricular goals. What is consistent across institutions, though, is the notion that coherence is always collaborative and rhetorical. In a discourse community, some level of coherence is achieved just by talking and writing to one another about our practices and theories. Yet more work is needed than simple discussion. The WPA must ensure there is a programmatic vision, a dwelling place that frames the work we do, at the center of a system that allows for instructors to venture forth together with rhetorical agency and academic freedom as their guides. Our transitions have taught us that, in a coherent program, WPAs should allow for productive variation in a way that demonstrates trust for faculty and adherence to a centralized mission.

Thus, the first order of business, when establishing direction for the writing program, was to bring everyone together to a common location, both literally and figuratively, so we could become a group who identifies "not as members of some abstract, organic, disciplinary community, but simply as interlocutors who have agreed to hear each other out at this time and in this place" (Harris 2001, 5).

While it is true we are all coming together in a single location, there is also a necessity for the writing program to get on the same page in some very basic ways. There is a need for us to create a localized discourse and a learning community that responds to the material conditions of our program. Therefore, if we are working with a definition of the writing program that includes a metaphor for discursive space/rhetorical positioning, then "coming together" also means we are speaking and thinking about writing in similar ways, sharing a lexicon, establishing common goals, and so forth. This work of coming together as a program began with the two of us coming together to think through our shared values and differences, and an analysis of our interactions has given us a way to move forward on a programmatic level.

As we have worked through these programmatic and personal transitions, it is clear we didn't get everything right. There were plenty of missed opportunities and unforeseen problems. Perhaps that is true of any writing program, no matter its institutional position and legacy. The balance between theory and practice and the experiences of working in GSU's unique context illuminated unanticipated complexities that required us to rethink the way we worked to administer the writing program. Donna Qualley and Elizabeth Chiseri-Strater too found this to be true: "We have come to realize, however, that this ongoing conflict between our most tightly-held theories and our practical realities may be a positive thing. The vulnerability that often leaves us feeling unsure and off-balance as administrators and teachers is also what keeps us positioned as learners continually having to renegotiate our positions" (Qualley and Chiseri-Strater 2007, 172).

As we separately prepared our syllabi for the fall 2015 semester, the second time we taught Writing Studies 1, the effects of our rhetorical action began to emerge. When we compared the finished drafts, we learned we had influenced one another quite a bit. While Brad opted not to use grading contracts, Kerri adopted them for her sections. At the heart of our program is a strategy for being WPAs in transition, choosing ethical, rhetorical tactics to build a community of writing teachers. That work has begun in earnest in the space of our Composition Steering Committee, a group made up of those faculty most heavily invested in shaping the values of the program. In time, we will continue this work across the entire program. Soon, our roles will be reversed. Now that Brad has been awarded tenure, he will become the writing program coordinator in the fall of 2016, and Kerri will be a writing teacher among writing teachers.

References

Adler-Kassner, Linda. 2008. *The Activist WPA: Changing Stories about Writing and Writers.* Logan: Utah State University Press.

Adler-Kassner, Linda, and Peggy O'Neill. 2010. *Reframing Writing Assessment to Improve Teaching and Learning.* Logan: Utah State University Press.

Duffey, Suellyn. 2007. "Defining Junior." In *Untenured Faculty as Writing Program Administrators: Institutional Practices and Policies,* edited by Debra Frank Dew and Alice Horning, 58–71. West Lafayette, IN: Parlor.

Harris, Joseph. 2001. "Beyond Community: From the Social to the Material." *Journal of Basic Writing* 20 (2): 3–15.

Johnstone, Henry. 1981. "Toward an Ethics of Rhetoric." *Communication* 6 (2): 305–14.

Qualley, Donna, and Elizabeth Chiseri-Strater. 2007. "Split at the Root: The Vulnerable Writing Program Administrator." *WPA: Writing Program Administration* 31 (1–2): 171–84.

Werder, Carmen. 2000. "Rhetorical Agency: Seeing the Ethics of It All." *WPA: Writing Program Administration* 24 (1–2): 7–26.

Wiley, Mark. 2001. "Rehabilitating the 'Idea of Community.'" *Journal of Basic Writing* 20 (2): 16–33.

18
WRITING CENTER PROFESSIONALS, MARGINALIZATION, AND THE FACULTY/ADMINISTRATOR DIVIDE

Molly Tetreault

Part of this story is that I didn't want to tell this story. I remember saying to a colleague as I started my current position directing the Connors Writing Center (CWC), "I don't really want to concentrate on marginalization. I want to think about writing center work in other ways." At the time, I was reading and rereading as much writing center scholarship as I could, trying to glean whatever might relate to my new role. It was winter in New Hampshire—the days were short, and I spent many dark, cold evenings being reminded that issues of marginalization play a central role in the field. I'd trek out of the abandoned writing center across the abandoned campus in five-degree weather, headed home to read about budget cuts, dungeon-like basement offices, expectations for grammar fix-it shops, metaphors of student writers as sick, and writing centers as quarantine wards. It was a bleak January. And yet, however grim the picture of writing center work, I didn't feel those situations fit my own.

But I got my first taste of marginalization that spring, as I attended my first conference since starting the position, leading me to reconsider my reluctance to engage with issues of marginalization. Walking into a writing center session, I saw a scholar I admire standing toward the front of the room. Despite my usual reserve in these types of situations, I decided I was going to introduce myself. I stood behind him as I waited for his conversation to wrap up, silently practicing what I'd say. I led with my name, hand outstretched. He returned the shake, and we exchanged pleasantries. But I was taken aback as the conversation unfolded.

Me: "I just started a new position directing the UNH writing center."
Him: "Faculty or administration?"
Me: "Administration."
Him: "That's too bad."

DOI: 10.7330/9781607326335.c018

He turned away and headed across the room to take a seat.

I went to find my own seat, wondering what he meant. *Too bad? Too bad for whom?*

During the session, I found myself speaking up too much as the audience engaged in discussion. I hated that I did it, but I was on the defensive, contributing to show I know something about writing centers and writing instruction, that I'm familiar with the scholarship, that I can engage. I said one thing, but I was really saying, *I belong here. It's not "too bad" that I'm sitting in this room.* And as I tried to show I could add something of value to the conversation, I realized that moment was the first time I had felt marginalized as a writing center director, a feeling that had been prompted by someone within the field. And now, more than two years into my position, I know my experience is not unique.

I spent the trip home from the conference thinking about the exchange, trying to make sense of the interaction. My fellow conference attendee could have meant a number of things by his comment, from dismissing me because of my position's administrative status to suggesting the university ought to recognize my work with a tenure-line faculty position. Whatever the intention—even if to express my fitness for a faculty position—I was still stunned that my first engagement within the professional community was met with a question about my job status.

Then again, I probably shouldn't have been so surprised. Marginalization has long been a major focus within writing center studies, reflecting the long history—and current reality—of many writing center directors who are overworked, underpaid, and misunderstood on their campuses. Discussions of marginalization tend to focus around the administrator/tenure-line faculty divide.

Indeed, it is such a common lens for understanding marginalization that both of the 2014 International Writing Center Association award-winning publications attempt to crack open this binary. In examining the implications of their study of midcareer writing center professionals (WCPs), Anne Ellen Geller and Harry Denny set up the issue this way: "Again and again, when new writing center director positions are created or established writing center positions are advertised, we hear a familiar question: Why isn't this position tenure track? From everything we heard in our interviews, we suggest a deeper conversation that transcends such framing" (Geller and Denny 2013, 111). One of their findings—that "the lived experiences of writing center professionals are not as different as their position configurations might suggest"—underscores the necessity of reframing and reconsidering the conversation (Geller and Denny 2013, 101). Similarly, Jackie Grutsch McKinney argues, "If we put aside our rhetorical and visual habits that have us continually wrapped in discussing and seeing ourselves as marginal or not marginal, we might see other perfectly viable, perhaps even more useful representations" (Grutsch McKinney 2013, 56). This perspective—grounded in Jerome Bruner's work on the narrative construction of reality—is similar to Linda Adler-Kassner's suggestion that the activist WPA work to change the "frame" through which our narratives are produced and read, "permitting 'alternative' interpretations" (Adler-Kassner 2008, 12).

To avoid the tunnel vision that leads to the tenure-line faculty/administrative divide, both Grutsch McKinney and Geller and Denny offer a similar approach. Grutsch McKinney argues that we need a focus on the "ecologies" of writing centers (Grutsch McKinney 2013, 55). Although Geller and Denny do not identify their solution as such, their recommendation that conversations about status "revolve around consideration of what institutional or departmental cultures will support and what WCPs need for individual, institutional, and disciplinary evolution" echoes Grutsch McKinney's call for an ecological perspective (Grutsch McKinney 2013, 111). These suggestions align with recent WPA scholarship that has also called for attention to the ecologies of writing programs and WPAs. As Mary Jo Reiff, Anis Bawarshi, Michelle Ballif, and Christian Weisser explain, "An ecological perspective shifts the emphasis away from the individual unit, node, or entity, focusing instead on the network itself as the locus of meaning. All the acts, actors, and objects in an ecology are connected, both in space and time, and the interactions among them reverberate throughout and beyond the system itself" (Reiff et al. 2015, 6). The way meaning reverberates throughout an ecology suggests the importance of sharing narratives of our work—our personal and local experience influences the larger web of our disciplinary knowledge and relationships, and vice versa.

An ecological perspective can be especially helpful in times of transition, as a WPA attempts to unravel the web of relationships that affects their understanding of their position and identity. Counseling theory posits that "moving through a transition requires letting go of aspects of the self, letting go of former roles, learning new roles," and "people going through transitions inevitably must take stock as they renegotiate these roles" (Anderson, Goodman, and Schlossberg 2014, 30). This chapter is my way of "taking stock" of the transition into my position.

My story is, of course, my own. In telling it, I take up Grutsch McKinney's call for WCPs to tell their stories, especially when those stories do not conform to what she describes as the "writing center grand narrative," or the story about writing center work most typically shared. As she writes, "Taking the effort to acknowledge how the narrative operates, writing transgressions of the narrative, allowing the suppressed and peripheral pieces to surface, and re-envisioning the boundaries of writing center work will allow us to dislodge our established rhetorical and visual ways" (Grutsch McKinney 2013, 89–90). These individual perspectives can thus become "instantiations of counterstories" that widen our perspective and provide glimpses into the reverberations across an ecology (Grutsch McKinney 2013, 86). Individual experience interacts with, is informed by, and informs nodes in the larger system.

To capture the reverberations in an ecology, I examine aspects of my personal, institutional, and disciplinary transition into writing center work and how these transitions have interacted with the narrative of marginalization. More specifically, I use my own narrative to argue that, by focusing on job status as a measure of marginalization, the field often reproduces traditional notions of academic and administrative success, undermining attempts to bring WCPs out of the margins.

~

When I applied for my position, I explained in my cover letter that it was my dream job. I love writing center work, and the position would also offer much greater stability and more opportunity to impact students and the writing culture on campus than I'd had in my three years as contingent faculty. My time as an adjunct emphasized to me the social nature of writing and teaching writing. While I witnessed every day the role community played in supporting student writers, I also felt what the lack of community and professional connections within my working environment did to me as a teacher. I taught at a number of different colleges but didn't feel connected at any. I was stagnating, left alone with the questions and ideas that emerged from my teaching.

No news here: adjuncting came with terrible pay and terrible working conditions. I remember conferencing with students in the main lobby of one of the colleges. We sat in the only seats available, outside the men's bathroom. A full-time staff member walked by, then doubled back to ask me why I was working in that spot. "People visiting the main office can see you here outside the bathroom," she explained. I responded, "The former adjunct office is now the student orgs office, so I don't really have another place to meet with students." I didn't add I had only found out about the loss of space after coming in to photocopy my syllabi the day before the semester began. No one had bothered to notify the adjuncts.

Members of the English department at one community college encouraged me to apply for a full-time position—if one ever opened up. A two-million-dollar budget cut and hiring freeze during the Great Recession meant that as full-time faculty retired, they were not replaced (and most still haven't been). I loved teaching within the community college system, but I was worried about the long-term realities of adjuncting. I thought about returning to graduate school for a PhD in composition. But after much consideration, I opted to continue adjuncting while completing a second master's degree, this time an MEd in teaching writing that would lead to secondary certification. By that point, a public-school teacher's pay, benefits, and teaching load sounded fantastic, and if I did decide to pursue a PhD after the MEd, I'd have more options for employment if a job search didn't go well.

As I neared the end of the MEd program, I applied for the writing center position and was thrilled to be offered it. Wanting to be thorough in my vetting of the program, I requested a meeting with Edward Mueller, director of the university writing programs, who would be my direct supervisor. Among other questions, I was curious about the position's evolution since I would be the first full-time administrative director in the center's twenty-year history. As Ed and I spoke, I got my first inkling of the work that had gone into making the position so secure.

From my perspective, I was moving from contingency into a stable position with institutional status that would enable me to become a member of a professional community—or so I hoped. In this sense, the position fit Neal Lerner's classification of directorships as "an active, enfranchised group with faculty status or secure status" rather than the "part-time contingent—and largely silent—group doing the best they can under very difficult conditions" (Lerner 2006, 10). Lerner argues that secure positions can be "just as influential in an institution as can a tenured faculty member (or both can be equally lacking in influence)" (Lerner 2000, 44). And, yet, as my first attempt to engage within the profession at large indicates, this taxonomy does not account for the hierarchies around which WCPs can—and do—arrange themselves.

The irony of the situation is this: compositionists often decry the ways they are marginalized within English departments—the root, as Robert J. Connors indicates, of composition as an "underclass" (Connors 1990, 108). But, as Lerner's historical work points out, the role of writing centers as an "outlet valve" for the conditions affecting composition positioned—and continues to position—WCPs as even lower down on the university hierarchy than composition's underclass (Lerner 2009, 30). That bottom-level status extends to writing center scholarship as well. Even a quick glance at *WPA* or *CCC* indicates how little writing center scholarship is cited or published. Trying to escape the margins, WCPs sometime shift and reenact the same marginalization they feel from composition studies or WPAs on those WCPs whose job status does not reflect the ultimate signifier of institutional status at the university—tenure. Paired with the tensions between faculty and administration within the modern, corporate university, administrative status can be a further marker of writing center directors as outsiders. If nothing else, that first conference interaction made this hierarchy very clear to me.

~

I started in January. Coming in midway through the academic year, I sometimes felt like an intruder. The staff had already established connections with each other and had functioned on their own for a whole semester before I arrived. My sense of place was so unsure. To settle in, I observed. I conferenced with student writers, sat at the staff table, listened to the staff. The CWC's associate director, Sarah Franco, helped me learn the ins and outs of the CWC's operations and get to know the staff. I tried to act as support to what was already going on, to honor the work the staff had already been doing.

So when Patty Wilde, one of the graduate students who worked for the writing program, invited me to join her in exploring the Robert J. Connors Writing Center Files—an archive of writing center documents housed in UNH's Dimond Library—I jumped at the opportunity. Still trying to find my footing, I went to the archive looking for connections—to the past staff and its work, to Robert J. Connors, the founding director. I had already spent considerable time going through the informal archive that is my office, examining the documents that showed the considerable work of the part-time and graduate assistant directors who had come before me. Those documents reminded me of "the backs I stand on," as Nancy Grimm writes; they are the "network of relationships" that are the foundation of my own work (Grimm 1999, 24).

Once in the archive, my need for connections led me to a collection of Connors's administrative documents, which illustrated the precarious position of the early center. It may be something of a cliché in the writing center world, but nothing signaled the early center's marginality quite like Connors's *gratefulness* to find a permanent location for the center in the basement of the English department building. That basement location—which Lisa Ede links to writing centers' position as peripheral—"our second-class status . . . symbolized by our basement offices and inadequate staffs"—was an upgrade from Connors's perspective, a stop to semesterly bouncing from location to location (Ede 1989, 7). At a time when I was helping orchestrate the writing center's move to the main branch of the UNH Library, to almost the exact spot

Connors had requested for the writing center when it opened in 1994, I couldn't help but notice how far the center had come over the course of twenty years.

I do not mean to impose a neat history of progress upon the UNH writing center. The twists and turns of the program are messy. What's more, bearing a name like the Robert J. Connors Writing Center means our center has a tendency toward hero worship. The writing assistants hope to "make Bob proud." I do too. But as easy as it is to think about the writing center past, present, and future in such ways, it's also important to avoid what Peter Carino has pointed out are the pitfalls of narratives of progress or simplified hero tales. Instead, he argues for a cultural model of history that offers "thicker descriptions of context" that "deconstruct oversimplified notions" (Carino 1996, 39).

Here is part of that context: Like many writing centers, the UWC faced budget cuts. The cuts were deep, especially considering how small the UWC's budget was to begin with. Connors fought hard against those cuts. Eventually, he opted to resign his position in protest, and three drafts of his resignation letter are housed in the archive. His final draft ends, "I have played my best cards, and I have failed. I have only this one card left, and I must finally play it. My last service to the writing center will be to leave it, and to hope that my resignation will convince the administration to reexamine funding priorities (Connors 1999, B.3 F.17). Reading those lines, I was struck by Connors's sacrifice, a form of faculty activism and protest, one last plea to the English department and the university to fund a growing campus-wide initiative.

Connors was a nationally known and respected scholar, tenured faculty at UNH, and a founding member of the Northeast's regional writing center association; as a writing center director, however, he described his situation as "marginal despite my best efforts" (Connors 1999, B.3 F.17). I, on the other hand, do not have to fight for an adequate budget or appropriate compensation for my position. I feel respected and listened to by the academic unit I work for. That's a very different relationship to the institution than Connors's, who ends his letter with these lines: "But I feel that no one is listening to us anymore. My effectiveness has been used up in shouting to try to make myself heard, and I have no voice left for it anymore." And to further complicate the typical narrative, in the intervening years between Connors's directorship and my own, so much of the work to stabilize the center and my position was done, and continues to be done, by undergraduate and graduate writing assistants, graduate-student administrators, part timers, nonstatus employees—and yes, people with administrative status.

We know the directing-a-writing-center-is-difficult narrative. That story is so well established that Rebecca Jackson, Jackie Grutsch McKinney, and Nicole I. Caswell make note of it in their chapter in this collection. Discussing one of the potential reasons most WCPs in their study primarily discussed the difficulties of their positions, they explain, "[The participants] may have (subconsciously) felt compelled to tell a story that resembled internalized disciplinary narratives" (122). Just as their participants may have felt compelled to tell particular sorts of stories, I worry that relaying moments of difficulty will lead to easy, knee-jerk interpretations. The victim narrative. The narrative of impotence. The *if-you-were-tenured-this-never-would-have-happened* response.

But conflict, challenges, and difficulties are part of people's working lives. Maybe it shouldn't be that way, but it is. Exploring how an administrative WCP learns to navigate the trickier moments of the position might be the only way to complicate the typical representation of those occupying nontenurable and nonfaculty positions as weak and powerless.

An e-mail arrived in my inbox the same month as the conversation at the conference. It was one piece of a longer exchange about the writing center's operations. Up to that point, the messages from this faculty member had been professional, courteous, collegiate—albeit with an increasing edge of dissatisfaction. Imagine my surprise when I read the first line.

"You are hurting UNH faculty and students."

It stung, but I quickly noted the order of stakeholders within that sentence. It gave me a sense of why she was angry. This faculty member's belief that students should have already learned how to write prior to arriving in her course lurked behind the whole of our exchange. But feeling as if I understood the source of her anger didn't provide an immediate path toward making the situation better.

I followed my typical inflammatory e-mail protocol: sleep on it and draft a response the next day. In my draft, I tried to reexplain my perspective and asked the faculty member to meet face to face so we could discuss the situation.

But I wasn't satisfied, and I wasn't sure the e-mail would accomplish much. I considered dropping by the faculty member's office to chat. Given that e-mail can feel like a faceless, disembodied form of communication, I wondered whether the tone would change if the conversation occurred face to face. Now that I am more seasoned, I might tell my new-to-the-job self, *generally a good approach, but not always effective.* I've experienced a number of turnarounds to these conversations when conducted in person, but I've also, on a few occasions, experienced further deterioration as well.

Three days passed with no follow-up on my end or hers. Wanting an outside perspective, I took the situation to Ed. After bringing him up to speed, he asked me, "Do you have to respond?"

Oh, I thought. *No. I don't.* Perhaps the faculty member was blowing off steam. Perhaps that was the way she chose to deal with her inability to convince or force me to run the writing center according to her wishes. Perhaps her e-mail was meant to be her final word on the subject. Whatever her reason for responding as she did, the wording and tone was inappropriate and unprofessional. I had already explained—multiple times—the situation from my perspective. I don't like to abandon any relationship and typically view these moments as an opportunity to convince, collaborate, reconsider; however, I didn't see much good coming from additional engagement and decided to let the situation cool off for a while. Maybe I'd visit her in the fall. Or maybe I wouldn't. Whichever route I took in the future, our immediate exchange was no longer a conversation. I didn't respond.

Ed's question—and his own leadership by example—illustrated what Anne Ellen Geller, Michele Eodice, Frankie Condon, Meg Carroll, and Elizabeth H. Boquet call "an administrative rhetoric that celebrates not only writing . . . but a kind of teaching and learning that accomplishes its goals by saying less and doing more, in subversive and deliberate ways" (Geller et al. 2007, 118). Cheryl Glenn and Krista Ratcliffe have identified this application of Glenn's work on silence as "one of the most powerful implementations of silence as pedagogy" (Glenn and Ratcliffe 2011, 5–6). In general, Glenn's and Ratcliffe's research—both collectively and individually—on the rhetorics of silence and listening have pointed to their "marginalized status" while challenging the idea that silence and listening are less powerful rhetorical arts (2). While silence can be a mark of marginalization and subjugation, it can also be a rhetorical strategy with remarkable power.

I want to be clear: I am not saying administrative WCPs (or anyone) should be limited to silence and listening. I am often quite vocal. I see myself as the guardian of and advocate for the writing center and the staff who work here. I speak out and speak up. I write. But in always figuring and representing one type of position as invested with the ethos and power to speak, we ignore the ways others within writing centers (who actually hold the majority of positions) perform their work, whether that be through speaking or deliberate use of silence and listening.

In the wider context of writing center studies, the conversation about job status is also a conversation about the discipline—what is the discipline's status at the university and within larger conversations about writing, literacy, and education? That conversation is often myopic, the tunnel vision Grutsch McKinney (2013) identifies, focusing on the faculty/administrator divide. To move beyond this tunnel vision is not an easy task. For example, despite their attempt, I am not convinced Geller and Denny are able to transcend the binary. When they write, "Participants who held administrative positions didn't appear overly concerned about whether their jobs might undermine the potential for or promise of tenure-stream faculty positions in writing centers for others" (Geller and Denny 2013, 105), we are back to the faculty/administrator divide. Their comment highlights the extent to which conversations about status often come down to an implicit belief that tenure should be our main concern and our main goal.

As a result, if your job configuration appears to others as working against that goal, you may be viewed as not having the best interests of the field at heart. And yet, both tenure-line and administrative positions are a part of, as Joseph Harris reminds us, "the structures of academic professionalism . . . [that] encourage us not to identify with our coworkers but to strive to distinguish ourselves from one another—and, in doing so, to short-circuit attempts to form a sense of our collective interests and identity" (Harris 2000, 52). By focusing on job status as a measure of marginalization, we reinscribe that structure, isolating us as individuals—or as groups according to job status—undermining what we might achieve as a whole.

How might we avoid the tenure-line faculty/administrator divide? How do we come together despite the individualistic structure of academic professionalism?

As a starting point, it's important for WCPs to recognize, as Ann M. Penrose describes, "what we're aiming for" (Penrose 2012, 122). Writing about contingent faculty's inclusion (or lack thereof) in composition as a profession, Penrose suggests "a more historically grounded understanding of professional as collaborative and contributing" (122). Contribution and collaboration are what Geller and Denny are calling for when they highlight their study participants' attitudes about scholarship. Participants "craved intellectual labor as scholarship for self-actualization and personal and professional status," but "effective program administration and leadership did not require making a case for the importance of published scholarship" (Geller and Denny 2013, 118). This observation leads them to an important question: "If advancing a field and oneself within it involves the consumption, production, and dissemination of new knowledge, whether through conference proposals and presentations, or, more importantly, vetted publication, what might it mean to exempt oneself or for significant parts of a community of professionals not to participate in its own collective/social construction of knowledge?" (118). The question isn't directly answered, but the implication isn't good. I do agree—engagement within the broader community is critical to the development of the field and the professionals who work within it. But my own experience speaks to some of the social factors that may work against some members engaging. If you're worried about how your job status will be read, you may be less likely to engage at professional meetings and conferences, let alone write and publish. That's a lot of work to be reminded you don't quite belong.

We need, in other words, a community that understands the importance of contributing while also fostering an environment that doesn't make some feel as if they aren't welcome to. Along the lines of what Liliana M. Naydan recommends for "building solidarity among workers of different kinds" (291) in her contribution to this collection, WCPs might turn to Krista Ratcliffe's trope of rhetorical listening as a way of working toward such a community. Ratcliffe defines rhetorical listening as "a stance of openness that a person may choose to assume in relation to any person, text, or culture; its purpose is to cultivate conscious identifications in ways that promote productive communication, especially but not solely cross-culturally" (Ratcliffe 2005, 25). Rhetorical listening is especially important among WCPs—if we want the academy to listen to what we have to say about writing, writers, and learning, we ought to practice that sort of listening among ourselves, too.

Listening, collaborating, contributing—these are pillars of writing center work. WCPs have much to share about all three. We witness the power of coming together across hierarchies and job statuses in our centers each day—tutors and students, tutors and directors, students and teachers, and so forth. But we undermine our knowledge and contributions as a field if we do not challenge academia's adherence to traditional hierarchies and definition of success as individual. By consciously working to dismantle those hierarchies, we can begin to blur the faculty/administrator divide. That's a transition writing centers would certainly benefit from.

References

Adler-Kassner, Linda. 2008. *The Activist WPA: Changing Stories about Writing and Writers.* Logan: Utah State University Press.

Anderson, Mary, Jane Goodman, and Nancy K. Schlossberg. 2014. *Counseling Adults in Transition: Linking Practice with Theory.* 4th ed. New York: Springer.

Carino, Peter. 1996. "Open Admissions and the Construction of Writing Center History: A Tale of Three Models." *Writing Center Journal* 17 (1): 30–48.

Connors, Robert J. 1990. "Overwork/Underpay: Labor and Status of Composition Teachers since 1880." *Rhetoric Review* 9 (1): 108–26. https://doi.org/10.1080/07350199009388919.

Connors, Robert J. 1999. Robert J. Connors Writing Center Files, 1994–2010. Milne Special Collections and Archives, University of New Hampshire.

Ede, Lisa. 1989. "Writing as a Social Process: A Theoretical Foundation for Writing Centers." *Writing Center Journal* 9 (2): 3–13.

Geller, Anne Ellen, and Harry Denny. 2013. "Of Ladybugs, Low Status, and Loving the Job: Writing Center Professionals Navigating Their Careers." *Writing Center Journal* 33 (1): 96–129.

Geller, Anne Ellen, Michele Eodice, Frankie Condon, Meg Carroll, and Elizabeth H. Boquet. 2007. *The Everyday Writing Center: A Community of Practice.* Logan: Utah State University Press.

Glenn, Cheryl, and Krista Ratcliffe, eds. 2011. *Silence and Listening as Rhetorical Arts.* Carbondale: Southern Illinois University Press.

Grimm, Nancy. 1999. "The Way the Rich People Does It: Reflections on Writing Center Administration and the Search for Status." In *Kitchen Cooks, Plate Twirlers and Troubadours: Writing Program Administrators Tell Their Stories,* edited by Diana George, 14–25. Portsmouth, NH: Boynton/Cook.

Grutsch McKinney, Jackie. 2013. *Peripheral Visions for Writing Centers.* Logan: Utah State University Press.

Harris, Joseph. 2000. "Meet the New Boss, Same as the Old Boss: Class Consciousness in Composition." *College Composition and Communication* 52 (1): 43–68. https://doi.org/10.2307/358543.

Lerner, Neal. 2000. "Confessions of a First-Time Writing Center Director." *Writing Center Journal* 21 (1): 29–48.

Lerner, Neal. 2006. "Time Warp: Historical Representations of Writing Center Directors." In *The Writing Center Director's Resource Book,* edited by Christina Murphy and Byron L. Stay, 3–12. Mahwah, NJ: Lawrence Erlbaum.

Lerner, Neal. 2009. *The Idea of a Writing Laboratory.* Carbondale: Southern Illinois University Press.

Penrose, Ann M. 2012. "Professional Identity in a Contingent-Labor Profession: Expertise, Autonomy, Community in Composition Teaching." *WPA: Writing Program Administration* 35 (2): 108–26.

Ratcliffe, Krista. 2005. *Rhetorical Listening: Identification, Gender, Whiteness.* Carbondale: Southern Illinois University Press.

Reiff, Mary Jo, Anis Bawarshi, Michelle Ballif, and Christian Weisser, eds. 2015. *Ecologies of Writing Programs: Program Profiles in Context.* Anderson, SC: Parlor.

19
TRANSITIONING FROM CONTINGENT TO TENURE-TRACK FACULTY STATUS AS A WPA
Working toward Solidarity and Academic-Labor Justice through Hybridity

Liliana M. Naydan

To employ a bit of labor-movement speak, any writing program administrator (WPA) job sort of positions the WPA who holds it as *The Man*—as the proprietor of power in a derogatory sense. In part, and perhaps especially as perceived by writing-program instructors who observe WPA work from the outside, WPAs indeed do have great power over their programs. They often hire, opt against renewing, fire, rehire, and administrate part- and full-time contingent faculty who have emerged as part and parcel of a twenty-first-century higher education workforce that is shaped by corporate motives, such as those explored by Marc Bousquet (2008) in *How the University Works: Higher Education and the Low-Wage Nation*.[1] They either help determine or determine outright the course offerings and course assignments; they perhaps provide insight into or even control instructors' compensation per course; and they assess and refashion writing programs according to visions they develop in accord with institutional missions and stakeholders in their institutions and programs. Yet, as Gary A. Olson and Joseph M. Moxley note, WPAs also lack the sort of power that they may believe themselves to have or that they may appear to have (Olson and Moxley 1989).[2] They occupy middle-managerial roles,[3] and, as evidenced by the publication of Debra Frank Dew and Alice S. Horning's *Untenured Faculty as Writing Program Administrators: Institutional Practices and Politics* (Dew and Horning 2007), as well as by the growing membership in the Conference on College Composition and Communication's (CCCC) Untenured WPA Special Interest Group (SIG),[4] many WPAs engage in administration prior to

DOI: 10.7330/9781607326335.c019

or sometimes at the expense of attaining tenure and the greater job security that accompanies it. They often become WPAs in times of professional transition before they feel they necessarily have substantial influence at their institutions.

This essay aims to expose the complex power dynamics involved in WPA work through the lens of social class as a phenomenon determined by "power and authority people have at work," a definition that Michael Zweig provides in *The Working Class Majority: America's Best Kept Secret* (Zweig 2000, 3). This essay also exposes these complex power dynamics through theorizing WPA identity as *hybrid*, a term that Homi K. Bhabha discusses in *The Location of Culture* (Bhabha 2004). I put Zweig's work into conversation with Bhabha's by telling the story of my own transition away from working as a contingent-faculty WPA who ran a writing center at an institution with a labor union for contingent faculty into a tenure-track assistant-professor WPA position at an institution that lacks a faculty labor union. In many ways, the story I tell is a story of struggling to position myself as an activist academic of the sort that Harry C. Denny (2010) describes in *Facing the Center: Toward an Identity Politics of One-To-One Mentoring*; that Patricia M. Malesh and Sharon McKenzie Stevens describe in *Active Voices: Composing a Rhetoric for Social Movements* (Malesh and Stevens 2009); and that Linda Adler-Kassner (2008) theorizes and idealizes in *The Activist WPA: Changing Stories about Writing and Writers*. Hence I tell the story of encountering peculiar and sometimes unfamiliar and unsettling power dynamics and existing in a state of flux with regard to my own power on and beyond the job.

Ultimately, I argue that in order to work effectively toward labor justice from middle-management tenure-line WPA positions, and in order to overcome crises of identity that may accompany transitions such as the one I experienced, WPAs who have made transitions similar to my own might recognize transitional moments, the identities that they produce, and the power dynamics that Zweig would certainly argue that they involve as hybrid, to use Bhabha's term. They might benefit from actively remembering and learning more about the contingent-faculty experience via rhetorical listening while they are working on the tenure track, and they might also benefit from engaging in a process of exchanging stories with contingent-faculty employees and with other WPAs and administrators about experiences they have had as workers of different ranks—experiences that shape them as always already hybrid, even long after transitional moments pass. These stories will, I hope, help unearth solidarity among faculty of different ranks and also help transitioning WPAs at the assistant-professor rank begin the process of engaging in transformations of their respective fields, their professional organizations, and the narrative that binds together fields, professional organizations, and everyday work.

POWER ON THE JOB: THE PARADOX OF CONTINGENT-FACULTY WPA STATUS AND THE BENEFITS OF ACTIVISM

Zweig defines working-class members as having "relatively little control over the pace or content of their work" and as not being "anybody's boss" (Zweig 2000, 3). I argue here that Zweig's definition provides great insight into academia's working-class majority of contingent faculty, even though power dynamics can emerge as hazy in contemporary academic contexts. In accord with Zweig's definition, contingent rhetoric and composition faculty very much lack power on the job, and, likewise, they often lack supervisory roles. Contingent faculty at times lack control over the material they teach, especially when writing programs commit themselves to specific textbooks or distribute common syllabi for all faculty. As for job security, WPAs often lack control over whether colleges and universities will rehire them from one semester to the next. And they almost always lack control over the means by which colleges and universities make decisions about hiring faculty on tenure or contingent lines. Yet WPAs hired on contingent-faculty lines reveal complexity in Zweig's social-class distinctions. By definition, WPAs obviously administrate something or someone—at least to some degree on the surface. Therefore, they retain a working-class status in academia even though they may masquerade as middle-class employees to populations of faculty or staff whom they appear to supervise.

The everyday realities of the social-class paradox of the contingent-line WPA emerged for me in the first position I accepted on completing my PhD in English in 2011. Having finished my doctoral degree amid the academic labor crisis that persists to this day, I was excited to get any job whatsoever fresh out of graduate school, especially a WPA position via which I was able to help run a writing center and via which I was able to get involved with a lecturers' union that had formed several years before. In ways, while on this job, I had power of the sort that Zweig (2000) describes non-working-class workers as having. I administered and led writing center staff meetings and communicated with writing consultants about their work on a daily basis. I also created my own syllabi for the tutor-education courses that I taught. Yet in other ways, I completely lacked power. My supervisors held the real power—the power over the budget and the power to fire me or not renew my contract at any point, for any reason. My everyday pedagogy and administration were subject to approval by the powers that be in ways quite different from those that I often heard tenure-line faculty in my profession speaking about. Academic freedom wasn't mine to exercise as long as I remained at constant risk of losing my job as a contingent faculty member—even if the staff I supervised failed to recognize the precariousness of my position.

And yet I managed to see great benefits in the full-time and precarious contingent-faculty position for which I was hired—benefits that some members of my profession certainly may not see—in particular because of the presence of my influential contingent-faculty union, which provided empowerment of a sort in the absence of power on the job as Zweig (2000) characterizes it. On the one hand, my union allowed me to develop as a professional in the field of writing center studies because it guaranteed me professional-development funding and relatively fair teaching loads—at least in comparison to the course loads that non-unionized contingent faculty have. With professional-development support, I attended regional conferences as well as national ones such as the National Conference on Peer Tutoring in Writing and the International Writing Centers Association Conference. I also published in my field to make myself a more appealing candidate for other positions should the clock ever run out on my contingent-faculty line or should I have the opportunity to make the sort of transitional professional move into a tenure-line position that I ended up having the opportunity to make. My scholarly work never counted per se as part of my job, which was by contractual definition teaching focused. It also never counted as part of what my superiors might review in quantifying my success, so it never gave me power on the job necessarily. But it counted toward my professional identity as a professional identity may transcend any given job—even an academic job—especially in the case of contingent-faculty employment. It gave me a certain power in my field beyond the job, to stretch Zweig's (2000) discussion of power a bit.

On the other hand, with my contingent-faculty WPA position, I also had an opportunity to develop my identity as an activist and organizer. And hence I had an opportunity to further find empowerment beyond my field and beyond the job in the absence of having power on the job as Zweig (2000) discusses it. In other words, I had the opportunity to unearth power via non-academic-job-oriented means, and the overlap among activist work, organizing work, and WPA work that I exposed for myself continues to animate my scholarly and my activist imagination. Denny (2010) gestures toward this overlap when he describes his undergraduate experience at the University of Iowa as providing him with "a new language and ways of thinking" that

> were turning [him] into a new kind of activist, not one who touted placards or bumper stickers, not one who would march on offices, but one who would discover everyday teaching and learning moments led to change every bit as important and sustainable as the more dramatic forms of protest in the streets or speeches from podiums. (7)

Similarly, Malesh and Stevens (2009) gesture toward this overlap when they characterize the contemporary activist academic's charge as involving "exposing students"—and, I would add, all members of academic communities—"to their own personal agency and encouraging them to assert it by helping them learn to use intersecting tools of analysis, critique, and action" (16).

My empowering academic-activist identity manifested in an array of practical ways while I inhabited my paradoxical and disempowering contingent-faculty WPA position. I brought what I knew about effective multimodal communication, a subject of my research, to the labor movement by cochairing and eventually chairing the Communications Committee and coediting our union's newsletter. I organized a flash mob as a rhetorical act that animated our collective message of increased pay for contingent faculty. I recorded digital video of the flash mob and posted it as a piece of multimodal writing that could reach a wider audience. And, eventually, I ran for the union's executive council and was elected as a campus cochair. I learned how to employ my knowledge of rhetorical situations to listen to my fellow contingent-faculty colleagues and talk to them about their employment conditions and their rights on the job—rights that in theory should include opportunities for academic freedom and self-governance. I learned how to employ collaboration as writing centers understand and value it to organize alongside my colleagues to improve our working conditions and to counter the pull-yourself-up-by-your-bootstraps American Dream mythology that continues to impede solidarity in workplaces.

In turn, my activist identity informed my academic identity—and my on-the-books professional work. I may not have had power on the job as Zweig (2000) theorizes it, but I gained a sense of empowerment that I needed to talk to my students about the injustices implicit in the formation of academic hierarchies. I told them I was a contingent faculty member because everyday education of the sort that Denny (2010) mentions creates meaningful change, and I didn't fear that they would see me as lesser in some way because of my status in the academic hierarchy. Instead, I trusted that they would show solidarity with me and respect the everyday work that they observed me doing for their benefit. Likewise, my scholarship transformed as a result of my activism. I saw connections, for instance, between religious faith, which I write about it in my scholarship on the rhetoric of fiction, and social justice. And I saw that the narrative of my academic identity as I articulated it in annual-review materials and in job applications I submitted in an effort to attain a new position had evolved to include shadows of activism. I saw that the sort of activist WPA about which Adler-Kassner (2008) writes does not just have to be a WPA who uses "strategies developed by community organizers and media strategists" to "shift frames" for stories about teaching writing (Adler-Kassner 2008, 5). An activist WPA might instead emerge as a WPA who sees the dynamic interplay among writing program administration, research, teaching, service, and activism.

TRANSITIONING INTO HYBRID TENURE-LINE ACTIVISM AND PROFESSIONALISM: TELLING STORIES, LISTENING RHETORICALLY, AND CHANGING THE PROFESSION

In transitioning from a contingent-faculty WPA to a tenure-track WPA job, I realized that the change in identity that I perhaps at moments imagined I'd experience didn't manifest as I thought it might because further complexity exists in Zweig's (2000) delineation of social classes as they pertain to academic contexts. Although tenure-track faculty typically have more power on the job, more inherent institutional respect, greater job security, benefits, and significantly higher pay than do contingent faculty, they don't *entirely* differ from contingent faculty, at least in terms of their everyday lived anxieties. They don't have power on the job, as Zweig (2000) describes it, unequivocally. Like contingent faculty, tenure-track faculty exist, at least until they earn tenure, as potentially disposable personnel and at risk of losing their jobs[5]—as contingent faculty of a sort who are *in medias res* in the narratives of their professional lives.[6] They exist as akin in ways to the kinds of liminal WPAs that Talinn Phillips, Paul Shovlin, and Megan Titus describe in their contribution to this collection. And they exist in the sorts of tenuous situations that M. J. Braun (2011) describes in noting that universities that have been "long touted as embodying the democratic principles of academic freedom and the free exchange of ideas" can, in reality, "be dangerous place[s] indeed for a rhetorician to teach and practice the political arts of democracy" (Braun 2011, 137). Hence I suggest that tenure-line faculty members exist as hybrid in Bhabha's sense of the term: as "neither the one thing nor the other" (Bhabha 2004, 49). Moreover, these tenure-line faculty exist as hybrid doubly so if they experience transitional moments that move them from contingent-faculty lines to tenure-track lines. For faculty members who have experienced these kinds of transitions, contingency emerges not only as a job status but as a residual and pervasive feeling or affect. And, notably, it is a feeling or affect that could potentially help formerly contingent and newly minted tenure-line WPAs sustain activist identities to help contingent faculty they employ.

For me, the challenge of transitioning into tenure-line WPA status involved sustaining everyday activity as an activist that would make manifest the sort of hybrid identity that I felt I now had. Like Denny (2010), I've come to realize that being an activist doesn't always require or necessarily involve participation in flash mobs or in-your-face grade-ins—examples of activities that helped define my contingent-line-faculty activist days. Activism can and should involve a wide range of rhetorical acts, some of them perhaps politically safer than others given the rhetorical situations in which tenure-track faculty members find themselves. It can and should involve acts that speak to different conceptions of rhetoric[7] and that help to establish the hybrid identity of the formerly contingent and newly tenure-line WPA as an empowering one despite problems that some theorists see with associating hybridity with a rhetoric of liberation.[8]

Activism of the sort that Denny (2010) describes might, first, involve formerly contingent tenure-line faculty recognizing everyday opportunities to speak about personal contingent-faculty experiences of disempowerment on the job—to use Zweig's (2000) terms—to foster hybridity as a reality. Upon seeing such opportunities in my own rhetorical situations, I fostered my own identity as hybrid by telling an array of stories about my experiences to contingent faculty in the first year of my tenure-line work. My hope in sharing my own stories was that contingent faculty would see me as an ally, not just as *The Man*—especially since I didn't at all feel like an oppressive authority. Among the stories I found myself telling about my pretransition, contingent days is one about how I used to spend a majority of my paycheck on gas to commute to and home from a job, but I had to keep the job for fear of the impression made by a lapse in employment and what it might do to my chances of finding a full-time position. This story spoke to situations akin to those in which I know my contingent-faculty employees found themselves. I also spoke about my own pretransition experience of grappling with the potentially high cost of a negative teaching evaluation given by a student who seemed hostile toward my tutor-education course from day one. Depending on the standards an employer holds for a contingent faculty member, a negative teaching evaluation could cost an employee a future professional opportunity if not a job, and I know well that contingent faculty who work for the writing program that I administer worry about their evaluations. I likewise spoke of my pretransition emotions about undergoing teaching observations amid threatening conditions that created constant anxiety about my future employment. I could understand with great clarity how contingent employees I was set to observe felt because when I worked as a contingent faculty member myself, I constantly feared that an unexpected event in class might be characterized in the wrong way and might make me less desirable to rehire. And, perhaps most important, I spoke of addressing within myself what I once called, in an article I wrote for my former union's newsletter, "the ever-open wounds that speak to the paradox that defines [contingent faculty]: pride in our work and love of our jobs but an uncomfortable awareness of our low status in the academic hierarchy and utter discomfort in addressing it" (Naydan 2013, 1).

Second, to further function as effective allies and to build solidarity among workers of different kinds to form a hybrid front against corporatizing forces in the university, formerly contingent tenure-line WPAs might practice rhetorical listening of the sort that Krista Ratcliffe (2005) describes in *Rhetorical Listening: Identification, Gender, Whiteness*: they might create respectful space for contingent faculty to share *their* stories of contingency and hybridity—stories of present-day realities that complement the value of institutional and personal histories of the sort that Molly Tetrault describes as key to identity formation in her contribution to this collection. According to Ratcliffe, who makes her argument about rhetorical listening with regard to gender and race, "*Rhetorical listening* is defined generally as a trope for interpretive invention and more particularly as a code of cross-cultural conduct" (Ratcliffe 2005, 17). It "signifies a stance of openness that a person may choose to assume in relation to *any* person, text, or culture," and it avoids gravitating "toward places of common ground," instead locating "our identifications in places of commonalities *and* differences" (Ratcliffe 2005, 17, 32). Furthermore, when "listening metonymically," rhetorical listeners can "avoid the trap of [developing] unfair generalizations and stereotyping" (Ratcliffe 2005, 98, 99). In other words, rhetorical listening is never comfortable or easy, yet new tenure-line WPAs—especially those hybrid kinds of WPAs who have worked as contingent faculty themselves prior to their transitions—will, in listening rhetorically to contingent faculty, be more likely to hear what they need to hear to emerge as activist leaders.

What formerly contingent and now tenure-line WPAs may hear certainly varies, and some of what I've heard in response to questions I've asked and via my own rhetorical-listening practice I probably shouldn't repeat. But these kinds of WPAs might hear, for instance, about the complex situations that keep contingent faculty in their positions—realities that they understand because of their pretransition experiences. I've heard in my tenure-line job about horrifying medical issues that family members of contingent faculty struggle with and contingent faculty members' utter desperation to make ends meet and pay medical bills. I've likewise heard about the range of pay that contingent faculty make at different campuses and about broken promises by institutions—narratives that counter the dominant ones that serve the maintenance of the status quo. I often can't do much about what I hear—at least not yet—but hearing about what I can't yet change helps me to think strategically about what I might be able to do in the future. And, on a more positive note, I've heard about the exciting classroom experiences that contingent faculty create for students—even if these contingent faculty members lack substantial institutional respect or support. Indeed, formerly contingent tenure-line WPAs who ask questions and listen rhetorically will realize how much they can learn or relearn from contingent faculty who bring with them to their work knowledge from a wide array of fields and work experiences—contingent faculty who may well exist, statistically, as the best teachers of college student writers.[9]

Finally, to emerge as effective allies to contingent faculty and effective activist academics at the tail end of their transitions, formerly contingent WPAs who define themselves through the lens of hybridity might engage in activist work that aims to challenge and to ultimately bring about change in professional organizations that dodge responsibility for the working conditions that their members face and that reinforce the existing status quo. I remember vividly that in the time between leaving my contingent-faculty position and beginning my tenure-line one, I wondered what shape my hybridized tenure-line activist identity would take. And soon after making my transition, I discovered the CCCCs Labor Caucus, a group composed of both contingent and tenure-line composition workers who focus on labor issues in rhetoric and composition. Likewise, I saw and answered an e-mail about an organization called MLA Democracy that went out on the WPA listserv, and in doing so, I realized that opportunities for labor activism for those in transitional situations like my own when we seek them out and make time for them as part of our everyday tenure-line missions and visions. As one of several early organizers for MLA Democracy, I helped shape it as a "movement that aims to place activists into MLA governance and to ensure the organization is responsive to the concerns of all members"—especially contingent faculty who form the new majority (MLA Democracy 2015). And when the Modern Language Association threw support behind National Adjunct Walkout Day (NAWD) in the form of MLA Action for Allies,[10] I saw a small victory for MLA Democracy and the labor movement as a whole—even though the MLA, like too many other professional organizations, has yet to provide enough support to contingent faculty who so need them.

CONCLUSION: A NEW NARRATIVE FOR WPA WORK

Certainly, social responsibility and WPA work interplay with one another in a number of ways, and I imagine that their interplay in part prompts Adler-Kassner to suggest that activist WPAs must generate and narrate stories that "tell about *why* we do the work that we do and motivate us to persist in it" (Adler-Kassner 2008, 10). The stories that Adler-Kassner (2008) encourages speak to the kind of robust social responsibility that any WPA takes on, or at least should take on, even in transitional moments. But as I think about the staunch challenges that lie ahead for academic-labor activists who work in rhetoric and composition, I realize that what Adler-Kassner (2008) suggests simply isn't enough, and I argue that formerly contingent WPAs must complement what she proposes by changing—or transitioning—the visible and audible story of what it means to be a tenure-line or perhaps even a tenured WPA. To appropriate Adler-Kassner's (2008) language in what I see as the main message of this chapter, formerly contingent WPAs must work to produce hybrid stories that tell about *how* we do the work that we do in the face of and in response to labor exploitation that now characterizes the field.

These hybrid stories of thorny realities can and should contain evidence of the never wholly comfortable local rhetorical acts and outcomes of speaking with and listening to contingent faculty. They likewise can and should contain evidence of the equally uncomfortable and wider-reaching rhetorical acts and outcomes of engaging professional organizations in the labor crisis in more profound ways. Only via such a revised, revisionist narrative can formerly contingent WPAs, any and all transitioning WPAs, and all rhetoric and composition professionals come to recognize that they always already lack a robust and meaningful engagement with the profession if they lack an activism-oriented engagement with it. To be in the profession in a meaningful way is to change the profession for the better, to transition it into something better just as we as WPAs ceaselessly transition through our careers among different positions and circumstances. Only via such a revised and revisionist narrative might academics realize that addressing questions of labor and working toward labor justice in solidarity across disciplines is part and parcel of twenty-first-century scholarly work and as a means by which to transition into having *actual* power on the job.

Notes

1. As Marc Bousquet puts it, "Over the past forty years, the administration of higher education has changed considerably. Campus administrations have steadily diverged from the ideals of faculty governance, collegiality, and professional self-determination. Instead they have embraced the values and practices of corporate management" (Bousquet 2008, 1).
2. According to Gary A. Olson and Joseph M. Moxley, "Despite their ostensible authority within the English Department, many freshman English directors possess little administrative power" (Olson and Moxley 1989, 51).
3. Some degree of debate exists about the nature of the role that WPAs occupy. See, for instance, Rita Malenczyk's 2004 "Doin' the Managerial Exclusion: What WPAs Might Need to Know about Collective Bargaining," in which Malenczyk states that

    our professional conversation notwithstanding, there is outside of that conversation a slightly more complicated—and exceedingly local—way of looking at what WPAs do and where they fit in the academic hierarchy. We employ terms like "management" and "labor" in conference discussions and in essays (see, for example, Miller, Horner, Bousquet, Mountford); yet, with some exceptions, the use of those terms is theoretical, which is fine (and desirable) in the context of academic argument but not so helpful when it comes to helping someone understand their own job and its politics—or, I would argue, the facts of how WPAs are situated. . . . But seen in the context of how labor boards or courts define "management" and "labor"—in other words, when trying to decide who is or is not entitled to collective bargaining—such a claim becomes harder to support. Any assertion that one "hires and fires" is complicated by the reality of who actually makes final hiring and firing decisions, and whose recommendations are followed, at any given institution. (Malenczyk 2004, 30)

4. See the UWPA SIG Facebook group for information about the Conference on College Composition and Communication's SIG, accessed June 11, 2016, https://www.facebook.com/groups/1573867772898062.
5. For an example of the kinds of risks that WPAs face, see Rita Malenczyk's "Fighting Across the Curriculum: The WPA Joins the AAUP," in which Malenczyk describes her tenure-line reappointment as being "quashed by a member of the higher administration" (Malenczyk 2001, 13).
6. I point out this similarity between contingent and tenure-track faculty not to disregard the harsh realities that accompany actual, on-the-books contingent-faculty status. I know those realities well and I know well, too, that minimizing them does nothing to solve the labor crisis at contemporary colleges and universities.
7. I rely implicitly here on two definitions of rhetoric that Patricia M. Malesh and Sharon McKenzie Stevens underscore in their introduction to *Active Voices: Composing a Rhetoric for Social Movements* (Malesh and Stevens 2009, 1–20). The first, Aristotle's (2007), defines rhetoric as "an ability, in each particular case, to see the available means of persuasion" (36). The second, Kenneth Burke's, defines rhetoric as "the use of words by human agents to form attitudes or to induce actions by other human agents" (Burke 1969, 41).

8. For example, as Anjali Prabhu (2007) explains in her critique of hybridity, "Hybridity is an enticing idea in current postcolonial studies. In its dominant form, it is claimed that it can provide a way out of binary thinking, allow the inscription of agency of the subaltern, and even permit a restructuring and destabilizing of power" (Prabhu 2007, 1). But, as she continues, "these assertions need to be tested" (Prabhu 2007, 11).
9. According to E. Ian Robinson's "Teaching Equality: What the Principle of Equal Pay for Equal Work Means for Lecturer Pay at the University of Michigan," research alone does not function to enrich teaching. An array of factors enrich teachers' pedagogies. And "on average, [University of Michigan] Lecturers are somewhat more likely than TT faculty to be seen as excellent teachers" (Robinson 2012, 34).
10. MLA Action for Allies invited members to "show [their] support for adjunct faculty members and find resources for starting discussions in . . . department[s] about the use of contingent faculty" (Chang 2015).

References

Adler-Kassner, Linda. 2008. *The Activist WPA: Changing Stories about Writing and Writers.* Logan: Utah State University Press.
Aristotle. 2007. *On Rhetoric: A Theory of Civic Discourse.* 2nd ed. Translated by George A. Kennedy. New York: Oxford University Press.
Bhabha, Homi K. 2004. *The Location of Culture.* London: Routledge.
Bousquet, Marc. 2008. *How the University Works: Higher Education and the Low-Wage Nation.* New York: New York University Press.
Braun, M. J. 2011. "Against Decorous Civility: Acting as if You Live in a Democracy." In *Activism and Rhetoric: Theories and Contexts for Political Engagement*, edited by Seth Kahn and JongHwa Lee, 137–46. New York: Routledge.
Burke, Kenneth. 1969. *A Rhetoric of Motives.* Berkeley: University of California Press.
Chang, Anna. 2015. "MLA Launches Action for Allies Campaign." MLA Commons. https://news.mla.hcommons.org/2015/02/18/mla-launches-action-for-allies-campaign/.
Denny, Harry C. 2010. *Facing the Center: Toward an Identity Politics of One-To-One Mentoring.* Logan: Utah State University Press.
Dew, Debra Frank, and Alice S. Horning, eds. 2007. *Untenured Faculty as Writing Program Administrators: Institutional Practices and Politics.* West Lafayette, IN: Parlor.
Malenczyk, Rita. 2001. "Fighting Across the Curriculum: The WPA Joins the AAUP." *WPA: Writing Program Administration* 24 (3): 11–24.
Malenczyk, Rita. 2004. "Doin' the Managerial Exclusion: What WPAs Might Need to Know About Collective Bargaining." *WPA: Writing Program Administration* 27 (3): 23–33.
Malesh, Patricia M., and Sharon McKenzie Stevens. 2009. "Introduction: Active Voices." In *Active Voices: Composing a Rhetoric for Social Movements*, edited by Sharon McKenzie Stevens and Patricia Malesh, 1–20. Albany: SUNY Press.
MLA Democracy. 2015. "Occupy the Profession." MLA Democracy, January 3. https://mlademocracy.net/category/information/.
Naydan, Liliana M. 2013. "LEO as a Community of Practice: Organizing Now for 2018." *LEO Matters* 21 (1): 1. http://www.leounion.org/files/LM21.pdf.
Olson, Gary A., and Joseph M. Moxley. 1989. "Directing Freshman Composition: The Limits of Authority." *College Composition and Communication* 40 (1): 51–60. https://doi.org/10.2307/358180.
Prabhu, Anjali. 2007. *Hybridity: Limits, Transformations, Prospects.* Albany: SUNY Press.

Ratcliffe, Krista. 2005. *Rhetorical Listening: Identification, Gender, Whiteness.* Carbondale: Southern Illinois University Press.
Robinson, E. Ian. 2012. "Teaching Equality: What the Principle of Equal Pay for Equal Work Means for Lecturer Pay at the University of Michigan." Lecturers' Employee Organization. http://www.leounion.org/documents/teachingequalityatum.pdf.
Zweig, Michael. 2000. *The Working Class Majority: America's Best Kept Secret.* Ithaca, NY: ILR.

Conclusion
TRANSITIONS AND TRANSFER

Brian Ray

The narratives in this collection have dealt not only with transition but also with struggle and contingency. When faced with new situations, WPAs have revisited their prior knowledge and assumptions and adapted them in order to succeed. Sometimes they have even abandoned notions of what worked in the past in favor of embracing new principles. For example, Laura Davies writes about her need to rework her civilian style of leadership when she began as WPA at the United States Air Force Academy (USAFA). In her chapter, "Command and Collaboration," she recounts how her new institution prompted her to theorize leadership as well as the idea of command in a way that led to a stronger set of goals and expectations. At USAFA, models of collaborative administration and decentered authority did not fit as well as one based on command—with its emphasis on responsibility, authority, communication, and decidedness.

In many ways, what Davies describes mirrors the narratives of transfer in work by Kathleen Blake Yancey, Liane Robertson, and Kara Taczak (2014), Rebecca Nowacek (2011), and Elizabeth Wardle (2007). Transfer has become a familiar idea in writing studies, one that applies easily to writing program administration. Briefly defined, transfer refers to the development of knowledge and practices that can be drawn upon, used, and repurposed in new settings (Yancey, Robertson, and Taczak 2014, 2). Scholars have identified five main types of transfer, outlined below and explained in terms of their significance to WPAs.

Near Transfer: When WPAs face a situation similar to previous ones. Near transfer could occur when someone moves to a similar kind of institution or takes on a responsibility closely aligned with ones they already have.

Far Transfer: When WPAs face a relatively unprecedented situation that seems very different from prior experiences. Far transfer might involve moving from a large land-grant university to a small liberal arts college (SLAC) or transitioning from a TA to an assistant director.

Low-Road Transfer: The application of concrete knowledge to new contexts. Assistant directors of composition programs often conduct teaching observations and write evaluation letters, and this basic practice tends not to vary across institutions and faculty rank.

High-Road Transfer: The application of abstract knowledge to new contexts. Although many aspects of teaching observations and evaluation letters remain constant across ranks and institutions, WPAs still must theorize the genre and think about differences between evaluating graduate or less experienced faculty and part-time and full-time faculty who might have significant teaching experience.

Negative Transfer: Prior knowledge and practices that interfere with a WPA's performance. Often, procedures and even models of administration that worked in a previous position may not transfer well at all into a new institution or level of position. A WPA might grow used to reporting directly to a dean at an SLAC, but doing so at a large university may appear to breach the chain of communication and offend their department chair.

These five points of transfer offer a tentative framework to assist WPAs when adapting to new positions, new responsibilities, or changing contexts at their institutions. Ideally, awareness of the types of transfer grants us greater agency during times of professional transition. Every contributor in this collection has needed to repurpose knowledge from other disciplines or careers during their transition into, out of, or between WPA positions. The prior knowledge, habits, and skills they brought with them helped but also at times hindered their transitions. Although I do not intend to discuss every single contribution here, I draw from several of them in which transfer figures prominently. Readers may want to read or reread others to look for other latent instances of transfer.

Perhaps no better example of far transfer exists than the first one WPAs experience, their initial administrative appointments after or during graduate school. In "An Exercise in Cognitive Dissonance," Talinn Phillips, Paul Shovlin, and Megan Titus explore the transitions of graduate students into the role of what they call "liminal WPAs," those who "are asked to engage in work incommensurate with their institutional status—an institutional status that marks them as impermanent and thus lacking the power senior WPAs have to do their jobs effectively" (70). Furthermore, liminal WPAs "may be doing the work of seasoned WPAs, but without . . . an accurate conceptualization of the scope of the position by those supervising them, and without the personal and disciplinary experience to anticipate concerns and negotiate them effectively" (74). The authors' discussion of one such WPA named Pat provides an excellent case in point. Pat, who quickly becomes overwhelmed by his responsibilities as an AD, begins to seek advice and help from other graduate students rather than from his supervisors. His experiences might qualify as both far and negative transfer. The strategies that may have served him well as a graduate student did not necessarily help him transition into his role effectively.

As Phillips, Shovlin, and Titus point out, the liminal WPA experience is a fraught one in which senior WPAs must play an active role as mentors. In this vein, I propose that WPAs introduce liminal WPAs in their programs to transfer theory and encourage structured reflection regarding what prior knowledge and practices they can repurpose for their roles. Many graduate students have work experience from other jobs, sometimes as supervisors. They may have helped raise younger siblings or otherwise found themselves in positions of authority and responsibility over others. These previous roles can provide reference points for their WPA work if theorized appropriately.

Distinguishing between high- and low-road transfer can also help WPAs at the onset of new jobs or duties. Trivial tasks—sometimes derisively called *administrivia*—come to mind regarding low-road transfer. For example, once a WPA has learned how to process a registration override, or evaluate a course for transfer credit, these practices transfer easily from one institution to another. Other such low-road activities might include building course schedules, ordering textbooks, hiring new instructors, and the logistical aspects of event planning (arranging catering, etc.).

Other practices we learn may not seem as readily applicable and require abstraction before they can be useful. Attending to high-road transfer becomes especially important when moving between institutions and even disciplines. Andrea Scott discusses the importance of self-awareness and reflection in multiple types of transitions in her chapter "Defining Disciplinarity at Moments of Transition." Scott shifted not only between the role of program and writing center director but also between types of institutions and even disciplines. As she writes, "Directing a writing center at a progressive SLAC on the West Coast feels radically different from associate directing a first-year writing seminar program at a highly selective research institution on the East Coast." She refers to "leadership configurations, institutional cultures, and often separate discourse communities engaging in scholarship about writing centers, first year composition, and literature" that shape how "WPA work is enacted, framed, and understood by its practitioners" (91).

Paying attention to such differences, as Scott does, facilitates the kind of high-road transfer required of WPAs in order to succeed over the course of their careers. High-road transfer becomes apparent in the comparison of her very different roles at her two very different institutions. She compares running a writing program to "steering a large cruise ship" and directing a writing center to guiding a more "nimble" vessel, one that makes it "easier to fine tune and change course." Another key difference lies in a need for "more curricular reinvention." In terms of power structure, in her early months directing the writing center, she "marveled at how, as an assistant professor, [she] reported directly to the dean of faculty." Theorizing her work at these two institutions has enabled her to take advantage of the flat power structure she describes.

Scott's transition into WPA work from an entirely different discipline counts as a particularly appropriate instance of high-road transfer. Her PhD work on postwar politics in Germany did not apply, at least immediately, to her WPA work and may have worked against her without critical reflection. However, her immersion in the scholarly discourse community of one discipline appears to have attuned her to the importance of disciplinary discourse. As such, she describes a three-year period in which she read as much about writing studies as possible while following WPA-L threads in order to become versed in her new discipline. In short, Scott theorized her experiences from political science and applied the abstract knowledge to her new discipline. This transition enabled the subsequent, more direct application of her background in German politics to her current research project, "Anglo-American Writing Studies in Germany, Switzerland, and Austria."

Scott's use of the sailing-ship analogy is but one of many metaphors used by WPAs to describe their work, both in this collection, as we noted in the introduction, and throughout WPA scholarship. Metaphor serves as an essential tool in the transfer of knowledge and was recognized by classical rhetoricians as a way of explaining one thing in terms of another. We might think of metaphors as setting the stage for transfer. If we think of writing program administration in terms of a journey, we might be more likely to transfer what we know from prior experiences and jobs that fits that particular metaphor—for instance, what in our work would fit the image of driving a car down a long road, reading a map, hiking a trail, packing a suitcase, or boarding an airplane? Different metaphors may catalyze different kinds of transfer. In this sense, it may help to think of writing program administration through as many metaphors as possible, stopping to consider the different paths of transfer they enable.

Metaphor serves a key function in Jennifer Campbell and Richard Colby's chapter, "Servers, Cooks, and the Inadequacy of Metaphor." Although the authors admit that "creating a comprehensive metaphor for the work of a WPA is probably futile," they nonetheless advocate for the value of metaphor in facilitating reflection: "We see . . . how our personalities and the nonacademic jobs we have had inform how we see the work [we do], and that is ultimately what metaphorical comparisons have led us to—seeing where we can excel in the vast landscape of WPA work" (67).

Using metaphor, the authors describe their respective positions in terms of service and cooking. In some ways, Campbell may have experienced less satisfaction in her WPA position precisely because she was defining it in terms of only service, a metaphor that influenced what she chose to transfer from prior employment. She became overwhelmed by the administrivia of her position, a situation she was ultimately unable to overcome. By contrast, Colby describes the process of conducting teaching observations in terms of one cook watching another at work and relishing the experience. The metaphor helped him transfer knowledge from his time in the restaurant business to administration in a way that enabled a more positive conception of his task. On the other hand, his desire for spontaneity—perhaps an asset elsewhere—did not transfer successfully into the drafting of annual-review letters, such as the one influenced by Star Wars. Both narratives illustrate how different metaphors influence the manner and extent of transfer.

Metaphor occupies the work of Rebecca Jackson, Jackie Grutsch McKinney, and Nicole I. Caswell's chapter "Metaphors We Work By," for which the authors coded narratives of writing center directors according to metaphors they used to describe their work. One participant, Katerina, described her experience directing a writing center as like being a teenager, elaborating that "you try to figure out what you are doing in this world/life/school/WrC; you have to prove that you are worth appreciation/understanding/being listened to/etc.; you are against someone else's rules but you definitely want to set your own rules" (116).

The teenager metaphor is fascinating in its cuing of uncertainty and constrained authority. What habits, knowledge, or skills could Katerina transfer from her own past as a teenager into her administrative work? What did she remember about being a teenager that could have induced negative transfer and therefore interfered with her performance? We might think about what strategies and tactics teenagers use to navigate and negotiate such contingency and constraint. Some would certainly be useful, while others would be better left untapped.

Moments of negative transfer also occur throughout the narratives of transition. Instead of seeing them as tragedies, however, realizing when negative transfer has happened (or is about to) leads to teaching moments and eventually success. Steven Corbett's chapter, "Performance Attribution and Administrative (Un)Becoming," addresses this kind of productive failure directly, drawing on transfer theory. According to Corbett, WPAs could theorize more deeply about what it means to fail as a WPA. In his case, that realization meant not performing as the WPA his first institution wanted. Knowledge and practices that interfered with Corbett's success, as he points out, included working-class roots and background as a returning, nontraditional student. These differences made it difficult for him to interact with some colleagues and to perform the politics required by his institution.

However, Corbett's failure resulted in a new self-awareness, and those aspects of his identity that had been weaknesses at one point became strengths as Corbett theorized his failure, later enabling a kind of high-road transfer. His experiences prompt us to recognize the importance of defining expectations with colleagues and upper administration at our institutions and trying to learn from failure when it seems inevitable. Doing so requires the motivation, self-efficacy, and self-regulation Driscoll and Wells (2012), whom Corbett cites, consider integral to transfer.

Negotiation and bargaining serve as two of the most vital tools for WPAs. Just as WPAs have different metaphors for their work, they also have different styles that reflect their identities. To what extent does one negotiation style transfer among positions, institutions, and subject positions? Chris Blankenship's chapter, "Suddenly WPA," takes up these questions as he reflects on the social privilege that afforded him a particular set of negotiation strategies and ultimately enabled him to bargain for better compensation and course releases before assuming an administrative role at his institution. We can read his meditation on his privilege in terms of transfer, a kind of theorizing about the extent to which someone of a marginalized gender, ethnicity, or social class would need to repurpose their strategies in order to achieve a similar outcome—or whether such an outcome would even be possible. As Blankenship himself concedes, his assertive discourse style may not transfer easily to those in marginalized subject positions. We are all familiar with the way assertive women are stereotyped in workplace cultures. Readers might study Blankenship's actions via high-road transfer, considering how they might need to adapt his decisions in order to fit their own circumstances.

Having read this collection and thought deeply about transfer, my own transitions between roles and institutions now make more sense to me. I see how certain types of knowledge or practices I learned at UNC–Greensboro during graduate school needed significant adaptation in order to fit with the culture, power structures, and needs of a regional midwestern institution in a town with a population of barely over thirty thousand people. I had to adjust from assisting a composition program staffed largely by TAs to a department in which composition was taught largely by full-time faculty and part-time instructors. At that institution, I had to build a composition program from one that had a history of passivity and a fragile sense of community.

Three years later, I had to adjust again to a program with a robust set of practices and procedures, well-trained faculty, and a strong sense of community. I had to shift into a very different kind of directing—not inventing things anew but instead orienting myself to existing norms. Whereas I had previously had to enact a command model of administration, at my current institution I had to learn a type of collaboration and develop the ability to delegate tasks. Certain arguments and positions I spent a great deal of time justifying at one institution—such as the place of literature in composition—become moot points at my new institution.

Attending to transfer has also helped me understand the experiences of other WPAs and jWPAs at my institution. For example, one of our assistant WPAs at my current institution came in with extensive experience in the restaurant industry. I watched him transfer his multitasking and organizational abilities from managing a restaurant to his duties as assistant director, such as managing textbook orders, assessment folders, and room reservations for various program events. His extensive time in the service sector also helped him manage his time effectively, balancing his teaching and thesis alongside administrative tasks.

The five types of transfer can and should inform readers' interpretations of the transition narratives in this collection. No matter how compelling, or how much we identify with one story, no single experience will match our own. Most important, none of the authors of these chapters describe seamless moves between careers, institutions, or phases in their careers. Every transition presents its own series of expected and unexpected challenges. To learn from these transition narratives requires the ability to theorize them, abstract from the lessons, and repurpose them for our own local contexts. As our collection has shown, we hope, reflecting on transitions in scholarship on writing program administration is necessary as we and others step into and between these positions. No one should have to transition on their own without a robust discourse to guide the process.

References

Driscoll, Dana Lynn, and Jennifer Wells. 2012. "Beyond Knowledge and Skills: Writing Transfer and the Role of Student Dispositions in and beyond the Writing Classroom." *Composition Forum* 26. http://compositionforum.com/issue/26/beyond-knowledge-skills.php.

Nowacek, Rebecca S. 2011. *Agents of Integration: Understanding Transfer as a Rhetorical Act.* Carbondale: Southern Illinois University Press.

Wardle, Elizabeth. 2007. "Understanding 'Transfer' from FYC: Preliminary Results of a Longitudinal Study." *WPA: Writing Program Administration* 31 (1–2): 65–85.

Yancey, Kathleen Blake, Liane Robertson, and Kara Taczak. 2014. *Writing Across Contexts: Transfer, Composition, and Sites of Writing.* Logan: Utah State University Press.

ABOUT THE AUTHORS

COURTNEY ADAMS WOOTEN is an assistant professor and first-year writing program administrator at Stephen F. Austin State University in Nacogdoches, Texas. She also serves as the book-review editor for *WPA: Writing Program Administration*. In the English and Creative Writing department, she teaches a variety of courses from first-year writing to upper-level rhetoric and writing studies to graduate-level writing pedagogy. She studies feminist rhetorics, writing program administration, and first-year composition. Her work has previously appeared in *Composition Studies*, *Harlot*, and *WPA: Writing Program Administration*.

JACOB BABB is assistant professor of English and writing program coordinator at Indiana University Southeast. He is also the associate editor for *WPA: Writing Program Administration*. He publishes on composition theory and pedagogy, writing program administration, and rhetoric. He has published articles in *Harlot*, *WPA: Writing Program Administration*, and *Composition Forum*, and he also has published chapters in several edited collections.

BRIAN RAY is assistant professor of rhetoric and writing at the University of Arkansas at Little Rock, where he also directs the composition program. He is author of the book *Style: An Introduction to History, Theory, Research, and Pedagogy*. His articles have appeared in *Written Communication*, *Rhetoric Review*, *Computers and Composition*, and *Composition Studies*.

MARK BLAAUW-HARA is professor of English and writing program coordinator at North Central Michigan College in Petoskey, Michigan. His writing has appeared in *Composition Forum*, the *Community College Journal of Research and Practice*, *Currents in Electronic Communication*, *The Writing Center Journal*, and *Teaching English in the Two-Year College*, where he is also the reviews coeditor. Mark currently serves as the vice president of the Council of Writing Program Administrators.

CHRIS BLANKENSHIP is an assistant professor in the English Department at Salt Lake Community College, where he teaches courses in writing, rhetoric, and linguistics. His recent scholarship includes work on composition pedagogy, writing assessment, and labor practices in higher education.

JENNIFER RILEY CAMPBELL is a teaching associate professor in the writing program at the University of Denver and served as assistant director for first-year writing for three years. Her interest in writing program administration began at Auburn University, where she was assistant to the director of composition while earning her PhD in English with concentrations in rhetorical theory, composition pedagogy, and twenty-first-century fiction and film. In addition to her ongoing interest in those areas, Campbell studies and teaches about civic and political rhetorics, mental health, and zombies.

NICOLE I. CASWELL is assistant professor of English and director of the University Writing Center at East Carolina University. Her research interests include writing centers, writing assessment, and emotional labor/work. Nicole's research has been published in the *Journal of Writing Assessment*, *Academic Exchange Quarterly*, the *CEA Forum*, and various edited collections. Her book *The Working Lives of New Writing Center Directors* (coauthored with Jackie Grutsch McKinney and Rebecca Jackson) was published by Utah State University Press in fall 2016.

ABOUT THE AUTHORS

RICHARD COLBY teaches in and is assistant director of the University of Denver Writing Program. He coedited the collection *Rhetoric/Composition/Play through Video Games* and a special issue of the journal *Computers and Composition Online* on gaming and composition. His work on using games in teaching has been published in *Computers and Composition, Computers and Composition Online,* and various edited collections. He teaches courses on the rhetoric of games and disciplinary research.

STEVEN J. CORBETT is director of the University Writing Center and assistant professor of English in the Department of Language and Literature at Texas A&M University–Kingsville. He is the author of *Beyond Dichotomy: Synergizing Writing Center and Classroom Pedagogies*; coeditor (with Michelle LaFrance and Teagan E. Decker) of the collection *Peer Pressure, Peer Power: Theory and Practice in Peer Review and Response for the Writing Classroom*; and coeditor (with Michelle LaFrance) of the forthcoming *Student Peer Review and Response: A Critical Sourcebook*. His work in writing studies research and pedagogy has appeared in a variety of academic journals and collections.

BETH DANIELL retired in the summer of 2015 after eleven years as WPA in the English department at Kennesaw State, where she also directed the writing-across-the-curriculum program in the College of Humanities and Social Sciences. She is author of *A Communion of Friendship: Literacy, Spiritual Practice and Women in Recovery* and coeditor of *Women and Literacy: Local and Global Inquiries for a New Century* and *Renovating Rhetoric in Christian Tradition*. Her work on such topics as rhetoric, literacy, religion, pedagogy, and writing program administration has appeared in *CCC, College English, JAEPL,* and *Pre-Text,* as well as in several collections.

LAURA J. DAVIES is associate professor of English and director of campus writing programs at SUNY Cortland, where she teaches in the English education and professional writing and rhetoric programs. Her areas of research include writing program administration, writing teacher pedagogy, and student reading and writing practices.

JAQUELYN DAVIS is a master's student at the University of Nevada, Reno, where she studies writing and teaches first-year composition. She also serves as the master's representative on the WPA Graduate Organization (WPA-GO). Before graduate school, Jaquelyn worked for three years at the Center for Writing Across the Curriculum at Saint Mary's College of California, where she developed interests in service-learning and writing program administration. At UNR, she continues to explore these interests through research focused on WPA work, collaboration, student empowerment, and the intersections of these topics with ecological pedagogy. After earning her master's, Jaquelyn will go on to pursue a career in teaching writing at the community college and high-school levels in her native Sierra Nevada foothills. She collaboratively hosted the September 2016 *The WCJ* blog.

HOLLAND ENKE currently works in training and organizational development. During her time at Saint Mary's College of California, Holland worked in the Center for Writing Across the Curriculum and served on the editorial teams for the literary journals *riverrun, Spectrum,* and *The Undergraduate*. Holland looks to her service-learning roots as she collaborates with coworkers on their career development, creating or organizing training that provides employees with the skills needed to be successful in their jobs and future careers. A writer at heart, Holland has volunteered for many writing and editing opportunities at her company.

LETIZIA GUGLIELMO is professor of English and Interdisciplinary Studies and coordinator of the Gender and Women's Studies Program at Kennesaw State University. Her research and writing focus on feminist rhetoric and pedagogy, gender and pop culture, the intersections of feminist action and digital communication, and professional development for students and faculty. She is editor and author of *MTV and Teen Pregnancy: Critical*

Essays on 16 and Pregnant *and* Teen Mom (Rowman & Littlefield), coauthor of *Scholarly Publication in a Changing Academic Landscape: Models for Success* (Palgrave), and coeditor of *Contingent Faculty Publishing in Community: Case Studies for Successful Collaborations* (Palgrave).

BETH HUBER earned her PhD in composition, rhetoric, and history from the University of Missouri, Kansas City, and is currently associate professor of English at Western Carolina University in Cullowhee, North Carolina. Her research interests include Cold War and political rhetoric and the rhetoric of the Beat-generation writers. Her most recent publication, "National Interest: Composition's Response in a Time of Cold War," examines the effects of foreign-policy rhetoric on the composition classroom during the 1950s and 1960s. In addition, her film short *Angelic in America* recently premiered at the European Beat Studies Network.

KAREN KEATON JACKSON a native of Detroit, Michigan, began her academic career at Hampton University, earning a bachelor of science in English secondary education with summa cum laude distinction. She went on to receive her master's and PhD in English composition from Wayne State University. While pursuing her PhD, she taught courses on multicultural literacy at LeMoyne College in Syracuse, New York, as a predoctoral fellow. Since arriving at North Carolina Central University in 2004, she has become director of the Writing Studio, coordinates the University Writing Program, and has served on the International Writing Center Association and the Southeastern Writing Center Association executive boards. Currently, she serves on the executive board of the Council of Writing Program Administrators. She maintains an active research agenda on the interrelated notions of literacy, race, and identity in the writing classroom, and more recently she has focused on composition studies at historically black colleges and universities (HBCUs).

REBECCA JACKSON is professor of English and director of the MA rhetoric and composition program at Texas State University. She is coauthor, with Jackie Grutsch McKinney and Nicole Caswell, of *The Working Lives of New Writing Center Directors* (Utah State UP, 2016), which recently won the 2017 International Writing Centers Association's Best Book Award. She has published widely in both writing center and composition studies and is currently working on a longitudinal study of writing center director job satisfaction and migration (with Jackie Grutsch McKinney and Nicole Caswell).

TEREZA JOY KRAMER directs the Center for Writing Across the Curriculum at Saint Mary's College of California, near San Francisco, a combined writing center and WAC faculty-support program. Her areas of scholarship include collaboration, writing centers, writing across the curriculum, and service learning. She's also a poet, having earned an MFA in creative writing and then a PhD in rhetoric and composition at Southern Illinois University Carbondale. Her poetry chapbook was published in 2016 by Finishing Line Press. She's published academic research singly in *Writing on the Edge* and *WLN: A Journal of Writing Center Scholarship* and collaboratively in *The WCJ* blog and *Marginal Words, Marginal Work? Tutoring the Academy in the Work of Writing Centers*, edited by William J. Macauley and Nicholas Mauriello, published by Hampton Press.

JACKIE GRUTSCH MCKINNEY is writing center director and professor of English at Ball State University. She is the author of two books, *Strategies for Writing Center Research* and *Peripheral Visions for Writing Centers*, the latter of which won the International Writing Centers Association prize for Outstanding Major Work in 2014. Her third book, *The Working Lives of New Writing Center Directors*, was coauthored with Becky Jackson and Nikki Caswell.

KERRI K. MORRIS is an associate professor at Governors State University, where she was hired to direct writing across the curriculum and to help build the university's first general education program. Her background is in historical rhetoric, with a special interest in the epideictic genre. She is also interested in WAC research and rhetorics of health. She is at heart a writing teacher and a writer.

LILIANA M. NAYDAN, PhD, is assistant professor of English at Penn State Abington. She researches writing centers and contemporary American fiction, and her work on these subjects has appeared in journals including *Praxis: A Writing Center Journal*, *Forum: Issues about Part-Time and Contingent Faculty*, and *Critique: Studies in Contemporary Fiction*. Her book, *Rhetorics of Religion in American Fiction: Faith, Fundamentalism, and Fanaticism in the Age of Terror* (Bucknell University Press, 2016), examines fiction that dramatizes and works to resolve impasses between believers after 9/11. She is currently researching contingent writing center workers via an International Writing Centers Association research grant.

REYNA OLEGARIO currently works in communications and marketing for a nonprofit organization. While working at Saint Mary's College of California's Center for Writing Across the Curriculum (CWAC) for four years, she discovered a knack for mentorship and developed editorial skills working on the university's two academic journals and CWAC's online platforms. Reyna draws on these experiences as she shapes digital communications in her current position. Though writing social media copy, newsletters, and press releases resides at the heart of her position, Reyna's inclination toward collaboration has led her to mentor other departments in embarking on their own digital-communication adventures.

KATE PANTELIDES is an assistant professor at Middle Tennessee State University and the Codirector of General Education English. She has taught rhetoric, composition, and technical communication courses at the undergraduate and graduate levels. Her research interests include rhetorical genre studies, discourse analysis, computer-mediated communication, writing program administration, and the experience of parents in academe.

TALINN PHILLIPS is associate professor of English at Ohio University, where she also directs the writing certificate and the Graduate Writing & Research Center. Her research focuses on multilingual writers, writing centers, and liminal writing program administrators. She is a founding board member of the Consortium on Graduate Communication and coedited *Supporting Graduate Student Writers: Research, Curriculum, and Program Design* from University of Michigan Press.

ANDREA SCOTT is assistant professor of academic writing and director of the writing center at Pitzer College. Her research focuses on the culture of writing at small liberal arts colleges and the history of writing research and pedagogies in German-speaking countries. Her articles have been published in *WPA: Writing Program Administration*, *WLN: A Journal of Writing Center Scholarship*, *Journal of Academic Writing*, *Zeitschrift Schreiben*, the *CEA Forum*, and the *Journal of Response to Writing*. Translations have appeared in the *Chicago Review*, *jubilat*, and *Henryk Broder: A Jew in the New Germany* (Illinois UP). In 2014 she received a Fulbright/DAAD award to attend the Leipzig Summer Academy for US faculty in German.

Director of the writing initiative, first-year writing, and the writing center at Binghamton University (SUNY), PAUL SHOVLIN earned his PhD in rhetoric and composition from Ohio University, where he also earned his MA and BA in English language and literature. Prior to joining the faculty in 2010, he held the position of interim director of the Center for Writing Excellence at Ohio University, taught English as a second language for the Peace Corps in Eastern Europe, and supported community literacy programs in Brooklyn, New York. His scholarly interests include new media studies, critical pedagogy, writing program administration, and popular fiction studies. His coauthored piece "Thinking Liminally: Exploring the (com)Promising Positions of the Liminal WPA" was recently published in *WPA: Writing Program Administration*.

About the Authors

BRADLEY SMITH is associate professor of English and director of first-year writing at Governors State University whose scholarship is focused on first-year writing pedagogy and writing program administration. His most recent publications include a vignette titled "Writing in Transit" published in *College Composition and Communication* and an article titled "A Study of the Journey Metaphor's Entailments for Framing Learning" in the *Journal of the Assembly of Expanded Perspectives on Learning*.

CHERI LEMIEUX SPIEGEL is professor of English at Northern Virginia Community College's Annandale Campus, where she teaches composition courses and served as assistant dean of Composition from 2011 to 2016. She received the 2016 award for Outstanding Service to the College for her work as assistant dean of composition. She serves on the executive board for the Council of Writing Program Administrators and has published articles in *TETYC* and *Computers and Composition Online*.

SARAH STANLEY is associate professor of English and directs university writing at the University of Alaska, Fairbanks. This chapter is the first about her experience as a WPA. She has published in the *Journal of Basic Writing*, *Radical Pedagogy*, and several book collections. A sustained academic interest has been the phenomenon of "noticing," or how learning becomes conscious, and she threads this interest into collaborative curricular design for diverse audiences, including students enrolled in Academic Recovery, a women's writing workshop at Fairbanks Correctional Center, and at community writing events around Fairbanks.

AMY RUPIPER TAGGART was professor of English and associate director of the Office of Teaching and Learning at North Dakota State University. Formerly, she ran NDSU's first-year writing program for four and a half years. She coedited (with Gary Tate, Kurt Schick, and H. Brooke Hessler) the *Guide to Composition Pedagogies* and coauthored (with Rebecca Moore Howard) the first-year research-writing textbook, *Research Matters*. Her articles have appeared in *WPA: Writing Program Administration*, *Reflections*, the *Michigan Journal of Community Service Learning*, and edited collections. Amy passed away in 2017.

MOLLY TETREAULT is director of the Connors Writing Center at the University of New Hampshire. She also teaches first-year writing and writing center theory and practice. Her research interests include writing centers, first-year writing, the transition from high school to college, and writing across the curriculum.

MEGAN L. TITUS directs the composition program at Rider University, where she is associate professor of English. In the English department, she teaches a variety of courses, ranging from first-year to advanced writing and rhetoric. She is also on the faculty for the gender and sexuality studies program. Her research interests include writing program administration and gender, and gender and popular culture. Her work has appeared in *WPA: Writing Program Administration* and *Praxis: A Writing Center Journal*. She recently coedited the textbook *Gender: A Reader for Writers* with Wendy L. Walker for Oxford University Press.

CHRIS WARNICK is associate professor of English and first-year writing coordinator at the College of Charleston. His research has appeared in the *Journal of Basic Writing* and *Across the Disciplines*, and he coedits the open-access journal *Literacy in Composition Studies*.

INDEX

academia, 148; activism, 285, 288; and parenting, 100–106
academic freedom, 287
Academic Jobs Wiki, 6
accelerated learning program (ALP), 254–55
accessibility, 57
accomplishments, acknowledging, 47
accreditation, 47
Active Voices: Composing a Rhetoric for Social Movements (Malesh and Stevens), 285
activism, 17–18; academic, 285, 290; labor, 292–93; power relations and, 287–88
Activist WPA: Changing Stories about Writing and Writers, The (Adler-Kassner), 285
adjuncts, adjuncting, 30, 252, 254; hiring and supporting, 65–66; marginalization of, 275–76
Adler-Kassner, Linda, 89, 93, 261, 274, 285, 289, 293; on community formation, 268, 269
"Administration as a Design Art" (Phelps), 253
administrators, administration, 6, 40, 63, 100, 134, 157, 235, 253, 265, 267; collaborative, 117, 189–91; graduate students as, 70, 71; marginalization of, 272–73; and parenting, 106–8; and scholarship, 219–20
administrivia, 299, 301
advisors, advising, 55, 149; student, 209–10, 211
advisory boards, in writing-across-the curriculum, 211–12
African Americans: at HBCUs, 28–29; marginality of, 30
agency, 14–15, 101, 202; rhetorical, 261–62
allegiances, disciplinary, 97
ALP. *See* accelerated learning program
ambivalence, 62–63
Anderson, Virginia, 163
Anson, Chris M., 165, 167(n3), 191
antiprofessionalism, 92
anxiety, in program consolidation, 171, 181–83, 184, 185
apprenticeships, associate directorships as, 94

argumentative discourse style, 44
Aristotelian rhetoric, 128, 129, 131
assessment, 79, 107, 159, 177, 255; of coordinator positions, 226–27; of identity, 174–75; protocol, 39; writing, 276
assessment programs, in community colleges, 249–50
assistant directors (ADs), 52, 53, 66, 72; ambivalence toward, 62–63; classroom observation, 63–64; leaving position, 60–61; relationships with colleagues, 57–60; responsibilities of, 54–56, 67–68, 298–99
assistant professors, 6, 100; activism, 285–86
associate directors, 93, 94, 100
associate professors, 53
attribution theory, 142, 143
authoritarian stance, 207
authority, 40, 78, 92, 93; collective, 217; in collaborative leadership, 196–97; command, 193–94, 197–98, 201; of Illinois Articulation Initiative, 265–66, 267
autoethnography, 154–56
autonomy, 88, 250
awareness, 19
Azziz, Riccardo, 172–73

Balliff, Michelle, 274
bargaining. *See* negotiation(s)
Bawarshi, Anis, 274
Bazerman, Charles, 97–98
"Becoming a Warrior: Lessons of the Feminist Workplace" (Phelps), 195–98
benefits, 70
Berlin, James, 128, 137(n4), 137(n5), 236
Bhabha, Homi K., 285
Bishop, Wendy, 239, 240
Bloom, Lynn, 52, 256
boarding schools, 117–18
boundaries, 57, 73
Boquet, Elizabeth, 212, 280
Bourdieu, Pierre, on habitus, 143, 148
Bousquet, Marc, 27, 62, 243, 284
Boyer model, 134–35
Brandt, Deborah, 220
Braun, M. J., 289
breaking ground transition, 11–12

"Breathing Lessons, *or Collaboration is . . .*" (Eodice), 206–7, 217
Bruner, Jerome, 113, 274
Burke, Kenneth, 101
Burnham, Christopher, 156
businesses, leadership, 7

Cain, Charol, 171
Campbell, Corbin M., 235
career development, 111
careers, 4, 6; and family, 250–51
Carino, Peter, 278
Carroll, Meg, 212, 280
CCCC. *See* Conference on College Composition and Communication
CEB. *See* Corporate Executive Board Company
chain of command, 193
Charlton, Colin, 149, 153
Charlton, Jonnika, 153
cheerleaders, 32
Chiseri-Strater, Elizabeth, 57, 59, 270
circles, CWAC student advisor, 215–16
Classical (Aristotelian) rhetoric, 128
cognitive dissonance, 71
coleading, faculty and student, 205–6
collaboration(s), 16–17, 96, 117, 176, 189, 207, 212, 281; faculty-student, 209–10, 216; with other WPAs, 257–58; in writing program development, 256–57
collaborative teams, 160
colleagues, 96, 267, 299; negotiating relationships with, 58–60; observation of, 63–64; relationships and, 147–48; support and resentment from, 46–47
command, commanders, 189, 197, 202; and collaboration, 17, 200–201; leadership, 191–94, 297
committees, internal review, 64
Communicating to Succeed program, 32
communication, 32, 56, 47, 148, 224; e-mail, 279–80; open, 205–6
community, 303; teaching, 200–201
community building, first-year composition, 268–69
community colleges, 151, 245; accelerated learning programs, 254–55; adjuncts at, 275–76; assessment programs in, 249–50; collaborative programming, 256–57; teaching at, 248–49, 251–52; WPAs in, 246–47
community of practice (CoP), 228, 247; framework of, 245–46; WPA, 254, 257–58
compensation, 70

competition, academic, 88
complaints, 58
Composition Committee, 37, 39; committees, 176
composition discussion groups, at community colleges, 256–57
composition programs, 38, 62, 88, 129, 132, 175, 205, 261; consolidation of, 178–81; coordinators of, 145, 262; directors of, 37, 39, 40–42, 176–77, 234–39; marginalization of, 276–77; moral charge of, 159–60
composition resource group, 256
Composition, Rhetoric, and Disciplinarity: Shadows of the Past, Issues of the Moment and Prospects for the Future (Malencysk, Wardle, and Yancey), 93
composition studies, 157; disciplinarity of, 92–93; as discipline, 87, 88–89
"Composition Studies: Dappled Discipline" (Lauer), 93
computer use, as generational change, 131–32
Condon, Frankie, 212, 280
conducting, as metaphor, 117
Conference on College Composition and Communication (CCCC), 11, 254, 284, 292
conflicts, teaching and assessment, 159
Connors, Robert J. (Bob), 159, 277–78
Connors Writing Center (CWC), Robert J., 272, 277–78
consolidation, 16–17; emotional responses to, 181–83; grieving in, 183–84; identities during, 171–72, 184–85; institutional contexts and, 173–74; program, 178–80
consultants, 31–32, 35
"Contemporary Composition: The Major Pedagogical Theories" (Berlin), 128
contingent faculty, 292, 294(n6); power relations, 286–87, 288–89; teaching evaluations of, 290–91
contracts, 135; negotiating, 41–44, 46, 165
contributions, of writing center professionals, 281
control: command, 193; lack of, 118–19
cooking, as metaphor, 62, 301
coordination, 40, 145
coordinators, 224; composition and rhetoric, 260, 262; first-year-writing, 222–23, 226–27; writing program, 247–48
Core Curriculum Habits of Mind Working Group, 208
Core Undergraduate Learning Experience (CULE), 159, 160

Corporate Executive Board Company (CEB), 11
Council of Writing Program Administrators (CWPA), 5, 46, 93, 134, 196, 226, 254, 256
counseling theory, 274
course releases, 223
creative repurposing, 143
creative writing, extracontractual work on, 46–47
creativity, command, 193
creativity theorists, 149
credentials, 70
credit transfer, standards for, 265–66
critical incidents: failure to fit, 144–49; knowledge transfer and, 142–43
CULE. *See* Core Undergraduate Learning Experience
Culture Shock and the Practice of the Profession: Training the Next Wave in Rhetoric and Composition (Anderson and Romano), 163
culture shocks, 163
current traditional (positivist) rhetoric, 128, 129
curriculum, 195, 199, 208, 222, 250, 268; collaborative creation of, 196, 197; first-year writing coordinator, 226, 227; shared, 247–48
curriculum committees, credit transfer standards, 265–66
customers, students as, 116
CWAC. *See* Center for Writing Across the Curriculum
CWPA. *See* Council of Writing Program Administrators

Dartmouth Conference, 129
debates, departmental, 222–23
"Decentering the WPA" (Gunner), 191
decision making, 58, 185
Delli Carpini, Dominic, 54
Denny, Harry C., 112, 273, 285, 287–88
departments, 38, 164; debates over WPA hiring, 222–23; internal relationships, 147–48
departure, 235
dialogues, 16–17
digital media, 147
directing, as performance, 114, 116–18
director of composition: accomplishments of, 47–48; negotiations for, 41–44; responsibilities of, 37, 38–39, 40–41, 48–50
director of university writing, 241–42

directors, directorships, 18, 53, 95, 157; composition, 176–77, 234–35, 276–77; first-year writing course, 198–201; interviews for, 175–76; and liminal WPAs, 76–77; as mentors, 72, 73, 74–75; writing center, 111, 273–74
disciplinarity, 87, 90, 91; in rhetoric and composition studies, 92–93
discipline, connection to, 165
discourse: academic, 222; as space, 261
discourse communities, 91, 141, 149, 150; fitting into, 145, 147; negotiations between, 142–44; programmatic vision in, 269–70
discourse style, argumentative, 44
discrediting, 148
dispositions, theorizing of, 148
disruption, 10, 18
Do Babies Matter? Gender and Family in the Ivory Tower (Mason, Wolfinger, and Goulden), 102–3
doors: as locational boundaries, 242; as metaphors, 236–39, 240
Driscoll, Dana, 142, 148
Duffey, Suellyn, 126, 268
Duranleau, Lauren J., 10–11
duties, 54, 56, 78, 247. *See also* responsibilities

ecology, of writing centers, 274–75
Ede, Lisa, 258, 277
efficiency, 182
egalitarianism, 97
Elbow, Peter, 87, 265
e-mails, responses to, 57, 279–80
emancipation narratives, 88–89
emotional intelligence, 55
emotions, 97; in literacy brokering, 224–25; and position demands, 57, 58, 78–79; during program consolidation, 181–83
emotion work, 55, 56
employees, at online writing centers, 116
English, as discipline, 92
English departments, 205, 268; composition directors in, 276–77; debates over WPAs, 222–23; valuing teaching, 161–62; and writing programs, 88, 147, 180
Enos, Theresa, 54
environmental factors, in faculty action, 235–36
Eodice, Michele, 206–7, 212, 217, 280
ethics: labor, 95; management, 61–62
ethics of care, 97

ethos, 156
"Evaluating the Intellectual Work of Writing Administration" (CWPA), 46, 134
evaluation, 79, 134, 176; of peers, 58–59; teaching, 290–91
evaluator reports, 234–35
Everyday Writing Center, The (Geller et al.), 212
exiting, 226, 227, 235
expectations, 12, 150; of writing center directors, 122–23
exploitation, 62
expressionist (neo-Platonic) rhetoric, 128, 129, 131, 132, 133
extracontractual work, 46–47

Facing the Center: Toward an Identity Politics of One-to-One Mentoring (Denny), 285
faculty, 28, 53, 66, 76, 93, 133, 186, 198, 208, 213, 252, 254, 256, 284, 286, 294(n6); collaboration with students, 209–10; community college, 248–49, 251; as community of practice, 245–46; course design, 89–90; key outcomes for, 235–36; relationships with, 18, 57–58, 133, 177, 245–46, 279–80; responding to, 64–65; and student coleaders, 205–6; tenure-track/line, 38, 53, 289–90; and Writing Studio services, 30–32
faculty development workshops, 206, 208
Faculty Retirement: Best Practices for Navigating the Transition (Van Ummersen, McLaughlin, and Duranleau), 10–11
failure, 142; coping with, 139–40; to fit with institution, 144–49
families: and careers, 250–51; dual-career, 100, 104–5, 108–9
far transfer, 297, 298, 299
fatherhood, 106; professional punishment and, 104–5
fear, in program consolidation, 181–83
feelings, 96, 97; in program consolidation, 181–83
femadmin, 100
females, as mother figures, 29
feminism, 100; leadership, 195–98
field groups, 96
Field of Dreams, A (O'Neill, Crow, and Burton), 9
first-year-composition (FYC), 131; community building, 268–69; curricular approach, 89–90

First-Year Writing Committee, role of, 222, 225
first-year writing (FYW) programs, 6, 32, 89, 177, 222, 262; assistant directors of, 53, 67–68; building, 263–64; seminars, 93, 94; writing cultures and, 90–91
flight attendant, metaphor of, 51
Flower, Linda, 158
following a train wreck transition, 11, 12
Forms of Talk (Goffman), 144
Fox, Steve, 45–46, 190
Framework for Success in Postsecondary Writing, 143
freedom(s): academic, 287; intellectual, 88; vs. rules, 132–33
Freire, Paulo, 133
front-of-house work, 56
funds, funding, 26, 33, 95, 103, 176, 287; English department, 173–74; higher education, 135–36, 137(n10)

Gallaher, Robin, 242–43
gardening, metaphor of, 241–42
Gates, Henry Louis, 30
Gebhardt, Richard, 64
Geller, Anne Ellen, 112, 212, 273, 280
GenAdmin, 153, 166, 233, 242
GenAdmin: Theorizing WPA Identities in the Twenty-First Century (Charlton et al.), 153, 233
gender roles, 29, 104–5
general education (GE), 157, 164, 226; outcomes-based models, 160–61
general education (GE) outcomes, 260
General Education Council, 162, 180
General Education Revitalization Committee, 240
General Education Task Force (GSU), 264
generational changes, 16, 128; in pedagogy, 127, 131–36
George, Diana, 9, 51, 61, 220
Georgia, university consolidation in, 171, 172–73
Gladstein, Jill, 90, 96, 208
Glau, Gregory, 253–54
Glenn, Cheryl, 280
Goffman, Erving, 140, 144
Goulden, Marc, 103
governance, 53; campus, 163–64
Graban, Tarez, 153
grading contracts, 266
grading weights, 265, 266
graduate schools, disciplinarity at, 91
graduate students, 163, 166(n2), 209, 240, 243, 299; as consultants, 30, 35; as

liminal WPAs, 70, 71–81; mentoring, 81–82; as acting directors, 72–73
graduate-student WPAs, at University of Alaska Fairbanks, 239–40
graduate teaching assistants (GTAs), 38, 39
Green, Susanne, 156
grief, grieving, in program consolidation, 183–84
Grutsch McKinney, Jackie, 273–74, 281
GTAs. *See* graduate teaching assistants
Gunner, Jeanne, 126, 191

habits of mind, 143
Habits of Mind Working Group, 213
habitus, 143, 148
Hairston, Maxine, 88
Hansen, Kristine, 184
Harbrace College Handbook, 131, 133
"Hard Work and Hard Data" (Glau), 253–54
Harrington, Susanmarie, 190
Harris, Joseph, 87, 234, 281
Haviland, Carolyn Peterson, 217
HBCUs. *See* historically black universities
health issues, 57, 177, 292; and identity, 154, 155
Hesse, Douglas, 9, 53, 56, 60, 63, 106, 157, 165
hierarchies, academic, 191, 195, 196, 200, 288–89, 294(n3)
higher education, 219; funding cuts, 135–36
Higher Learning Commission, 39, 47, 260
high-road transfer, 298, 299–300, 302
hiring, reasons for, 130
historically black universities (HBCUs), 26, 33; founding of, 27–28; teaching at, 28–29
Hodin, Rachel, 139
Hogue, Tere Molindar, 190
Holland, Dorothy, 171, 172
Horning, Alice S., 37, 284
housekeeping tasks, 55–56
How the University Works: Higher Education and the Low-Wage Nation (Bousquet), 284
"How We Do What We Do?" (Scott), 36
Hult, Christine, 234
Hussey, Trevor, 219
hybridity, 208, 295(n8); of identity, 285, 289–90
hyperprofessionalization, 92

IAI. *See* Illinois Articulation Initiative
Ianetta, Melissa, 88, 97, 205
incongruity, perspective, 102

identities, identity, 6, 15–16, 18, 78, 154, 155, 253; academic-activist, 288–89; during consolidation, 171–72; hybrid, 95, 285, 289–90; as literacy brokering, 220–21, 225; loss of, 183–84; metaphors and, 51–52; negotiation of, 60, 150; professional, 93–94, 149, 166, 178, 225, 242; program consolidation and, 184–85; reassessment of, 174–75; and role playing, 156–57
Identity and Agency in Cultural Worlds (Holland et al.), 171
identity performance theory, 142
Illinois Articulation Initiative (IAI), 265–66, 267
independent writing programs, 9
indisciplines, 92
information technology, 7, 8
Inoue, Asao, 265
institutional: contexts, consolidation and, 173–74; cultures, 91; history, 66; intelligence, 55; status, 70
institutions, 235; change at, 236, 243; fitting into, 144–49; retiree support, 10–11
instructors, 6, 40, 199; parental role of, 28–29
integrity, personal, 150
intellectual freedom, 88
intellectual work, 56
intent to leave, 235
interdisciplinary departments, 180
interdisciplinary teams, 160
interim positions, and program consolidation, 179–81, 186
internal hires, 66
International Writing Centers Association, 273, 287
interruption(s), 100, 221; dual-career families, 108–9; in parenting and academia, 102–8; as practice, 101–2
interview process, 130; for directorships, 175–76
investment: emotional and professional, 78–79; personal and professional, 80–81
isolation, 18, 197. *See also* marginalization

Jewell, Richard, 191
job ads, 6
job application, 240
job descriptions, 55, 72, 80
job market, 78, 240
jobs, 100, 113, 115, 119–23; community college, 247–52; and life balance, 165;

negotiations over, 73–74; as public performance, 114, 116–18; security of, 286; status of, 18
job title, 70
Johnson, Mark, 52, 113
Johnstone, Henry, 263, 269
jump starting transition, 11, 12
junior faculty, 45

Kitchen Cooks, Plate Twirlers and Troubadours (George), 9, 51, 220
Klausman, Jeffrey, 245, 252
knowledge transfer, 141–42, 300; and critical incidents, 142–43; types of, 297–303; in writing studies, 140–41
Koerber, Amy, 105–6
Koontz, Kristen, 182, 183
Kopelson, Karen, 87
Kotter, John, 27

labor, 17, 62, 90, 95, 107, 252; activism, 18, 292–93; writing center directors, 114, 121
labor justice, 294
Lachiotte, William, 171
"Ladybugs, Low Status, and Loving the Job, Of" (Geller and Denny), 112
Lakoff, George, 52, 113
Lauer, Janice, 93
leaders, leadership, 4, 6, 7, 9, 10, 11, 17, 61, 91, 154, 157, 167(n4), 252; collaborative, 189–91; command, 191–92, 297; feminist, 195–98; as liminal space, 29–30; and management, 26–27, 29, 32–33; and organization, 34–35; transfer of power, 188–89
Leadership Transition Institute, 8
learning, 140, 141, 158; collaborative, 207, 209–10
learning communities, 270
leaving positions, 75–76, 81
lecturers, 53, 57, 295(n9); observation of, 58–59, 65
Lerner, Neal, 276
lesson planning, 60
liberal arts colleges, small, 90
liberatory pedagogy, 132
liminality, liminals, 15, 29–30, 94; characteristics of, 70–71; graduate students as, 71–82
limitations, on work preparation, 163
listening, 280; rhetorical, 282, 292
literacy brokers, brokering, 17, 220–21; assessment, 226–27; emotions in, 224–25

literacy work, 88, 158
literature, literary studies, 87, 88, 89, 91, 92, 131, 147
Little Red Schoolhouse, 91
Location of Culture, The (Bhabha), 285
logistical tasks, 55, 73
loneliness, 18
Lounder, Andrew, 235
low-road transfer, 298, 299
Lunsford, Andrea A., 258

Maid, Barry, 88
Maimon, Elaine, 260
Malenczyk, Rita, 45–46, 93, 176, 251, 294(n3)
Malesh, Patricia M., 285, 287
management, managers, 13, 63, 131, 133; community college jobs as, 250, 251; and leadership, 26–27, 32–33; as liminal space, 29–30; and organization, 34–35
management ethic, 61–62
managerial intellectuals, 27
managerial tasks, 55
managerial unconscious, 27
marginalization, 18, 29–30, 183; of adjuncts, 275–76; of administrators and directors, 272–74; of composition directors, 276–77; of writing center professionals, 277–78
Marginal Words, Marginal Works? Tutoring the Academy in the Work of Writing Centers (McCauley and Mauriello), 35, 205
Marquez, Loren, motherhood and academia, 103–4
Marxism and Literature (Williams), 96
Mason, Mary Ann, 102–3
Mauriello, Nicholas, 35, 205
McCauley, William, 35, 205
McLeod, Susan, 9, 166; "Moving Up the Administration Ladder," 156
medical issues, of contingent faculty, 292. *See also* health issues
men: fatherhood, 104–5; social privilege, 39–40
mentors, mentoring, 97, 249, 251, 253, 254; directors as, 35, 72, 73, 74–75; of graduate WPAs, 81–82; identity and, 156–57
merger, of university programs, 172
metaphors, 3–4, 62, 127, 261; doors as, 236–39, 243; gardening, 241–42; identity through, 51–52; literacy brokering and, 221, 227; role of, 300–301; for writing center director jobs, 113–23

Micciche, Laura R., 101, 191, 221, 236
middle manager roles, 284
Mihut, Ligia, on literacy brokering, 221, 224–25
military, 200; change-of-command, 188–89; leadership theories, 192, 193
Miller, Richard, 53
miscommunication, impacts of, 224
mistakes, owning, 60
MLA. *See* Modern Language Association
MLA Action for Allies, 293
MLA Democracy, 292–93
mobilization, 269
Modern Language Association (MLA), 293
moral charge, of discipline, 158, 159–60
motherhood, 107; and academia, 100–105; professional pressures, 105–6
"Moving Up the Administrative Ladder" (McLeod), 9, 156
multidisciplinary perspectives, 89, 90
multidisciplinary writing programs, 89, 90, 93, 95
multitasking, 51

Naming What We Know: Threshold Concepts in Writing Studies (Adler-Kassner and Wardle), 93
National Adjunct Walkout Day (NAWD), 293
National Conference on Peer Tutoring in Writing, 287
National Survey of Student Engagement (NSSE), 159
National Writing Project (NWP), 72
NAWD. *See* National Adjunct Walkout Day
negative transfer, 298, 299, 301–2
negotiation(s), 18, 38, 40, 220, 222, 267, 302; for director position, 41–44; in discourse communities, 142–44; among stakeholders, 73–74
neo-Platonic (expressionist) rhetoric, 128
new (social epistemic) rhetoric, 128, 131
new transfer, 297
non-tenure-track faculty, 53
novices, writing center directors of, 117–18
NSSE. *See* National Survey of Student Engagement
nursing, as metaphor, 7, 8
nurturing, 51
NWP. *See* National Writing Project

observation: classroom, 63–64; of lecturers, 58–59; of teachers, 291, 301
office management, 55

Olson, Gary A., 111
ombudsperson, 55
O'Meara, Kerry-Ann, 235
O'Neill, Peggy, 9
online for-profit institutions, 116
open-door policy, 240
open rank positions, 6
opportunities, doors of, 243
organization(s), 54, 251; role in, 34–35
"Organizational Design as Improvisation" (Weick), 253
orientation, 66
outsiders-within, 35

Paese, Matt, on internal politics, 12–13
Palin, Sarah, 105–6
parental identities, 15–16
parenting, 51, 100–103; and administrative duties, 106–8; as gendered institution, 104–5
parents: students as, 107–8; teachers/instructors as, 28–29, 100–107
participant leadership, 31
partnering, partnerships, program, 207–8, 212–13
Passing the Leadership Baton (Mullins), 8
patriarchal structures, 191
pedagogy, 65, 226; generational changes in, 127, 128–29, 131
peer review, 147; observations as, 63–64
peers: negotiating relationships with, 58–60; observation of, 63–64
Penrose, Ann M., 281
people pleasing, 58
performance, 107, 148; directing as, 114, 116–18; of self, 145–46, 149
performance theories, 140
permanence, institutional, 70
personal investment, of graduate WPAs, 80–81
personal issues, 9, 250–51; resolving, 223–24
persuasion, as tool, 162–63
Phelps, Louise Wetherbee, 189, 191, 194, 202; feminist leadership of, 195–98; mentorship of, 253, 254
philosophical miscommunication, 130–31
pieties, 101–2, 109
place, 233
placement, 40
plagiarism, 64
players, 32
politics, internal, 12–13
portfolio-assessment program, 39, 250

Portland Resolution, 25–26
positivist (current traditional) rhetoric, 128, 131
power, 14–15, 17, 40, 192; commanders, 193–94; liminals' access to, 71, 76, 78; transfers of, 188–89
power dynamics, 285, 286–87
power of no, 44
power structure, 134, 234
pragmatism, 158–59
"Praxis and Allies" (Sura et al.), 51
preparation, 153–54, 163
presentation, self, 145–46, 149
Presentation of Self in Everyday Life, The (Goffman), 144
president, as metaphor, 116–17
Presidential Transition in Higher Education: Managing Leadership Change (Martin and Samels), 8
prioritization, 54
privilege, social, 39–40, 44–45, 302
problem solving: command and, 193; dispositions to, 143–44
professional development, 53, 66, 164, 287; community colleges, 251, 255; Illinois Articulation Initiative, 265–66
professional investment, in graduate WPAs, 78–79, 80–81
professionalism, 131
professionalization, 92, 132, 134, 197, 234, 255, 236; of graduate students, 78, 91
professional lives, 9; family and, 250–51; motherhood and, 102–6
professional progress, 103
professional-writing courses, 181–82, 255
professor of practice, 155; support for, 156–57
professorships, 6; teaching, 53, 64
program assessment, 39
programmatic vision, of discourse community, 269–70
programs, 79, 228; partnerships, 207–8, 212–13
"Progress of Generations, The" (Baker et al.), 126
Promise and Perils of Writing Program Administration, The (Enos and Borrowman), 220
promotions, internal committee reviews, 64
psychorhetorical forces, 144
public purpose, 134
publishing, contingent faculty, 287
punishment, for fatherhood, 104–5
pure civilians, 198

qualifications, position, 6
Qualley, Donna, 57, 59, 270
quasi-administrators, 162–63, 164, 223–24
QUEST model, outcomes-based, 160–61

race, and teacher/instructor roles, 28–29
rank, 70
Ratcliffe, Krista, 280, 282, 291
reflection, 19
registration, as responsibility, 55
Reiff, Mary Jo, 274
rejuvenation, 101
relationships: with colleagues, 147–48; faculty, 18, 57–58, 133, 254; within organizations, 34–35
renegotiation, 274
replacing an icon, 11, 12
representation, 107
research, 205, 246
research institutions, first-year writing seminars, 90–91
resentment, of colleagues, 46–47
resources, for writing programs, 95
responsibilities, 46, 222; for adjuncts, 65–66; administrative work, 219–20; of assistant directors, 54–56, 67, 298–99; of coordinators, 223–24; of director of composition, 37, 38–39, 40–41, 48–50, 176–77; for writing center directors, 111–12, 117
restaurant industry, as metaphor, 62
retirement, retirees, 186; support for, 10–11
reviews, annual, 56, 145, 176–77, 301
revolving door, 234
rhetoric(s), 88, 89, 189, 280, 282, 294(n7)
rhetorical agency, 261–62, 267, 269–70
rhetorical listening, 292
Rhetorical Listening: Identification, Gender, Whiteness (Ratcliffe), 291
rhetorical sensitivity, 158
rhetorical systems, 91, 128–29
rhetoric and composition studies/programs, 157, 205; disciplinarity of, 92–93
"Rhetoric and Ideology in the Writing Classroom" (Berlin), 128
Rhetoric for Writing Program Administrators, A (Fox and Malenczyk), 45–46, 93
rhetoricity, 160–61
Robertson, Liane, 89, 140
roles, roleplaying, 25, 118, 274; identities and, 156–57; leadership and management, 34–35
rollercoaster, as metaphor, 118, 119

Romano, Susan, 163
Rose, Shirley, 54, 186, 222
Rossman Regaignon, Dara, 90, 96, 208
roundtables, WID faculty, 216
rules, in composition program, 132–33
Ryan, Kathleen J., 153, 181

Safferstone, Todd, 12, 13
salaries, for liminals, 70, 71
scheduling, 54; of Writing Studio use, 30–32
Schell, Eileen E., 190, 192
scholarly discourse, 91, 92
scholarship, 60, 87, 88, 93, 94, 97, 135, 246; and administrative duties, 219–20
scholarship of teaching and learning (SoTL), 157–58, 162
Schön, Donald, 159
Schwalm, David E., 9, 160, 162, 222, 253
Scott, Tony, 36; on managers and leaders, 26–27
self: assessment, 47; awareness of, 299; performance/presentation of, 145–46, 149; preservation of, 227
self-governance, 182
self-reflection, 236, 299
self-sacrifice, 97
self-starters, 80
sensemaking, 235, 236, 241
sensibility, 236
server, serving, as metaphor, 51, 54, 56, 62, 301
services, 39; accessing, 31–32, 33–34
Signifyin' Monkey: A Theory of African-American Literary Criticism, The (Gates), 30
silence, 280
Skinner, Debra, 171
SLACs. *See* small liberal arts colleges
Sledd, James, 62
small-group conferences, 147
small-group workshops (circles), 214–15
small liberal arts colleges (SLACs), 96; writing centers at, 90, 93, 95
SME. *See* statement of mutual expectation
Smith, Patrick, 219
smooth sailing transition, 11, 12
social classes, 289
social contexts, 97
social control, 144
social epistemic (new) rhetoric, 128
sociorhetorical forces, 144, 148
soft money, 33
space, discourse as, 261
staff, 18; parental roles of, 29

staffing changes, 79; in program consolidation, 179–80
stakeholders, 12, 131, 226; negotiating among, 73–74
state governments, funding cuts, 135–36, 137(n1)
statement of mutual expectation (SME), 46, 165
status(es), 70, 78
staying put, 17–18, 235–36
steering a ship, writing center directorship as, 119, 300
STEM teaching, 160
Sternberg, Robert, 150
Stevens, Sharon McKenzie, 285, 287
Stolley, Amy, 153
storytelling, stories (narratives), 220, 236, 261; of writing-center professionals, 121–22, 274–75
stress, 10, 177
Strickland, Donna, on managers and leaders, 26–27
structures of experience, 96
structures of feeling, 96
students, 35, 58, 176, 215–17, 237, 250, 255, 261; assistant directors and, 55, 60; coleading with, 205–6; collaboration with faculty, 209–10; at HBCUs, 28–29; hostility of, 290–91; as parents, 107–8; as writing advisors, 211, 212, 213–14; writing programs, 263–64; and writing studio services, 30–32, 33–34
stuff, and worldview, 126–27
subjectivities, 15–16
superparents, 105–6
supervision, 40, 65, 252; of liminal WPAs, 76–77
SuperWPA, 105–6
support, 46
support networks, peer-to-peer, 13
sustainability, of intellectual work, 97–98

Taczak, Kara, 89, 140
tasks, prioritization of, 54
teaching, teachers, 63, 64, 95, 159, 164, 295(n9), 301; in community colleges, 248, 255; parental role of, 28–29; student evaluations of, 290–91; valuing, 158, 161–62
teaching assistants (TAs), 53, 176
teaching-centered institutions, 26, 38
teaching community, 200–201
teaching demonstration, 237
teaching load, 175, 267
teaching practicum, 41

technology, 147
teenagers, as metaphor, 117–18, 301
temporary positions, 15
tenure-track positions, 6, 30, 174, 177, 265, 294(n6); Boyer model for, 134–35; composition, 38, 41, 88–89
Tetris, as metaphor, 118, 119–20
Thoune, Darci, 250, 256
time management, 103, 104, 199–200
timing, of transitions, 199–200
Title III grants, 33
topic-based programs, 89, 90
Toth, Christie, 251
training, 16, 72, 77, 93, 163, 176, 215
transdisciplinary work, 164
transfer, types of, 297–303
transfer research, 142–43
transition curve, 111
transitions, 4, 5, 7, 26; defining, 219; types of, 11–12
Transitions between Faculty and Administrative Careers (Henry), 10
travel, metaphor of, 3–4
travel funds, 34
trust, 30
turnover, 235
tutorial sessions, 33

unions, 288
university duties, 40
Untenured Faculty as Writing Program Administrators: Institutional Practices and Politics (Dew and Horning), 284
Untenured WPA Special Interest Group, 284
upper-division classes, and program consolidation, 181–82, 184
US Army Command Policy, 193

values, 89, 226
Van Buren, Mark E., 12, 13
Van Ummersen, Claire A., 10–11
vision, 127, 131

WAC. *See* writing-across-the-curriculum programs
Wardle, Elizabeth, 93, 143, 148
WCDs. *See* writing center directors
wearing different hats, 117
Weick, Karl, "Organizational Design as Improvisation," 253
Weisser, Christian, 274
Wellins, Richard S., internal politics, 12–13
Wells, Jennifer, 142, 148
Werder, Carmen, 267, 269

West, Cornel, 158
"What Leaders Really Do" (Kotter), 27
White, Edward M., 14, 54, 171, 192
white male privilege, 39–40
whole-class workshops, 208
WID. *See* writing-in-the-disciplines programs
Wieck, Karl, 236
Williams, Raymond, 90, 96
Wolfinger, Nicholas H., 102–3
women, in academia, 100–105
Women's Ways of Making It in Rhetoric and Composition (Ballif, Davis, and Mountford), 102, 109
work, conditions of, 25, 56
worker-manager ethos, 63
working class, 286
Working Class Majority: America's Best Kept Secret, The (Zweig), 285
work portfolios, 72
workshops, 204, 226, 265; for adjuncts, 65, 66; faculty-development, 206, 208; student advisors and, 209–10; WPA, 54, 167(n3); writing, 91–92
worldview, 127, 128–29
"WPA as Father, Husband, Ex, The" (Hesse), 9
WPA evaluator reports, 234–35
WPA Outcomes Statement for First-Year Composition, 93, 180
writing-about-writing curriculum, 226, 268
Writing Across Contexts: Transfer, Composition, and Sites of Writing (Yancey, Robertson, and Taczak), 89–90, 140
writing-across-the-curriculum (WAC) programs, 6, 90, 146, 204, 206; advisory boards, 211–12
writing advisors, students as, 209–10, 211, 213–14
"Writing and Transfer" (Weisser, Ballif, and Wardle), 140
writing center directors (WCDs), 111, 273–74; colleague and student relationships, 279–80; expectations of, 122–23; marginalization of, 277–79; metaphors used by, 113–21; storytelling by, 121–22; study of, 112–13
writing center professionals (WCPs), 273, 273–74, 281–82; marginalization of, 276–79
writing centers, 6, 183, 272; directors of, 93, 95, 300; ecology of, 274–75. *See also* Connors Writing Center
writing cultures, 90–91
writing intensive (WI) programs, 29, 32

writing-in-the-disciplines (WID) programs, 208, 210, 213, 216
"Writing Program (Administrator) in Context: Where Am I, and Can I Still Behave Like a Faculty Member?, The" (Schwalm), 253
"Writing Program Administration as Preparation for an Administrative Career" (Schwalm), 9
Writing Program Administration at Small Liberal Arts Colleges (Gladstein and Ragaignon), 90, 96
Writing Program Administrator as Researcher, The (Rose and Weiser), 158–59
Writing Program Administrator Interrupted, The (Strickland and Gunner), 101

writing programs, 5, 9, 53, 95, 147, 166(n2), 185, 300; collaboration in, 256–57; in community colleges, 245–46; multidisciplinary, 89, 90; Syracuse University, 196–98
writing studies, 91–92, 300; as discipline, 88–89; knowledge transfer, 140–41; professional identity in, 93–94
Writing Studio, 26, 29, 33; services and use of, 30–31

Yancey, Kathleen Blake, 89, 93, 140

Zaleznik, Abraham, 32, 34–35
Zweig, Michael, 285, 286, 289